Undefeated

Acknowledgments: The author owes much to the Sanskrit scholar
Hélène Flacelière, to the philosopher G. Granger, to the historian
H. I. Marrou, and to the archaeologist George Ville (1929–1967).
Mistakes are his alone; they would have been more numerous if
J. Molino had not agreed to go over the typed copy of this book,
bringing to it his rather frightening encyclopedic knowledge. I have
discussed this book a great deal with J. Molino. Furthermore, the
enlightened reader will find, in many places in this book, implicit
references to—and, no doubt unintentional reminiscences of—the
Introduction à la philosophie de l'histoire of Raymond Aron, which
remains the basic work in this field.

Writing History: Essay on Epistemology was originally published
under the title *Comment On ecrit l'histoire: essai d'épistémologie*
in 1971 by Éditions Seuil.

All inquiries and permissions requests should be addressed to
University Press of New England, Hanover, New Hampshire
03755.

Library of Congress Cataloging in Publication Data

Veyne, Paul, 1930–
    Writing history: essay on epistemology.
    Translation of: Comment on écrit l'histoire.
    Includes index.
    1. History—Methodology.   2. History—Philosophy.
3. Historiography.   I. Title.
D16.V4613   1984   901   84-7281
ISBN 0-8195-5067-1 (alk. paper)
ISBN 0-8195-6076-6 (pbk. : alk. paper)

5 4 3

To Helen
whose lovable theoretism has long been
an indispensable balance-weight
for an obsolete empiricist

Contents

Prologue

What is history? Judging by what we hear around us, this is a question that needs to be asked again.

"History, in this century, has understood that its real task was to explain"; "Such and such a phenomenon cannot be explained by sociology alone: wouldn't recourse to the historical explanation give us a better idea of it?" "Is history a science?" This is useless debate! "Isn't the collaboration of all researchers desirable and alone fruitful?" "Shouldn't the historian apply himself to building up theories?" No.

No, such history is not that in which historians deal. At the very most, it is that in which they think they deal or that they have been persuaded they ought to regret not having dealt with. No, it is not useless to know if history is a science, for "science" is not a lofty word, but a precise term; and experience proves that indifference to the debate about words is usually the accompaniment of a confusion of ideas on the matter. No, history has no method—just ask to be shown that method. No, it explains nothing at all, if the word "explain" has any meaning; as for what it calls its theories, they need a closer examination.

Let us understand each other properly. It is not enough to affirm once again that history speaks of "what will never be seen twice"; neither is there any question of claiming that it is subjective, a matter of perspective, that we query the past starting from our own system of values, that historical facts are not things, that man understands himself and does not explain himself, that of him there can be no science. In a word, there is no question of confusing being and knowing; human sciences exist and are good (or at least those of them that really deserve the name of science), and human physics is the hope of our century, as physics was that of the seventeenth century. But history is not that science, and never will be; if it can be bold, it has undefined possibilities for renewing itself, but in another direction.

History is not a science, and has little to expect from sciences; it does not explain, and has no method. Better still, history, about which much has been said for two centuries, does not exist.

Then what is history? And what do historians, from Thucydides to Max Weber or Mark Bloch, really do, once they have gone through their documents and proceeded to the "synthesis"? Is their work the scientifically conducted study of the various activities and the various creations of men in other days? the science of men in society? human societies? Much less than that; the answer to the question has not changed over the 2,200 years since the successors of Aristotle found it—historians tell of true events in which man is the actor; history is a true novel. A reply that at first sight seems innocuous.

Part One

The Aim of History

Chapter I

Only a True Account

Human Events

Human events are true occurrences with man as the actor. But the word "man" must not frighten us. Neither the essence nor the goals of history require the presence of that character; they depend on the perspective chosen. History is what it is, not because of some nature of man, but because it has decided on a particular way of knowing. Facts are considered either as individualities or as phenomena behind which a hidden invariable is sought. The magnet attracts iron, volcanoes erupt: physical facts in which something is repeated; the eruption of Vesuvius in 1779: a physical fact treated as an event. The Kerensky government in 1917: a human event; the phenomenon of double power in a period of revolution: a phenomenon that can be repeated. If we take the fact for an event, it is because we judge it to be interesting in itself; if we are interested in its repeatable nature, it is but a pretext for discovering a law. Whence the distinction that Cournot makes between the physical sciences, which study the laws of nature, and the cosmological sciences, which, like geology or the history of the solar system, study the history of the world; for

The curiosity of man has not only as its aim the study of the laws and forces of nature; it is still more promptly roused by the spectacle of the world, by the desire to know its present structure and past revolutions. . . .[1]

The human presence is not necessary for events to rouse our curiosity. It is true that human history has the peculiarity that the operations involved in knowing others are not the same as those through which we

Notes are on pages 291–332.

understand physical phenomena; geological history, for example, has a very different aura from human events. Thus we speak of meaning, of understanding, but the correct term is much simpler: finality. In the world as it appears to us, the conduct of human affairs and the understanding of them are dominated by the fact that we know in ourselves, and recognize in other people, the existence of an expectation that determines a plan, and of a plan that leads to modes of action. But this human finalism entails no consequences for the epistemology of history; it is not introduced by the historian when he makes a synthesis; it belongs to actual experience, and is not peculiar to the account the historian gives of that experience; it is found both in the novel and in the merest bit of conversation.

Events and Documents

History is an account of events: all else flows from that. Since it is a direct account, it does not revive,[2] any more than the novel does. The actual experience, as it comes from the hands of the historian, is not that of the actors; it is a narration, so it can eliminate certain erroneous problems. Like the novel, history sorts, simplifies, organizes, fits a century into a page.[3] This synthesis of the account is not less spontaneous than that of our memory when we call to mind the last ten years through which we have lived. To speculate on the interval that always separates the actual experience and the recollection of the event would simply bring us to see that Waterloo was not the same thing for a veteran of the Old Guard and for a field marshal; that the battle can be related in the first or the third person; that it can be spoken of as a battle, as an English victory, or as a French defeat; that from the start one can drop a hint of the outcome or appear to discover it. These speculations can produce amusing experiments in aesthetics; to the historian, they are the discovery of a limit.

That limit is that in no case is what historians call an event grasped directly and fully; it is always grasped incompletely and laterally, through documents or statements, let us say through *tekmeria*, traces, impressions. Even if I am a contemporary and a witness of Waterloo, even if I am the principal actor and Napoleon in person, I shall have only a perspective of what historians will call the event of Waterloo; I shall be able to leave to posterity only my statement, which, if it reaches them, they will call an impression. Even if I were Bismarck deciding to send the Ems dispatch, my own interpretation of the event would perhaps not be the same as that of my friends, my confessor, my regular historian, and my psychoanalyst, who may have their own version of my decision and think they know better than I do what it was I wanted. In essence, history is knowledge through documents. Thus, historical narration goes beyond all documents, since none of them can be the event; it is not a documentary photomontage, and does show the past "live, as if you were there." To repeat the useful distinction of G. Genette, it is *diegesis* and not *mimesis*.[4] An authentic dialogue between Napoleon and Alexander I, had it been preserved in shorthand, will not be "stuck" in the account. The historian will most usually prefer to talk about this dialogue; if he quotes it verbatim, the quotation will be a literary effect, designed to give life—let us say *ethos*—to the plot, which would bring history thus written close to the historical novel.

Events and Differences

Being the account of events, history, by definition, does not repeat itself, and is only the history of variations; men will tell of the 1914 War, but not of the war as a phenomenon. (Imagine a physicist who did not seek out the law of falling bodies, but talked about falls and their different "causes.") Of the text of man, the historian knows the variations but never the text itself; the greater part of what may be known about man—the most interesting part, perhaps—must not be asked of history.

An event stands out against a background of uniformity; it is a difference, a thing we could not know a priori: history is the daughter of memory. Men are born, eat, and die; but only history can tell us of their wars and empires. They are cruel and commonplace, neither completely good nor completely bad; but history will tell us if, at a given period, they preferred indefinite profit to retirement once their fortune was made, and how they perceived or classified colors. It will not teach us that the Romans had two eyes and that to them the sky was blue; on the other hand, it will not leave us ignorant of the fact that where we talk of colors when speaking of the sky in fine weather, the Romans used another category and spoke of the *caelum serenum* rather than of the blue sky; that is a semantic event. As for the night sky, they saw it with the eyes of common sense, as a solid vault and not too distant; we, on the other hand, have seen it as an infinite abyss since the discovery of the Medicean planets, which caused the atheist to whom Pascal lends voice the terror familiar to us. An event of thought and of sensibility.

No event exists in itself, but in relation to a conception of the eternal man. A history book is a little like a grammar; the practical grammar of a foreign language does not record all the rules of the language, but only the rules different from those of the language spoken by the reader for whom the grammar is destined, rules that might surprise him. The historian does not exhaustively describe a civilization or a period, or make a complete inventory of it, as if he had just arrived from another planet; he will tell his reader only what is necessary so that the latter can picture that civilization starting from what is always taken to be true. Does that mean that the historian is never obliged to enunciate primary truths? Unfortunately, primary truths have a troublesome tendency to be substituted for real truths; if we do not know that our conceptions of the sky, of colors, and of profit—whether justified or not—are not at least eternal, we will not think of questioning the documents on these matters—or, rather, we will not understand what they tell us.

Because of its paradoxical and critical aspect, the "historicist" side of history has always been one of the most popular attractions of the subject; from Montaigne to *Tristes tropiques* or to *L'Histoire de la folie* of Foucault, the variety of values from nation to nation and from century to century is one of the great themes of Western sensibility.[5] Since it is opposed to our natural tendency to anachronism, it also has a heuristic value. For example, in the *Satyricon*, Trimalcion, after drinking, speaks at length, proudly and joyfully, of a magnificent tomb he has had built for himself; in a Hellenistic inscription, a public benefactor whom the state wants to honor sees in the greatest detail what honors his country will confer on his corpse on the day he is cremated. This involuntary gruesomeness will make real sense when we read, in Father Huc, that the attitude of the Chinese is the same in this matter:

People in comfortable circumstances, who have something left over from their spending money, do not fail to provide in advance a coffin to their taste, and a well-cut one. Until the time comes to lie in it, it is kept in the house like a fine piece of furniture that cannot fail to be a pleasant and consoling sight in suitably decorated apartments. The coffin is above all for well-born children an excellent means of showing the intensity of their filial piety to the authors of their days; it is a great and soothing consolation to the heart of a son to be able to purchase a coffin for an old father or an old mother, and to . . . offer it to them at a moment when they least expect it.[6]

Reading these lines written in China, we understand better that the abundance of funeral things in classical archaeology is not solely due to the chance of finds; the tomb was one of the values of Greco-Roman civilization, and the Romans were as exotic as the Chinese. That is not a great revelation from which to draw tragic pages on death and the West, but it is a true little fact that gives more relief to a picture of civilization. The historian never brings a resounding revelation that upsets our view of the world; the banality of the past is made up of insignificant details that, as they multiply, nonetheless form a very unexpected picture.

Let us note in passing that, if we were writing a Roman history with Chinese readers in mind, we would not have to comment on the Roman attitude toward tombs; we could be content to write, like Herodotus: "On this point, the opinion of these people is almost like our own." So if, in order to study a civilization, we limit ourselves to reading what it says itself—that is, to reading sources relating to this one civilization— we will make it more difficult to wonder at what, in this civilization, was taken for granted; if Father Huc makes us aware of the exoticism of the Chinese about funereal things, and if the *Satyricon* does not bring us the same astonishment about the Romans, it is because Huc was not Chinese, whereas Petronius was Roman. A historian content to repeat in indirect speech what his heroes say of themselves would be as boring as edifying. The study of any civilization enriches the knowledge we have of another, and it is impossible to read Huc's *Travels in the Chinese Empire* or Volney's *Travels in Syria* without learning more about the Roman Empire. The procedure can be generalized; and, whatever the question studied, it can be approached systematically from the sociological point of view. By that I mean from the point of view of comparative history; the recipe is almost infallible for renewing any historical point, and the words of comparative study ought to be at least as hallowed as those of exhaustive bibliography. For the event is difference, and the characteristic effort of the historian's profession and what gives it its flavor are well known: astonishment at the obvious.

An event is anything that is not obvious. Scholasticism would say that

history is interested in matter no less than in form, in individual details
no less than in essence and definition; scholasticism also adds that there
is no matter without form, and we shall see that the problem of universals is put to historians too. Provisionally we can adopt the distinction
made by Dilthey and Windelband:[7] On one side there are the nomological sciences, which have as their goal to establish laws or types, and
on the other, the ideographical sciences, dealing with the individual;
physics and economics are nomological, and history is ideographical. (As
for sociology, it isn't too sure what it is. It knows that there is a place
for a nomology of man, and it would like to be that; but often, under
the flag of sociology, authors produce what is in reality a history of
contemporary civilization—and that is not the worst that is done.)

Individualization

But to say that the event is individual is an equivocal qualification;
the best definition of history is not that its object is what is never seen
twice. It may be that some considerable aberration of the orbit of Mer-
cury, due to a rare conjunction of the planets, will not be repeated, but
it is also possible that it will be in a distant future; the chief point is to
know whether the aberration is related for its own sake (which would
be to write a history of the solar system) or whether it is seen only as a
problem of celestial mechanics. If, as if moved by a spring, John Lackland "came this way a second time," to imitate the example, the historian
would relate the two comings and would feel no less a historian for doing
so. That two events are repeated, even repeated exactly, is one thing;
that they are nonetheless two is another, and that alone counts for the
historian. Similarly, a geographer writing a regional geography will consider two glacial cirques as distinct, even if they are enormously alike
and represent the same type of relief; the individualization of historical
or geographical facts by time or space is not contradicted by their
eventual subsumption into one species, one type, or one concept. History
lends itself to a typology, and one can hardly describe well-characterized
types of revolutions or of cultures as a variety of insect is described; but
even if it were otherwise, and there were a variety of war the description of which would cover several pages, the historian would continue to
relate individual cases belonging to that variety. After all, direct taxation
can be considered as a type, and so can indirect taxation; what is his-

torically pertinent is that the Romans had no direct taxation and the taxes were imposed by the Directory.

But what individualizes events? It is not their difference of detail, their "matter," what they are in themselves, but the fact that they happen—that is, that they occur at a given moment; history would never repeat itself, even if it happened to say the same thing again. If we were interested in an event for its own sake, outside time, like a kind of trinket,[8] we would vainly, like aesthetes of the past, take delight in what was inimitable about it. The event would nonetheless be a "sample" of historicity, connected to nothing else in time. Two passings of John Lackland are not a sample of a pilgrimage of which the historian had two copies, for the historian would not find it a matter of indifference that that prince, who has already had so many misfortunes with the methodology of history, had the further misfortune of having to pass the way he had already passed; when told about the second passing, he would not say "I know," as does the naturalist when he is brought an insect he has already seen. This does not imply that the historian does not think in concepts like everyone else (he does indeed speak of "the passing"), or that historical explanation should not have recourse to types, such as "enlightened despotism." It simply means that the soul of a historian is that of a reader of news items; these are always the same, and are always interesting because the dog that is run over today is different from the one run over yesterday—and, more generally, because today is not yesterday.

Nature and History

Because a fact is made singular, it does not follow that by right it is not capable of scientific explanation; despite what is often said, there is no radical difference between the facts studied by the physical sciences and historical facts. All are individualized at a point in space and time, and it would be a priori as possible to treat the latter scientifically as the former. One cannot oppose science and history like the study of the universal and the individual. To begin with, physical facts are not less individualized than are historical facts; then the knowledge of a historical individuality supposes its being related to the universal: "This is a riot and that is a revolution, which can be explained, as always, by class struggle, or by the resentment of the mob." That a historical fact is what "will never be seen twice" does not a priori prevent its being explained. Two passings of John Lackland are two distinct events. Each will be explained, and that is all there is to it. History is a fabric of processes, and science only explains processes; if heat is diffused twice, on 12 March and a second time on 13 March, along an iron rod in the Place de l'Étoile (renamed Place du Général de Gaulle), each individual fact of diffusion will be explained.

It is poetical to set the historical character of man against the repetitions of nature, but it is an idea no less confused than poetical. Nature, too, is historical, has its history, its cosmology; nature is no less concrete than man, and all that is concrete exists in time. It is not the physical facts that are repeated, it is the abstraction without place or date that a physicist extracts from them; if submitted to the same treatment, man repeats himself just as much. The truth is that concrete man has other reasons than nature for not repeating himself (he is free, he can accumulate knowledge, and so on); but it is not because man has his own way of being historical that nature cannot have its own manner of being so.

Cournot is absolutely right to make no difference in principle between the history of nature and of man. It happens, too, we must admit, that the history of the cosmos and of nature is scientifically explicable and that the history of man is not, or practically not. But, as we shall see at the end of this book, that difference is in no way due to the special manner man has of being historical, nor to the individualized character of historical facts—or, rather, of every fact, historical or natural. It is not absolutely impossible a priori for the historian to imitate the physicist and to extract from a human fact an invariable, which, being abstract, is eternal and will be valid in all future concrete cases, as the law of Galileo is valid for every future fall of a body. Did not Thucydides, it is said, write his *History* to give eternal lessons of this kind? We shall see later why that operation cannot be realized, and we shall also see that its impossibility comes from causality in history, and not from the individual character of human events.

The true difference is not between historical facts and physical facts, but between historiography and physical science. Physics is a body of laws, and history is a body of facts. Physics is not a body of physical facts related and explained; it is the corpus of the laws that will be used to explain those facts. To the physicist the existence of the sun and the moon, even of the cosmos, is an anecdote that can be used only to establish Newton's laws; in his eyes those heavenly bodies have no greater value than an apple.[9] For the historian that is not the case; if there were (supposing there could be) a science that was the corpus of the laws of history, history would not be that science; it would be the corpus of facts that those laws explained. It remains to be seen whether, if there were a science of historical laws, one would still be interested in the facts themselves; no doubt one would be satisfied to establish them and historiography would be reduced to historical criticism.

True Events

History is anecdotal, it interests by recounting, as the novel does. It differs from the novel on only one essential point. Let us suppose I am being told about a riot and that I know that the intention of this account is to tell me some history that happened at a given moment, to a given people. I shall take as a heroine the ancient nation that was unknown to me a minute before, and it will become for me the center of the story (or, rather, its indispensable support). And this is what the novel reader does. Except that here the novel is true, which does away with the need for it to be exciting. The history of the riot can afford to be boring without losing its value. That is probably why, in consequence, imaginary history has never caught on as a literary genre (except among aesthetes who read *The Buccaneering Grail*) any more than has the imaginary news item (save among aesthetes who read Félix Fénéon); a story that wants to captivate savors too much of the false, and cannot be anything more than an imitation. The paradoxes of individuality and authenticity are known; for a fanatical admirer of Proust, this relic must be the very fountain pen with which the *Temps perdu* was written and not another absolutely identical fountain pen because mass-produced. The "museum piece" is a complex notion bringing together beauty, authenticity, and rarity; neither an aesthete, nor an archaeologist, nor a collector will in his raw state make a good curator. Even if one of the forgeries painted by van Meegeren were as beautiful as an authentic Vermeer (say as a youthful Vermeer, a Vermeer before Vermeer), it would not be a Vermeer. But the historian, by contrast, is neither a collector nor an aesthete; beauty does not interest him, nor does rarity. Only the truth does.

History is the relating of true events. In terms of this definition, a fact must fulfill a single condition to be worthy of history: it must really have taken place. Let us admire the deceptive simplicity of this definition in which the genius of Aristotelianism is made manifest, perceiving the essential and the unseen evidence; we know that at first sight a great philosophy does not seem deep, obscure, or stirring, but insipid. History is the relation of true facts, and not seemingly true ones (as in the novel) or unlikely ones (as in the tale). This implies, among other things, that the historical method that is dinned into us does not exist. History has a criticism, which Fustel de Coulanges called analysis and which is difficult; everyone knows that it takes "ten years of analysis for one day of synthesis." But synthesis does indeed take only a day. The word "analysis" is deceptive; let us say "the use of documents and the criticism of them." Now, historical criticism has only one function: to answer the question asked of it by the historian: "I believe that this document teaches me this; may I trust it to do that?" Its task is not to tell the historian, who would only have to make a synthesis of it, what the documents teach us; it is up to the historian himself to see that, and his synthesis is made by just taking cognizance of the documents. Similarly, the rules for historical synthesis are blank pages;[10] other than the techniques of handling and checking documents, there is no more a method of history than one of ethnography or of the art of traveling.

There is no method of history because history makes no demands; so long as one relates true things, it is satisfied.[11] It seeks only truth, in which it is not science, which seeks exactness. It imposes no norms; no rule of the game subtends it, nothing is unacceptable to it. That is the most original characteristic of the historical genre. Do we imagine that it is sufficient to state the "great theorem" of Fermat and then to verify it by using electronic computers to do arithmetic? to establish that the magnet attracts iron in order to do physics? At most it would be doing natural history. There is indeed a "field" of physical phenomena; and movement, for example, from Aristotle to Einstein, has always been considered as part of that field. But it is not enough for the reality of a phenomenon in that field to be recognized for it to become ipso facto part of the corpus of physics, save as a problem. In contrast, this would be fully sufficient if a historical fact were involved.

History is a deceptive knowledge that teaches about things that would be as banal as our lives if they were not different. Yes, it is picturesque; yes, ancient towns were full of odors, the smell of bodies too close together, of gutters, smells from the dark shops selling meat and skins, and whose beauty could not be seen because of the narrowness of the streets and the projecting roofs (*suggrundationes*); towns in which we rediscover the attractiveness of the primary colors red and yellow, and the childish taste for shiny things. It is a bit boring, like the memories of a man who has traveled too much; it is not rigorous or mysterious; but it is undeniably true. History is a city visited for the pleasure of seeing human affairs in their diversity and naturalness, without seeking in it any other interest or any beauty.

History Is Mutilated Knowledge

More exactly, we visit what is still visible of that city, the traces of it that remain; history is mutilated knowledge.[12] A historian does not say what the Roman Empire was, nor what the French Resistance in 1944 was, but what it is still possible to know about it. It certainly goes without saying that one cannot write the history of events of which there remains no trace, but it is curious that that goes without saying. Is it not still maintained that history is, or should be, the integral reconstitution of the past? Are there not books entitled *History of Rome* or *The Resistance in France*? The illusion of integral reconstitution comes from the fact that the documents, which provide us with the answers, also dictate the questions to us; in that way they not only leave us in ignorance of many things, but they also leave us ignorant of the fact that we are ignorant. For it is almost an effort against nature to go on imagining that a thing can exist when there is no evidence that it does exist; before the invention of the microscope, no one had the very simple idea that there could be animals even smaller than those we can see; before Galileo's telescope, no one had taken into account the possible existence of stars invisible to the naked eye.

Historical knowledge is cut on the pattern of mutilated documents; we do not suffer spontaneously by that mutilation and we have to make an effort to see it, precisely because we measure what history must be by the pattern of the documents. We do not approach the past with a preestablished set of questions (what was the population? the economic system? the childish, honest politeness?), having decided to refuse to examine any period that left blank the answers to too many questions; neither do we demand of the past a clear explanation of itself. We also do not refuse to call any event a historical fact on the pretext that its causes remain unknowable. History has no threshold of knowledge, no minimum of intelligibility; nothing of what has been, so long as it has been, is inadmissible for it. Thus history is not a science; it has no less rigor, but that rigor applies to the level of criticism.

Chapter II

History Does Not Exist

The Incoherence of History

The field of history is thus completely undetermined, with one exception: everything in it must really have taken place. For the rest, whether the texture of the field is tight or loose, intact or with gaps, is of no moment. A page of history on the French Revolution is of a weave close enough for the logic of the events to be almost wholly understandable and a Machiavelli or a Trotsky could deduce from it a whole art of politics; but a page of history of the ancient East, which is reduced to a few meager chronological data and contains all that is known of one or two empires of which there remains little but the names, is still history. The paradox has been sharply highlighted by Lévi-Strauss:

History is a disconnected whole, formed of areas each of which is defined by a frequency of its own. There are periods when numerous events present to the historian the characteristics of differential events; others, on the contrary, when for him . . . very little and sometimes nothing happened. All those dates do not form a series, they belong to different species. Coded in the system of prehistory, the most famous episodes of modern history would cease to be relevant, except perhaps . . . certain massive aspects of demographic evolution seen on a global scale, the invention of the steam engine, of electricity and of nuclear energy.[1]

To which there corresponds a kind of hierarchy of modules:

The relative choice of the historian is never anything but history that teaches more and explains less and history that explains more and teaches less. Biographical and anecdotal history, which is lowest on the ladder, is *weak* history that does not contain . . . its own intelligibility, which it only gets when transported wholly into a history stronger than itself; yet it would be wrong to believe that these dovetailings progressively reconstitute a total history, because what is gained on one hand is lost on the other. Biographical and anecdotal history is the least explanatory, but it is richer from the point of view of information because

15

it considers individuals in terms of what is special to them and goes into details, for each of them, the shades of character, the circuitous nature of their motives, the phases of their deliberation. This information is simplified, then abolished when we pass on to increasingly stronger history.

The Incomplete Nature of History

To every reader with a critical faculty and to most professionals[2] a history book appears in a very different light from what it seems to be; it does not treat the Roman Empire, but what we can still know about that empire. Below the reassuring surface of the account, the reader, from what the historian speaks about, from the importance he seems to attribute to particular sorts of facts (religion, institutions), can infer the nature of the sources he has used, as well as the gaps in them. That reconstitution finally becomes a reflex; the reader can guess where the badly filled gaps are; he is aware that the number of pages devoted by the writer to the different moments and aspects of the past is an average between the importance of those aspects to him and the richness of the documentation; he knows that the people said to have no history are merely people whose history is unknown and that the "primitive peoples" have a past, as everyone else has. Above all, he knows that from one page to the next the historian changes tense without warning, according to the tempo of his sources; that every history book is in this sense a fabric of incoherences, and it cannot be anything else. This state of things is certainly unbearable for a logical mind, and is enough to prove that history is not logical, that there is—and can be—no remedy.

Might the remedy lie in modifying the chapter titles? One chapter might, for example, be called "What We Know of the Rural History of Rome" instead of "The Rural History of Rome." One might, at least, give a preliminary definition of the sources according to their nature (historizing history, anecdotal history, romantic history, dry chronology, administrative documents) and their tempo (a page covering a day or a century). But how can we resolve the difficulty of the existence of aspects of the past that the sources do not give us and that we do not know are not given to us? Moreover, we would have to decide the importance that the historian attributes to the various aspects—the political history of the first century B.C. is often known almost month by month; only the broad outlines of the second century are known. If history were really "codified" methodically according to "frequencies," logic would demand that the two centuries be written of with the same rhythm; since we cannot relate the detailed events of the second century—we do not know them— we could only abbreviate the detail of the first. Indeed, one could say, is it not fitting to consult sources for important facts and leave out the dusty details?

But what is important? Is it not, rather, a question of what is interesting? Then, how regrettable it would be to level from below, as it were, in the name of coherence! Why refuse to see, in the first-century sources, the abundance of interesting details? The key word is "interesting"; to speak of historical importance would be too serious. The intrigues round Cicero are certainly no longer important to us, but they are curious in themselves and for the reason that they did occur—just as, to the naturalist, the most unimportant and valueless insect is interesting because it exists, and, to Alpinists, a peak is worth climbing because, as one of them[3] said, "It is there." Thus, since one cannot make history tell more than the sources reveal, it only remains to write it as it has always been written: with unequal tempo in proportion to the unequal preservation of traces of the past. In short, for historical knowledge, it is enough for an event to have occurred for it to be worth knowing.

Thus, we will see a history of the Roman Empire, in which political life is little known and social life fairly well known, follow without warning on a history of the end of the Republic, in which it is rather the reverse, and precede a history of the Middle Ages that, in contrast, will show that the economic history of Rome is almost unknown. In saying that, we do not claim to emphasize the obvious fact that, from one period to the next, the gaps in the sources do not bear on the same subjects; we merely note that the heterogeneous character of the gaps does not prevent us from writing something that can still be called history, and that we have no hesitation in putting the Republic, the Empire, and the Middle Ages into the same tapestry, even though the scenes we embroider on it clash. But the most curious thing is that the gaps in history close over spontaneously before our eyes and we can discern them only with difficulty, so vague are our ideas on what we must a priori expect to find in history, so much do we come to it unprovided with a prepared questionnaire. One century is a blank as far as our sources are concerned; the reader hardly notices the gap.

The historian can dwell for ten pages on one day and pass over ten years in two lines; the reader will trust him, as he trusts a good novelist, and will presume that those ten years are uneventful. *Vixere ante nos Agamemnones multi* is not an idea that comes naturally to us; think of Marx and Engels peopling thousands of years of prehistory with their monotonous primitive Communism, or of the type of "likely history" that archaeologists use to reconstruct, more or less, the history of far-distant centuries. The latter type is the reverse of the utopia and has the same overly logical insipidity, the rule of the game being to make as few suppositions as possible (the historian must be prudent), to account as economically as possible for the few traces that pure chance has chosen and allowed to come down to us. Our familiarity with the past is like that with our grandparents; they are alive, so that time passes and we never think that their life story, about which we know practically nothing, is full of events as entrancing as our own and cannot be perfectly reconstructed. Science is de jure incomplete; history alone can be allowed de facto to have gaps—because it is not a fabric, it has no weave.

The Notion of the Non-event

Therefore historians, in every period, are free to divide history as they please (into political history, scholarship, biography, ethnology, sociology, natural history[4]), for history has no natural joints. It is time to distinguish between the "field" of historic events and history as a genre, with the different ways these have been conceived through the centuries. For in its successive avatars the historical genre has been variously extended and, in certain periods, has shared its domain with other genres, such as accounts of journeys or sociology. So let us make a distinction between the field of events, which is the virtual domain of the historical genre, and the realm of variable extension, which the genre has carved out for itself in this domain over the centuries. The ancient East had its lists of kings and its dynastic records; with Herodotus, history became political and military, at least in principle, relating the exploits of the Greeks and the barbarians—yet Herodotus the traveler did not separate it from a kind of historical ethnography. In our own time, history has annexed demography, economics, society, and mentalities; it aspires to become "total history," to reign over all its virtual domain. Deceptive continuity is established among these successive realms; whence the invention of an evolving genre, continuity being assured by the word "history" (but it is thought that sociology and ethnography are to be considered separately) and by the unchanging heading, political history; all the same, today the role of heading tends to pass to social history or to what is called civilization.

What, then, is historic, and what is not? Later we shall have to ask ourselves this; but let us say at once that to draw the distinction, we cannot trust the frontiers that are those of the historical genre at a given moment—we might as well believe that Racine's tragedies or Brecht's dramas are the incarnation of the essence of the theater. It is impossible, in our reasoning thus far, rightly to establish the distinction between history, ethnography, biography, and the common news item; it is impossible to say why the life of Louis XIV would be history and that of a Nivernais peasant of the seventeenth century would not; it is impossible to state that the reign of Louis XIV related in three volumes is history but in one hundred volumes is not. If we try to make the distinction, to lay down a definition (history is the history of societies, the history of what is important, of what matters to us . . .), German historicity has proved and—even more—has involuntarily confirmed by its failure, that no definition holds good; the only frontiers remain, for the moment, the variable conventions of the genre.

At the most one may remark that the genre, since the time of Voltaire, has tended to spread out more and more; like a river in very flat country, it spreads out widely and easily changes its course. In the end historians have made a doctrine of that sort of imperialism; they have recourse to a forest metaphor rather than a river metaphor—in word or act, they affirm that history, no matter when it is written, is only a clearing in the middle of a huge forest, which, by night, belongs entirely to them. In France the School of Records, grouped round the review founded by Marc Bloch, strove to clear the frontier zones of that open space. According to those pioneers, traditional historiography studied too exclusively the fine, big events always recognized as such; the school made a "history of treaties and battles," but there remained to be cleared a huge stretch of "non-events" whose limits we cannot perceive. The non-events are events not yet recognized as such—the history of territories, of mentalities, of madness, or of the search for security through the ages. So the non-events will be the historicity of which we are not conscious as such; the expression will be used in that sense in this book—and so it should be, for the school and its ideas have given good proof of their fruitfulness.

Facts Have No Absolute Dimensions

Within the clearing that the conceptions or the conventions of every period carve out in the field of historicity, there is no constant hierarchy from province to province; no zone commands another or absorbs it. At most one may think that certain facts are more important than others, but that importance depends entirely on the criteria chosen by each historian and has no absolute size. It is convenient to distinguish between economic history, political history, technical history, and so on, but no rule of method teaches us that one of these histories precedes the others. If it did so teach, and if Marxism were demonstrably true, it would be a very Platonic truth that would not affect the manner of relating history; the technical would not reabsorb the economic, nor economics, society; and there would always remain social, economic, and technical events for detailed description. Sometimes a clever producer sets a vast background: Lepanto, the whole of the sixteenth century, the eternal Mediterranean and the desert, where Allah alone exists. It is arranging in tiers going far back and juxtaposing, like a baroque artist, different temporal rhythms; it is not arranging determinisms in series. Even if, for a reader of Koyré, the idea that the birth of physics in the seventeenth century might be explained by the technical needs of the rising middle class was not inconsistent or even absurd.[5] The history of science would not disappear by being thus explained; in fact, when a historian stresses the dependence of the history of science in relation to social history, he is writing a general history of an entire period and is obeying a rule of rhetoric that prescribes the building of bridges between his chapters on science and those on society. History is the realm of juxtaposition.

Yet the impression remains that the War of 1914 is, all the same, a more important event than the fire at the Bazar de la Charité or than the Landru affair; the war is history; the rest are news items. That is only an illusion arising from our confusion of the series of each of these events and their relative size in the series; the Landru affair caused fewer deaths than the war, but is it disproportionate to a detail of Louis XV's diplomacy or a ministerial crisis in the Third Republic? And what is to be said of the horror with which Hitler's Germany spattered the face of humanity, of the gigantic news item of Auschwitz? The Landru affair is of major importance in a history of crime. But that history is less important than political history, and occupies a lesser place in the life of most people. The same can be said of philosophy, of science prior to the eighteenth century; has it fewer present-day consequences? has the diplomacy of Louis XV many more?

But let us be serious: If a genie granted it to us to know ten pages of the past of a civilization unknown until today, what would we choose? Would we prefer to know about major crimes or what that society was like, Melanesian tribes or British democracy? Obviously we would prefer to know if the society was tribal or democratic. But again we have confused the magnitude of events and their series. The history of crime is only one small part (but a very suggestive one in the hands of a clever historian) of social history; similarly the institution of permanent embassies, an invention of the Venetians, is one small part of political history. We should have compared either the importance of criminals with that of ambassadors, or compared social history and political history. Would we prefer to know if our unknown civilization was democratic and not tribal? Or if it was industrial or still at the Stone Age? Both, no doubt, unless we preferred to squabble about whether the political is more important than the social and whether seaside holidays are better than holidays in the mountains. Then there appears a demographer who proclaims that demography is most important.

What confuses ideas is the genre called general history. Alongside books entitled *The Dangerous Classes* or *Diplomatic History*, whose chosen criterion is evident from the title, there are others like *The Sixteenth Century* whose criterion is implied; but it is nonetheless there and is no less subjective. The axis of these general histories has long been political history, but it is today less event-based: economics, society, civilization. All the same, all is not settled. Our historian will no doubt reason thus: So as not to upset the balance of our account, let us speak of what matters most to the majority of Frenchmen in the reign of Henry III. Political history will no longer be of much account, for most of the king's subjects had no contact with authority save as taxpayers or as criminals; we shall speak mainly about the daily labors of Jacques Bonhomme.[6] One chapter will rapidly sketch the cultural life, but in it clever men will talk mostly about almanacs, booklets sold by peddlers, and the quatrains of Pibrac. But what about religion? A considerable gap for the sixteenth century. But are we applying ourselves to describing the average lines of daily life of the time or its emotional heights, which are obviously both intense and of short duration? Better still, shall we relate what is average about the sixteenth century or what differentiates it from the preceding and from the following centuries?

Geographers know this difficulty: In a given maritime province famed for its fishermen, it is nevertheless on record that fishing employs only a small percentage of the population. It is true that the province owes its character to the fishermen; it is equally true that fishing is perhaps the sensitive area, the weakest point of its economy. Thus, is it the average, the difference, or the strategic point?

Another historian appears, to whom what is most important is the duration of the events selected: the deep structures, the slow heartbeats, the secular cycles; it is a quantitative criterion, but quantity is now time, rather than the number of men or the number of hours in each man's day. A third historian prefers works to events—the seventeenth century consists of physics, the baroque, Cartesianism, and absolute monarchy. For a historian of antiquity, a no less conceivable criterion would be intelligibility—instead of offering the reader a history full of gaps like an edition of Sappho, he will reduce it to an anthology of events, chosen so as to be less full of gaps than others; the local history of Pompeii and the prosopographical study of government personnel will take up more pages than the city of Rome and the whole of the third century. Or he will define the civilization by its peaks rather than by its plains. Vergilian pieties will be one point of view on Roman pieties, about which it is so difficult to know.

It is impossible to decide that one fact is historic and that another is an anecdote deserving to be forgotten, because every fact belongs to a series and has relative importance only within its series. Is it the greatness of the consequences that makes one fact more important than another, as has been said?[7] Happy are those who are capable of isolating and following down to the present day the consequences of the defeat of Athens in 404; then, as we know, "origins are rarely beautiful." Moreover, the consequences themselves ought to be the subject of a choice, and into this comes the annoying question of the "meaning of history," the meaning we choose to give it: Vergil and the destiny of Rome, Marx and the middle class, Augustin Thierry and the Third Estate, Lavisse and French unity. But the criterion of the importance of consequences is only an invention created by a sense of the serious; history relates the wars of Louis XIV for themselves and not for the distant consequences they may have. Ought we, rather, to judge the relative importance of each event according to the values of the period itself? That means charitably taking as objectivity the subjectivity of the main people concerned; unfortunately, values are themselves events among other events. We do not write about the Treaties of Westphalia because of their interest to the men of that day; if those treaties had gone unnoticed, that very indifference would only be one more event. We are not interested in the circus in precisely the same way as the Romans were, but we are also interested in their interest in the circus. Thus, would what is historical not be individual, what concerns man as a social being? Let those speak who feel capable of making that distinction or of finding a meaning in it.

A cold of Louis XIV, though royal, is not a political event, but it concerns the history of the health of the French people. The field of events is an interlacing of series. So we can see to what regulating idea historiography is oriented: to a total history to which no event is foreign—indeed, no one is any longer astonished to find, in the summaries of reviews, a history of the sense of duration or a history of the perception (or of the classification) of colors. On the other hand, one can no longer see clearly what radical difference there might be between, on the one hand, a history of society under Louis XIV, of art in Pompeii or of Tuscan territory in the thirteenth century, and, on the other hand, a description of present Trobriand society, of North African workers in Paris suburbs, or of photography as a popular art: between history, descriptive ethnography, and sociology as the history of contemporary civilization, the distinction is purely traditional or based on university institutions.

Extension of History

Now, the more the horizon of events widens before our eyes, the more indefinite it appears. Everything that has made up the daily life of all men, including what was discernible only to a virtuoso in the art of the journal, is, by right, quarry for the historian; for one cannot see in what other region of being except in life, day by day, historicity might be reflected. Which does not at all mean that history should be history of daily life, that the diplomatic history of the reign of Louis XIV will be replaced by the description of the emotions of the people of Paris when the king made his solemn entrances, that the history of the technique of transport will be replaced by a phenomenology of space and of its intermediaries. No, it simply means that an event is known only by traces, and that every fact of everyday life is a trace of some event (whether that event is cataloged or still sleeps in the forest of non-events).

Such is the lesson of historiography since Voltaire or Burckhardt. Balzac began by competing with the registry office; then the historians competed with Balzac, who had reproached them, in the 1842 preface of the *Comédie humaine,* with neglecting the history of manners. They first dealt with the most obvious gaps, describing the statistical aspects of demographic and economic evolution. At the same time they made discoveries about mentalities and values; they saw that something more particular was to be done than giving details on madness in the Greek religion or on forests in the Middle Ages: to make readers understand how people of the period considered forests or madness, for there is no absolute way of seeing them. Each epoch has its own way, and professional experience has proved that the description of those ways of seeing offer the researcher rich material, material as subtle as he could wish for. With that, we are still far from knowing how to conceptualize all the little perceptions that make up actual experience. In the *Journal d'un bourgeois de Paris,* under the date of March 1414, we read a few lines so idiosyncratic that they might pass as the very allegory of universal history.

At that period little children sang in the evening, as they went to get wine or mustard:
> *Your clot has a cough, old crone,*
> *Your clot has a cough, a cough.*

It did happen, as a matter of fact, that in God's good time, foul, infected air fell on the world, which made more than a hundred thousand people in Paris lose their appetite for food and drink and their ability to sleep; this sickness brought so much coughing that High Mass was no longer sung. No one died of it but it was hard to cure.

Anyone content with smiling would be a dead loss as far as history was concerned; those few lines constitute a "whole social fact" worthy of Mauss. Anyone who has read Pierre Goubert recognizes in them the normal demographic state of preindustrial populations, among whom summer endemic diseases were often spread by epidemics of which, to their astonishment, they did not die and that they accepted with the resignation with which we accept car accidents (although more of them died). Anyone who has read Philippe Ariès will recognize, in the crude language of these little children, the effects of a pre-Rousseau system of education (or, if he has read Kardiner and believes that the basic personality . . .). But why were the children sent to buy wine and mustard? No doubt other provisions did not come from a shop, but from the farm, or had been prepared at home (as bread was) or bought in the morning at some herb market; that is economics, that is the town and the land, and the glory of the economist von Thünen. There would remain to be studied the children's republic that seems to have its own customs, candor, and likes and dislikes. Let us at least admire, speaking as philologists, the unusual form of their song, with its two stages of repetitions and its banter in the polite form. Whoever has had an interest in the fellowships, the pseudo relationships, and the joking relationships of the ethnographers will admire all that lies in the use of the words "old crone"; whoever has read van Gennep appreciates the pungency of that folkloric joking. Readers of Le Bras will feel themselves on known ground with those High Masses that serve as a standard for an event. Let us give up commenting on that "foul air" from the point of view of the history of medicine, on those "hundred thousand people" in the Paris of the time of the Armagnacs from the point of view of demographic conscience, and finally on that "God's good time" and the feeling of a *fatum*. In any case, would a history of civilizations in which nothing of all these riches appeared deserve its title, even if Toynbee were the author?

The gulf that separates ancient historiography, with its narrowly political point of view, from our economic and social history is enormous, but it is no greater than the one that separates history today from what it might be tomorrow. One good way of realizing this is to try to write a historical novel, just as the right way to test a descriptive grammar is to put it backwards into a translation machine. Our conceptualization of the past is so reduced and summary that the best-documented historical novel shrieks out its falsity as soon as the characters open their mouths or make a gesture. How could it be otherwise when we cannot even say what exactly is the difference that we feel between a French, an English, or an American conversation, when we cannot follow the clever meanderings of a conversation between Provençal peasants? We feel, by the attitude of two men chatting in the street and whose words we cannot hear, that they are neither father and son, nor strangers to each other: no doubt a father-in-law and son-in-law. We guess, from his bearing, that that other gentleman has just crossed the threshold of his own house, or of a church, or of a public building, or of an unknown house. Yet it is enough for us to take a plane and disembark in Bombay, for us no longer to be able to guess these things. The historian has still a great deal of work to do before we can turn over time's hourglass, and the treatises of tomorrow will perhaps be as different from ours as ours are from Froissart or Eutropius's *Breviarium*.

History Is a Boundary Idea

What can be equally well expressed as History with a capital H—that of the *Discours sur l'histoire universelle*, of the *Leçons sur la philosophie de l'histoire*, and of *A Study in History*—does not exist. There only exist "histories of. . . . " An event is meaningless except in a series, the number of series is indefinite, they are not hierarchically ordered, and we shall see that they do not converge toward a geometrical projection of all the perspectives. The idea of History is an inaccessible limit or, rather, a transcendental idea. That History cannot be written; historiographies believed to be complete unknowingly deceive the reader about what they have to offer, and philosophies of history are nonsense, akin to a dogmatic illusion—or, rather, they would be nonsense if they were not mainly philosophies of "a history of," among others, national history. The only good use to be made of History is a regulating one; that idea, Kant would say, "has an excellent use, an indispensably necessary one, that of directing the understanding toward a definite goal." Thus it has "an objective but indeterminate value" and we could not make of it "any determined empirical use, seeing that it does not indicate the slightest criterion." It is simply "a heuristic principle."

All is well so long as one is content to affirm, with St. Augustine, that Providence directs empires and nations, and that the Roman conquest was in conformity with the divine plan. We then know of what "history of" we are speaking; all goes wrong when History ceases to be the history of nations and is gradually inflated by all we can come to conceive about the past. Will Providence direct the history of civilizations? But what do we mean by civilizations?[8] Would God direct a *flatus vocis*? One does not see that bicameralism, coitus interruptus, the mechanics of central forces, direct taxation, the detail of rising lightly on one's toes when uttering a subtle or strong sentence (as M. Birotteau did), and other events of the nineteenth century must evolve with the same rhythm. Why should they? And if they do not, the impression that the historical continuum gives us of dividing into a certain number of civilizations is only an optical illusion, and it would be about as interesting to discuss their numbers as to discuss the grouping of stars in constellations.

If Providence directs History and if History is a whole, then the divine plan is indiscernible; as a whole, History escapes us and, as an interlacing of series, it is a chaos like the agitated movement of a large town seen from a plane. The historian does not feel very anxious to know if the agitation in question is leading in some direction, if it has a law, if it is evolving. It is very clear, in truth, that this law would not be the key; to discover that a train is going to Orléans does not sum up or explain what the passengers inside the carriages may be doing.

If the law of evolution is no mystic key, it can only be an indication, which would allow an observer who came from Sirius to tell the time on the dial of History and to tell that such a historic moment is later than another; whether that law is rationalization, progress, the passage from the homogeneous to the heterogeneous, technical development, or development of freedoms, it would allow one to say that the twentieth century is later than the fourth, but would not summarize all that may have happened within those centuries. An observer from Sirius, knowing that freedom of the press or the number of cars is a reliable chronological indication, would consider that aspect of reality in dating the spectacle of the planet Earth, but it goes without saying that the inhabitants of Earth would nonetheless go on doing many other things beside driving cars and cursing their government in their daily papers. The sense of evolution is a biological, theological, anthropological, sociological, and paraphysical problem, but not a historical one, for the historian is not concerned with sacrificing history to just one of its aspects, even if that aspect is an indication; physics and even thermodynamics cannot be reduced to the contemplation of entropy.[9]

So, if that vast problem does not interest the historian, what will interest him? One often hears that question[10] asked, and the reply cannot be simple; his interest will depend on the state of the documentation, his tastes, an idea that crosses his mind, an assignment from an editor, and many other things. But if thereby one means to ask what the historian ought to be interested in, then it becomes impossible to give a reply—

will it be right to give the noble name of history to a diplomatic incident and refuse it to the history of games and sports? It is impossible to fix a scale of importance without its being subjective. Let us end with a page of Popper, who puts things strongly.

I think the only way to resolve the difficulty is consciously to introduce a pre-conceived point of view of selection. Historicism wrongly takes interpretations for theories. It is possible, for example, to interpret "history" as a history of the class struggle, or of racial struggle for supremacy, or as the history of scientific and industrial progress. All these points of view are more or less interesting and, as points of view, beyond reproach. But historicists do not present them as such; they do not see that there are necessarily a number of fundamentally equivalent interpretations (even if some of them may be distinguished by their fruitfulness, an important point). Instead, . . . they present them as doctrines or theories declaring that all history is the history of class struggle, and so on. Classical historians, who rightly oppose this procedure, are, on the other hand, liable to fall into a still greater error: aiming at objectivity, they feel constrained to avoid all selective points of view; but, since that is impossible, they adopt points of view without, usually, realizing that they are doing so.[11]

Since History does not exist, one little mystery grows clear—how is it that ancient philosophy, scholastic philosophy, and classical philosophy never philosophized about History? The historism of the nineteenth century reckoned it had gone beyond classical philosophy; the discovery of the past would have been the discovery of a new continent that would be the place of all possible truth. We must, said Troeltsch, "fundamentally historize all that we think of man and of his values"; that is the modern version of the Pyrrhonian paradoxes. The truth is that classical philosophy had not ignored history—or, rather, histories; but, instead of philosophizing on History, it meditated either on Being and Becoming in general, or on a "history of" among several clearly defined ones—for example, on that of the succession of political regimes, royalty, democracy, tyranny.

History Takes Place in the Sublunary

Besides, classical philosophy did not personify History; it confined itself to stating that our world is one of becoming, of generating and of corruption. To Aristotle and the Schoolmen, indeed, the world includes two quite distinct regions, Earth and the heavens. The celestial region is that of determinatism, of law, of science—the heavenly bodies are not born, do not change or die; and their movement has the periodicity and the perfection of the works of a clock. On the other hand, in our world, situated below the moon, becoming reigns and everything is an event. There can be no sure science of becoming; its laws are only probable, for one has to reckon with the peculiarities that "matter" introduces into our reasoning about form and pure concepts. Man is free; chance exists, events have causes whose effect remains doubtful; the future is uncertain; becoming is contingent. We have a better understanding of this Aristotelian opposition of the celestial and the sublunary when we compare it with the opposition we readily make between the physical sciences and the human sciences. Man, we affirm, cannot be the object of science; human acts are not things.

It is the Aristotelian opposition, brought to another level of being; we shall see at the end of this book what can be believed about it, but it remains true that, to describe history as it is and as it will be so long as it merits the name of history, the Aristotelian conception is the most convenient instrument. In the sublunary world, each will recognize the world where we live and act, the world that we see and that novels, dramas, and history books describe, as opposed to the heaven of abstractions where physical and human sciences reign. The idea may shock us; we often believe, more or less vaguely, that freedom and chance are illusions of common sense that science repudiates. Thus the historian, if he wants to rise above common knowledge, ought to substitute determinism for chance and freedom, to leave the sublunary. That is to imagine that history is a human science, such are the two illusions: believing that human sciences are sublunary, believing that history is not sublunary. Against historism and against scientism in history, we have to return to classical philosophy, for which History does not exist and historical facts are not scientific. A study of historic epistemology can feed exclusively on a few crumbs fallen from the table of Aristotle and of Thucydides[12]—and, as we shall see, on the lessons of the *work* of historians over the last century.

Which Facts Are Historic?

Historism, from Herder and Hegel to Collingwood and Toynbee, is useless or false; it has raised difficulties, rather than solved or even set problems.[13]

To escape historism, it is enough to suppose that everything is historical; if this is pushed to the limit, historism becomes harmless. It limits itself to stating what is evident—it arrives continually at events of every kind, and our world is one of becoming; it is vain to think that some of those events would be of a particular nature, would be "historical," and would constitute History. The initial question put by historism was this: What distinguishes a historical event from another that is not? As it quickly became apparent that that distinction was not easy to make, that one could not rely on naive or national conscience to discriminate, but that one could not do better and that the object of the debate was escaping, historism concluded that History was subjective, that it was the projection of our values and the answer to the questions we are ready to ask it.

The merit of historism will have been to bring to light the difficulties of the idea of History and the limits of historical objectivity; it is even simpler not to begin to propose the idea of History and to admit right away that the sublunary is the realm of the probable. All that is said about the analysis of the historical object, about the crisis of history, about facts "that do not exist"—all that is at the heart of the present question of history (at least in Germany and in France: in England that heart is, rather, the human problem of historical causality) is only the consequence of the initial question: What is historic, what is not? Now it is enough to admit that everything is historic, in order for that question to become both evident and harmless. Yes, history is only the reply to our questions, because it is impossible to ask all the questions, to describe all the becoming, and because the progress of the historical questionnaire is situated in time and is as slow as the progress of any science. Yes, history is subjective, for it is undeniable that the subject of a history book is chosen freely.[14]

Chapter III

Plots, Not Facts or Geometrical Figures

If everything that has happened is equally worthy of history, does not history become chaos? How could one fact in it be more important than another? Why is it not all reduced to a grisaille of singular events? The life of a Nivernais peasant would be as good as that of Louis XIV; that beeping of horns rising from the avenue would be as good as a world war. Can one escape the historist questioning? There must be a choice in history, in order to escape a dispersion into singularities and an indifference in which everything is of equal worth.

The reply is twofold. First, history is not interested in the singularity of individual events, but in their specificity (as we shall see in the next chapter); second, facts, as we shall see, do not exist like so many grains of sand. History is not an atomic determinism; it takes place in our world, where a world war is more important than a concept of car horns unless—everything is possible—that concert itself sets a world war in motion. For "facts" do not exist in isolation; the historian finds them organized in wholes in which they act as causes, objectives, opportunities, risks, pretexts, and so on. Our own existence, after all, does not appear to us as a grisaille of atomic incidents; it immediately has a meaning, and we understand it. Why should the position of the historian be more Kafka-like? History is made of the same substance as the lives of each of us.

Facts thus have a natural organization that the historian finds ready-made, once he has chosen his subject and it is unchangeable—The effort of historical work consists precisely in discovering that organization—causes of the 1914 War, the goals of the belligerents, the Sarajevo incident; the limits of the objectivity of historical explanations partly return to the fact that each historian succeeds in pushing the explanation more or less far. Within each subject chosen, this organization of facts confers

31

on them a relative importance; in a military history of the 1914 War, a surprise attack on forward posts is of less importance than an offensive that filled the newspaper headlines; in the same military history Verdun counts more than Spanish flu. Of course, in a demographic history the reverse will be true. The difficulties would begin only if one took it into one's head to ask whether Verdun or flu is absolutely more important from the point of view of History. Thus, facts do not exist in isolation, but have objective connections; the choice of a subject in history is free but, within the chosen subject, the facts and their connections are what they are and nothing can change that; historical truth is neither relative nor inaccessible, as something ineffable beyond all points of view, like a "geometrical figure."

The Notion of a Plot

Facts do not exist in isolation, in the sense that the fabric of history is what we shall call a plot, a very human and not very "scientific" mixture of material causes, aims, and chances—a slice of life, in short, that the historian cuts as he wills and in which facts have their objective connections and their relative importance: the beginnings of feudal society, the Mediterranean policy of Philip II or only one episode of that policy, the revolution of Galileo.[1] The word "plot" has the advantage of reminding us that what the historian studies is as human as a play or a novel, *War and Peace* or *Anthony and Cleopatra*. That plot is not necessarily arranged in chronological order; like an interior drama, it can unfold from one plane to another. The plot of Galileo's revolution will place Galileo against the framework of thought about physics at the beginning of the seventeenth century, against the aspirations he vaguely felt within himself, against the current problems and references, Platonism and Aristotelianism, and so on. The plot may thus be a transversal cut of different temporal rhythms, a spectral analysis. It will always be a plot because it is human, sublunary; because it will not be a bit of determinism.

A plot is not a determinism in which atoms called the Prussian army would overthrow atoms called the Austrian army; its details then assume a relative importance called for by the development of the plot. If plots were little determinisms, then, when Bismarck sends the Ems dispatch, the working of telegraphy would be given in detail with the same objectivity as the decision of the chancellor, and the historian would have begun by explaining to us what biological processes had brought about the coming into the world of that same Bismarck. If details did not assume relative importance, then, when Napoleon gives an order to his troops, the historian would explain each time why the soldiers obeyed him (we remember that Tolstoy puts the problem of history almost in those terms in *War and Peace*). It is true that if the soldiers had disobeyed once, that event would have been pertinent, for the course of the drama would have been changed.

Then what are the facts worthy of rousing the interest of the historian? All depends on the plot chosen; in itself, a fact is not interesting or uninteresting. Is it interesting for an archaeologist to go and count the number of feathers on the wings of the Victory of Samothrace? Will he give proof, as he does so, of a praiseworthy rigor or of a superfluous exactitude? It is impossible to say, for the fact is nothing without its plot; it becomes something if it is made into the hero or the supernumerary in a drama of the history of art in which the classical tendency not to use too many feathers and not to split hairs about the rendering, the baroque tendency to overload and to seek the detail and the taste of barbarian arts to fill space with decorative elements, will be made to follow each other.

Let us notice that if our plot mentioned above had not been the international policy of Napoleon, but the Grand Army, its morale, and its attitudes, the customary obedience of the Old Guard would have been relevant and we would have had to say why. But it is difficult to add up the plots and make a total; either Nero is our hero and it will suffice for him to say, "Guards, carry out my orders," or else the Guards are our heroes and we will write another tragedy. In history as in the theater, to show everything is impossible—not because it would require too many pages, but because there is no elementary historical fact, no eventworthy atom. If one ceases to see the events in their plots, one is sucked into the abyss of the infinitesimal. Archaeologists know this well—you discover a rather rough bas-relief representing a scene whose meaning escapes you; since the best photograph cannot replace a good description, you undertake to describe it. But which details are to be mentioned, which are not? You cannot say, since you do not understand what the figures in the scene are doing. And yet you foresee that a particular detail, insignificant to you, will provide the key to the scene for a more ingenious colleague than yourself—that slight inflection at the end of a sort of cylinder that you take for a stick will make him think of a serpent; it is indeed a serpent the figure is holding, so the figure is a genie. Thus, in the interest of science, is all to be described? Try to do so.

There Is No Atomic Fact

Unfortunately, even if we refuse to treat the historical event as depersonalized behavior, even if we do not cover our eyes so as not to see its meaning, we are not at the end of our difficulties; we shall find an event-worthy atom by following this course, and we shall be sucked down by two abysses instead of only one. An event, whatever it is, implies a context because it has a meaning; it refers back to a plot of which it is one episode—or, rather, to an indefinite number of plots—conversely, one can always divide an event into smaller events. What may constitute an event? The German breakthrough toward Sedan in 1940? It is a whole strategic, tactical, administrative, and psychological plot. Will the atom of a historical fact be the conduct of each individual soldier in the two armies? It is a vast labor to understand a single individual. Or each action of each soldier, each step of each soldier. But a step is not a spatiotemporal behavior that can be recorded by means of an ingenious apparatus. It has a meaning; a soldier does not walk like everyone else— he walks in step, even in goose step; Frederick II is not far off, nor is Frederick William I. What are we to choose? Which drama shall we prefer? One cannot speak of everything, neither can one tell the life story of all the pedestrians who pass each other in the street.

It is impossible to describe a totality, and all description is selective; the historian never draws the map of the eventworthy—at the very most he can multiply the routes that cross it. As F. von Hayek says[2] (more or less), it is a misuse of language to talk of the French Revolution or of the Hundred Years' War as if they were natural units, which makes us think that the first step in the study of those events must be to determine what they resemble, as is done with a stone or an animal. The object of the study is never the totality of the phenomena observable at a given time and place, but only certain aspects of them; according to the question we ask, the same spatiotemporal situation can contain a certain number of different objects to be studied. Hayek adds that according to those questions, what we are accustomed to consider as a unique historic event may split into a multitude of objects of knowledge; it is a confusion on this point that is principally responsible for the doctrine, so fashionable today, according to which all historical knowledge is necessarily relative, determined by our "situation" and bound to change with the passage of time; the kernel of truth contained in the assertion concerning the relativity of historical knowledge is that at different times historians will be interested in different objects, but not that they will hold different opinions on the same object.

Let us add that if the same "event" can be dispersed among several plots, then data belonging to heterogeneous categories—social, political, religious—can compose one and the same event; it is even very frequently the case. The majority of events are "total social events," in the opinion of Marcel Mauss; indeed, the theory of the total social fact merely means that our traditional categories mutilate reality.

Indeed, there comes to my mind a little enigma: Why is it so often a question of the decomposition of the historical object, the crisis in the objectivity of history so often brought up, and so rarely a question of the decomposition of the geographical object, a subjectivity of geography? And what about the "total geographical fact"? Yet it is clear that a region has no more objective existence than has an event; we divide it at will (a Toynbee of geography would decree that there are 43 or 119 "regions" on the globe and that all *should be regarded as philosophically equivalent*). An area is broken down into geological, climatological, botanical, and other data, and the region will be what we make of it by the questions we choose to put to it: Shall we attach importance to the question of the open field, and shall we ask it? A civilization, it is said, questions history starting from its own values and loves to admire itself in its past; if it is true that civilizations have those existential needs and that they satisfy them in history, they will satisfy them even more in geography, which will allow them to admire themselves in their present. Consequently, one is astonished that there is not a geographism as there has been a historism; must we think that geographers had less philosophical minds than historians, or that philosophers had more historical than geographical minds?[3]

It is obviously impossible to relate the whole of becoming, and a choice must be made; nor does there exist a particular category of events (political history, for example) that would be History, and our inevitable choice. So it is literally true to state, with Marrou, that all historiography is subjective. The choice of a historical subject is free, and by right all subjects are of equal value; there is no History, nor is there a "sense of history"; the train of events (drawn by some engine of really scientific history) does not move forward on a fully laid track. The itinerary chosen by the historian to describe the eventworthy field can be freely chosen, and all the itineraries are equally legitimate (though not all are equally interesting). Having said that, the configuration of the eventworthy territory is what it is, and two historians who may have taken the same road will see the territory in the same way, or will discuss their disagreement very objectively.

Structure of the Eventworthy Field

Historians relate plots, which are like so many itineraries that they mark out at will through the very objective field of events (which is infinitely divisible and is not made up of eventworthy atoms); no historian describes the whole of this field, for an itinerary cannot take every road; none of these itineraries is the true one, is History. In short, the eventworthy field does not comprise spots to be visited and that would be called events; an event is not a being, but an intersection of possible itineraries. Let us consider the event called the 1914 War—or, rather, let us take up a more precise position: the military operations and the diplomatic activity; that is an itinerary as good as any other.

We can also take a wider view and move into neighboring zones; military needs brought state intervention in economic life, raised political and constitutional problems, changed customs, increased the number of nurses and women workers, and brought about a complete change in the condition of women. We are now on the itinerary of feminism, which we can follow more or less far. Some itineraries pull up short (the war has had little influence on the evolution of painting, unless we are mistaken); the same "fact" that is a deep-rooted cause on a given itinerary will be an incident or a detail on another. All these connections in the eventworthy field are perfectly objective. So what will be the event called the 1914 War? It will be what you make of it according to the scope that is freely given to the concept of war: the diplomatic or military operations, or a greater or lesser part of the itineraries that cross that concept. If the view is wide enough, the war will even be a "total social fact."

Events are not things, consistent objects, substances; they are a découpage we freely make in reality, an aggregate of the processes in which substances, men, and things interact. Events have no natural unity; one cannot, like the good cook in *Phèdre,* cut them according to their true joints, because they have none. Simple as it is, that truth did not become well known before the end of the last century, and its discovery produced a certain shock; people spoke of subjectivism, of the decomposition of the historical object. It can hardly be explained other than by the very eventworthy character of historiography up to the nineteenth century and by its narrowness of vision. There was great history, especially political history, which was sacred; there were "accepted" events. Non-eventworthy history has been a sort of telescope that, by letting us see in the sky millions of stars other than those known to astronomers of old, would make us understand that our dividing the starry sky into constellations was subjective.

Thus, events do not exist with the consistence of a guitar or a soup tureen. It must still be added that, whatever is said, they do not exist in the manner of a "geometrical figure"; it is popular to affirm that they exist in themselves, in the manner of a cube or a pyramid. We never see all the faces of a cube simultaneously, we never have more than a partial point of view; on the other hand, we can multiply those points of view. It may be the same with events; their inaccessible truth would integrate the numberless points of view we could have of them, each of which would be a partial truth. That is not so; to compare an event to a geometrical figure is deceptive, and more dangerous than convenient. We shall first develop at some length an example (we shall do so two or three times in the course of this book—no more than that), so that we may see of what this so-called plurality of points of view consists.

An Example: Public Benefaction

In Roman society the gift—or, rather, all that can be designated by that vague word—had as big a place as in potlatch societies or in those that have a redistributive fiscal policy and aid the Third World; bread and circuses, distribution of land to veterans, New Year's presents, "gifts" from the emperor to his officials, baksheesh raised to the rank of an institution, wills by which a man's goods are distributed to his friends and his servants, banquets to which the whole town is invited, patronage of the leading citizens who make up the ruling class. (The importance of that patronage is such that in a Greco-Roman town, one of those whose ruins in North Africa or in Turkey are visited by tourists, most of the buildings we would call public were offered to the city by a leading citizen—that is the case with most amphitheaters. Let us imagine that in France, most of the town halls, the schools, and hydraulic dams are due to the wealth of the citizens and that, moreover, they might offer drinks and a cinema to the workers.) How can we interpret that confused mass of data in which the most unusual modes of behavior (the presents to officials are their salary, patronage takes the place of income tax) and the most diverse motives are combined—unscrupulous ambition, paternalism, monarchic style, corruption, munificence, local patriotism, taste for rivalry, desire to hold one's own, conformity to opinion, fear of uproar?

In some of these modes of conduct one can discern the ancient equivalent of public assistance and of charity.[4] There arise from this plot free bread, distribution of land and the founding of settlements, public feasts (when the poor had the opportunity to eat meat and sweets), pensions given to "clients" in good houses, the duty of philanthropy according to the Stoics or, rather, according to popular morality. Certainly the words "poor" and "charity" are unknown in the vocabulary of pagans; they are Jewish and Christian concepts. The pagans said they acted out of generosity or patriotism, and welfare relief was supposed to be destined for all citizens; it was the Roman people who had a right to public corn, "the citizens" who were sent to colonies. But let us not be deceived by values; in fact, only the poor citizens would benefit from corn and land, but the phraseology nonetheless continued to dissolve the economic category of the poor in the civic universality of the law. Thus universalism did not prevent the poor from being helped—or, rather, certain poor: those who could declare themselves to be Roman citizens; the others were abandoned to poverty and to private philanthropy. So the distribution of corn was not exactly what ancient values said it was, nor was it the equivalent of modern welfare; it was a singular event. It would be false to think that public assistance is a function that, in deceptive phraseology, is found, ever the same, throughout history; the values are not the mirror of modes of conduct, and modes of conduct do not fall into line with functions.

Other plots that are not superimposed on that of assistance and that produce other modes of conduct and other motives, are conceivable—for example, public benefaction. This concept, invented by Marrou in 1948, designates the attitude of the governing class, composed of landed gentry who live in town and who believe the government of the city is a right and a duty to the state. Thus, they feel that they have to keep things going, even at their own expense, and to make themselves popular by their generosity; if necessary, the people could bring them back to their duty by making a commotion. Monuments, amphitheaters, public banquets, circus and arena spectacles. . . . Thus, the subject of the plot is the mechanism that made the pagan governing class the prisoner of its own privileges. That class considered it a duty to ruin itself for the city, for nobility has its obligations. Which is a third plot: aristocratic munificence; the noble distributes pensions to his dependents, remembers friends and servants in his will, builds an amphitheater, patronizes arts and letters; having become a Christian, he gives alms, frees his slaves, embellishes the basilica, multiplies pious and charitable works. Other itineraries again are conceivable in the same eventworthy field: economic rationality in antiquity, the utilization of the "surplus," "collective goods." (How did ancient societies procure the goods that cannot be expected of a selfish *homo oeconomicus* and that modern men expect to get principally from the state?)[5] All these plots, each of which has its own objectivity, do not concern the same modes of conduct, the same values, and the same actors. We could even have discussed differently all the modes of conduct concerning the gift; scattered them, as is usually done, among public rights, ideology, and customs; or not mentioned many of them as being too anecdotal.

Criticism of the Idea of the Geometrical Figure

So where will our geometrical figure be? Although they cross and recross, these different plots do not converge, except in the measure that everything touches on everything; those so-called perspectives themselves open onto numberless points of view (public beneficence opens up perspectives on the state as a provider, the genesis of bureaucracy, sumptuary waste). It would not even have occurred to us to bring together all those modes of conduct like so many so-called partial points of view, were it not for the existence of the word "gift" and a general impression of exoticism ("all that is a far cry from our customs; it is Roman potlatch"). When we believe in a geometrical figure, we are the victims of a semantic trap; if, instead of speaking of "gift" because we have read

Mauss, we have spoken, like the Greeks, of the desire to compete and of patriotism, or, like the Romans, of liberality and a seeking after popularity, or again, like the Indians, of ceremonial gifts, we should have divided the eventworthy field in a totally different way, and the vocabulary would have made us imagine other geometrical figures. Would the "true" geometrical figure be that of the persons concerned? Is it not fitting to study a society starting from one's own values? The result would be ridiculous. To study the modes of conduct of a society is one thing, to study its way of dividing the eventworthy field is another; it is true that the Romans looked on distributions of corn as civic duties and that they were a form of assistance. We have seen the paradox before; as far as these distributions are concerned, the ancient idea of civic universalism does not correspond to the facts and concept of public benefaction, which on the contrary fits them like a glove (it was cut from them), dates from 1948.

If one insists on speaking of geometrical figures, let that term be reserved for the perception of one event by different witnesses, by different living individuals: the battle of Waterloo as seen by the monad Fabrice, the monad Marshal Ney, and a monad canteen keeper. As for the event "the battle of Waterloo," as a historian will write it up, it is not the geometrical figure of these partial views; it is a choice from what the witnesses have seen, and a critical choice. For, if duped by the expression "geometrical figure," the historian was content to integrate the evidence, one would find, in that battle, several romantic whiffs coming from a young Italian and a lovely young peasant girl, whose origin would be identical. The historian carves out in the evidence and the documents the event as he has chosen to make it; that is why an event never coincides with the *cogito* of its actors and witnesses. It will even be possible to find, in a battle of Waterloo, grumblings and yawns coming from the *cogito* of a veteran. That will be because the historian has decreed that "his" battle of Waterloo will not be only the strategy, and will also include the mentality of the combatants.

When all is said and done, it seems that in history only a single authentic geometrical figure exists: History, total history, the totality of all that happens. But that geometrical figure is not for us; God alone, if He exists, Who sees a pyramid from every angle at once, must be able to contemplate History "like one and the same town looked at from different sides" (thus does monadology express itself). On the other hand, there are small geometrical figures that God Himself does not contemplate because they exist only in words: the potlatch, the French Revolution, the 1914 War. Would the First World War then be only words? Men do indeed study "the War of 1914 and the evolution of manners," "the 1914 War and the planned economy"—is not the war itself the integral of all these partial views? Precisely, it is a total, a lumber room; it is not a geometrical figure; one cannot say that the rise of feminism between 1914 and 1918 is the same thing as the strategy of frontal attacks seen by other eyes.

But what about the logic of war, the terrible totalitarian logic of modern conflicts? But what do you mean by the word "war"? The choice is: Either you speak of the military and diplomatic conflict, or else of all that happened during that conflict. Total wars are like terrible storms. Storms are climatic and meteorological phenomena. When a storm breaks on a mountainous mass, nature feels it in all aspects: relief, glacial contours, erosion, hydrography, flora, fauna, magnetic field, human habitat. Everything suffers the consequences or tries to protect itself from them; you can call a storm just the single meteorological phenomenon or the sum total of its consequences, but, in this second case you must not believe that there is a geometrical figure of the storm integrating all the points of view. To speak of a geometrical figure is to take a partial view (all views are partial) for a point of view of a totality. Now "events" are not totalities, but knots of relationships; the only totalities are words— "war" or "gift"—that one freely extends widely or narrowly.

Is it really worthwhile to use up our munitions like this against an inoffensive way of speaking? Yes, because it is at the origin of three illusions: that of the depth of history, that of general history, and that of the renewal of the object. The words "point of view" have made subjectivity and inaccessible truth resound like harmonics: "All points of view are equal and the truth will always escape us; it is always deeper." In fact, the sublunary world has no depths anywhere, it is only very complicated; we do reach some truths, but they are partial (that is one of the differences that separate history from science; the latter also reaches truths, but provisional truths, as we shall see later). Since no geometrical figure gives them unity, the distinction between "the history of" and the history called general is purely conventional. General history does not exist as an activity leading to specific results; it confines itself to putting special histories within one binding and to proportioning the number of pages allowed to each according to personal theories or public taste; it is the work of an encyclopedist when it is done well. Who can doubt that the collaboration of the "generalist" and of the specialist is desirable?[6] It can hardly do any harm; but it is not the collaboration of the blind and the paralyzed. The generalist may have penetrating views, like everyone; they will enlighten a specialized "history of," but they will not bring about a wonderful synthesis.

The third illusion, that of the renewing of the object, is the paradox of origins, which has caused much ink to flow. "Origins are rarely beautiful"—or, rather, by definition what we call origins is anecdotal. The death of Jesus, a mere anecdote in the reign of Tiberius, was soon to be transformed into a gigantic event; and who knows if, at this very moment. . . . The paradox is troubling only if one imagines that there is a general history and that an event, in itself, is historic or is not. A historian who died at the end of the reign of Tiberius most probably would not have mentioned the passion of Christ; the only plot in which he could have placed it was the political and religious agitation of the Jewish people in which Christ would have played, as he wrote of it, and as He still plays for us, the part of a mere figure in the crowd—it is in the history of Christianity that Christ has the main part. The signification of His passion has not changed with time; it is we who change plots when we pass from Jewish to Christian history. Everything is historic, but there are only partial histories.

Historical Nominalism

In conclusion, when Marrou writes that history is subjective, one may agree with the spirit of that affirmation and accept it as a *ktéma es aei* of historical epistemology; in the perspective of the present book, we will formulate the letter of it otherwise: Since everything is historic, history is what we will choose. Finally, as Marrou reminds us, subjectivity does not mean arbitrariness. Let us suppose that from our window (the historian as such works in a study) we gaze on a crowd demonstrating in the Champs-Elysées or the Place de la République. First, it will be a human spectacle, and not an infinitely divisible behavior, of arms and legs; history is not scientist, but sublunary. Second, there will be no elementary facts, because each fact has meaning only within its own plot and has reference to an indefinite number of plots: a political demonstration, a certain way of walking, an episode in the personal life of each protester, and so on. Third, one may not decree that only the plot "political demonstration" is worthy of History. Fourth, no geometrical figure will include all the plots that can be said to be in that event-worthy field. In all of this, <u>history is subjective</u>. It remains that all that the substances—men—do in the street, in whatever way it is considered, is absolutely objective.[7] So we can see what the word "subjectivity," coming from the pen of Marrou, means—that word which has raised so many protests (the virtue of Clio must not give rise to suspicion): not "idealism" but "nominalism." And, as I hope by now to have persuaded my reader, nothing is more reasonable than a nominalist conception of history.[8]

The Problem of Historical Description

The nominalist conception allows us to realize the illusion of an enrichment of the past, of the impression that the past retroactively receives a feeling of the future, that the future triumph of Christianity modifies the meaning of the life of Christ or that masterpieces grow with humanity as an inscription carved in the bark grows with the tree. In *La pensée et le mouvant,* Bergson studies this apparent action of the future on the past; on the concept of preromanticism, he writes:

If there had not been a Rousseau, a Chateaubriand, a Vigny, a Hugo, not only would one never have noticed, but also there would never have been, a romanticism in the classics of former days, for this romanticism of the classics is realized only by cutting out of these works a single aspect, and the cutting, with its particular form, no more existed in classical literature before the appearance of romanticism than there exists in the passing cloud the amusing drawing that the artist sees in it when he organizes the amorphous mass according to his fantasy.

But isn't that taking a conceptual découpage for a substantial form? The themes one can one day qualify as preromantic already existed, without bearing the name, in classicism; they can't be introduced into it after the event, for God Himself cannot make what has not taken place to have taken place; the future had to bring the possibility of linking those themes with romanticism, when there was a romanticism, but it did not create them; a fact is not created when it is discovered.

It is not romanticism that, in its day, creates preromanticism retroactively; it is the historian of literature, at whatever period he lives. Thus time plays no part in Bergson's paradox, despite appearances; the same enrichment of the object works, but in the opposite direction, when, in the twentieth century, we undertake to describe romanticism as a post-classicism. The real problem posed by the paradox is that of historical découpage, of the constitution of the event as one will call it into being. One can write countless things on romanticism, on classicism; one can describe classicism as preromanticism; one can also cut from it a thousand other plots that will all be acceptable. For one does not describe in the absolute; every description implies the choice, most often unconscious, of features that will be deemed pertinent. The "fact" that the 1914 War is, for example, can be described—or, rather, constituted—in a thousand different ways that range from a chronicle of the diplomatic and military events, to an analysis of the political, social, mental, economic, and strategic conditions implied in those events, to a sort of analysis "in depth," to a "sociology" of that conflict in which the name of Verdun will scarcely be spoken, unless by way of an example.

These two extreme manners obviously do not meet the same interest, do not rest on the same choice of relevant features, are not addressed to the same public. So it must never be forgotten, when we begin to write, that the chronicle of events is not the only way of writing history, and that it is not even an indispensable part of it; that it is, rather, a lazy way out. The historian is not reduced to a procession of well-known episodes, the Marne and Verdun. He must feel, around the "fact" (as it comes to us from the documents of the day, from the collective memory and from school tradition), a thousand other possible structures, and he must be ready to change the descriptive level, if expediency demands it. Expediency—that is, internal coherence: All descriptive courses are good; the essential thing is, once a course has been chosen, to keep to it. A book devoted to the 1914 War, and to that alone, must be narrative and tell of Verdun; within a general history the 1914 War must be represented only by its global, "sociological" features.

The Difficulty of Coherent Synthesis

Internal coherence and nimbleness in shifting the descriptive level of "facts" are fine, difficult, and rare things; most often a history book is made up of a juxtaposition of descriptions that are not at the same level. A book of Roman history will set out the military events in a narrative way; the facts that contrast the strategy of the ancients wih that of the moderns (see Ardant du Picq on this) and the fatal sequence of Roman imperialism will be deemed to be implied in the details of their manifestations; political history will be written, sometimes from day to day, sometimes from a distance; the account of literary life will suppose that the literary phenomenon is always and everywhere the same, and will be content to enumerate works and authors; the social life, on the contrary, will be seen from much higher. In short, the historian will appear to address himself now to a specialist to whom the Roman atmosphere, the non-eventworthy data, are familiar and are almost as easily understood as they were by the Romans (who were steeped in them and who were interested only in the day's news); now to an ignorant but intelligent reader who has everything to learn, beginning with the ever-present non-eventworthy data. The latter will want to have brought out for him the features that differentiate or liken Roman civilization and contemporary civilization and other great civilizations in the framework of universal history; he will accept with difficulty being offered in bulk, within one binding, pages of "sociology" and pages of chronology.

To satisfy so exacting a reader about coherence would be a Herculean task; it would need a Max Weber—perhaps several of him. It would be necessary to say what distinguishes Rome from other civilizations seen on the same scale—to analyze, for example, what distinguishes the Roman religion from other religions; that analysis obviously presupposes a comparative typology of the religious phenomenon. It would be necessary to do the same for administration, at the cost of a synthetic and comparative view of the administrative phenomenon in history. Roman society itself would have to be set in the comparative study of preindustrial civilizations, and that comparison would make us aware, for Rome, of a thousand details that until then had remained implicit and hidden in the obvious. In exchange for all these fine things, our exacting reader would consent to let us leave out the details of the wars between Caesar and Pompey.

Thus, writing a general history is a task to make the boldest tremble, for it is not a question of summarizing "facts," but of arranging them differently and of being coherent with the level adopted. To do it well, there wil have to remain no residue of eventworthy data that has not been rethought and that would be relevant only to the scale of a chronicle or a monograph. In short, what, since Fustel de Coulanges, has been called historical synthesis is nothing but the effort of incorporating the fact at a descriptive level that is not necessarily that of the document. To pass from the monograph to the general history does not consist in retaining in the latter only the main features of the former, because when we pass from the one to the other, the main features are no longer the same; thus, for example, an abyss is created between the republican religion and the imperial religion within Roman history that is not the same as that between the Roman religion and the other religions. To write a good general history would, finally, be an undertaking so difficult that today it does not seem to have been a success for any civilization; that is because the day has not yet come. When, thanks to some future Weber, the great differential features of universal history have become a topic familiar to us, we shall more opportunely speak of it again.

In the meantime, three consequences can usefully be deduced from historical nominalism. First, every history is in some way a comparative history. For the features considered relevant, in relation to which an individual fact is described, are universal in that way. When we find the existence of sects in the Roman religion relevant and interesting, we are in a position to say whether any other religion does or does not present the same feature; and, conversely, to note that another religion has a theology leads us to realize that Roman religion has none, and to be astonished that it is what it is. Next, every "fact" is surrounded with an implicit margin of the non-eventworthy, and it is that margin that leaves room to arrange it otherwise than has been done traditionally. Finally, since the "fact" is what one makes of it if one has the necessary flexibility, the discipline with which history can be compared is literary criticism. For we well know that what textbooks say about Racine is the least part of what could be said about that writer; a hundred critics writing a hundred books on Racine would write them all more differently, more truthfully, and more subtly than each other. Only the ungifted critics would be satisfied with the school Vulgate, with the "facts."

Chapter IV

Pure Curiosity about the Specific

If humanism is understood to be the fact of being interested in the truth of history insofar as the latter includes beautiful deeds, and in those beautiful deeds insofar as they teach the good, then history is certainly not humanism, for it does not confuse transcendentals; nor is it one, if we mean by humanism the conviction that history would have particular value for us because it speaks to us of men—that is, of ourselves. We do not mean to decree, so saying, that history should not be a humanism, or to forbid anyone from finding his pleasure in it (though the pleasure of history is fairly limited when we read it and seek in it anything else but itself); we only consider that if one looks at what historians do, we will see that history is no more a humanism than are the sciences or metaphysics. Then why does one take an interest in history and why does one write it? Or, rather (for the interest in it by each person is his personal affair: taste for the picturesque, patriotism . . .), what sort of interest does the historical genre, by its nature, seek to satisfy? What is its finality?

A Historian's Words: "It Is Interesting"

An archaeologist I know, a man deeply interested in his work and a clever historian, looks pityingly at you when you congratulate him on discovering in his dig a sculpture that is not bad; he refuses to explore the more marvelous sites, and declares that digging in a refuse dump is ordinarily more instructive. He wishes never to find a Venus de Milo, for, he says, it would teach nothing very new and art is a pleasure "outside work." Other archaeologists reconcile their work and their sense of beauty, but more through personal uniting of the two than by an essential unity. The favored term of my archaeologist, who is against the beautiful, is the main phrase of the historical genre: "It is interesting." This adjective does not apply to a treasure, to the crown jewels; it would be preposterous for the Acropolis, out of place for the site of a battle in the last two wars. The history of every nation is holy in its eyes, and one cannot say "The history of France is interesting" in the tone with which one praises Maya antiquities or the ethnography of the Nuers; it remains true that the Maya and the Nuers have their historians or ethnographers.

There is a popular history that has its time-honored repertoire—great men, famous episodes. That history is everywhere around us, on street signs, at the base of statues, in the bookseller's window, in the collective memory, and in school curricula; such is the "sociological" dimension of the historical genre. But the history of historians and of their readers sings that repertoire to a different tune when it takes it up; moreover, it is very far from confining itself to that repertoire. There has long existed a privileged history: a bit of Greece through Plutarch, especially Rome (the Republic rather than the Empire, and much more than the Byzantine Empire), a few episodes of the Middle Ages, modern times; but, in truth, scholars had always been interested in the entire past. Gradually, as ancient and foreign civilizations have been discovered— the Middle Ages, the Sumerians, the Chinese, "primitives"—they have come within the compass of our interest with very great ease, and if the Romans bore the public a bit, it is because they have been made into a "value people" instead of seeing how exotic they were. Since we are interested in everything, we no longer understand that barely sixty years ago Max Weber could base the interest we have in history on the famous "relation to values."

Weber: History as Related to Values

That expression, which becomes sibylline in proportion to its distance from the great period of German historism, simply means that what would distinguish the events we deem worthy of history from other events would be the value we attribute to them; we would maintain that a war between European nations is history and that a "fight between Bantu tribes" or [American] Indians would not be.[1] We would not be interested in all that happened, but would traditionally attach interest only to certain peoples, certain categories of events, or certain problems (quite independently of the favorable or unfavorable value judgments we may make regarding those people or those events); our choice sets history within its frontiers. A choice that varies from people to people and from century to century; let us take the history of music: "The central problem of that discipline, *from the point of view of the curiosity of the modern European* (there is the relationship with values!), no doubt resides in the following question: why does harmonic music, arising almost everywhere from popular polyphony, develop only in Europe?" (The italics, the parentheses, and the exclamation point are Weber's own.)[2]

It is to prejudge the curiosity of that modern European and to confuse the sociology of history with its finality. It does not seem that a specialist in Greek history at the École Normale Supérieure believes that his discipline is of an essence different from that of his colleague studying American Indians; if tomorrow there appears a book entitled *History of the Iroquois* (I think I remember such an empire existed), no one will be able to deny that the book is there and that it is history. Conversely, it suffices to open a Greek history book for Athens to cease to be that "high point of the past" about which we were dreaming the moment before, and for there to be no more difference between the Iroquois Confederacy and the Athenian (or Delian) League, whose history is no more or less deceptive than the rest of universal history.

Obviously, Weber does not see things otherwise, but how can he maintain another distinction he makes between the "justification" and the "reason for knowing"? The history of Athens would interest us in itself; that of the Iroquois would only be material for knowing problems with which we have to deal in relation to values—for example, the problem of imperialism or of the beginnings of society.[3] That is very dogmatic; if we look around us, we note that some treat the Iroquois as sociological material, that others treat the Athenians in the same way (as Raymond Aron does in his study on internal warfare, through Thucydides), and that still others study the Iroquois for love of the Iroquois and the Athenians for love of the Athenians. But we suspect that the thought of Weber is more subtle than these objections; he writes approximately this:

The fact that Frederick William IV renounced the imperial crown constitutes a historical event, whereas it is a matter of indifference what tailors made his uniform. It will be answered that it is indifferent to political history, but not to that of fashion nor to professional tailors; true, but even from that point of view, the tailors will not be personally important unless they changed fashion or the tailor's profession; otherwise their biography will only be a means of knowing the history of fashion or of their profession. Thus it happens that an inscribed potsherd tells us of a king or an empire: the potsherd is not thereby an event.[4]

The objection carries weight, and the reply we shall try to give will be a long one.

First of all, the distinction between value fact and document fact depends on the point of view, on the plot chosen, far from determining the choice of plot and the distinction of what would or would not be historic. Then there is some confusion between the plot itself and its characters and "bit players" (let us say between history and biography); there is also some confusion between the event and the document. Whether it is a potsherd or a tailor's biography, what is called a source or a document is first of all an event, great or small; the document can be defined as any event having a material trace to come down to us.[5] The Bible is an event in the history of Israel, and at the same time its source; a document of political history, it is an event in religious history; an inscribed potsherd, found in an ancient quarry on Sinai, which reveals the name of a pharaoh, is a document for dynastic history; it is also one of the many small events that make up the history of the solemn use of writing, of the habit of raising monuments for posterity, epigraphic or otherwise. That being said, it is with that potsherd as with any other event: It may play, in the plot of which it is an event, the most important parts or be only part of a crowd scene; but, in spite of what Weber says, there is no difference of nature between the main parts and the figures in the crowd—mere shades separate them, one goes gradually from one to the other, and in the end sees that Frederick William IV himself is basically one of a crowd.

The history of the peasantry under Louis XIV is that of the peasants; the life of each of those peasants is that of a "bit player" and the actual document will be, for example, the identity hook of that peasant. But if, in a peasantry, each peasant serves only to add to numbers, it is enough to pass on to the history of the upper middle class for the historian to designate by name the middle-class families and to pass from statistics to prosopography. We reach Louis XIV: the value man, the hero of the political plot, history incarnate. But no, he is only a "bit player"—alone on the stage, but a "bit player" all the same; it is as the head of state that the historian speaks of him and not as the platonic lover of La Vallière or as the patient of Purgon. He is not a man, but a part—that of monarch who, by definition, permits only one "bit player"; on the other hand, as a patient of Purgon, he counts in the history of medicine and our "reason for knowing" is in this case the diary of Dangeau and the documents relating to the health of the king. If the evolution of fashion is taken as the plot, that evolution is made by the tailors who upset it and also by those who keep it in the old ruts; the importance of the event in its series decides the number of lines the historian will devote to it, but does not decide the choice of the series. It is because we have chosen the political plot that Louis XIV plays the main part; we did not necessarily choose that plot to add one more biography to the hagiography of Louis XIV.

The Heart of the Problem: Weber and Nietzsche

In truth, up to now we have quite intentionally looked at Weber's theory through the wrong end of the opera glasses, to see if it agreed with the real activity of the historian; for it is its agreement with facts that judges a theory. But the problem that it sought to solve is not thereby settled; for Weber, who was fundamentally a follower of Nietzsche, this problem was expressed in Nietzschean terms. When he says that history is a relation to values, he does not think of definite values (classical humanism, for example) in whose name we would prefer Greek history to that of American Indians: He only wants to note that in fact, until his time, no conception of history has been interested in the total past, that each has sorted out, and he calls that selection "valorization." One does not prefer the Athenians to the Indians in the name of certain established values; it is the fact that one prefers them that makes them into values; a tragic gesture of unjustifiable selection would serve as a basis for every possible vision of history.

Thus Weber raises to the level of tragedy a state of historiography that was to reveal itself as very temporary; the metamorphosis of the historical genre into total history (which, by a curious coincidence, became obvious just after Weber's generation) was indeed to show it. In other words, this conception of historical knowledge implies the refusal to consider historiography as an activity depending on a norm of truth; it would be impossible for the historian to appeal to some tribunal of reason, for that tribunal could only be set up by an unjustifiable decree. Such seem, at least, the ideas that underlie Weber's pages, which are not very explicit.

Unfortunately, if the norm of truth is driven out through the door, it comes in again through the window; Weber himself cannot fail to lay down laws concerning historiographical matters. After noting that the vision of the past is valorization, he imposes that valorization as a norm. The writers of a textbook of general history had decided to attach as much importance to African and American history as to that of the Old World (which would today be only banal); instead of bowing to this valorizing gesture, Weber criticizes the textbooks in the name of what history should be: "The idea of a sort of politico-social equity in history which would want—at last! at last!—to give Bantu and [American] Indian peoples, so outrageously despised up to now, a place at least as important as to the Athenians, is quite simply naïve."[6] Tragedy is degraded into academism; after showing that nothing rightly permits one choice rather than another, Weber concludes that one must keep to the established order. The passage from tragic radicalism to conformity does not date from Weber; if I am not mistaken, the first to practice it was the god Krishna. In the *Bhagavad-Gita* he teaches Prince Arjuna, who is getting ready to go to war, that since life and death are the same thing, he has only to do his duty and join battle (instead of not joining it or seeking a *via media,* as prudence suggests). So one understands how, to Weber, the doctrine of Nietzsche serves as a link between his epistemological thought and his political stance before and during the First World War, which were often surprising in so reasonable a historian: nationalism tinged with Pan-Germanism, *Machtpolitik* raised to a norm.

It is not for us to investigate whether Nietzsche marks the end of Western philosophy or is only the first of the contestants. At least, our problem has advanced a step; valorization, according to Weber, has nothing to do with the settled values of a given period, which is enough to eliminate the widespread idea that our vision of the past is the projection of the present, the translation of our values and of our inquiries— the great Nietzschean tragedy has nothing in common with existential pathos. Valorization draws the frontier of history, it does not organize the inside like a theater for psychodramas; within its limits, history is its own valorization. For realism wants us to recognize that the scientific ideal exists de facto among our motives as well as the artistic ideal or the ideal of law,[7] and that that ideal orders scientific activity; this activity is always more or less imperfect in relation to the ideal but, without it, the activity would become incomprehensible.

Man has always recognized that science, law, art, and ethics are singular activities that have their own rules and are to be judged by those rules; we may discuss the rules, dispute their application, but not the principle that there are rules. What is interesting to a historian is not what interests his civilization, but what is historically interesting, just as "the" Middle Ages (or, rather, some periods in the Middle Ages) showed particular interest in strange and exotic animals. The medieval zoologists were occupied, or ought to have been occupied, with what is zoologically interesting: all animals. They could have been more or less conscious of the ideal of their science, and at any moment a zoologist could have risen among them to appeal to that ideal; it may also be that the zoologist's ideal has evolved. But that evolution will by right have been purely scientific and have constituted something that science had within itself.

Historical Interest

The proximate sociological cause of the birth and duration of a discipline has always been, as Gramsci and Koyré have said, the existence of a small, specialized group (drawn from priests, professors, technicians, publicists, parasites, persons of independent means, people on the fringes of society, good-for-nothings) that takes as its aim self-knowledge and is often the only audience it has. It is not otherwise with historical knowledge. It extricates itself, as a curiosity for specialists, from its "sociological" implications, from the records in which are inscribed the names of kings or from the monuments that perpetuate the memory of national exploits and dramas. It is not because "our" civilization makes a valorizing choice that the past is not for us a grisaille in which no fact is more important than another; it is because facts exist only in and through plots in which they have the relative importance imposed by the human logic of the drama.

The nature of real historical interest is deduced from the essence of history. The latter relates what took place just because it did take place;[8] thus it ignores two centers of interest: values and examples; it is not hagiographic or instructive and delightful. It is not enough that Louis XIV suffered from gangrene for history to be greatly concerned with that illness, except to register the death of the king, who to the historian played only the part of a monarch and had no value as an individual. History will not concern itself either with a striking action or with a startling catastrophe, both events of value as examples.

Can one really believe that all that has happened is interesting? Is it worthy of history that men cut their nails, peeled apples, or struck matches? Yes, just as to report that the Seleucids finally conquered Coele-Syria from the Lagids in 198. For, curiously, to peel fruit half of humanity brings the knife to the fruit held still and finds it natural to act thus, whereas the other half twists the fruit on the knife held still and declares that that is the only rational way to peel fruit; to strike matches, Westerners move the matches from front to back or from back to front, depending on whether they are men or women. This inspires some thoughts on techniques, on the nature-culture dialectic, masculine and feminine "roles," imitation, the diffusion of techniques and their sources; how long have matches been in use? What other technical gesture, itself different according to the sex of the person who performs it, served as a model when matches were first struck? Certainly a very curious plot underlies it. As for the singular importance of a match struck by Dupont one September morning in a given year, the historic aspect is the importance it has in the life of Dupont, if one takes as the plot the relative period of that life.

For a paragraph or two let us think in archetypes (for uncivilized thought has good points, as being classificatory not structural). History as it is written can be referred to two archetypes: "This action is worthy of living on in our memory" and "Men are different from each other." Let us open the most famous of the Indian chronicles, the *Rajatarangini;* in it we read of the glory and the catastrophe of King Harsha and of the unforgettable glory of the court in his reign. Let us open Herodotus; he wrote his inquiry, he said, so that "time would not carry exploits into forgetfulness and that no brilliant action by the Greeks or the barbarians should one day lose its fame." But Herodotus had too much genius to limit himself to history considered as a citation in humanity's dispatches; in fact, the book he wrote resulted from the second archetype: "Peoples differ from each other" in space or time and "In Egypt the women urinate standing up and the men squatting" (which foreshadows the study of the technics of the body by Marcel Mauss). He is the father of the art of travel, which is today called ethnography (one even gets round to imagining that there is an ethnographical method), and of non-event-worthy history. It is thus that history has ceased to exist in relation to values and has become the natural history of men, a work of pure curiosity.

Comparison with the Origins of the Novel

History has some likeness to the novel (or lying history), for the novel has similarly passed from the relationship with values because it relates for the sake of relating. It begins, as much among the Greeks as in the Middle Ages and in modern times, with novelized history that speaks of men-values, kings or princes: *Ninos et Sémiramis, le Grand Cyrus;* for one cannot unceremoniously fling the name of someone into the commercial world unless that someone is well known, a king or a great man. Public figures write their memoirs and let their lives be written, but the public is not entertained with the life of an ordinary person. To be well known is to be someone whose actions and passions are interesting merely because they are his. Aristotle said that the characteristic of history is to tell of the actions and passions of Alcibiades; the latter cut off his dog's tail to get himself spoken about—or, rather, the cut-off tail was spoken about only because the dog belonged to Alcibiades. The weekly *France-Dimanche* speaks either of interesting adventures that happened to some unknown person or of insipid adventures that are of interest because they happened to Elizabeth of England or to Brigitte Bardot; half of this paper is related to values, the other half is a collection of examples.

Therein lies the whole problem of history and of the novel. When the novel ceased to speak of Cyrus to relate the adventures of unknown people, it had first to justify itself, which it did in several ways: the account of a voyage in which a common man tells less of his life than of what he has seen; the confession, in which the least among the faithful confesses his story for the edification of his brethren, for he bears within himself the human condition; finally, the account through a mediator, in which a third person, who is none other than the author, relates a story that he gets from a stranger or that he has found among papers—he is there as a guarantee to the readers of the interest and truth of the story ("Adolphe, a Story Found in the Papers of an Unknown Man").

Finally, the question of knowing what is the interest specific to history can be formulated thus: Why do we affect to read *Le Monde,* and why are we embarrassed to be seen with *France-Dimanche* in our hands? In what way are Brigitte Bardot and Soraya more worthy or unworthy than Pompidou to live in our memory? For Pompidou, his place is secure; since the birth of the historical genre, heads of state have been inscribed in the archives for their qualities. As for Brigitte Bardot, she becomes worthy of great history if she ceases to be the woman-value and becomes a mere "extra" in a scenario of contemporary history dealing with the star system, the mass media or that modern religion of the star that Edgar Morin preaches; it will be sociology, so to speak, and it is under that serious heading that *Le Monde* speaks of Brigitte Bardot on the rare occasions that it happens to mention her.

History Is Interested in the Specific

It will be objected, with some appearance of reason, that there is a difference between Brigitte Bardot and Pompidou; the latter is historic for himself alone, the former only serves to illustrate the star system, as the tailors of Frederick William do the history of costume. We are here at the heart of the problem, and here we shall discover the essence of the historical genre. History is interested in individualized events—none of which, as far as it is concerned, serve a dual purpose—but it is not interested in their individuality; it seeks to understand them—that is, to find among them a kind of generality or, more precisely, of specificity. It is the same with natural history; its curiosity is inexhaustible, all the species matter to it and none is superfluous, but it does not propose the enjoyment of their singularity in the manner of the bestiaries of the Middle Ages, in which one could read the description of noble, beautiful, strange, or cruel animals.

We have just seen that, far from being related to values, history begins with a general devaluation—Brigitte Bardot and Pompidou are no longer well-known individualities, admired or desired, but the representatives of their category; the first is a star, the second is divided between the species of teachers who turn to politics and the species of heads of state. We have moved from individual singularity to specificity—that is, to the individual as understandable (that is why "specific" means both "general" and "particular"). Such is the seriousness of history: It proposes to tell of past civilizations and not to preserve the memory of individuals; it is not a vast collection of biographies. The lives of all the tailors under

Frederick William are very much alike, so history will relate them as a whole because it has no reason to be interested in one particular one; it does not deal in individuals, but in what is specific about them, for the good reason that, as we shall see, there is nothing to say of individual singularity, which can only serve as an unutterable support to valorization ("because it was he, because it was I"). Whether the individual is an outstanding figure in history or a crowd figure among millions of others, he counts historically only for his specificity.

Weber's argument about the king's tailors and the relationship to values hid the true position of the question, which is the distinction between the singular and the specific. The distinction is innate, and we make it everywhere in our daily lives (the indifferent exist only as the representatives of their respective species); it is because of it that our purist archaeologist did not want to find a Venus de Milo—he did not reproach the statue with being beautiful, but with being too much talked about, while teaching us nothing, with having value but no interest. He would have restored her interest from the moment that, behind the singularity of the masterpiece, he saw the contribution it made to the history of Hellenic sculpture by its style, its workmanship, and its beauty. All that is specific is historic; everything is understandable except the singularity that makes Dupont not Durand and individuals to exist one by one—That is an indisputable fact but, once enunciated, there is nothing more to be said about it. On the other hand, once given the singular existence, all that can be said of an individual possesses a kind of generality.

Only the fact that Durand and Dupont are two prevents the reality from being reduced to the intelligible speech about it; everything else is specific, and that is why all is historic, as we have seen in chapter II. Here is our archaeologist on the site of his dig; he excavates the most boring Roman house possible, a dwelling of the usual type, and wonders what is worthy of history in those bits of walls. Thus he seeks either events in the ordinary sense of the word—but the building of that house was assuredly not great news in its time—or customs, manners of the "collective"—in a word, something "social." That house is like thousands of others, it has six rooms; is it historic? The facade is not quite drawn with a tracing line, it is a bit sinuous, there are just five centimeters of sag—so many singularities due to chance and without historical interest. If that interest exists, this carelessness is a specific detail of the current building technique; for us, the product of mass production shines rather by its monotony and its pitiless regularity. The five centimeters of sag are specific, they have a "collective" sense and are worth remembering; everything is historic, except that of which one does not yet understand the reason. At the end of the dig, there will perhaps be no detail of the house unconnected with its species; the only incontrovertible fact will be that the house in question is itself and that it is not that other one rising beside it. But history has no use for that singularity.[9]

Definition of Historical Knowledge

Thus we reach a definition of history. Historians have always felt that history was about man in the group rather than about the individual, that it was the history of societies, nations, civilizations—indeed, of humanity, of what is collective in the vaguest sense of the word; that it did not concern itself with the individual as such; that if the life of Louis XIV was history, that of a Nivernais peasant during his reign was not, or was only material for history. But the difficulty is to reach a precise definition; is history the science of collective facts that would not amount to a collection of tiny individual facts? Is it the science of human societies? Is it the science of man in society? But what historian, or what sociologist, is capable of separating what is individual from what is collective, or even of attaching a meaning to these words? The distinction between what is historic and what is not is nonetheless made immediately and as if by instinct.

In order to see how approximate these attempts at a definition of history are, multiplied and successively crossed out, without ever having the impression that one has "got it," it is enough to seek to state them precisely. The science of what sort of societies? The whole nation, even humanity? A village? At least an entire province? A group of bridge players? A study of what is collective: Is it heroism? The fact of cutting one's nails? The argument of the sorites here finds its proper use, which is to denounce as being badly put every problem where it can be used. Indeed, the question is never asked thus; when we are in presence of a singularity come down from the past and suddenly understand it, there is produced in our mind a click that is of a logical order (or, rather, ontological) and not sociological. We have not found something collective or social, but something specific, comprehensible individuality. History is the description of what is specific—that is, comprehensible—in human events.

As soon as it is no longer valorized, the singularity is obliterated, because it is incomprehensible. Among the 90,000 epitaphs contained in the corpus of Latin inscriptions, here is that of a man named Publicius Eros, who was born, died, and in between married one of his freedwomen; peace to his ashes, and he falls back into the nothingness of oblivion—we are not novelists, and our job is not to take an interest in Dupont for the sake of Dupont and to interest the reader in Dupont. Only it happens that we can, without too much difficulty, understand why Publicius had married one of his freedwomen—formerly a public slave himself (we would say a municipal employee), as his name reveals, he married among his own; his freedwoman must have been his concubine for a long time, and he had only freed her to have a wife worthy of him. He may have also had very personal motives for doing so; she was perhaps the woman in his life or the most famous local beauty.

None of his motives would be singular; all are inscribed in the social, sexual, and conjugal history of Rome. The only fact of no difference to us—but important for those round him—is that Publicius was himself and no other; instead of being centered on the interesting personality of this Roman Dupont, our true novel bursts into a series of anonymous plots. Slavery, concubinage, intermarriages, sexual motivations in the choice of a wife—the whole of Publicius will be found there, but in pieces; he will have lost only his singularity, about which there is exactly nothing to say. Thus historical events are never confounded with the *cogito* of an individual, and that is why history is knowledge through traces, as we have seen in chapter I. We must only add that by pulling Publicius to pieces in plots, we shall separate universal truths (man is sexual, the sky is blue), for the event is difference.

The historical is that which is not universal and not singular. For it not to be universal, there must be a difference; for it not to be singular, it must be specific,[10] it must be understood, for that sends us back to the plot. The historian is the naturalist of events; he wants to know for the sake of knowing, but there is no science of singularity. To know that there has existed a singular being named Georges Pompidou is not history, so long as one cannot say, in the words of Aristotle, "what he did and what happened to him"; if one can say that, he is thereby raised to specificity.

History of Man and History of Nature

If history can thus be defined as the knowledge of the specific, then the comparison becomes easy between that history—I mean the history of human facts—and the history of physical facts, such as the history of the Earth or of the solar system. One willingly affirms that there is nothing in common between these two kinds of history; it is said that the history of nature does not matter much to us unless it is about something considerable, as big as our globe. But no one will tell in a chronicle what happened on a bit of Earth without men (there was a great storm one day, an earthquake the next year; a century and a half later a colony of marmots settled on the bit of Earth). On the other hand, the slightest incidents in the life of human societies are judged to be worthy of recollection. We ought to conclude from that that we would give special, anthropocentric attention to human history, because that history tells us of people like ourselves.

It is not so. True, if we write the history of the terrestrial globe, we do not bother to keep a meteorological and zoological chronicle of the various parts of our globe—meteorology and zoology, which study their subjects in a nonhistorical way, are sufficient for us, without giving ourselves the trouble of recounting the history of marmots and that of storms. But if that is so, if our globe has its historians, whereas marmots do not have theirs, it is for the same reason that causes us to write the history of Nivernais peasants under Louis XIV, but not the biographies of those peasants individually: interest for the specific alone. History is not existential, neither is historiography humanism. Our attitude is exactly the same to human events and natural events: Only their specificity interests us; if that specificity varies in time, we write the history of those variations, of those differences; if it does not vary, we draw a nonhistorical picture of it.

We have seen above that when a historian writes about Nivernais peasants or Roman freedmen, his first concern is to remove the singularity of each person, to scatter it in specific data that regroup themselves into items (standard of living, matrimonial customs of the population under study); in place of a juxtaposition of biographies, he obtains a juxtaposition

of items, the whole of which constitutes "the life of Nivernais peasants."
At most he will not mention that those peasants took food and were sexed,
for that is true at all times.

Now the same two criteria, specificity and difference, are enough to
explain in what measure we write the history of natural facts and why
we write it less than that of human facts. Here is a little part of our
globe. It rains and it snows there, but it also happens that it rains in the
neighboring areas; since we have no reason for preferring that area to
any other, the rainfalls will regroup in a single item, whenever they fell.
And since rain has hardly changed for some millions of years, we have
no history of it to relate; we shall make a sempiternal picture of this
mechanical meteor. On the other hand, the climate and relief of that
district have changed between the Secondary period and the Tertiary
period; that will be a little event in the history of our globe, whose
records we are keeping.

Finally, the only nuance that separates the history of man and that of
nature is quantitative; man varies more than nature and even than the
animals, and there are more stories to tell about him. For he has, as we
know, a culture, which means that he is both reasonable (he has goals
and deliberates on the best way of attaining them; his recipes and his
works are transmitted to his posterity and are susceptible of being understood by the latter in their rationality and taken up "in the present" as
being still valid) and unreasonable, for he is arbitrary (for example, he
eats, as animals do; but, unlike them, he does not always and everywhere
eat the same thing—each culture has its traditional cuisine and finds that
of neighboring people detestable). The historian will not relate, meal by
meal, all the luncheons and dinners of all men, for those meals, like the
rains mentioned above, regroup in items, the whole of which constitutes
the culinary ways of each civilization. Nor will the historian take the
trouble to say "man eats," for that is not a differential event. But he will
tell the history of cooking through the ages, in the same way as the
history of the terrestrial globe.

The opposition between the history of nature and human history is
unessential, no less than the opposition between the past, which alone
would be "historical," and the present. Against Heidegger, against historism, without forgetting existentialism and the sociology of knowing,
we have to reaffirm the intellectualist character of historical knowledge.
Assuredly, nothing of what is human is foreign to the historian, but

neither is anything animal foreign to a biologist. Buffon thought that the fly should not hold a greater place in the concerns of the naturalist than it occupies in nature; on the other hand, he maintained a value relationship with the horse and the swan—in his own way he was a disciple of Weber. But zoology has changed a great deal since then and, after Lamarck had pleaded the cause of the lower animals, every organism became of interest in the science; it attaches no particular value to the primates, because it feels its attention slackening slightly once beyond the tarsier specter and becoming almost nonexistent as it reaches the fly.

Weber was indignant that the history of the Bantus could be studied as much as that of the Greeks. Let us not retort that times have changed, that the Third World and its nascent patriotism . . . , that the awakening of the African people who are taking an interest in their past . . . ; it would be a fine time to see that patriotic considerations should be the criterion of intellectual interest and that the Africans have more reasons to despise Greek antiquity than Europeans had to despise Bantu antiquity; anyhow, today there are many more Africanists than there were in the time of Weber and of Frobenius. And who still dares to state that the study of the Nuers or of the Trobiand Islanders is not as instructive as that of the Athenians and the Thebans? It is exactly as instructive, given equality of documentation, for we see the same motives playing there; let us add that if the Bantu *Homo historicus* proved to be a more primitive organism than the Athenian, it would only add to the interest, for it would thus reveal a less known part of the plan of Nature. As for knowing—Weber also asks the question—how many pages are to be devoted to Bantu history and how many to Greek, the answer is simple, as was seen in chapter II: It all depends on the volume of documentation.

Knowledge has its goal in itself and is not related to values. The proof of it is the manner we have of writing Greek history. If it is naïve to put the fights of the Bantus on the same footing as the wars of the Athenians, what reason could we really have for being interested in the Peloponnesian War, were not Thucydides there to make it interesting? The influence of that war on the destiny of the world was practically nil, whereas the wars between the Hellenistic States, which in France are known only to five or six specialists, played a decisive role in the destiny of the Hellenistic civilization in regard to Asia and, thereby, in the destiny of Western and world civilization. The interest of the Peloponnesian War is like that of a war between Bantus if an African Thucydides had related it. It is thus that naturalists are particularly interested in a definite insect if there exists a particularly well-written monograph on it; if that is a relation to values, the values in question are exclusively bibliographical.

History Is Not Individualizing

History is not related to values; furthermore, it is interested in the specificity of individual events rather than in their singularity. So if it is ideographic, if it relates events in their individuality, the War of 1914 or the Peloponnesian War and not the phenomenon of war, it is not from aesthetic taste for individuality or faithfulness to remembrance. It is because it cannot do better; it would only like to become nomographic, if the diversity of events did not make that mutation impossible. We have seen in the first chapter that singularity is not a privilege that historical facts have over physical facts; the latter are no less singular. Now the dialectic of knowledge is subtended by a mysterious law of economy of effort. By virtue of that law, if the revolutions of peoples were as entirely reducible to general explanations as physical phenomena are, we would lose interest in their history; all that would matter to us would be the laws governing human evolution; satisfied with knowing through them what man is, we would omit historical anecdotes, or else we would be interested in them only for sentimental reasons, comparable with those that make us cultivate, alongside great history, that of our village or of the streets in our town. Unfortunately, historic events cannot be compressed into generalities; they only very partially reduce to type, their succession is neither directed to some end nor regulated by laws known to us; everything is different and everything has to be said. The historian cannot imitate the naturalist, who is occupied only with the type and is not concerned with describing each representative of the same animal species. History is an idiographic science, not because of us, and our taste for the detail of human events, but because of those events themselves, which persist in keeping their individuality.

The Charter of History

Each event is like a species in itself. And it is from the founder of natural history that we can borrow the charter of plain history. In one of the most inspired pages we owe to Greek genius, Aristotle contrasts the study of stars, which are gods, with that of the plots of Nature, which are the living organisms of our sublunary world:

Among the natural individualities, some have neither beginning nor end, and have existed from all eternity; the others are subject to appearing and disappearing. The study of both kinds has its own interest. For the eternal beings, the little knowledge we have of them brings more joy than all the sublunary world, by reason of the eminence of that contemplation: furtively to glimpse the loved one similarly brings the lover more joy than the detailed knowledge of important things. But, on the other hand, for certainty and extent of knowledge, sublunary science has the advantage; and since we have already treated of divine beings and said what we thought of them, there remains for us to speak of living nature, leaving out, if possible, no detail, whether exalted or lowly. It must be admitted that some of these beings do not present a very aesthetic sight, but the knowledge of the plan of Nature in them reserves, for those who can see the reason for things and who really love to know inexpressible pleasures. So we must not give way to a childish repugnance and turn away from the study of the least of these animals: in all parts of Nature there is something to admire.[11]

One sees the impartiality of the historian; it goes further than good faith, which may be partisan and is generally widespread. It resides less in the firm purpose of telling the truth than in the goal one sets oneself— or, rather, in the fact of no longer proposing to oneself any aims at all, save that of knowing for the sake of knowing. It is identical with mere curiosity, the curiosity that gives rise in a Thucydides to the known split between the patriot and the theorist,[12] whence the impression of intellectual superiority given by his book. The virus of knowing for the sake of knowing goes so far as to give its carriers a kind of enjoyment when they see the convictions that were dear to them being contradicted. Thus there is something inhuman about it; like charity, it develops for itself, in addition to the biological will to live whose value is prolongation.[13] And so it generally horrifies, and one knows what a fluttering of wings was stirred to defend the capitol of values, which J. Monod appeared to attack when he recalled that old truth that, as St. Thomas says, knowing is the only activity that has its goals in itself.[14] And what does man become, in all that? We can be reassured: Through contemplation one does not become less of a man, one eats, one votes, one professes sound doctrines; this vice not always unpunished—that is, pure curiosity—scarcely risks becoming as contagious as zeal for the values that are indispensable to us.

The Two Principles of Historiography

If that is so, the age-long evolution of historical knowledge seems to be stressed by the appearance of two principles, each of which marked a turning point. The first, dating from the Greeks, is that history is disinterested knowledge, and not national or dynastic memories; the second, which has at last become clear in our time, is that every event is worthy of history. These two principles follow from each other; if the past is studied out of mere curiosity, knowledge will be directed to the specific, for it has no reason to prefer one individuality to another. Consequently, every kind of fact becomes quarry for the historian, as soon as the historian has at his command the necessary concepts and categories to think so; there will be an economic or a religious history as soon as one has means to conceive economic or religious facts.

It is, however, probable that the appearance of total history has not yet had all its effects; it is no doubt destined to upset the present structuration of human sciences and to explode sociology in particular, as will be seen at the end of this book. There is at least one question to be asked at once. Since any event is as historic as any other, the eventworthy field can be carved out with complete freedom. How is it, then, that too often it is persistently carved out traditionally, according to space and time, "history of France" or "the eighteenth century," according to singularities instead of specifics? How is it that books entitled *Revolutionary Messianism in History, The Social Hierarchies from 1450 to Today in France, China, Tibet and the U.S.S.R.,* or *Peace and War Among Nations,* to paraphrase the titles of three recent books, are still too rare? May it not be a survival of the original attachment to the singularity of events and to the national past? Why this preponderance of chronological selection, which seems to carry on the tradition of royal pomp and of national records?

Yet history is not that kind of dynastic or national biography. We may go further: Time is not essential to history, any more than is the individualizing of events that it undergoes in spite of itself. Anyone who "truly loves to know" and wants to understand the specificity of facts attaches no particular price to seeing unrolled behind him, in its continuity, the majestic carpet that links him with his ancestors the Gauls; he needs only a little time to see some plot or other unfolded there. If, on the contrary, one holds, with Péguy, that historiography is "memory" and not "inscription"; that, for the historian, "remaining positioned in the same race, . . . carnal, . . . spiritual, . . . temporal, and eternal is merely a question of evoking and invoking the Ancients," then one will not condemn only Langlois and Seignobos, but all serious historiography since Thucydides.

It is deplorable that from Péguy to *Sein und Zeit* and to Sartre, the justified criticism of scientism in history has served as a springboard for all the anti-intellectualisms. In truth, it is difficult to see how Péguy's demand could be translated into acts and what it would give as historiography. History is not the past of the "race," as Croce says with profundity.[15] It may seem paradoxical to deny time in history, but it is no less true that the concept of time is not indispensable to the historian who has need only of that of the intelligible process (we would say, of the concept of plot). These processes are of an indefinite number, for it is thought that carves them out, that denies chronological succession to one single line. Time, from the pithecanthropus to today, is not that with which history is told; it is only a setting in which historical plots develop freely. What would become of a historiography that finally freed itself from the last traces of singularities, the unities of time and place, to devote itself entirely to the single unity of plot? That will be seen in the course of this book.

Appendix

Axiological History

History is interested in what has been because it has been; a point of view to be carefully distinguished from that of the history of literature or of art, which is an axiological discipline, defined within its frontiers with reference to values: It is interested in great artists, in masterpieces. This axiological history, writes Max Weber, "is not directed to searching out facts causally important for a historical connection," but "conceives its objects for themselves" and "envisages its objects starting from points of view totally different from those of history." To this first distinction a second one must be added. Axiological history itself includes two moments: a preliminary evaluation ("here are the great writers"), a history of objects thus evaluated; the second moment—which is literary and art history as we read it—is no longer in any way distinct from just history. So much so that we may express it thus: A literary history of the seventeenth century, written from the nonaxiological point of view of pure history, would be a "literature of the seventeenth century in its time," whereas a literary history written from the axiological point of view, as it is very generally written, would be the equivalent of a "literature of the seventeenth century from the point of view of twentieth-century taste." One can understand that the famous paradox of the "renewal of the masterpieces" is proper and normal for axiological history, and for it alone.

The distinction of these three elements (evaluation, axiological history, pure history) is one of the most unquestionable merits of Max Weber; we are going to develop it here as best we can (Weber's texts are not absolutely clear: *Essais sur la théorie de la science,* trans. Freund, pp. 260–264, 434, 452–453; compare the section on Weber in chapter IV of this volume). These enlightening distinctions are too frequently unknown, to the great prejudice of the problem of the neutrality of values. When we want to deny the final character of the distinction between factual judgments and value judgments, we usually invoke literary history as the supposed proof of the impossibility of this distinction. It is to the great prejudice, as well, of the methodological clarity of literary history; a history of literature is usually presented as a "history of masterpieces" in which is mingled, capriciously and without strong principles, a "history of literary life and taste" that belongs to pure history and is developed either the better to explain the history of masterpieces or for its own sake. Whence arises hostility between historical and literary temperaments, people hurling at each other the words "mere aesthete" or "common philologist," and appearing to think these are great insults; each, in fact, is judged to belittle what he has not chosen.

First, pure history, when applied to literature, to art, to science, and so on, obviously calls for value judgments, but in indirect speech—to express it differently, for factual judgments. The pure historian must know that, to men, art is art and that *Iphigenia* is not a geometrical proof, a political tract, or a lay sermon, bearing "witness" or "messages." How will he treat the literary history of the seventeenth century, for example, if he gives a picture of society and civilization in Louis XIV's reign? I do not know if the problem has ever been posed in print, but, when we hear the historians on the *Records* staff spoken of, we know that there could be no question of introducing, into a picture of the seventeenth century, a heterogeneous chapter in which a literature textbook had been summarized from the point of view of "men of letters" and of making a gallery of the portraits of great men, which, to a historian, would be parrotry; literary history must be rewritten from a really historical point of view and a sort of "sociology" of literature under Louis XIV must be made. Who read, who wrote? What was read and what was the conception of literature and writers? What were the rituals, the roles, and the roads taken by literary life? What writers, great or lesser, created fashions, were imitated?

It is impossible not to find this point of view of pure historians right and coherent; it is enough to bear in mind the abyss separating literary production as it is today and as it will look to posterity; anyone dealing with secondhand book

dealers knows that a good half of what was read in the seventeenth century consisted of pious works and collections of sermons. That is an important fact, and
it would be inconceivable for a historian not to emphasize it; but will he then,
using the same pen, spin out an aesthetic phrase on Racine's purity? No, except
for saying that that purity, of which contemporaries were (or were not) aware,
is (or is not) explained by the literary moment and had (or did not have) consequences for contemporary production. He will also say whether contemporaries felt they were living in a period of literary brilliance, and will add that
posterity was to invalidate or confirm that judgment.

The idea of a pure history of value-activities, not very clear where literature
is concerned, is on the other hand familiar to archaeologists and to the historians
of science. Roman art has left countless sculptures, a certain number of paintings,
and a very few masterpieces; archaeologists publish all they find, good or bad—
their finds bear witness to the artistic life and the evolution of styles. They study
art from a "sociological"—or, rather, a civilization point of view: a setting for
life, a sculpture for a room, funeral art, the hideous rock decorations of the gar-
dens in Pompeii, popular art—that is, the art of pieceworkers as clumsy as clog-
makers, Pompeiian paintings the equivalent of our wallpapers or tapestries for
chair backs depicting Raphael's "Fair Gardener."

In truth, since the early 1950s the pure history of literature and the arts has
developed a great deal, under the name of sociology of art (it is known that
"sociology" is frequently a synonym for social history or non-eventworthy history); the epoch-making book was that of Antal on the historical background of
Florentine painting, however questionable his methods and conclusions may be,
as is generally the case with a pioneering book. Closer to us, let us cite, as an
example of a pure literary history, the *Carrière de Jean Racine* by Raymond
Picard or the pages dedicated by Pierre Goubert to Louis XIV literature in *Louis
XIV et vingt millions de Français*.

Second, axiological history is the history of works that deserved to live on,
treated as living, everlasting, not as relative to their time; it is nonetheless their
temporal history being written. They are considered in their singularity, because
they are valorized, and their period is referred to them, instead of their being
used to put together the history of their period—the axiologist historian will
speak of literary life under Louis XIV to explain the life and work of Racine; he
will not see Racine as an "extra" in that literary life, as would the pure historian.

The work of A. Koyré consisted, in some ways, in making the history of science
pass from an axiological history to a pure history, to a history of science "in its
time." Before him, the history of science was mainly a history of great discoveries
and inventions, a history of established truths and how they were arrived at;
Koyré has put in place a history of errors and truths, a history of the too human
progression of eternal truths (Kepler discovering one of his laws on the basis of
Pythagorean lucubrations and at the cost of two mistakes in calculation that
cancel each other out; Galileo feeling obliged to define his position between
Platonists and Aristotelians, believing he must reclaim the thought of Plato, and

imagining, perhaps, that he is inspired by that philosophy, just like a contemporary physicist thinking he owes his discoveries to Marxism).

Ceasing to be axiological, the history of science ceases to be a prize-giving and becomes as fascinating as a novel based on fact; Weber was quite right to say that the irruption of axiology into pure history usually ends in catastrophe. When, instead of explaining and understanding baroque art historically, men begin to say axiologically, like the Duchess of Guermantes, "That cannot be beautiful because it is dreadful," they cease at once to understand it, seeing in it only a "degeneration of art"—a judgment that, axiologically, is open to discussion, and is historically meaningless. It would be the same with the history of science. Astrology would be seen only as a superstition, a counterfeit science, forgetting that it was at most a false science and that in its day belief in the mathematical, determinist theory that astrology represented was the position of deeply scientific minds—just as, with us, psychoanalysis was viewed favorably by scientific minds and rejected in the name of ordinary common sense.

Third, axiological history is thus founded on evaluations, on authentic value judgments; but—a distinction in which Weber's insight is evident—it is something other than those evaluations, "a distinction frequently not made" (*Essais*, p. 434; cf. p. 453), and that explains the known paradox that a historian of literature may have poor taste. It will be enough, in order to be a good axiological historian, for him to borrow from public opinion a canonical list of great writers, after which he will know that he has to analyze the life and work of Baudelaire rather than of Béranger.

The preliminary evaluation, whether it be the work of the historian himself or whether he adopts that of his readers, thus determines what writers are worthy of being discussed, which in turn requires that he have taste. After that, axiological history is no longer substantially different from pure history, except that it is centered on what makes the writers stand out. But it no longer calls for taste, for a feeling for belles-lettres, nor for some affinity with the work of art; it only demands the main faculty of the historian, which is not sympathy but *mimetic* faculty, and also some virtuosity in writing—any college student could do it. This mimetic faculty is also all that is needed by the curator of an art gallery, who can do without taste, which will allow him to follow better the taste of his clients; on the other hand, it is indispensable, in speaking to amateurs, for him to know how to look at works of art, where values come in: As Weber says, "The axiological interpretation, not to be confused with evaluation, consists in developing the different, significant attitudes that are *possible* before a given phenomenon" (p. 434, Weber's emphasis).

In other words, to perceive values is one thing; to judge them is another. A historian of Roman portraits may have an infallible eye for arranging the works in their stylistic series, yet have no idea of the true artistic value of those portraits.[16]

That does not matter, for history, even if axiological, speaks of masterpieces because they are beautiful, but not according to their beauty. Whether it is

Baudelaire or Béranger, the themes to be treated will be the same: style, methods, poetics, themes, nature of sensibility, and so on. The share of evaluation is necessarily reduced to the opinion "it is beautiful" or "it is not beautiful," which would be a bit short for a textbook of literary history. A value judgment cannot be longer than an exclamation. Thus, once the preliminary evaluation is over, axiological history is absolutely like history, and we understand how historians of literature felt no need to make certain distinctions and to bring out the postulates implicit in their work. We also understand what their outstanding faculty is: not taste and feeling, but a mimetic faculty allowing the perception of values, without judging them from the perspective of the absolute. And that is enough, so long as a certain type of problem is not set: the problems of authenticity; that is the test of truth. Let homage be paid to Roberto Longhi, or to André Breton, the author of *Flagrant délit*.

Chapter V

Intellectual History

Writing history is an intellectual activity. Yet it must be acknowledged that such a statement will not be universally believed today; it is more commonly thought that historiography, in its origins or in its aims, is not a body of knowledge like others. Man, being in historicity, would feel a particular interest in history, and his relation with historical knowledge would be more intimate than with any other knowledge; the object and the subject of knowledge would be difficult to separate. Our vision of the past would express our present situation, and we would be painting ourselves when painting our history; historical temporality, having as a condition of possibility the temporality of the *Dasein*, would sink its roots into the inmost being of man. It is said, too, that the idea of man in our times has suffered a radical change; the idea of an eternal man has given way to that of a purely historical being.

In short, everything happens as if, in the sentence "History is known by a being who is himself in history," a short circuit occurred between the first proposition and the second because both contain the word "history." Historical knowledge is only half intellectual; there is something radically subjective about it, it would partake partly of consciousness or of existence. However widespread they may be, all these ideas appear to us to be false—or, rather, they seem to be the exaggeration of a few much less dramatic truths. There is no "historical" or "historian" consciousness; if the word "consciousness" is avoided with regard to historical knowledge, all these fogs will scatter.

Consciousness Has No Knowledge of History

Spontaneous consciousness has no notion of history, which calls for intellectual elaboration. Knowledge of the past is not an immediate

datum, for history is an area in which there can be no intuition but only
reconstruction, and in which rational certainty gives way to a knowledge
of fact whose source is foreign to consciousness. All that the latter knows
is that time passes; if a *Dasein* gazes at an old sideboard, it can say to
itself that the piece of furniture is worn, old, older than itself; but, contrary to what Heidegger claims, it cannot say that the piece of furniture
is "historical." History is a bookish, not an existential, notion; it is the
organization by the intelligence of data relating to a temporality that is
not that of the *Dasein*. If "historical" presupposes "old," there is nonetheless, between "old" and "historical," all the abyss of the intellect. To
identify these two adjectives, to assimilate the time of the ego and that
of history, is to confuse the condition of possibility of history with the
essence of history; it is to telescope the essential, to go in for edifying
style.[1]

All that consciousness knows of history is a narrow fringe of the past
whose memory is still living in the collective memory of the present
generation;[2] it also knows—Heidegger seems to set great store by this—
that its existence is existence with others, collective destiny, *Mitgeschehen*
("by this word we designate the community, the *Volk*"). It is insufficient
to know history and arrange its plot. Beyond the fringe of the collective
memory, consciousness is content to assume that present duration can
be prolonged by recurrence; my grandfather must have had a grandfather, and the same reasoning can be used about the future—this is not
often thought about.[3]

We also are aware—at least in principle—that we live among things
that have their history and that made conquests. A townsman may well
imagine that an agrarian landscape, the development of which has called
for the toil of ten generations, is a bit of nature; a nongeographer will
not know that scrubland or the desert originated in the destructive
activity of man. On the other hand, everyone knows that a city, a tool,
or a technical process has a human past; we know, said Husserl, with
a priori knowledge, that cultural works are human creations. Likewise,
when the spontaneous consciousness thinks of the past, it is to envisage
it as the history of the building of the present human world, taken as
completed, as a house already built or a full-grown man who has only
old age to look forward to;[4] such is—it has not generally been acknowledged—the spontaneous conception of history.

Consciousness sees in the past the building of the present, because action is in the present and takes no interest in the past. At every period men, "primitive" as well as civilized, have always known that their destiny would partly be what they made it by their action. They also knew that time had elapsed before them; but they have no knowledge of that time because action does not include the knowledge of the past and does not have the use of that knowledge. True, one always acts and thinks starting from a body of acquired knowledge that, even if one wanted to, cannot be wiped out; Crusoe-like adventures that aim at reinventing the world regularly end in rediscovering the commonplace things of yesterday or the day before.

For man is so naturally historical that he cannot distinguish the beginning of what comes to him from the past. With that, he is not naturally historiographical; this body of knowledge is less a treasury of memories than a stage reached. He treats a piece of land or a custom without any more thought than if it were a bit of nature. Historicity means only that man is always at some stage of his road, that he can only go on from the point he has reached, and that he finds it very natural to be at that stage of his cultural way. Action has no need to know the genesis of the recipes, tools, and customs that it uses. Certainly, if we are geometers, we belong, said Husserl, to the community of geometers past and future; but Husserl also said that the sense of cultural works "formed a sediment"; that, far from the present referring to the past, it was the past that had to be "reactivated" in order to be alive and present. Likewise, it is taking things the wrong way to raise tradition as the norm. What is the good of insisting on traditionalism, since it is impossible for men not to have a tradition and since it is useless to preach to them one they don't have or no longer have? After all, traditions are not to be had to order.

No Historicist Mutation

Since the knowledge of the past, both in its origin and in its virtues, is foreign to consciousness and indifferent to action, it is difficult to believe that, as has frequently been affirmed, the development of historical science over the last two centuries, as well as the discovery of the historicity of man and nature, has constituted a revolution; that modern man has received a shock from it; that the present age is that of history; that since man is considered finite, it is no longer known what he is. Was more known about it before? That historicist trauma did not take place, at most there was a world weariness;[5] indeed, considerable richness in the knowledge of man has been produced, but there has been no change in that area.

The clearest lesson of present-day history and ethnography seems to be that of human variability. Our conviction that man changes has become a reflex; if you assure a present-day historian that the sky looked like an infinite gulf to the Romans, that their pregnant matrons had "longings," or that their heads of family preferred their own children to those of others, he will on principle begin by doubting, for he knows that perception, psychopathology, and paternal instinct vary from culture to culture. It may appear to him, on examination, that on a given point there has been no change (men think to establish, today, that there is often a connection between homosexuality and a mother fixation; that remark is found in Seneca's *Phaedra*). He will register that constant fact as noteworthy; it does not presuppose being, but becoming. It is one of the most sensitive points of friction between the temperament of historians and the "literary" temperament; faced with a historical enigma, the latter will seek the solution in the knowledge of the human heart, and the former will undertake an "arrangement in series" starting from period data.

For why should man be more invariable than mountains or living species? He may be relatively stable, in a given environment, for more or less time; he will be so only for a time. That stability can last as long as the species; it will nonetheless be a question of fact to know if it will last for a long time or forever. Is it definitively human to make war? No one knows. Likewise, it is vain to make a distinction between historical and anthropological explanations; it is but a question of greater or lesser duration. Are the revolutionary attitude and the freedom of antireligious minds phenomena proper to the Enlightenment, or are they found in every age under a thousand avatars, as natural to man? It is of little importance, for the distinction between that attitude and its historical avatars is deceptive; neither does clothing in itself exist independently of period costume. There exists only that which is determined.

The increase of historic and ethnographical knowledge has, over the last two centuries, given us pictures of man in all the forms of his development, with his rationalism and his rites, with the irreducible diversity of his aims and the naturalness he brings to the most opposite kinds of behavior. Becoming what his culture, his class, or the dynamics of the group he is in makes him what he is: taking from what he does a consciousness more like a period curio than an everlasting light; always busy with enterprises and caught in institutions; never alone, always busy—without there being for him any royal road or point of no return. Everything is contemporary and everything is always possible.

Does this mean that all this has completely upset our vision of man? The supposed mutation of the idea of man that is tumultuously treated in *Les noyers de l'Altenburg*[6] amounts to very little. We have not passed from an eternal man to a man in the process of becoming; rather, one image of man, so poor that it could be called eternal without meaning very much, has been replaced by an image much richer in details. We have neither better nor worse knowledge of what man is, but we have more details; documented knowledge has devalued an empty affirmation. If we aired an idea at the same level as well-informed knowledge, we might no less legitimately hail Epicurus as the ancestor of our atomic scientists. How could one translate for oneself that famous idea of an eternal man? Either by a definition of essence (a reasonable animal), to which we still have nothing to object or to add, or else by mechanical statements (as when we declare that man will always make war) that, not being verifiable in fact, remained harmless and were corrected by themselves if contradicted by fact.

Thus, when Thucydides affirms that "Past and future events will present, by reason of their human character, likenesses or resemblances," he does not compromise himself because he does not say which ones. There has been no historicist revolution, for the simple reason that an eternalist anthropology and a historical anthropology have never really clashed over a given problem; we have only seen prejudices arising from a lack of information give way to documented knowledge without a fight. It is not true, for example, that before Sombart it was believed that the economic attitude toward profit was eternal and natural to man; it was not even thought about, there were not those concepts. As for the principle that man varies according to time and place, it is one of those that has always been known; thus, in anthropology, things did not happen as in natural history, in which the discovery of the evolution of species and of the ages of the globe marked a real mutation and at first gave rise to polemics.

The quantitative change in the knowledge of man provoked no moral shock. To learn that humanity began a million years ago rather than in 5200 B.C. is like learning that the heavens are infinite or that the universe is a curve; the pace of the world is not changed by it, and peoples cling no less strongly to their values on the pretext that their intellectuals think those values are not eternal. Perhaps our grandnephews will laugh at us and say, "They ended up by being persuaded that they were obsessed by the idea of history, but they were not all that much so." Historical knowledge has no consequences other than the purely cultural; it deprovincializes, it teaches that in human things all that is, might not be. As the *Divan occidental* says:

> Wer nicht von drei tausend Jahren
> Sich weiss Rechenschaft zu geben
> Bleibt im Dunkel unerfahren,
> Mag von Tag zu Tage leben.

The Goals of Historical Knowledge

History does not concern the inmost being of man and does not upset his feelings about himself. Why, then, does he take an interest in his past? It is not because he is historic, for he is no less interested in nature. There are two reasons for that interest. In the first place, our belonging to a national, social, or family group may give the past of that group a particular attraction for us; the second reason is curiosity, either for the anecdotal or for accompanying a demand for intelligibility.

We usually invoke the first reason: national feeling, tradition; history would be people's consciousness of themselves. What serious-mindedness! When a Frenchman opens the work of a Greek or a Chinese historian, when we buy a widely circulated history magazine, our aim is entertainment and knowledge. The Greeks of the fifth century were already like us—Why do I say the Greeks? The Spartans might have been thought to be more nationalistic. When the sophist Hippias lectured to them, they liked to hear him talk of "heroic or human genealogies, of the origin of different peoples, of the founding of cities in the primitive period and, in general, of everything relating to ancient times. That is what they listen to with most pleasure." "'In short,' Socrates answers him, 'your way of pleasing the Spartans is to let your vast erudition play the part that dear old women play with children: you tell them enjoyable stories.' "[7] That explanation is enough; history is a cultural activity, and culture free of charge is an anthropological dimension. If it were not so, it would be difficult to understand why unlettered despots have protected arts and letters and why so many tourists come to the Louvre to be bored.

Not only has the taste for history always had a good share of gratuitousness, but it has always insisted on veracity. Even if the hearers are disposed to be credulous, so as not to spoil their pleasure, history is not listened to like a tale and, if its truth cannot be believed, it loses its delight. Likewise, the interest in the past of our *Volk* plays only a minor role in this: an optional, inessential, secondary role, subordinate to truth and, above all, limited—for our curiosity is not confined to our own national history. The nationalist valorization of the past is not a universal fact, and there are other possible forms of alcohol: "Our people prepare for a radiant future," "We are the new barbarians, with no past behind them, and we will revive the youth of the world." There is something deliberate about such collective binges, it is not found ready-made in the essence of history. Indeed, they proceed from the inverted logic of ideologies; it is national feeling that gives rise to their historical justification, and not the reverse—it is the primary fact; the invocation of the land and the dead is only orchestration. The most chauvinistic historiography can thus appear objective at no great cost, since patriotism has no need to falsify truth in order to be; it is interested only in what justifies it, and leaves all else alone.[8] Knowledge is not affected by the aims, disinterested or practical, assigned to it by each man; those aims are added to it and do not constitute it.

A False Problem: The Genesis of History

That is why the origins of the historical genre pose a purely philological problem and are without interest for the philosophy of history. As in all history, the birth of historiography is an accident without necessity; it does not flow essentially from the consciousness of self in human groups, does not, like a shadow, accompany the appearance of the state or the rise of political awareness. Did the Greeks begin to write history when they constituted themselves into a nationality?[9] Or when democracy made them effective citizens? I do not know, and it does not matter; it is only a point of literary history. Elsewhere it will be the magnificence of the royal court under a memorable monarch that will incite a poet to perpetuate its memory in a chronicle.[10]

Let us not set up the history of ideas or of literary genres as a phenomenology of the mind, let us not take accidental sequences for the displaying of an essence. All has always been in place for history to be written one day; accidents have decided whether it would effectively be written down and in what form. The knowledge of the past has always fed both curiosity and ideological sophisms; men have always known that humanity is in a state of becoming and that their collective life is made up of their actions and their passions. The only new thing has been the use, in writing and before that by word of mouth, of those omnipresent data; there was a birth of the historical genre, but not of a historian's consciousness.

Historiography is a narrowly cultural event implying no new attitude to historicity, to action. We shall finally be convinced of this if we open a parenthesis to discuss a quite widely held ethnographical myth. The primitives, it is said, had no idea of becoming; time, as they saw it, was a cyclic repetition. According to them, their existence only repeated as the years went by, an unchanging archetype, a mythical or ancestral norm. And it was that conception of time that prevented them from thinking history and, a fortiori, from writing it. Let us for a moment pretend to believe this pompous melodrama,[11] since there is so much of it in the history of religions, and let us only ask ourselves what can be the meaning of the verb "prevented"—how can an idea, that of an archetype, prevent that of history from forming? That way the mere existence of the Ptolemaic system should have sufficed to prevent the appearance of that of Copernicus; yet, does it not happen that one idea supplants another?

But that is the point—since it is concerned with primitives, people don't want the archetype to be an idea, a theory, a cultural product like our own theories; it has to be more visceral, to be on the order of mentality, of consciousness, of living experience. The primitives are too close to original authenticity to have, in their visions of the world, the slight perspective and the touch of bad faith that we have about our most strongly asserted theories. And then, of course, they are not people to have theories. So we pull down their cultural and philosophical productions to the level of consciousness, which finally confers on that consciousness the weight of a pebble;[12] thus, we will have to believe that the primitive, about whom it cannot be doubted that he sees with his own eyes that one year is not like the preceding year, continues nonetheless to see everything through archetypes—and not just profess to do so.

In fact, a primitive sees reality exactly as we do; when he sows, he wonders what the harvest will bring; and, like us, he has philosophies by which he tries to describe or to justify reality—the archetype is one of them. If the archetypal thought was really lived out, it might for a long time prevent a historian's thought. When one's brain is made in a certain way, it is difficult to change it. On the other hand, it is not difficult to change ideas—or, rather, it is useless, for the most contradictory ideas can coexist as peacefully as possible; we do not think, indeed, of extending a theory outside the field for which it was specially worked out. There was once a biologist who saw knives as "made for cutting," who denied finality in the field of biological philosophy, who believed in a sense of history so long as political theory was in question, and who gave proof of activism as soon as it became a matter of applied politics.

A primitive, in the same way, will see that tomorrow is not like today, and even less like yesterday; will profess that corn is planted in a certain way because the god, on the first day, planted it thus; will curse young people who intend to plant it otherwise; and finally will tell those same young people, listening intently to him, how, in the time of his grandfather, the tribe, through the guile of a high statesman, overcame a neighboring people. None of these ideas prevents another, and we cannot see why that primitive man should not compose the history of the struggles of his tribe. If he does not do so, it is perhaps simply because the news of the existence of a historical genre has not yet reached him.

Birth of the Historical Genre

In fact, it is not sufficient for it always to be possible to invent the historical genre; you have to think of doing it, and how do you manage that? The psychological processes of invention are unforeseeable and remain obscure for us; innovation will be made easier if, for example, there already exists a scientific prose, if the public is accustomed to reading in order to learn, if the economic-social structure is such that that public can exist. As always, numberless modest causes will come into play—"the" fact taken as the whole of the birth of a historiography will not have one essential cause corresponding to it as a whole; correlatively, since there is no historiography in itself, a different form of historiography will correspond to a different mix of causes. The tradition of a historical genre will be founded on the day when a work has proved to readers that the narration of events can produce a coherent, intelligible book; from that day it will become as difficult to break with that tradition as it was to create it.

The authority of example causes the evolution of the historical genre to be full of singularities, in which it would be useless to look for profound explanations of it. The history of the theater, of philosophy, and of constitutions dates from Aristotle, that of fine arts from Pliny; on the other hand, the history of music was not written before the middle of the nineteenth century because there had not been a man of goodwill to do it. Why has India had practically no historians, though she has had scholars, philosophers, and grammarians? Surely not because of the profits of production or because the Indian soul is interested only in the eternal. Why didn't our seventeenth century invent economic history? Because the structure of its thinking prevented it from thematizing economics and from thinking of it as history? The idea is no doubt correct, but unsubstantial. Was there not enough love of realities to judge them worthy of History?

Yet that century did not disdain to write the *History of the Great Roads of France* and that of a thousand trifles. When the men of letters of the day gazed over the countryside, they obviously knew that that land had not always looked the same; what they did not know, because they had not yet seen an example of it, was that by systematically pursuing the history of a piece of land, they would end up by formally writing a work. Indeed, such a work, with all the new concepts it would have called for, could not be achieved by one man alone; the creating of economic history was at the mercy of a fortunate accumulation of perilous progress. It was begun, in the eighteenth century, by learned men who compiled histories of prices in the nations of antiquity.

Since only that which is determined exists, the problem of the birth of historiography is not distinct from that of knowing why it was born in a particular form. There is no proof that the Western way of writing history as a continuous account according to duration is the only conceivable way or the best way. We are so accustomed to thinking that history is that, that we forget there was a period when it was not yet understood that it would be that. When it began, in Ionia, what would one day be the historical genre hesitated between history and geography; Herodotus uses the stages of the Persian conquests to tell of the origins of the wars of the Medes in the form of a geographical review of the conquered peoples, recalling the past and present ethnography of each of those peoples. It is Thucydides, whose turn of mind is close to that of natural philosophers, who, taking the plot of a war as a pattern for the study of the mechanisms of politics, involuntarily gave the impression that history is the account of events happening to a nation. We shall see, at the end of this book, why he was led to give the results of his research in the form of an account rather than of a sociology or a *techné* of politics. Finally, it is the mechanical continuation, by Xenophon, of the Thucydidean account that sealed the tradition of Western history, born of a misunderstanding perpetrated by a mediocre follower. But things might have ended in something other than national histories; from Herodotus there could have arisen a *historia* like that of the Arab geographers or like a geographic-sociological review in the manner of the *Prolegomena* of Ibn Khaldun. Once history had become the history of a people, it remained that—so much so that if someday a historian opens up another path and writes, as Weber does, the history of an item, that of the city through the ages, it is labeled sociology or comparative history.

The Existentialist Conception

Let us recapitulate. History is an intellectual activity that, through time-honored literary forms, serves the aims of mere curiosity. If we have been able to convince the reader of this, we may pass more rapidly over another interpretation of history that is quite famous: Historiography is the reflection of our situation, the backward projection of our idea; the vision of the past is the reflection of our values; the historical object does not exist independently of the spectator of history; the past is what we understand as our prehistory.[13] The canonical text of every meditation on historical knowledge thus would be "Lafayette, we are here!" It is no exaggeration to say that only ten years ago such themes formed the "course question" in the philosophy of history.

It is difficult to discuss a conception that, in addition to having an un-verifiable character, is absolutely foreign to the feeling that historians and their readers have about what they are doing and has interest only for an analysis of nationalistic myths in the historiography of the nineteenth century. In what way is the assertion that Antigonus Gonatus made himself master of Macedonia in 276 B.C. (it is a great date) a projection of our values or the expression of my idea? No doubt historiography has a social dimension and an ideological role, just like physics and psychoanalysis; but, no more than those disciplines, is it reduced to its popular image, nor does it take that as a norm. No doubt, too, if science is chaste, its servants and users are only more or less so; it is good never to forget it, and it is certainly more healthy to recall that unpleasant truth than to fall into a corporative apologia.

It nonetheless remains true that, whatever the aims that written history is made to serve, it is written with only itself and its truth in view; otherwise it is no longer history. *Omnes patimur Manes*—every nation has its Brichots to publish a book on the *Führertum* among the Romans in 1934, on the idea of the *Reich* among the same people in 1940, and on the defense of the medieval West against the Eastern threat in 1950. But the blunder goes no further than the title of the book, whose contents remain true; if they were not, they would be discussed very objectively. As for the projection of our values on the past, has it never happened that a historian published a book that did not deal with the anxieties of the day? Unless it is simply meant that history, as knowledge, develops in time, that it does not immediately ask all the questions it might ask itself, and that it is postulated that the questions it asks itself in every period are precisely those that form the spirit of the time, supposing that there is any meaning in this last expression.

It will be said that "Economic history was born at the moment when the economy became an obsessive dimension." This is certainly not true; it is materially false,[14] and arises from a simplistic conception of intellectual life. Ideas are born where they can be: from current events, fashion, chance, reading in the ivory tower; they are most often born of each other and also from the study of the object itself. To cut this short and put an end to this nonsense, the existential theory of history consists in gathering some banal or vague observations on the social conditions of historical knowledge and in claiming that they are *constituents* of the historical object; the past could not be considered without seeing through the cares of the present, just as, in Kant, a physical phenomenon cannot be considered without seeing its extensive magnitude.

To this two objections will be raised. First, no one will think of trying to see physical phenomena other than as extensive—how, indeed, could one tackle it? On the other hand, if a historian is told that he is projecting the values of the present on the past, he will take that as a reproach, which he will wish to escape by being more objective in the future. Now, if he wishes, he can do so, according to the existentialists themselves; the latter are so wholly convinced that historiography *is* different from our idea, that they declare that it *ought* to be that idea and that, in future society, it will fulfill that duty.[15] They know basically that it is so objective that they reproach it with being objectivist.

The Historical Catharsis

In fact, the existentialists mistrust history because it is depoliticized. History is one of the most harmless products ever elaborated by the chemistry of the intellect; it devalues, takes away passion, not because it reestablishes truth against partisan errors, but because its truth is always deceptive and because the history of our land rapidly appears as boring as that of foreign nations. We remember Péguy's shock when he heard one of the dramas of two days previous becoming "history" on the lips of a young man; the same catharsis may be achieved with regard to the most burning question of the day, and I suppose that this bitter pleasure is one of the attractions of contemporary history. It is not at all that passions were false in their own time, or that the passing of time makes regrets sterile and brings the hour of forgiveness; unless they are called indifference, these feelings are played with rather than felt. It is simply that the contemplative attitude is not confused with the practical attitude; one can relate the Peloponnesian War with perfect objectivity. ("The Athenians did this and the Peloponnesians did that") while being an ardent patriot, but not if one relates it as a patriot, for the sound reason that a patriot has nothing to do with this account. As Kierkegaard said, the most perfect knowledge of Christianity will never be the same thing as feeling that Christianity concerns us; no consideration of an intellectual order will ever peremptorily make us pass to the plane of action.

That is one of the reasons—and it is far from being the only one—that accounts for a paradox: Even if, in politics, one has the most decided opinions, it is very different to say for what party one would have opted during the Fronde, in the time of the Marmousets, or under Augustus—

or, rather, the question is childish and leaves us cold. It is not enough to find in the past a political category that is ours for our passion to be inclined to it; one has no passions by analogy. On the other hand, the most dreadful tragedies of contemporary history, those that haunt us continually, do not release in us the natural reflex to avert our gaze, to wipe out the memory of them; they appear to us to be "interesting," however shocking that word may be. In effect, we read and write their history. The shock felt by Péguy would be that felt by Oedipus if he were present at a performance of his own tragedy.

The theater of history makes the audience feel passions that, being lived in an intellectual mode, undergo a kind of purification; their gratuitousness makes every sentiment vain that is not apolitical. There remains only a general compassion for dramas about which it is not for an instant forgotten that they were lived in the most real way. The tonality of history is that saddened knowledge of evil that Dante experienced, on Easter Wednesday in 1300, when he could contemplate, from the height of Saturn, the globe in its roundness: "that bit of earth that makes us so ferocious," *l'aiuola che ci fa tanto feroci.* It is obviously not a lesson in "wisdom," since writing history is an activity of knowledge and not an art of living; it is a curious particular of the historian's job, and that is all.

Part Two

Understanding

Chapter VI

Understanding the Plot

It is often said that history cannot be content to be an account; it explains, too—or, rather, it should explain. This amounts to admitting that in fact it does not always explain, and that it may allow itself not to explain without ceasing to be history—for example, when it just brings to our notice the existence, in the third millennium, of some Oriental empire of which we barely know the name. To which it can be retorted that the difficulty for history would, rather, be not to explain, for the slightest historical fact means something; it is a king, an empire, a war. If tomorrow the capital of Mitanni is excavated and if the royal archives are deciphered, it will suffice us to go through them for events of a familiar type to be classified in our minds—the king made war and was conquered; these are, indeed, things that happen. Let us further extend the explanation: through love of glory, a very natural thing, the king made war and was conquered by reason of his numerical inferiority, for, with some exceptions, it is usual for small battalions to retreat before big ones.

History never goes beyond this level of very simple explanation; it remains fundamentally an account, and what is called explanation is nothing but the way in which the account is arranged in a comprehensible plot. And yet, at first sight, explanation is something very different; for how can this ease of synthesis be reconciled with the very real difficulty in performing that synthesis, a difficulty residing not only in criticism and in the use of documents? And with the existence of great problems, the hypothesis "Muhammad and Charlemagne" or the interpretation of the French Revolution as the taking of power by the middle class? To speak of explanation is to say too much or too little.

"To Explain" Has Two Meanings

In other words, the word "explanation" is taken sometimes in a strong sense in which it means "to assign a fact to its principle or a theory to a more general theory," as science or philosophy does, sometimes in a weak and familiar sense, as when we say, "Let me explain to you what happened, and you will understand." In the first meaning the historical explanation would be a difficult scientific conquest, accomplished at this time on only a few points of the eventworthy field—for example, the explanation of the French Revolution as the taking of power by the middle class. In the second meaning one wonders what page of history might not be explanatory, so long as it is not reduced to mere gibberish or to a chronological list, and so long as it has some meaning for the reader.

We shall subsequently show that in spite of certain appearances and certain hopes, there is no historical explanation in the scientific meaning of the word, and that these explanations amount to explanations in the second sense of the word; those "familiar" explanations, of the second type, are the true—or, rather, the only—form of historical explanation, and we are going to study them now. Everyone knows that when he opens a history book, he understands it, as he understands a novel or what his neighbors are doing; put in other words, explaining, for a historian, means "to show the unfolding of the plot, to make it understood." Such is the historical explanation: entirely sublunary and not scientific at all; we will keep the name "comprehension" for it.

The historian explains plots. Since we are talking about human plots and not, for example, geological dramas, their province will be human— Grouchy came too late; the production of madder declined because of a lack of new outlets for it; a cry of alarm arose from the Quai d'Orsay, where, anxiously, they followed the selfish but clever policy of the bicephalous monarchy. Even an economic history like that of the Popular Front by Sauvy remains a plot that stages theorems on productivity but also the intentions of the actors, their illusions, and it does not lack the little accident that changes the course of things. (Blum did not recognize the economic recovery of 1937 because, in the statistics, it was hidden under a seasonal depression.) The historian is interested in events solely because they occurred, and they are not an opportunity for him to discover laws. At most he brings them up when the opportunity occurs;

what he is keen on discovering are the unknown events or the misunderstood aspect of events. The human sciences penetrate the historical account as alleged truths, and their intrusion cannot go very far, for narration gives little opportunity of going deeply into things—economic history will speak of investments, markets, the flight of gold; will explain the supposed decline of Roman Italy as a result of the competition of the provinces of the Empire (which is only a word, for sources do not permit the specification of the comparative advantages and the terms of trade);[1] it can hardly go any further. The economic life of a nation does not coincide with the system of economic laws, and cannot be explained by it.

It is difficult to imagine the existence of a textbook entitled *Textbook of Historical Synthesis* or *Methodology of History* (we do not say *of Criticism*). Would that textbook be a summary of demography, of political science, of sociology? It is exactly that. For, first, to what chapter of that textbook would these data belong: "Grouchy arrived too late" and "John Hus was burned at the stake"? To a treatise on human physiology in relation to the effects of cremation? Historical explanation utilizes the professional knowledge of the diplomat, the soldier, the elector—or, rather, the historian goes through, via documents, the apprenticeship of a diplomat or a soldier of earlier times. It also utilizes, in the form of traces, some scientific truths, chiefly about economic and demographic matters. But it utilizes above all truths that are so much part of our daily knowledge that there is no need to mention them or even to notice them—fire burns, water flows. As for "Grouchy arrived too late," these words remind us that in addition to causes, history includes "deliberations," that we must bear in mind the intentions of the actors; in the world as we see it, the future is contingent and, consequently, deliberation has its justification.[2] Thus Grouchy can arrive "too" late. Such is the sublunary world of history, in which reign side by side liberty, chance, causes, and ends, as opposed to the world of science, which knows only laws.

To Understand and to Explain

Since such is the quintessence of historical explanation, it must be agreed that it does not deserve so much praise and that it is hardly distinguishable from the kind of explanation in use in everyday life or in any novel in which that life is related. It is but the light emanating from a sufficiently documented account; it offers itself to the historian in the narrative and is not an operation separate from the latter, any more than it is for a novelist. All that is related is comprehensible, since it can be related. Thus, we can conveniently reserve for the world of the true-to-life, of causes and ends, the word "comprehension" dear to Dilthey; that comprehension is like the prose of M. Jourdain, which we use as soon as we open our eyes on the world and on our fellow men. To put it into practice and to be a true historian, or nearly so, it is enough to be a man—that is, to let oneself go. Dilthey would very much have liked to see the human sciences, too, have recourse to comprehension; but wisely they (or at least those among them that, like pure economic theory, are not sciences only in words) refused. Being sciences—that is, hypothetico-deductive systems, they wanted to explain exactly as physical sciences do.

History does not explain, in the sense that it cannot deduce and foresee (only a hypothetico-deductive system can do that); its explanations are not the referral to a principle that would make the event intelligible, but are the meaning that the historian gives to the account. In appearance, the explanation sometimes seems to be drawn from the sky of abstractions—the French Revolution is explained by the rise of a capitalist middle class (let us not investigate whether that middle class was not, rather, a group of shopkeepers and of lawyers), which simply means that the Revolution *is* the rise of a middle class, that the story of the Revolution shows how that class or its representatives seized the levers of state. The explanation of the Revolution is the *summary* of it, and nothing more.

Without undertaking to record all the conceivable uses of the word "explain" in history, let us take one that is famous: by the hypothesis that the word sibylline is traditionally applied to "Muhammad and Charlemagne," Pirenne was able to explain the economic collapse of the Carolingian period. What the word "explain" introduces here is that Pirenne has thrown light on a new fact, the rupture of commercial relations between the West and the East as a result of Arab conquests. If that rupture had always been familiar knowledge, the causal connection would be so obvious that the explanation would not be distinct from the factual account.

The False Idea of Causes

When we ask for an explanation of the French Revolution, we do not crave a theory of revolution in general, from which 1789 could be deduced, nor an elucidation of the concept of revolution, but an analysis of the antecedents responsible for the outbreak of that revolution; the explanation is nothing but the relating of those antecedents, showing as a result of what events the event of 1789 came about. And the word "causes" designates those same events; the causes are the different episodes of the plot. In everyday life, if I am asked "Why were you angry?" I shall not enumerate causes, but will begin a little narrative, woven of intentions and chances. So people are astonished that several books are devoted to causality in history: why specially in history? Wouldn't the study be easier to do in daily life, when we explain why Dupont was divorced and why Durand went to the seaside rather than to the mountains?

Even more conveniently we could study causality in *l'éducation sentimentale;* the epistemological interest of it would be identical with causality in Pirenne or in Michelet. It is a prejudice to believe that history is something apart and that the historian indulges in mysterious operations ending in historical explanation. The problem of causality in history is a survival of the paleoepistemological era; men have continued to suppose that the historian gave the causes of the war between Anthony and Octavius in the same way that the physicist was presumed to give those of falling bodies. The cause of the falling is the attraction that also explains the movements of planets, and the physicist goes back from the phenomenon to its principle; he deduces from a more general theory the behavior of a more limited system, for the explanatory process goes from top to bottom. The historian, on the other hand, confines himself to the horizontal plane: the "causes" of the war between Octavius and Anthony are the events preceding that war, exactly as the causes of what happens in Act IV of *Anthony and Cleopatra* are what happened in the first three acts. And so the word "cause" is much more used in books on history than in history books, in which you can go through five hundred pages of narrative without coming across it even once.

Seignobos declares that an event has causes, that all causes are of equal value, and that it is impossible to designate some as the principal ones; all have contributed to producing the effect, all are fully causes. This point of view is doubly a fiction. The historian does not pick out causes whose conjunction produces the effect; he unfolds a narrative whose episodes succeed each other with the actors and makers articulating their acts. It is permissible, and may be convenient, to consider one of those episodes separately and to call it a cause, but to amuse oneself by cutting the plot into pieces baptized "causes" would be a schoolboy exercise whose only value would be in the ordering of the speech. By cutting up this continuum, it would be possible to make it into many or few causes, according to conventions (the Grand Army en masse or soldier by soldier) and the exhaustion would be unthinkable, not only because each causal series would go back to the beginning of time, but above all because it very quickly loses itself in the non-eventworthy; the historians of future centuries, who will be much more subtle than we are, will perceive, in the souls of the old soldiers of the Grand Army, subtleties that we do not even suspect. Only the physicist, because he has supported legislation on abstractions, can enumerate exhaustively the variables and discrete parameters of a problem.

Second, Seignobos, like Taine, seems to suppose that the historian begins by gathering facts, that he then seeks their causes and is not pleased if he does not find them. That is a mistake, for the historian resembles the journalist rather than the detective; he has completed his task when he has told what he has seen in the documents; he will discover the guilty one only if he can. But is the detective the "good" historian? Certainly, but no one is expected to perform the impossible; if the documents are insufficient to allow the guilty one to be discovered, the historian is no less a historian for that. All that the historian relates is professionally satisfying; we do not spontaneously sense causal gaps— or, rather, if we perceive them, it is a positive discovery that we have made while we think of "further" questions to ask ourselves. The riddle, therefore, is this: how does it come about that history, remaining history, can indifferently seek causes or put little enthusiasm into finding them, can tell of superficial ones or discover profound ones, and, for one and the same event, can bind together at will several plots that are equally explanatory although very different—the diplomatic history, or the economic or psychological or prosopographic history of the origins of the 1914 War? Must we conclude from this that there are "limits to historical objectivity"?

The solution of the riddle is very simple. In the world as we see it, men are free and chance reigns. The historian can each moment let his explanation dwell on a liberty or a chance, which is so often a center of decision. Napoleon lost the battle, what is more natural? These are misfortunes that happen, and we ask nothing more; there is no gap in the narration. Napoleon was too ambitious; any man is free to be so— in fact, that explains the Empire. But was he, rather, put on the throne by the middle class? If so, that class carried the main responsibility for the Empire; it was free, because it was responsible. The non-eventworthy historian then grows indignant. He knows that history is made of *endechomena allôs echein,* of "things that might be different," and he wants the reasons for the free decision of the middle class to be analyzed, what were formerly called its maxims of high policy to be separated, and so on ad infinitum. That is, in history, to explain is to make explicit; when the historian refuses to linger over the first liberty or the first chance he comes across, he does not substitute a determinism for them, but he makes them explicit by discovering in them other liberties and other chances.[3] One can perhaps remember the controversy between Khrushchev and Togliatti about Stalin, after the publication of Khrushchev's report; the Soviet statesman would very much have liked to stop the explanation of Stalin's crimes at the first coming of freedom, that of the general secretary, and at the first chance that made him the general secretary; but Togliatti, as a good non-eventworthy historian, retorted that for that freedom and that chance to be and to work havoc, it was also necessary for Soviet society to be such that it could engender and tolerate that kind of man and chance.[4]

History "In Depth"

Every historical account is a plot out of which it would be artificial to cut discrete causes, and this account is directly causal, comprehensible; only the comprehension it gets is more or less deep. "To look for the causes" is to relate the fact in a more penetrating way, to bring to light the non-eventworthy aspects, to pass from the comic strip to the psychological novel.[5] It is pointless to oppose a narrative history to another that aspires to be explanatory; to explain more is to narrate better, and in any case one cannot relate without explaining—the "causes" of a fact, in the Aristotelian sense, the agent, the matter, the form, and the end are, in truth, the *aspects* of that fact. It is toward this deepening of the account, this making explicit data, aims, and means of action, that today's historiography is often oriented; it ends in analyses (in the sense in which one speaks of the analytical novel)—which, though not accounts in the usual sense of the word, are nonetheless plots, for they include interaction, chance, and goals. It is usual to call this kind of analysis, in a metaphor coming from the theory of economic cycles, the study of the different temporal rhythms: in the foreground, the policy of Philip II day by day; as background, the Mediterranean data, which hardly change. The poles of the action thus serve to construct a temporal scenography in depth, and it is understandable that a baroque artist like Braudel enjoyed this. In the same way, the history of science will be that of the relations between the biography of a scientist, the techniques of his time, and the categories and problems limiting his field of vision at that time.[6]

What justifies the metaphor of the multiple temporal rhythms is the unequal resistance to the change in the different poles of action. At every period unconscious diagrams, *topoi* that are in the air of the time, impose themselves on a scientist or an artist, *geprägte Formen* that classical philology studied in the time of its greatness:[7] those "ready-made forms" that impose themselves with surprising strength on the imagination of artists and that are the matter of the work of art. For example, Wölfflin discloses, beyond the quite varied personalities of the artists of the sixteenth century, the passage from a classical structure to a baroque structure and the "open form." For all is not possible at every moment of history; an artist expresses himself through the visual possibilities of his time, which are a kind of grammar of artistic communication, and that grammar has its own history, its slow rhythm, that determines the nature of styles and the manner of the artists.[8]

But, since a historical explanation does not descend by parachute from the sky, it remains to be concretely explained how the "ready-made forms" could almost imperatively impose themselves on an artist, for the artist does not "submit" to "influences"; the work of art is a doing, which uses sources and "influences" as material causes, in the same way that the sculptor uses marble as the material cause of his statue. So we shall have to study the education of painters in the sixteenth century, the atmosphere of the studios, the demands of the public that made it more or less difficult for an artist to break with the fashionable style, the authority of recent works, as opposed to the works of the previous generation. The influence of visual grammar, of the "pedestal" supporting figuration in the sixteenth century, which Wölfflin analyzes so brilliantly, passes through the psychosocial mediations which are taken up by historical study and of which the art historian cannot be ignorant.

But if there is mediation and interaction, other mediations will function in the opposite sense and will explain that the baroque structure of figurative space and the open form may have appeared, lasted a long time, and disappeared; if ready-made forms are a material cause of the work, the work is the material cause of those forms. The grammar of forms, in slowly passing time, would be a realized abstraction, if it existed otherwise than through and among the artists who make it last, by continuous creation, in swiftly passing time or among those who revolutionize it. At most one can say that these two poles of artistic activity evolve at different speeds, that forms die less quickly than artists, and that we have more difficulty in being conscious of the existence of that grammar of forms than of the personality of the artists.

The plurality of historical times is a manner of speaking that means two things: that the innovators who upset the data of their period are fewer than the imitators, and that the historian must react against a laziness urging him to be satisfied with what the documents say in black and white or with the facts as conceived by the most eventworthy history.

Every fact is both causing and caused; the material conditions are what men make of them, and men are what the conditions make of them. Thus, since Ranke's *Wallenstein*, we see in biography the account of the interactions of a man and his time; interaction is today called "dialectic," which means that the individual whose life is being written about will be considered as the son of his century (how could he not be?), but that he also acts on his century (for one does not act in a void) and that, in order to do so, he takes into account the data of his century, for one does not act without a material cause.

Chance, "Matter," and Liberty

To sum up: historical explanation advances the explication of factors more or less far; and, in this sublunary world, those factors are of three kinds. One is chance, also called superficial cause, incident, genius, or opportunity. Another is called causes, or conditions, or objective data;

we will call it material causes. The last is liberty, deliberation, which we will call final causes. The slightest historical "fact" includes these three elements, if it is human; each man at birth finds objective data that are the world as it is and that make him a proletarian or a capitalist. For his own ends man uses these data as material causes; he joins a trade union or he breaks the strike; he invests his capital or consumes it, just as the sculptor uses a block of marble to make a god, a table, or a basin. Finally there is chance, Cleopatra's nose or the great man. If we stress chance, we shall have the classical conception of history as a theater where Fortune plays at upsetting our plans; if we insist on the final cause, we end up with the so-called idealist conception of history—for Droysen, for example, the idea, formulated in pseudo-Hegelian terms, is that in the last resort the past is explained "by moral forces or ideas."[9]

We may prefer to insist on the material cause—do not our liberties bring into play the data of the environment? This is the Marxist conception. It is fairly pointless to perpetuate the conflict of these conceptions; it is a problem settled a good two millennia ago. However ingenious or revolutionary a historian may be, he will always find the same material and final causes. Everything happens as if the property of philosophical truth, as opposed to other truths, is to be very simple—we might say almost truistic, if its property is not equally to be unceasingly misunderstood under the pressure of the history of ideas. To decide whether one will prefer the material or the final causes, there is no need to labor over history books; everyday life ought to be enough to enlighten our choice, and the most acute historian will never find anything other, when his work is done, than what he found at the beginning: "matter" and liberty. If he found only one of these two causes, he would have passed surreptitiously into a paraphysical beyond. It is pointless to hope that by going into Max Weber's problem (Is Protestantism the cause of capitalism?), we will finally succeed, documents in hand, in establishing scientifically that in the last resort matter controls everything or that, on the contrary, minds do. However deeply the historical explanation penetrates, it will never find limits; it will never open on mysterious forces of production, but only on men like you and me, men who produce and, to do so, put material causes into the service of final causes, if chance doesn't interfere. History is not a tiered construction, in which a material and economic foundation would bear a social ground floor surmounted by superstructures for cultural uses (the studio of a painter, a gaming

room, the historian's study); it is a monolith in which the distinction between causes, goals, and chances is an abstraction.

So long as there are men, there will be no goals without material
means; the means will be means only in relation to goals, and chance will
exist only for human action. The result is that every time a historian
halts his explanation on goals, or on matter, or on chance, his explanation
must be considered incomplete; in truth, so long as there are historians,
their explanations will be incomplete, for they can never be a regression
ad infinitum. Thus, historians will always use the terms "superficial
cause," "objective conditions," "mentalities," or synonyms, according to
the fashion of their century. For wherever they stop the explanation of
causes, wherever they are at the moment, they give up going further into
the non-eventworthy; their halt will necessarily produce one of these
three aspects of all human action. According to the period, they have a
heuristic opportunity to stress one or another of these aspects; the study
of mentalities seems at present to be the most opportune, the prejudice
of eternal man not being dead and the materialist explanations having
become familiar to us. The important thing, beyond the heuristic plane,
is not to believe that the three aspects of action are three levels or three
separate essences; as "a discipline of historic reasoning" let us study the
origin of three conceptions of history corresponding to these three aspects: the materialist theory of history, the history of mentalities, the
distinction between superficial and profound causes. We do not intend
in any way to refute them, but just to show their relative nature in relation to human action, which is a whole, and their temporary character
in relation to the historical explanation, which is reference to the infinite.

Material Causes: Marxism

When the explanation halts at the material causes and when it is
imagined that with them the explanation is completed, we get Marxist
"materialism": men are what objective conditions make of them. Marxism
is born of the very vivid feeling of the resistance that reality offers our
will, of the slow march of history, which it tries to explain by the word
"matter." Then we know into what aporia this determinism plunges us.
It is very true, on the one hand, that social reality has a crushing weight
and that men generally take on the mentality of their condition, for no
one willingly exiles himself into utopia, rebellion, or solitude; the infra-

structure, it will be said, determines the superstructure. But, on the other hand, that infrastructure is itself human; there are no forces of production in a pure state, but only men who produce. Can it be said that the plow produces slavery and that the windmill determines serfdom? But the producers were free to adopt the windmill, out of love of efficiency, or to reject it, out of habit; so is it their mentality, enterprising or following a routine, that determined the forces of production? The false problem then begins to go round and round in our minds, around a Marxist axis (the infrastructure determines the superstructure, which determines the infrastructure) or around a Weberian or pseudo-Weberian axis (of capitalism and of the Protestant mind, which secreted the other?). We shall pour out declarations of principle (thought reflects reality, or conversely) and finishing touches that save an account (reality is a challenge; man answers it). In fact, there is not a vicious circle, but a regression ad infinitum; had the producers refused the windmill out of routine? We shall see later that that routine is not an ultima ratio; it explains itself, it is rational conduct in its own way.

The resistance of reality, the slowness of history, do not come from infrastructures, but from all the other men for each of them; Marxism tries to explain by journalistic metaphysics a very simple fact arising from the most everyday understanding. Let us consider the drama at present being lived by the underdeveloped countries that cannot "take off"; the impossibility of investing profitably in modern industries there perpetuates a mentality foreign to investment, and that mentality in turn perpetuates that impossibility. Indeed, a capitalist in those countries has little interest in investing, since speculation in land and lending at interest bring him profits as high, safer, and requiring less work; none of them is interested in breaking that circle. But let us suppose that it is broken by a traitor who "spoils the game," who begins to invest, and who changes the conditions of economic life—all the others will have to fall in line or give up. That means that each man, in turn, takes toward the rest the attitude corresponding to an impossibility of which the other men are, with regard to him, the authors; each is powerless so long as the others do not move with him. The whole forms a coalition of prudence in which each is the prisoner of the others, and it gives rise to a bronze law as inflexible as all historical materialisms—except that an individual initiative, which has no explanation in materialism, can break the charm and give the signal for another coalition. And one of the most frequent social processes is this, which is capable of contradicting all forecasts and causal explanations because it is an anticipation: the announcement of an action that *is going* to be undertaken by others modifies the data on which each bases his hopes, and causes him to change his plans.

Final Causes: Mentality and Tradition

Instead of halting the explanation at material causes, it happens that at other times it is halted at final causes; if they are taken as an ultima ratio, the explanation then cloaks one of those two mythical figures: the mentality (the rational, collective soul) and tradition. This is roughly what happens in the historian's mind. He begins with the cruel, daily experience of his inability to determine why this oppressed people revolts and that other does not. Why was there public benefaction in Hellenistic Athens and not in fifteenth-century Florence? We try to explain the political attitudes and the voting of western France in the Third Republic; too quickly for our taste we encounter the inexplicable.

The combinations of influences, the observation of which teaches us the value with precision, dictate to the candidate the rules of the game. In the Pays de Caux, it will be enough to have the landowners and the farmers for one, and all the rest will catch on. In western Maine, Anjou, Vendée, agreement between the noble and the priest will get you elected almost without a campaign. In Léon you can be content with the priest alone; on the other hand, you will pass over him almost with impunity in Lower Normandy, so long as you have the big farmers and a clean bill of health.[10]

These are empirical conclusions as subtle as they are solid.

But we come now to theoretical explanations, we touch the most delicate problem and the most impenetrable one; of course we are in a position to measure the intrinsic value of the various factors, but at the same time we prove that it is not the same everywhere. Why do the people of Anjou passively and seemingly naturally endure the political interference of the big landowners? Why do the Bretons only bear it angrily, and how does it come about that in often analogous circumstances most Normans will absolutely reject it? To these questions, the system of landowning, the social structure, the way dwellings are grouped, various other circumstances furnish the beginnings of an answer, but in the end we reach (and is it not an admission of defeat?) the mystery of ethnic personalities. Just as there are individual temperaments, so there are provincial temperaments and national temperaments.

But are not these mentalities only traditions? Another sociologist writes:

Let us take an example, and let us consider the electoral frontier that separates the departments of Allier and Puy-de-Dôme: to the north of that line they vote Left; to the south, Right. Yet the present socioeconomic structures are not very different. But history teaches us that that frontier coincides with the one that in the Middle Ages separated Auvergne, a land of freehold and peasant democracy, from the Bourbonnais, where reigned an arrogant feudal system that employed a people without hearth or home to cultivate the land.[11]

The essence of the historical explanation would be, then, to search in the existence of mental "microclimates," which means that the causes are lost for us in the mystery of the collective soul, and that within a distance of thirty kilometers that soul changes without our being able to say why; "microclimate" expresses well the narrowness of our capacity to explain. A Florentine and an Athenian had the same municipal patriotism, the same ease in giving, the same taste for rivalry, the same attitude of the leading citizen who holds the government of the city to be his personal affair; then why were there public benefactors in Athens and not in Florence? Is it a tradition peculiar to Athens or to the Greek cities in general, and one that goes back to some detail in the Hellenic past? But public benefaction spread throughout the Mediterranean basin, from the Persians, Syrians, and Jews to the Carthaginians and the Romans.

Here it would be amusing to see us making the complete inventory of the causes, having recourse to the method of remainders or that of concomitant variations.[12] The explanation of the difference is concealed in the mental climate of Florence and Athens, which means that we do not know it, but that we know that we do not know it and that we can represent our ignorance concretely to ourselves; we know that in the Assembly, in Athens, an orator could rise and cleverly propose that a rich man should make a sacrifice on behalf of the Public Treasury; we guess that in an assembly of the major arts, that would have been unthinkable. A difference of climate that documents hardly allow us to understand, but one that contemporaries, could we but question them, would express with the greatest vigor; no more than we, could they make clear the reason for it, but they would be explicit on the impossibility of risking such a proposal in Florence. Our action is unconsciously directed by shades of meaning that we cannot explain but that we know to be decisive: a particular proposition is or is not unthinkable. If we have to say why, two answers are possible. One is "People are like that," and so we will have sealed a fact about mentality. The other is "The proposition would be contrary to every custom, nothing like it had ever been seen," and we will have sealed a fact about tradition.

Chance and Deep-rooted Causes

The distinction we draw between superficial and deep-rooted causes may thus be taken in at least three ways. A cause may be termed deep-rooted if it is more difficult to see, if it appears only as the result of an effort at clarification; the depth is then in the order of knowledge—it will be said that the deep-rooted cause of public benefaction is the Athenian or the Greek soul; and, so saying, the impression will be given that the depths of a civilization are being touched. But, in a second way, the depth may really be in the being; the cause will be called deep-rooted, which in a word sums up a whole plot—the French Revolution is basically explained by the rise of a middle class. If the origins of the 1914 War are studied, once the plot is put together, it is possible to take a bird's-eye view of it and to conclude that, in the main, that war is explained by purely diplomatic causes and by the politics of powers, or by reasons of collective psychology—but not by the economic causes of which Marxists dream. That which is deep-rooted is global.

The idea of a deep-rooted cause has, finally, a third meaning; the most efficacious causes are called superficial, the ones in which the disproportion is greatest between their effect and their cost. This is a very rich idea implying a full analysis of the structure of a given action, one that implies a complete analysis of a given structure of action and whose meaning is strategic—one must know and judge a singular situation as a strategist in order to be able to say "That incident was enough to ignite the gunpowder," "This chance sufficed to block everything," or "So simple an action by the police very efficaciously put an end to the disorder." So it is a fiction to claim, like Seignobos, that all causes carry the same weight because the absence of only one would be equivalent to a veto. They would all have the same importance in an objective, abstract process in which one might, besides, hope to have enumerated them all; but then one would no longer be speaking of causes, but would only be laying down laws and their equations, variables on which unknowns would depend and parameters that would be the data of the problem.

When it is said that the firing in the Boulevard des Capucines was only the occasion for the fall of Louis Philippe, it is not claimed that Louis Philippe would of necessity have remained on the throne without that skirmish or that he would necessarily have fallen because of the general discontent; it is only being affirmed that that discontent was seeking a way to act and that it is never very difficult to find an opportunity when one is resolute. It is less costly, for the genius of history, to provoke an incident than to make a whole people furious; and the two causes, equally indispensable, do not have the same cost. The deep-rooted cause is the less economic; whence the discussions in the 1900 fashion on the role of "leaders"—who is responsible for social unrest, a handful of leaders or the spontaneity of the masses? In the superficial but effective view of a chief police commissioner, it is the leaders, because it suffices to put the masses in prison to stop the strike; on the other hand, it takes all the weight of bourgeois society to make a proletariat revolutionary. Since history is a play of strategy, in which the foe is sometimes man and sometimes nature, it happens that the post of chief police commissioner is occupied by chance—it is chance that gives Cleopatra her nose and Cromwell a grain of sand in his bladder; sand or a nose costs little, and these causes, as efficacious as they are economic, will be considered superficial.

"Economic" does not mean "easy to get" or "not improbable" (a chance will, on the contrary, be thought so much the more superficial as it was improbable), but "what attacks the breastplate of the opponent at its weak point": the bladder of Cromwell, the heart of Anthony, the cadres of the workers' movement, the nervous tension of the Parisian crowd in February 1848; if the most improbable of chances is enough to break a breastplate, it is because it had unknown weak points. It can be affirmed that, without the firing on the boulevard, the slightest incident could have brought about the fall of the Citizen King, but naturally one cannot swear that that incident would surely have taken place; chance and the chief police commissioner sometimes miss the opportunities to attack at the weak point, and opportunities are not always found again— Lenin must have told himself that in 1917, for he was much more intelligent than Plekhanov and had the most correct ideas on that incarnation of chance called the great man. Plekhanov, more a scientist than a strategist, began by stating that history had causes; he crushed the clever battle array that a historical situation is and, like Seignobos, reduced it to a certain number of battalions that he picked off one by one under the name of causes. But, unlike Seignobos, he believed that all causes do not have the same strength; if all causes were equal, how could the engine of history operate? Let us consider how it operated in 1799— the interests of the victorious middle class were curbed by lack of a great man, but the weight of those interests was so great that they would in any case have overcome the friction; even if Bonaparte had not been born, another saber would have been raised to take his place.

The distinction between opportunities and deep-rooted causes rests on the idea of intervention. Trotsky reasoned thus: with resolute police officers, no February 1917 Revolution; without a Lenin, no October Revolution;[13] Stalin could be counted on to wait a very long time for history to ripen, and Russia would today be a society of the South American type. Between 1905, when he made no gesture, and 1917, Lenin moved from the causal idea of ripening to the strategic idea of the "weak point in the capitalist chain," and that weak point gave way in the country that was causally the least ripe. Since history includes superficial causes—that is, efficacious ones—it is strategic; it is a succession of battles that include as many different arrangements and as many singular conjunctures. That is why the *Russian Revolution* of Trotsky, the masterly analysis of a great historical battle, is not a Marxist book, except for its professions of faith. There is no rule of action, there are no prefabricated strategies for typical situations; those who have made "pragmatic" history and tried to extract tactical recipes from the past attained the poor results we see in Polybius ("One must never be imprudent enough to introduce a big garrison into a fortress, especially if it is made up of barbarians"). Must we add "in Machiavelli"?[14]

The deep-rooted causes determine what happens, if it happens; and the superficial causes determine whether it will happen. Without the deficit of royal finances that caused the outbreak of the middle-class Revolution, there would be no mention of the thrust of the rising middle class; France would have become a conservative monarchy in which the enlightened gentry and the upper middle class would have mingled. The middle-class discontent at the nobility's power would have left no other traces than *Figaro* and a few anecdotes like those that could as well be quoted in Thackeray's England. Chance in history corresponds to the definition given by Poincaré of aleatory phenomena: mechanisms whose results may be completely upset by imperceptible variations in the initial conditions. When the mechanism in question is found in one camp (whether it is

called the Ancient Regime, Anthony, or tsarism) and the author of the
imperceptible variation is in the opposite camp (the deficit, chance, or
nature that makes noses pretty, the genius of Lenin), the disproportion
between what the first camp undergoes and the economy of effort in the
second camp is such that we say that the second struck the first at the
weakest point of its armor.

History Has No Broad Outlines

Since "superficial cause" does not mean a cause less effective than
another, it is not possible to discover main lines of evolution, any more
than they could be found in a game of poker lasting for a thousand years.
When speaking of historical chance or of one of its synonyms (leaders,
Masonic conspiracy, great man, sealed truck, or "mere accident on the
trip"), we must carefully distinguish a single event from history taken as
a whole. It is very true that certain events—the Revolution of 1789 and
that of 1917—have deep-rooted causes; it is not true that history, in the
last resort, is exclusively guided by deep-rooted causes rising from the
middle class or the historic mission of the proletariat—it would be too
easy. Thus, understanding history does not consist in being able to discern great underwater currents below the surface agitation; history has
no depths. It is well known that its reality is not rational, but it must be
known that it is no longer reasonable; there are no issues that are normal,
giving history, at least from time to time, the reassuring look of a well
tied-up plot in which what ought to happen does happen. The main lines
of history are not didactic; the landscape of the past does indeed present
some lines of relief that are much fuller than others: the diffusion of
Hellenistic or Western civilization, the technological revolution, the age-
old stability of some national groupings. Unfortunately, these mountain
chains do not reveal the action of reasonable, moderate, or progressive
forces; rather, they show that man is an imitative animal and a conservative one (he is also the opposite, but the effects of it have a different
tectonic aspect). The fullness of these lines is as stupid as a routine or an
epidemic.

Thus, it is a presumption to think that the history of each period has its
"problems" and is explained by them. In fact, history is full of failed possibilities, of events that did not take place; no one will be a historian if he
does not perceive, around history that has really happened, an indefinite

multitude of equally possible histories,[15] of "things that could have been otherwise." Discussing Syme's *Roman Revolution,* a census taker wrote something like this: "History cannot be reduced to the day-to-day politics and to the action of individuals; the history of a period is explained by its problems." That is false depth;[16] in history textbooks each period is thus busy with a certain number of problems that result in events called their solution; but this lucidity *post eventum* is not that of contemporaries, who have ample opportunity for proving that oppressive problems or ardently prepared revolutions end up lost in the obscurity of sand, while unexpected revolutions break out and, in retrospect, reveal unsuspected problems.[17] The merit of a historian is not to pass for profound, but to know at what a humble level history functions; it is not to have exalted or even realistic views, but to have sound judgment on mediocre things.

History Has No Method

History is a matter of understanding; its only difficulties are about details. It has no method, which means that its method is innate; in order to understand the past, it is sufficient to view it with the same eyes we use to understand the world around us or the life of a foreign people. It is sufficient to view the past in this way in order to see in it the three kinds of causes we discover around us as soon as we open our eyes: the nature of things, human freedom, and chance. Such are, according to the Peripatetics, and especially Alexander of Aphrodisias, the three kinds of efficient causes that rule the sublunary world and that Wilhelm von Humboldt, in one of the finest essays ever written on history, describes as the three kinds of motivating causes of universal history.[18] History is placed in this actual world, of which Aristotelianism remains the best description—this real, concrete world, peopled with things, animals, and men, in which men do and will, but do not do all they will, in which they have to inform a matter that is not informed haphazardly; this same world that others strive to describe less well, speaking of "challenge" or by crediting Marxism, under the name of praxis, with a philosophy more faithful to reality than that of Marx.[19]

Certainly, the historian must first reconstruct the past; the logic or the psychology of that reconstruction is in no way different from that of the sciences, for logic does not vary to a great extent. In his reconstruction of truth, the historian conforms with the same norms as scientists do; in his inferences, in the search for causes, he obeys the same general laws of thought as a physicist or a detective. No more than the detective does he use a special grid for events; he is satisfied with the eyes he has been given in order to see. May he only not refuse to see, nor pretend that he does not understand what he does understand! We know, in fact, that there is a temptation in superfluous methodology that urges us to find, badly and at the cost of laborious methods, data of understanding that we would not even seek if we did not already understand them; it is the scientist temptation to recompose that which is proximate. More than one sociologist

. . . will pretend to approach the social fact as if it were unknown to him, as if his study owed nothing to the experience he has, as a social subject, of intersubjectivity; under the pretext that in fact sociology is not yet made of that lived-through experience, that it is the analysis of it, the making explicit and objective, that it overthrows our initial consciousness of social relationships, he will forget that other evidence that we cannot broaden our experience of social relationships only by analogy or by contrast with those we have lived through, in short, by an imaginary variation of the latter.[20]

Thus, it is a relief to learn that sociologists have just perfected a method, called content analysis, which, when sociologically studying a collection of texts, consists in reading and understanding them; when a sociologist is dealing with the sociology of the press or of education, and whether he studies *Carnard enchaîné* or reports on the *agrégation*, his method is to read those writings in order to extract ideas and themes from them, just as other readers do.

The historical explanation thus consists of rediscovering in history a mode of explaining that we have, in some way, "always known"; that is why it may be called comprehension, that is why history is familiar to us, why with it we feel everywhere at home. Historiography has had no Galileo nor Lavoisier, and cannot have one. Thus, its method has made no progress since Herodotus or Thucydides, however surprising that affirmation may seem; what has made considerable progress, on the other hand, is historical criticism and above all, as we shall see later, the historical topic. The effort has often been made to go beyond the naive vision of things thanks to some discovery relating to the functioning of history; economic materialism is the classic example. These methodological attempts have never been successful, and the first concern of philosophers who profess to follow a historical methodology is, when they become historians, to return to the evidence of common sense. It is known how Taine, as a historian, does something else and something much better than as a theorist; it is known how Marxists "relax" their determinism; it is known that Auguste Comte, who speaks of the fatality of history, soon adds that it is a "modifiable fatality."

The historical explanation can appeal to no principle, to no permanent structure (each plot has its own particular causal device); so professional historians have far fewer ideas on history than do amateurs. However surprising that may appear, historical methodology has no fixed content; that is not because history stages economies, societies, and cultures that the historian knows better than others (he also has better knowledge of how they link together)—everyone knows it or, if you prefer, no one does. The public sometimes has a flattering but inexact idea of the preoccupations of historians; they are rarely in doubt about whether economic materialism speaks the truth, whether societies are structural, or whether cultures have an epistemic base. At the most they say to themselves that they ought to be up-to-date with these fine things, but, since they never succeed in finding the right way of going about it professionally, they conclude that it is philosophy and too hard for them, although certainly suggestive. Not that historians are usually more limited than the editors of literary magazines, but they never encounter these problems in their work, and cannot encounter them. At the risk of being disappointed, the public has to be warned that when they come across an interesting social or cultural fact, they must not bring it to the historian for an expert opinion, counting on his being able to apply the right method, lay bare the base, or connect the cultural with the economic. Also, nothing is more disappointing than to read historians, especially the greatest—they have no ideas. It is known that a physicist is much more interesting when, instead of talking physics, which is rather narrow, he tells us if the universe is curved and if indeterminism is the latest thing; similarly there is a tradition of history for nonhistorians. Hence the suspect popularity of certain books by great historians. The great Max Weber, in a book that is not his best, has thus raised a problem imagined to be that of the primacy of economics or of religion; the great Panofsky, in his *parerga*, imagined one day that there was a homology between the *Summa theologica* of St. Thomas and the structure of Gothic cathedrals: that is history as we like it. In the works of Marc Bloch, Pirenne, or Syme, unfortunately, there is only history: so the names of these authors are spoken with reverence, but they are not spoken about for very long.

We know, since Kant, that a science must be studied with scientists and that what they do must be considered, rather, what they eventually say they are doing; we see historians occupied with epigraphy or with parish registers, and concerning themselves much less with forming a general conception of the historical and the social. Indeed, what would they do with it? Their task is to make us understand the sublunary, and comprehension tolerates no other kind of explanation alongside it. Let us propose historical materialism to them. One of two things will happen: either the relationship between the economic and the social is understandable from the facts, and the materialist theory becomes useless, or it is not understandable and the theory is a mystique. For if it had to be supposed that the water mill produces serfdom by an operation as mysterious to us as that by which an excess of urea produces macabre hallucinations, in that case Marxism would be an article of faith; but it calls itself historical and affirms that the relationship between the mill and serfdom is discovered empirically. In that case the problem is no longer to hold that the infrastructure determines the superstructure, but to succeed in building up a coherent plot that connects the mill, in the first act, and serfdom, in the last act, and to do that without the intervention of any deus ex machina. If Marxism is speaking the truth, one will be brought, by the logic of the facts themselves, to build that plot, in the expectation of that happy day—let us put Marxism into the cupboard where we stow views on mind and pious desires. Either Marxism contradicts the concrete explanation of serfdom, and is false, or else it agrees with it, and is superfluous; there is no historical explanation except a concrete one; every other explanation will at best be a useless repetition of it. Marxism might be a true statement: "Throughout history, we find, when we study facts in detail, that economic causes are of exceptional importance"; but it cannot be a method to replace understanding. It can be at most a heuristic.

The Ontology of the Historian

That every historical explanation is concrete means that our world is made up of agents, centers of action, which alone can be efficient causes, excluding abstractions. These agents are either things (the sun that gives us light, water, a windmill) or animals and men (a serf, a miller, a Frenchman). For a historical explanation to be admissible, it must not present any interruption of continuity in causal relations that connect the agents involved in the plot: the miller, his master, the mill. These agents, otherwise called the substances, are like the pillars on which the road of the explanation rests. One has no right to replace one of those pillars by an abstraction playing the part of a deus ex machina; if the plot thus presents an impediment, the explanation is not admissible. Here are two examples.

First, it is known what a stir was made by Panofsky's book in which he sets forth the discovery he thinks he has made of a formal homology between the great theological summas of the thirteenth century and the structure of the Gothic cathedrals. I do not know if that homology exists, and is not one of the many phantoms raised by the combinative. But let us suppose it does exist; the real, the only question will then be to explain concretely how that homology between the book of a theologian and the work of an architect could have been produced. Panofsky certainly does not fail to try to explain it—could it be that architects and theologians associated with each other, and that a foreman wanted to transpose into his own art the subdivision procedures of the Scholastics, as Seurat and Signac wanted to apply to painting the physical theory of primary colors (which they had misunderstood, so much so that in their pictures those colors do not recombine and produce a grisaille)? Many other explanations are imaginable, but, as long as we do not have the right one, Panofsky's thesis will be an unfinished page, and not at all an example to be followed by the human sciences.[21]

Second, from a famous pen we see quoted with praise the following sociologism: "The mathematical rationalism of the eighteenth century, sustained by mercantile capitalism and the development of credit, leads men to conceive space and time as homogeneous and infinite environments." What plot could lead us, without impediment, from the letter of credit to infinitesimal calculus? If the scene took place among primitives, the following fable could be imagined: In a tribe whose village was surrounded by a circular fence, an ethnographer with the right training inquired about the natives' conception of space. One old man, considered to be a character, who had his own ideas and had always lived rather on the fringe, replied with a lucubration that he had elaborated in the course of his meditations. Letting his imagination soar on the wing of allegories and correspondences, he declared: "As for the great All that surrounds us, it is round like everything that is perfect, like a vase, like the uterus, like the fence surrounding a village." The ethnographer did not fail to conclude that the mentality of the primitives represents the idea of space by the model of the village in which they live. But when the scene is transferred to the Paris or the Turin of the eighteenth century, when the village fence is replaced by the time bargain or the effect of commerce, and when the old man is Dalembert or Lagrange, it becomes more difficult to invent a satisfactory plot.[22]

As a young historian, an Aristotelian without knowing it, said one day, with the vivacity of his age: "Every historical proposition into which one could not put the words 'things' or 'people,' but only abstractions like 'mentality' or 'middle class,' is likely to be nonsense." For the bill of exchange to give rise to infinitesimal calculus, the causation has to go through accountants and merchants, and it will be more difficult to relate these than to relate abstract words. Abstractions cannot be efficient causes, for they have no existence; as the Sophist says, "Only that which really exists has the power to act on something or to suffer because of something."

Only substances with their accidents, concrete beings with their ways of being, exist and can be actors in a plot. Snow and a swan are white, Socrates walks about—these are substances; white snow causes ophthalmia, but whiteness cannot. In order to kill Socrates, it takes hemlock or Anytus: Athenian demagogy or conservatism lacks that power, for there exist only demagogues or conservatives. France does not make war, for she does not really exist; there are only Frenchmen, of whom war may be the accident. No more do there exist forces of production; there exist only men who produce. There exist only the corporal things or people, the concrete, the individual, the specific.

For a historian, as for all men, what is really real is the individual. It is not relations, as has been the case in science since Newton's time. No more is it the Spirit (there is, among historians, those Sons of Earth, a naive, clumsy way of being attached to truth; their motto is "Realism first." For example, Hegelian ontology is in vain an ontology in motion; it is in vain, in the eyes of the philosopher, imperishable because of the rigor, the vigor, and the subtlety with which Hegel concluded his exem-

plary experience of thought: for the historian, Hegelian ontology is useless and unusable, because it is a false ontology; he sees no further.).

Abstraction in History

The philosophizing tradition inherited from historism gives the falsest
possible idea of history. Theories are the least lacking; in history the difficulty of a problem is never theoretical (whereas it may be in the sciences);
neither is it always in the criticism of documents. To explain either the
fall of the Roman Empire or the origins of the (American) Civil War,
the causes, scattered, are there; would we lack a doctrine showing us
how to wind up the mechanism and what part carried another? Will a
synthesis be erroneous when the mechanism has been wound up wrongly?
Things do not happen like that. The difficulty of history is that it stages
thousands or millions of substances, and in practice there is no question
of following the causal movements, taking them one by one; historiography is, inevitably, a shorthand. Now the subtle detail that changes
everything often slips through the mesh of this laconism. In history it is
as in politics: the difficulty is not to draft a decree or make a plan for
development, but to have it applied. Now, in the detail of things, the
decree may get bogged down in passive resistance as soon as it passes
through the gates of the capital; the plan for development will surely
meet the norms of the most liberal socialism or of the most progressive
free enterprise—unfortunately, if the managers lack initiative and the
workers lack know-how, the plan is only a false abstraction. The economics minister who signed it will have failed, and the historian who
judged it by its wording will have been mistaken.

Furthermore, that shorthand is written in abstract language, whence
the dangers that threaten it. "We must not underestimate the force of
abolitionist ideas in the outbreak of the (American) Civil War"; "feudal
society was born because, the central power being weak and far away,
each man looked for a protector close by": history books are inevitably
written in that style. But must we really underestimate abolitionist ideas?
Where do we get those ideas? The men of the North are dead, and besides
there would be too many of them; these "ideas" are held by all and by
none, and it is unlikely that they really knew what they thought; it is still
more improbable that they could have written it down or said it, had

they been questioned. "Weak and far-off power"—what power is not? From what degree of distance do men look for another protector? "Far-off power" may be the intuition of a great historian, and it may be the equivalent of political gossip in a café.

History is condemned to try to seize the reality in a network of abstractions. It also is constantly exposed to the temptation of reifying an abstraction, of lending to a word written by the historian the same causal role as things and men, even of considering that this abstract cause has itself not been caused, that it is unmoved and that nothing historical can happen to it; it will be presumed to arise and to disappear through some inexplicable caprice. In other words, historians are often tempted to separate, from the homogeneous foundation of interactions of substances that constitutes history, sorts of frameworks to explain historical development that would order it in the last resort or even cause it without in turn being caused. The great theories of history are usually nothing else: they consist in admitting that historical development has a structure, an anatomy; that the diagram of a mechanism that makes it move can be traced. It is remarkable that, at every period, the operation is repeated, to the profit of the level most recently reached in the conquest of the non-eventworthy. The eighteenth century thought it had found the motive power of history in climates, in laws, in mores;[23] the nineteenth century hypostatized the economy into an infrastructure; and our century, whose conquests are more subtle, is inclined to reify the aspect of an epoch or the frameworks of thought. We willingly suppose, in fact, that the culture of each epoch is determined by the frameworks (the visual grammar of the baroque, the mechanistic reading of the physical world, and so on) that limit it and confer on it a sort of stylistic unity; few ideas are as popular as that one, for it procures the type of morose delight given by historical relativism and it confers dizzying depths on history. Let us give an example of such frameworks and of the good use that can be made of them, as well as several examples of their abuses.

An Example: The Greek Religion

The evolution of the Greek religion, before and after the beginning of the Hellenistic period, like that of the Roman religion before and after the end of the Republic, and that of the religions of India, from the Vedic period to Hinduism, is dominated by the same change of framework. In the three cases we are first of all in the presence of religions made up of cults addressing themselves to all citizens and recurring to the rhythm of the official calendar; it is Brahmanism, the religion of Athens in the classical period, or the religion of the Roman Republic. Next come religions in which each of the faithful, if he so desires, selects a divinity to which he vows personal piety and that exists for him alone; it is the henotheism of "mystic paganism" in which, and against which, Christianity developed, it is Hinduism with its countless sects and universal tolerance. To put it in shocking but expeditious language, there was movement from a "set menu" religious framework to an "à la carte" religion—the invasion of the Roman Empire by Oriental religions (which, under Greek influence, became religions requiring initiation) is only one aspect, one consequence of this radical change of framework, which also affects the traditional divinities. From one framework to the other, a superficially identical fact—an invocation to Jupiter—changes meaning, even though that invocation is textually the same: in the first framework, Jupiter is addressed as an official personage; in the second, as a chosen master who moved the heart of the one who became his worshiper.

When a worshiper thus takes a god of his choosing, he does not thereby deny the existence of other gods; henotheism is not monotheism. That tolerance was, indeed, general in antiquity; it was thought that the gods are the same for all men, just as an oak is everywhere an oak. At most, each people named it in its own language—that is, the names of the gods can be translated from one language into another, like common nouns. But when the "à la carte" framework was established, that tolerance changed structure; the worshiper of a chosen god, without denying the other gods, professes that his is better than the others, that to him he is all the others, that the other gods are his god with erroneous names— just like a lover declaring that his beloved is the fairest and that to him she is all women, whose existence he does not deny, any more than their right to be loved in their turn. It is understandable that this universal tolerance, between individuals and between peoples, was to be transformed into intolerance vis-à-vis the monotheism or the exclusivism of Christians; what was the matter with the Christians, they thought, refusing their respect to the gods of others, and particularly to the divinity of the emperor, denying the existence of those gods—or, rather, considering them as devils (for such was then the view of Christians)? In the atmosphere of general tolerance, Christian exclusivism was incomprehensible, and consequently inspired horror; their impiety could be explained only by a hidden perversity, an unnatural vice, and it was thus that the monotheism of the Jews had already been interpreted.

Of course, this idea of two religious frameworks has hardly any value, save a didactic one; the passage from one framework to another was not brought about by a beat of the drum; it is explained by the very fact that it was progressive—or, rather, it is only a word that sums up this progressive change. From the time of the *Rig Veda* and Homer, we see personal faith existing in the shadow of the collective religion, and to the end of antiquity we see official religion surviving; as Saussure would say, "Passing from one system of relations to another was not willed; the modification has no bearing on the arrangement, but on the elements that are arranged."[24] However, there will be a great temptation to take advantage of a didactic abstraction and to reason thus: "In order for Oriental gods or the old pagan religion to be conceived of only as a matter of personal faith, the frameworks must first have been changed; it was not the invasion of Oriental religions that upset the system, it was that upsetting that made the invasion possible." It would then remain to explain why there was this upset; that is what people refrain from doing, which amounts to attributing the change to some tragic caprice of history.

The Frameworks: A Collection of Tales

The operation is carried out as follows. Let us suppose I want to intimate that in the sixteenth century clocks were few and did not keep good time, and that consequently people put up with some fluctuations in their day's program; in order to present the matter more vividly, I interiorize it and write that time, to people in the sixteenth century, was fluctuating time, a sleeping time. I will only have to declare that, far from the mediocrity of the clocks helping us to understand that the people conceived of time in this way, it was, on the contrary, the conception they had of time as fluctuating that prevented them from improving and increasing the number of their clocks. It is thus that, according to R. Lenoble,[25] antiquity's conception of nature was vitalist. Therefore it was not possible to conceive of phenomena as mechanistic, so long as nature was represented as a mother; there first had to be a passing from one of these representations to the other: a mysterious revolution, which the author compares with the sudden mutations of which biologists speak. It can be seen how the illusion that frameworks are one autonomous instance involves another illusion: an epoch has a style as a whole, an aspect, as Umbrian landscapes or the different quarters of Paris look to us.[26]

"Do we realize it?" Spengler reveals: "Between differential calculus and the dynastic kingship of Louis XIV, between antiquity's polis and Euclid's geometry, between the perspective in Dutch painting and the conquest of distance by the railway, the telephone, and the long-range weapons, between contrapuntal music and the credit system, there is a deep formal affinity." He left to others the task of finding what it was. After which we can go on to a third illusion, historicist relativism. Thirty years ago, Collingwood thus turned over the epistemological soil by proving, after Hegel, that Milesian physics presupposed certain underlying principles: that there are natural objects, that they form a single world, and that they are composed of the same substances.[27] He called "presuppositions" those principles that, by determining the questions one will decide to ask existence, also predetermine the answers; from which Collingwood came to the conclusion of radical historism: physics is the account of a dream, the history of the ideas formed about physics. The reasoning we have seen a hundred times is recognizable: all knowledge supposes a horizon of reference beyond which all examination is impossible, and this framework is not supported by reasoning, since it is the condition of all reasoning. Thus, history sees equally legitimate weltanschauungs follow each other, and their appearance remains inexplicable; they follow each other only by the breaking and changing of frameworks, reasoning that would be irrefutable if it did not consist of reifying abstractions.

History seems to have some difficulty in absorbing the principle of interaction that geography has assimilated since Humboldt. Everything hangs together and a cause can only be caused, unless it is the Prime Mover in person; Marxists are so aware of this that in the face of all coherence, scarcely have they taught that the infrastructure determines the superstructure than they hasten to add that the latter reacts on the former. There are no breaks in the eventworthy field; everything in it is in a gradual range of shades: the unequal resistance of reality, the unequal fluidity of temporalities, the unequal awareness that we have of this, the unequal probability of our forecasts.

Nothing is more concrete than history. The ideas, theories, and conceptions of history are certainly the dead part of a historical work, just as the theory of heredity is the dead part of the work of such a novelist. The ideas are not very interesting; it is an academic exercise or a worldly ritual like the fashion shows of great couturiers. History has neither structure nor method, and it is certain in advance that every theory in this domain is still-born.

Chapter VII

Theories, Types, Concepts

ither there is understanding, or else history is no longer history. But can there be more than understanding? Can one distinguish, in the explanation, an individualizing method and another moment that might be generalizing? Otto Hintze[1] assigned to the historian, as an instrument, if not as a goal, the apperception of *anschauliche Abstraktionen*, of intuitive abstractions, like enlightened despotism (of which he himself was the historian); these abstractions would have a relative generality, without being as completely separated from the singularity of phenomena as a law in physics or a chemical model is, and they would allow him to penetrate to the deep meaning of events. Thus, intuitive abstractions are what are at other times called historical theories: enlightened despotism, the English, French, and American revolutions as revolts of the middle class.

In what consists the attraction, power, understanding at first sight of the great theories that aim at explaining an entire historical movement? Is there something more to them than ordinary understanding? Rostovtsev, for example, proposed to consider that the political crisis experienced by the Roman Empire at the beginning of the third century, with the triumph of the "military monarchy," could be explained as a conflict between the army, representing the peasant masses and devoted to the emperor, and the municipal and senatorial middle class; in short, it was a conflict between the country and the town, and the Severian emperors were to be compared less with Richelieu than with Lenin. What is the nature of a theory of this kind, and in what way can the "town-country conflict" be considered as a type? We shall see that, under their sociological or scientist guise, theories and types simply come back to the eternal problem of the concept; for what is an "intuitive abstraction," except a sublunary concept?

An Example of a Theory

The conflict between town and country does not explain the crisis of the third century as one event explains another; this crisis is interpreted in a certain manner: the soldiers, supporters and favorites of the monarchy, had come from the poor peasantry and their political action could have been inspired by a solidarity they had preserved with their brothers in poverty. Thus, Rostovtsev's theory is the plot itself (or a way of writing, the truth of which it is not ours to judge), designated by a concise formula that suggests that town-country conflicts are common enough in history to merit the use of a special noun, and that one cannot be surprised to come across a representative of this species in the third century of our era. It is both a summary of the plot and a classification, as when the doctor says: "The illness whose development you have just described to me is common varicella."

Is Rostovtsev's diagnostic the right one? A priori (that is, reasoning backward, starting with the comparative probability of causes, as we shall see in the next chapter), we do not quite know what to think of it. Today, in the nations of the Third World, the army frequently plays an important political part because it is the only constituted political force, as it was in Rome; but that part varies from nonexistent to total, from one country to another. The army represents the interests of the peasants; it oppresses them; its anxiety to ensure national security makes it support a middle class policy of interior order; it brings about a coup d'état because of rivalries between groups of officers or between corps (it had been thus in Rome in the crisis of 69, after Nero's death). In any case, Rostovtsev's theory, being basically but a plot like any other, it can be judged only by historical criteria.

A Theory Is Only the Summary of a Plot

If the crisis of the third century proved in effect to be what Rostowzew said it was, it would then be one more town-country conflict: the theory sends us back to a typology. About 1925 this type of conflict was much discussed, and the Russian Revolution and Italian fascism were interpreted by it; it can be believed that this interpretation is not legitimate alongside tens of others that equally have some truth in them—is not history a descriptive science, not a theoretical one, and is not all description inevitably partial? Let us note that this "town-country conflict" is not really a type; it is only, in its turn, an understandable summary of a plot. When the organizers and the beneficiaries of agricultural activity reinvest the income from the soil in urban activities, the result is the animosity of peasants against city dwellers, and there is, so to say, a geopolitical plan for an economic divorce. The reader can then guess what must have happened in the mind of more than one historian who referred to this theory or to this type: he fell into the trap of abstraction.

When a plot is set up as a type and given a name, there is a tendency to forget the definite, to cling to the definition. It can be seen that there is a conflict here—we know that in Russia, in Italy, and in Rome there are towns and conjoint country districts. Thus, the theory seems to settle in place of itself; when it had been formulated for the first time in its general aspect, did it not produce the effect of a sociological revelation? Now that it is believed to be explanatory, it is forgotten that it is but the summary of a prefabricated plot and it is applied to the crisis of the third century, which amounts to advancing, as the explanation of an event, the summary of that same event. At the same time, people forget to reconvert this abstract summary into a concrete plot; they forget that the town, the country, and the army are not substances, that townspeople, peasants, and soldiers alone have existence. For the explanatory current to come through, the first thing was to establish that these soldiers in the flesh had preserved their class reflexes as former peasants, and had not forgotten their poverty-stricken brethren when they joined the army; rather, to speak like Sartre, those intervening stages would have been bypassed.

Certainly what confers on historical theories—that of Rostovtsev, that of Jaurès on the French Revolution—the prestige that surrounds them can be understood; they imply a typology with something solemn about it. Thanks to them, history becomes both intelligible and mysterious, like a play in which great forces, familiar yet invisible, struggle and always bear the same name: the Town, the Middle Class. The reader is plunged into an allegorical atmosphere if, as Musil says, by allegory we understand the state of mind in which everything takes on more meaning than it honestly ought to have. We can only sympathize with this inclination to dramatize; dramatic poetry, says Aristotle, is more philosophical and more serious than history, for it clings to generalities. Thus, history that seeks profundity has always been careful to get rid of its unforeseen and anecdotal banality, in order to assume the seriousness and majesty that constitute all the pleasure of tragedy. It now remains to be seen if a typology can be of any use in history—what is the use of noting, for the understanding of the plot of the *Choephori*, that it is the same as that of *Electra*, and that the Lagidian monarchy reminds us of the enlightened despotism of Frederick II? To all appearances, a typology can have considerable heuristic value, but it is not clear that it might add something to historical explanation. Can it nevertheless become an autonomous discipline, different from history? That is doubtful, but one should not be discouraged.

The Typical in History

It is always pleasant to find, in a description of China in the Sung period, a page on the paternalism of individual relationships and another on the artisans' colleges, which could be transported "as is" into a picture of Roman civilization: the page of Roman history is already written and, above all, the historian of China will have given ideas that the reader would never have had on his own, or will have let the reader perceive a significant difference. Furthermore, finding the same facts centuries and thousands of leagues apart seems to exclude all chance, and confirms that the interpretation of the Roman facts must be true because it is in conformity with a certain logic of things. Is there, thus, much that is typical in history? There are sciences, like medicine or botany, that describe a type in several pages: such a plant, such an illness; they are lucky that two corn poppies or even two cases of varicella are much more like each other than two wars or even two enlightened despotisms are. But if history, too, lent itself to a typology, it would have been known for a long time. Certainly there are diagrams that repeat, because the combination of possible solutions to a problem is not infinite, because man is an imitating animal, because he surely has instincts, because action also has its mysterious logic (as we see in economics). Direct taxation and hereditary monarchy are familiar types; there has not been only one strike, but many strikes, and Jewish prophetism counts four great prophets, twelve minor ones, and a host of unknown ones.

In short, not everything is typical, events do not reproduce themselves in species like plants, and a typology would be complete only if its understanding was very weak and it were reduced to an inventory of historical vocabulary ("war: armed conflict between powers")—that is, to concepts—or if it surrendered to conceptual inflation: if you set about it, you find the baroque, capitalism, and *homo ludens* everywhere, and the Marshall Plan is no more than a manifestation of the eternal potlatch. More than once an attempt has been made to establish a historical typology alongside history;[2] it is one of the many activities grouped under the vague name of sociology—this is true of part of the work of Max Weber and, in some ways, of that of Mauss. Experience seems to have proved that too often what has been thought to be typical is too brief to be of interest; typology soon gives way to a juxtaposition of historical monographs. Finally, these typologies are incomplete to the point of being unusable (including, it is unpleasant to admit, those of Weber); when a historian of antiquity consults the lists of groupings or of types of morality set up by Gurvitch, he almost regularly ascertains that nothing is there that is suitable for "his period."

The reason for these disappointments is a very simple one: mainly, it is only in the field of biology that differences between species and individuals are clearly found; in natural history, types have substantial supports, which are living organisms; the latter reproduce almost identically, and among them one can objectively distinguish the typical and individual peculiarities. In history, on the other hand, the type is what one causes it to be; it is subjective, in Marrou's sense; it is what is chosen as typical in the eventworthy field. We know that historical types do not exist in themselves, that events are not reproduced with the constancy of living species, that the typical in history is a choice; one can take an enlightened monarchy as a whole, or one aspect of it, or even the unenlightened aspects of a monarchy that is otherwise enlightened; and each man will define the type "enlightened monarchy" in his own way. In short, the types are infinite in number, since they exist only through us. Once again, we have to come to the conclusion of historical nominalism.

There are no natural objects in history, natural like a plant or an animal that might give rise to a typology or a classification; the historical object is what one makes it, and can be subdivided again according to a thousand criteria, all of equal importance. This excessively great freedom means that historians do not make typology without feeling ill at ease; when they regroup several events by the same partial criterion, they cannot help but add hastily that the other aspects of those events do not satisfy the chosen criterion—which seems, however, to be self-evident. If a historian declares that public benefaction, considered as a kind of gift, comes close to potlatch in this respect, he hastens to add that in other ways it is a tax; if another historian, on the other hand, studies the ways in which communities procure the resources they need, and compares in this respect public benefaction to taxation, he is careful to add very quickly that this comparison "lacks historical sense" and that public benefaction recalls potlatch in other ways.

Types Are Concepts

But because the type is set up, instead of being found ready-made, because the type is what one chooses it to be, it follows that invoking the type adds nothing to the explanation and also that, formulated thus, the idea of "using a typology" is only a scientist myth. Far from adding anything to the explanation, recourse to the typical allows it to be shortened, as we shall see. To call the Roman crisis of the third century typical means: "We well know that type of a conflict, it is the one already described as town-country conflict." Now, faced with the typical, the historian cannot have the same attitude as the naturalist; the latter has not much more to add when, at the sight of a corn poppy, he has said, "It is only a typical corn poppy." The historian must first verify at great length if the Lagidian monarchy really conforms to the type of enlightened despotism or if the documents do not impose another interpretation. And what will be gained by concluding that it is indeed enlightened despotism? Nothing that he did not already know and verify, but he will be able to abridge his description of the Lagidian regime by saying "it had all the characteristics of enlightened despotism"; as a good historian he will only have to finish filling in the blanks and to say in what circumstances the enlightened character of this despotism showed, and what special way it had of being so.

The type or the theory can thus be useful only in shortening a description; enlightened despotism or town-country conflict is spoken of in order to deal quickly with, as we say, "war" instead of "armed conflict between powers." Theories, types, and concepts are one and the same thing: ready-made summaries of plots. Thus, it is useless to prescribe for historians the construction or the utilization of theories or of types; they have always done this, they could not do anything else, save not saying a single word, and that doesn't get them any further.

Ought history to become generalizing, elaborating types and having recourse to them to interpret individual facts? The emptiness of this scientist language can be measured when what it comes back to is seen. Does "employing a type" mean having recourse to enlightened monarchy in order to understand Ptolemaic public benefaction? Would it be having recourse to a formula of enlightened monarchy, to a definition in four lines, in order to verify, word by word, whether it applies to the reign of that prince and whether it allows the resolution of the problem posed by his government? Is it not, rather, that having read a monograph on Frederick II or Joseph II, having understood the plot related there, we get from it ideas to understand Ptolemy and to ask questions about him that we would never have thought of asking otherwise?

And what does "constructing a type" mean? If this expression does not designate the academic operation that consists of summarizing a book in a striking formula (and a rather forced one, for none of the enlightened despotisms of the eighteenth century resemble each other, and each historian can "split" this diversity according to the plan he prefers), the constructing of a type is nothing more than the understanding of the politics of Frederick II or of Joseph II. It is true that by wanting to pursue to the end a certain idea of that politics one can discover misunderstood aspects of the action of those princes; the so-called elaboration of types is reduced to a heuristic process. Better understood, the politics of Frederick II will give ideas to a historian of the Ptolemies, for the utilization of types is nothing more than what is also called comparative history, and is neither history of a different kind nor even a method, but a heuristic device.

All in all, the history termed "generalizing" does nothing more than what mere history does: it understands and makes one understand. It is true that one feels it really means to push the understanding of facts further than a more traditional historiography would be content to go; "generalizing history" must be the German name for what the French call structural or non-eventworthy history. Finally, where does the typical begin? If enlightened monarchy is a type, will it not also be the same for mere monarchy? Will not everything in history be typical, and will not typology be mistaken for the dictionary? And so it is: types are nothing but concepts.

Comparative History

If that is so, what can still be the place for a discipline, comparative history, much cultivated today and that rightly seems very promising, even though the idea of it is far from clear? We are doing comparative history when we reflect on the Hellenistic monarchies while having in our minds the type of enlightened monarchy that stands out from a history of Frederick II. Then what is comparative history? A particular variety of history? A method? No, it is a heuristic device.[3]

The difficulty is to say where mere history ends, where comparative history begins. If, in order to study the manorial regime in Forez, we mention side by side facts relating to different manors—and how can we not do so?—are we writing a comparative history? And what if we are studying the manorial system in the whole of medieval Europe? Marc Bloch, in *La société féodale,* compares French feudalism with that of England, but does not speak of comparative history except when he compares Western feudalism with that of Japan; on the other hand, Heinrich Mitteis published a history of the medieval state in the Empire, in France, Italy, England, and Spain under the title *The State in the Middle Ages, an Outline of Comparative History.* When Raymond Aron analyzes the political life of industrial societies on both sides of the Iron Curtain, we speak of sociology, no doubt because contemporary societies are being dealt with; on the other hand, R. Palmer's book that analyzes the history of "the age of the democratic revolution in Europe and in America, 1760–1800" is considered a classic of comparative history.

Could it be that, among these historians, some stress national differences while others bring out the common features? But if the industrial democracies have so many common features, how is their history more comparative than that of the different manors in Forez? Either the history of two manors, of two nations, of two revolutions has so many features in common that there is no question of comparative history, or else they have histories very different from each other, and then the fact of bringing them together in a single volume and multiplying the likenesses or the dissimilarities between them has above all a didactic value for the reader, after having had a heuristic value for the author. Consider Mitteis: he devotes a chapter to each of the European states, one after the other, then in a collective chapter that might be called European history, he sums up the evolution of all those states taken together, bringing to light the analogies and the contrasts. Judging by the results, one can see hardly any difference between a book of comparative history and a book of history that is not comparative: only the geographical framework considered is more or less wide.

The truth is that comparative history (and the same could be said of comparative literature) is original less in its results, which are mere history, than in its elaboration; more precisely, the equivocal and falsely scientific expression "comparative history" (Cuvier and comparative grammar are, however, far apart) designates two or three different procedures: recourse to analogy to fill gaps in documentation; bringing together, for heuristic aims, facts borrowed from different nations or periods; the study of a historical category or of a type of event through history, without taking into account the unities of time and place.

We have recourse to analogy to explain the meaning or the causes of an event (what we shall later term "retrodiction") when the event in question reappears at another time and in another place where the relevant documentation allows us to understand its causes. This has been done in the history of religions since Frazer, when it explains the Roman facts whose meaning is obliterated by the analogy of Indian or Papuan facts whose explanation is known.[4] We equally have recourse to analogy when the gaps in documentation leave us in ignorance of the events themselves; we have practically no information about Roman demography, but the demographic study of modern preindustrial societies has made so much progress in the last few decades that by using its analogy as a base, it is possible to write several confident pages on Roman demography, the meager Roman facts that have come down to us playing the part of initial proofs of the matter.

The second step in comparative history, the heuristic comparison, is what every unblinkered historian does, when he is not imprisoned in "his period," but "thinks of thinking" about enlightened despotism when he is studying a Hellenistic monarchy, or of the revolutionary millenarisms of the Middle Ages or of the Third World when he is studying the revolts of slaves in the Hellenistic world, in order to "find ideas" by resemblance or contrast. He is then free either to keep to himself his comparative records, after his study has had the benefit of all the questions that it occurred to him to ask,[5] or to describe side by side the revolts of slaves and of serfs, and call the book *Essay in Comparative History*.

A step that is close to a third step is that of a history of items. In fact, it often happens that things can be pursued much further; instead of juxtaposing monographs in his head or within the same binding, one can often write a global study on the feudal system or on millenarism through history. It suffices for the common features to be prominent enough or for the differences to appear as so many different solutions to a common problem; it is a question of opportunity. That is what Max Weber did in his famous study of the city in world history; a history divided by space ("history of England") or time ("the seventeenth century") succeeds a history divided into items: the city, millenarism, "peace and war between nations," the monarchy of the Ancien Régime, industrial democracy. We shall see at the end of this book that the future of the historical genre surely lies along that road. But, even so, history "by items" or "comparative" remains history; it consists in understanding concrete events that are explained by material causes, by ends, and by chance. There is only one history.

It Is a Heuristic Device

We see in what respects comparative history seems to be different from ordinary history: taking documentation into account, on the one hand it has recourse to analogy to fill in gaps in the sources, taking the conventions of the genre into account, while on the other hand it breaks the unities of time and place. We shall have many opportunities, in the rest of this book, to use side by side the words "documentation" and "conventions of the genre," and we shall see that many of the falsely epistemological problems are mere pretenses raised by the nature of the sources or by conventions. Comparative history itself is one of those pretenses; it consists in doing one's whole duty as a historian—not getting imprisoned in conventional frameworks, but recutting them according to the pattern of events and using every means to understand.

But the result is not a history that is different, more explanatory, more general, or more scientific than the others. Comparative history reveals nothing that could not rightly have been discovered by a noncomparative study; it only facilitates the discovery. It is a heuristic device, but it does not make one discover anything else. Let us beware of believing that there is the slightest relationship between comparative history and comparative grammar; when the latter compares two languages, such as Sanskrit and Greek, it is not to make it easier, by analogy, similarity, or contrast, to penetrate either of these languages, but to reconstitute a third language, Indo-European, from which the other two derive. In contrast, when comparative history talks of millenarism or of the city, it says nothing but what is true of the different millenarisms and diverse cities that it has considered; from comparison knowledge is more easily born but, by right, a sufficiently penetrating mind could have gotten, from a monographic study, all that the comparison allows it to get more easily.

It follows that comparative history has nothing to do with the "method of differences." Will the good way to discover the cause of public benefaction be to compare the details of Hellenistic civilization, where that institution exists, and of Florentine civilization, which is ignorant of it, so as to find, by subtraction, which of these details was the cause? It is impossible or useless. Impossible, because one should be able to make clear all those details. Now it is likely that the details are mostly non-eventworthy for us; to phrase it differently, our comparative inquiry may come to this conclusion: "The cause of the existence of public benefaction in Greece and of its absence in Florence lies in the different mentalities or traditions of those two societies." On the other hand, suppose chance lets us get at the right cause. In that case the comparative inquiry, heuristically opportune, will nonetheless have been useless by right. Let us suppose that it is revealed that the main cause of public benefaction is the absence of direct taxation. Florence had that taxation and no public benefaction, and it was the contrary in Athens; but who does not *understand* the relationship here between cause and effect? A city usually needs money and takes it from where it is: in the purse of the taxpayers or, in their absence, in that of a wealthy benefactor. It was thus sufficient to reflect a bit about Athens to find the right explanation. Except to make one's task easier, what was the use of working up a so-called comparative method that makes one discover nothing but what is found in the terms of the comparison?[6]

Comparative history amounts to nothing more than mere history; we have already seen that it is the same with generalizing history. We have also seen that theories and types are the same thing: the summaries of ready-made plots, kinds of concepts. In other words, there is but one history, which always consists only in understanding and is written with words; there are not several kinds of history or several different intellectual operations, some of which are more general or scientific than others. What else do we do than understand plots? And there are not two ways of understanding.

The Concepts

The only real problem is that of concepts in history, and we are going into it at length. Like all speech, history does not speak by hapax legomenon, but expresses itself by means of concepts; and the driest of chronologies will at least tell us that at such a period there was war and at such another, revolution. These universals are sometimes ageless ideas—war or king—at others, recent terms that seem more scholarly—potlatch or enlightened despotism. That difference is superficial, and to say that the War of 1914 was a war is not to stand on more positive ground than to talk of potlatch. To understand how an idea as simple as that of war could rise for the first time in men's minds at a certain stage in the evolution of societies and their relationships, it suffices to see how recently the concepts of a revolutionary day or of the cold war were born. War is a whole ideal type, and we realize this when we have to distinguish it from private war, anarchy, the guerrilla, the Hundred Years War, or intermittent war, without speaking of the "flower war" of the Mayas and of the squabbles between endogamous primitive tribes; to say that the Peloponnesian war was a war is already to advance.

History is the description of the individual through universals, which, by right, raises no difficulty; to say that the Peloponnesian war took place on land and sea is not to struggle with the unutterable. Nonetheless, we find that historians are constantly constrained or deceived by the concepts or the types they use; they reproach them with sometimes being keys that are valid for one period but do not work with another, at other times with not being open enough and entailing associations of ideas that, plunged into a new setting, are made anachronistic. As examples of this latter source of annoyance, let us cite the notions "capitalism" and "middle class," which do not ring true when applied to antiquity (a Hellenistic or Roman person of note does not look at all like a capitalist bourgeois, even like a Florentine in the time of the Medicis). Examples of the first inconvenience are almost all the words in the history of religions; folklore, piety, feast, superstition, god, sacrifice, and even religion change values from one religion to another (*religio*, in Lucretius, means "fear of the gods" and translates the Greek *deisidaimonia*, which we, for lack of a better word, translate by "superstition," and these differences in semantic division correspond to the differences in the conceptions of the things).

In general these difficulties of conceptual origin exasperate good, professional workmen who do not like to complain of their bad tools; their job is not to analyze the idea of revolution, but to say who brought about that of 1789—when, how, and why. They see the refining of concepts as the failing of beginners. It remains true that the conceptual instruments are the causes of progress for historiography (to have concepts is to conceive of things); inadequate concepts give the historian a characteristic unease that is one of the episodes in the drama of his job. Every professional one day or another knows the feeling that a word will not do, that it sounds wrong, that it is unclear, that the facts have not the style to be expected of them according to the concept under which they are grouped; that unease is an alarm warning that the anachronism or the approximation threatens, but sometimes years pass before a selection is found under some sort of fresh concept.

Is not the history of historiography partly the history of anachronisms caused by ready-made ideas? The Olympic Games were not games, the philosophical sects of antiquity were not schools, henotheism is not monotheism, the changing group of Roman freemen was not a nascent middle class, the Roman knights were not a class, the provincial assemblies were only urban cultural colleges authorized by the emperor, and not intermediary bodies between the provinces and the government. To remedy these misunderstandings, the historian invents ad hoc types that in their turn become so many traps. When this quasi fatality of misunderstanding is recognized, working out fresh concepts will become a reflex for the historian. On the other hand, when we see L. R. Taylor explaining that the political parties in Rome were only cliques and clients, whereas, on the other hand, some maintain that they correspond to social or ideological conflicts, we can be sure in advance that it is not a careful study of sources that will advance the debate, by even a millimeter. One can say right away that the dilemma has to be bypassed, that we will have to be interested in the "sociology" of the political parties through history and try to invent, through heuristic comparativism, a "sociogly" to fit the political parties in the Roman Republic.

An Example: Hellenic Nationalism

In order to illustrate the role of concepts, here is an example that we shall develop at some length, because in it can be seen how a concept or an ideal type, that of nationalism, allows the better understanding of a historical movement, once one thinks of subsuming it under the concept—and also how that same concept had, on the other hand, begun by preventing that same inclusion. About the second century of our era, at the height of the Golden Age of the Roman Empire, there lived a Greek publicist famous in his day, Dion of Prusa; he enjoyed great fame in the Hellenic countries that had bcome "provinces" of the Empire (we would call them more or less colonies) and were faithful to their conquerors. Now Dion constantly developed ideas that, after centuries of Roman domination, seem curiously out of date: nostalgia for the ancient independence of Greece, respect for the old Hellenic customs, hostility toward Roman customs, appeals to "Greekness" to be aware again of its own identity and pride. Elsewhere we will show that he spent part of his life seeking a city that could assume the leadership of Greekness (despairing of Athens, he finally rested his hopes in Rhodes).

It has long been agreed—but more in France than in the Germanic countries—to speak of these aspirations as nonsense that could originate only in a literary man's mind. In fact, those aspirations are really those of Greek nationalism, and Dion is the representative of a Hellenic patriotism in the Roman Empire. Is that only to change the pejorative word "nonsense" for the noble word "patriotism"? No, it is to change the facts, for it is to encumber the idea of Hellenic patriotism with all the implicit contents that the concept of nationalism draws from its birthplace, the nineteenth century in Europe. The nationalism of Dion will be explained by the profound impetus that upset Central and Eastern Europe in the course of the nineteenth century; it was pregnant with the same political consequences; and the renaissance of Hellenic culture toward the end of the first century, which is called the "sophistic second," and even the linguistic purism that began to be rampant then (it even went as far as giving Latin proper nouns a Greek form) are comparable with the renaissance of national languages and literatures in the nineteenth century. The position of the Greeks in the Roman Empire is comparable with that of the Czechs and Hungarians under the domination of the Hapsburgs. Repudiating the ancient patriotism of the city-state, which has no real justification, since the Roman conquest had united "Greekness" in slavery, Dion makes present to us the birth of a Panhellenic nationalism that announces Byzantine patriotism and the rupture between the Western Empire and the Greek Empire.

But the dialectic of comprehension and of concepts does not stop there, for the nationalist idea seems to contradict other attitudes of Dion. How does it happen that this anti-Roman publicist is in other respects a convinced partisan of imperial power, that the sovereign he recognizes is a foreign master and that, not always disdaining lowly tasks, he also preached, with threats, to the Greeks of Alexandria, obedience to the Roman emperor? So we realize how much the idea of nationalism is confused: for centuries fatherland and state were not the same thing; a Magyar noble was the sworn enemy of Austrian ways, but devoted to his emperor to the death, although the latter was an Austrian. Hobbes discusses the advantages and the drawbacks of having a foreigner as a prince, in the tone in which we examine the place of foreign capital in the economic life of a nation. Better than French philologists, German scholars have understood how Dion, faithful to his Greek fatherland, could also be faithful to his Roman emperor.[7]

The Three Kinds of Concepts

Thus, historical concepts are strange tools; they allow us to understand because they are rich with a meaning that overflows every possible definition; for the same reason they are a perpetual incitement to misinterpretation. Everything happens as if they bore in themselves all the concrete wealth of the events that are subsumed in them, as if the idea of nationalism embodied all that is known about all nationalisms. It is indeed like that. The concepts of actual sublunary experience, especially those used in history, are very different from those of the sciences, whether they are the deductive sciences like physics or pure economics, or sciences in the process of being worked out, like biology. So there are concepts and concepts, and everything must not get mixed up (as in general sociology, which treats certain concepts that spring from common sense, those of social roles and controls, as gravely as if they were scientific terms). To recapitulate a classification that is in a fair way to becoming sanctioned, there are first of all the concepts of the deductive sciences: power, magnetic field, elasticity of demand, kinetic energy;

these are abstractions perfectly defined by a theory that permits their construction, and they appear only after long theoretical explanations. Other concepts, in the natural sciences, give rise to empirical analysis; we all intuitively know what an animal or a fish is, but the biologist will seek criteria to distinguish between animals and plants, and he will say whether the whale is a fish. In the end, the fish of the biologist will no longer be those of common sense.

Criticism of Historical Concepts

Historical concepts, on the other hand, belong exclusively to common sense (a town, a revolution) or, if they have a scholarly origin (enlightened despotism), they are no better because of that. They are paradoxical concepts: we know intuitively that this is a revolution and that that is only a riot, but we could not say what riot and revolution are; we will speak of them without really knowing them. Could we define them? That would be arbitrary or impossible. Revolution, sudden, violent change in the politics and government of the state, says Littré, but this definition does not analyze or exhaust the concept. In fact, our knowledge of the concept of revolution consists in knowing that this name is readily given to a rich and confused mass of facts that are found in books dealing with the years 1642 and 1789. To us, "revolution" has the look of all we have read, seen, and heard about the different revolutions of which a knowledge has come down to us, and it is this treasury of knowledge that governs our use of the word.[8] Also, the concept has no precise limits; we know much more about revolution than any possible definition, but we do not know what we know, and that sometimes gives us unpleasant surprises when the word does not ring true or is anachronistic in some of its uses. Yet we know enough about it to say, if not what a revolution is, at least if a given event is or is not one: "No, sire, it is not a riot. . . ." As Hume says:

We do not associate distinct, complete ideas with all the terms we use, and when we speak of government, Church, negotiations, conquest, we rarely develop in our mind all the simple ideas that make up these complex ideas. It is nevertheless to be remarked that, despite this, we avoid saying silly things on all these subjects and we are conscious of the contradictions that these ideas can present, just as well as if we understood them perfectly: for example, if, instead of saying that in war the conquered has only to resort to the armistice, we were told that he only had to resort to conquests, the absurdity of these words would strike us.[9]

A historical concept allows, for example, the designation of an event as a revolution; it does not follow that by using that concept, one knows "what" a revolution "is." Thse concepts are not concepts worthy of the name, complexes of necessarily connected elements; they are, rather, composite representations that give the illusion of intellection, but in reality are only kinds of generic images. The "revolution," the "city" is made up of all the already known revolutions and cities, and expects of our future experiences an enrichment to which it remains definitively open. Likewise, we can see a given historian who specializes in the seventeenth century in England complaining that his colleagues "have spoken of social classes without expressing reservations about that century; speaking of rising classes or of classes in decline, they apparently *had in mind* conflicts of quite a different nature."[10] In the same way, the expression "middle class" presents "far too many *deceptive associations* when applied to the social state in the time of the Stuarts" or "sometimes (but more rarely, precisely because of the vague character of this language) there has even been confusion of a hierarchical grouping and a social class, and *the reasoning has been pursued as if* such groups could increase, decrease, clash, become aware of themselves, have a policy of their own."

In short, as the *Critique of Pure Reason* has it:

An empirical concept cannot be defended, but merely explained; we never know for sure if, under the name indicating the same object, we do not think now of more, now of fewer, characters. Thus, in the concept of gold, besides weight, color, and strength, someone may think of the characteristic that gold has of not rusting, whereas someone else may be ignorant of that characteristic. One uses certain characteristics only insofar as they suffice to make a distinction, but fresh observations will cause some to disappear and some to be added, so that the concept is never enclosed within sure limits. Moreover, what would be the use of defining a concept of that kind? When we consider water, for example, we do not in fact stop at what we conceive under the word "water," but we have recourse to experiences and, in that case, the word, with the few characteristics attached to it, constitutes only a *designation* and not a concept of the thing; consequently, the supposed definition is nothing but the explanation of the word.[11]

If it was agreed to reserve the name of revolution only for revolutions that transfer property, a bit of order would surely be added in the majestic garden of the French language, but the theory and typology of revolutionary phenomena or the history of 1789 would in no way be advanced. The frequently expressed wish that history would precisely define the concepts it uses, and the affirmation that that precision is the first condition of its future progress, are good examples of false methodology and of useless rigor.

But the most cunning danger is that of words that raise false essences in our minds and people history with universals that do not exist. The public benefaction of antiquity, Christian charity, the relief of the moderns, and Social Security have practically nothing in common, do not benefit the same categories of people, do not meet the same needs, do not have the same institutions, are not explained by the same motives, and are not covered by the same justifications. Nonetheless, assistance and charity through the ages will be studied, from the Egypt of the pharaohs to the Scandinavian democracies; it will only be left to conclude that assistance is a permanent category, that it fulfills a function necessary to every human society, and that in that permanence there must be hidden some mysterious finality of integration of the whole body social. In this way one will have carried one's stone to the building of a functionalist sociology.

In that way deceptive continuities, mistaken genealogies, are established in history. When we utter the words assistance, gift, sacrifice, crime, madness, or religion, we are incited to believe that the different religions have enough common features for it to be legitimate to study religion throughout history; that there exists an entity called the gift or the potlatch that has constant, defined properties—for example, that of raising up countergifts or of giving the donor prestige and superiority to the beneficiaries. Sociology in former times often fell into the trap of the notional; through comparative history it began to raise entities of reason. Out of love for generalities (it is only the science of the general), it imagined a sociological category called criminality and put in the same bag the holdups of industrial societies, the uproars and rapes of the Far West, the vendetta in Corsica or in Renaissance Italy, and the banditry of poverty in Sardinia.

The Aggregates

It is not without disquiet that we see books entitled *Treatise on the History of Religions* or *Religious Phenomenology*: therefore, does something called religion exist? It is reassuring to find soon that, in spite of the generality of their titles, these treatises, if their design makes it possible to treat ancient religions, practically pass over Christianity and vice versa. That is understandable. The different religions are so many aggregates of phenomena belonging to heterogeneous categories, and none of these aggregates has the same composition as the other. One religion involves rites, magic, mythology, while another includes theological philosophy, has become bound up with political, cultural, and athletic institutions, with psychopathological phenomena, has produced institutions with an economic dimension (the panegyrics of antiquity, Christian and Buddhist monasticism); another has "captured" a particular movement that, in another civilization, would have become a political movement or a curiosity in the history of manners and customs.

It is a platitude to say that the hippies faintly recall early Franciscanism; at least we can see how a psychosocial possibility may be captured by a religious aggregate. The nuances separating a religion from a folklore, from a movement of collective fervor, from a political, philosophical, or charismatic sect will be imperceptible; under what can we classify Saint-Simonism or the group round Stefan George? With the "Lesser Vehicle" Buddhism, we have an atheistic religion. The historians of antiquity knew how uncertain the border between the religious and the collective (the Olympic Games) may be, and the Reformers saw, in papal pilgrimages, a pagan tourism. The famous phrase "In antiquity all that is collective is religious" is not an incitement to overestimate the religious element in antiquity by attributing to it the intensity it is known to have in Christianity; it means that the aggregate called the Greek religion was made up of much folklore.

The "plan" of any one religion resembles that of no other, just as the plan of each built-up area differs from all others: one built-up area includes a palace and a theater; another, factories; the third is a mere hamlet. It is a matter of degrees: from one religion to another, the differences are great enough to make, in a practical way, a textbook of the history of religions unfeasible unless it begins by a typology, as a book of general geography entitled *The Town* always begins by distinguishing between types of towns and by acknowledging that the difference between the town and the village will always be blurred. It is nonetheless true that the different religions must have something in common that causes them to be gathered into the same concept; it is no less certain that the historian must regard that something as essential, on pain of no longer understanding the fact of religion.

But the difficulty is to define that essential kernel: the sacred? religious feeling? the transcendent? Let us leave philosophers to tackle that problem, which is essentially regional; as historians, it will suffice us to be warned that the essential kernel of the aggregate is only the kernel of it, that we cannot prejudge what this kernel will be in a given religion, that this kernel is not an invariant, and that it changes from one culture to another (neither "sacred" nor "god" is a univocal word; as for religious feelings, there is nothing specific about them; ecstasy is a religious phenomenon when it relates to the sacred, instead of to poetry, as with a given great contemporary poet, or to the rapture of astronomical knowledge, as was the case with the astronomer Ptolemy). The whole remains sufficiently blurred and verbal for the concept of religion itself to be floating and merely a matter of appearance; thus, the historian must proceed very empirically and beware of investing his idea of a determined religion with all that the concept of religion retains from other religions.[12]

Classificatory Concepts

It can be seen where the danger lies: in the classificatory concepts. It is quite possible to find words to describe brigandage in Sardinia, banditry in Chicago, the Buddhist religion, or France in 1453; but we must not speak of "criminality," of "religion," or of "France" from Clovis to Pompidou. We can speak of what the Greeks called madness or of what the objective symptoms at that period were, of what we will call madness, but not of "madness" or of "its" symptoms. Let us not draw Nietzschean or tragedy-like conclusions from that; let us only say that every classificatory concept is false, because no event is like another and history is not the constant repetition of the same facts—it is only the play of illusions raised by classificatory concepts that makes us believe so.

Being and identity only exist by abstraction, but history wants to know only the concrete. It is not possible to give full satisfaction to that wish, but a great deal will have been done if the decision is taken never to speak of religion or revolution, but only of the Buddhist religion or of the revolution of 1789, so that the world of history is peopled exclusively with unique events (which may, however, be more or less like each other), and never with uniform objects. It remains true that all historical concepts will always be misunderstood in some way, since everything is in the process of becoming; but it is enough if they are not misunderstood in terms of the chosen plot. It is not dangerous to speak of "the middle class from the fourteenth to the twentieth century" if by "middle class" we mean all the plebians—who, however, are not the populace; it would be more dangerous if that term was understood to mean a class of capitalists. Unfortunately, without its being very well realized, we generally understand the term in all its meanings at the same time, for such is the fatal flaw of sublunary concepts.

Our intent is not to refuse all objectivity to the middle class, out of servility to capital, or to deny, through anticlericalism, that religion is an order in Pascal's meaning, or an irreducible essence; more modestly, we want to bring to light the difficulty in finding in the middle class or religion, a sign of recognition that is valid for all periods of history. Thus, if "religion" is the conventional name that we give to a mass of aggregates that are very different from one another, it follows that the categories used by historians to introduce a bit of order—religious life, literature, political life—are not eternal frameworks, and change from society to society; not only does the internal structure of each category vary, but even their mutual relationships and the distribution among them of the eventworthy field will not be the same. Here there are also religious movements that could as well be called social; there, philosophical sects that are more religious; elsewhere, politico-idealogical movements that are philosophico-religious—what is, in a society, readily stowed in the box "political life" will elsewhere correspond more exactly with the facts usually put into the box "religious life." That means that at every period each of these categories has a fixed structure that changes from one period to another. So it is not without anxiety that we find, in the table of contents of a history book, a certain number of drawers—"religious life," "literary life"—as if these were eternal categories, unimportant receptacles into which it would only remain to pour an enumeration of gods and of rites, of authors and of works.

Let us take the category "literary genres" throughout history. To us, the plaintive elegy is recognizable by its long mourning clothes; to us, all that is prose is not verse, and all that is verse is not prose. But in the literatures of antiquity, it was meter that distinguished the poetic genres; for, in the Indo-European languages, the phonological value of contrasting short and long syllables gave rhythm such importance that the attitude of a poet in antiquity to meter is comparable with that of our composers to a dance rhythm. Therefore, the elegy was any poetry written in the elegiac rhythm, whether it treated mourning, love, politics, religion, history, or philosophy. Moreover, along with prose and verse, there existed a separate category, the prose of art, which was very far removed from everyday language and often very obscure. The ancients had as much difficulty as we ourselves have in understanding Thucydides, Tacitus, or the *Brahmana;* the proses of Mallarmé give some idea of this prose of art (that is why ancient languages studied in literary texts are notoriously more difficult than modern languages).

Let us now consider the concept of realism or that of the novel. As readers of Auerbach know very well, in ancient literatures, as much in Indian as in Hellenistic-Roman literature, the account of everyday life, of what is serious, of what is neither tragic nor comic, was not allowable; to speak of the serious aspect of life was conceivable only in a satirical tone or as a parody. As a result, of two Roman writers who had the temperament of a Balzac, one—Petronius—was not able, in the novel, to achieve more than half success; and the other—Tacitus—vulgar and terrible like Balzac, and, like him, capable of making some glimmer of a storm spring from everything, became a historian.

Every historic proposition having the form "this event belongs to literature, to the novel, to religion" ought only to come after a proposition of the form "literature, or religion, at that time was this or that." The arranging of events in categories demands the prior historizing of those categories under pain of erroneous classification or of anachronisms. In the same way, to use a concept in the belief that it is self-evident is to risk an implicit anachronism. It is the fault of the vague and implicit character of sublunary concepts, of their aura of associations of ideas. When we utter the words "social class," which are innocent, we awaken in the reader the idea that that class must have had a class policy, which is not true in every period. When we utter the words "the Roman family" without further precision, the reader is led to think that that family was the eternal family—that is, our own—whereas with its slaves, its clients, its freemen, its minions, its concubines, and the practice of abandoning some newborn children (especially girls), it was as different from our own as the Islamic or the Chinese family. In a word, history is not written on a blank page; where we see nothing, we suppose that there was eternal man. Historiography is an unceasing struggle against our tendency to anachronic misinterpretation.

Becoming and Concepts

Sublunary concepts are perpetually false because they are vague, and they are vague because their object is constantly moving; we attribute to the middle class under Louis XVI and to the Roman family characteristics that the concept has retained of the Christian family and the middle class under Louis Philippe; it happens that from Rome to Christ and from Louis XVI to Louis Philippe, family and middle class are no longer the same. Not only have they changed, but they include no invariable that might support their identity through changes. Beyond all conceptions of religion and all historical religions, there is no definable kernel that is the essence of religion; religiosity varies like everything else. If we imagine a world divided among nations whose frontiers constantly change and whose capital is never the same, periodically drawn geographical maps would register those successive states; but it is clear that from one map to the next, the identity of "the same" nation could be decided only in terms of appearance or convention.

"In truth, Protarch," says the Philebus, "identification of the One and the Multiple, operated by language, prowls around everything we say; it is a thing that was not begun today and that will never end." The separation between the one and the multiple, between being and becoming, means that in history two approaches are equally legitimate and will always be rivals; they are those that for some little time it has been fashionable to call, using anglicisms, the regressive method ("the formation of French unity") and the recurrent method ("permanence of the Alsatian soul through one thousand years of political vicissitudes"). In the first approach you take as reference point the frontiers of the "nation" at a given moment; you can then study the formation or the dismantling of this conceptual territory. In the second, you take as reference point one of the "provinces," which will be assumed to keep its personality through all the upheavals of the conceptual map.

For example, in literary history the first approach will be to study the evolution of a genre: satire through the ages, its origins, its metamorphoses. The second approach will be to take as reference point "realism" or "raillery"; you will begin by smiling at the naive teleology of the previous approach, at the assimilation between the evolution of a genre and that of a living species, and you will thunder against its fixity: "Who still does not know that the satirical genre is only a false continuity, that this genre can be emptied of its wit and serve other functions, while the essence of satire will be reincarnated in another genre, such as the novel, which will then be the authentic descendant of satire?" That is quite fair. For the fixity of the satirical genre, you thus substitute the fixity of realism or of raillery; for the teleology of the regressive approach you substitute functionalism of the recurrent approach. Through a thousand avatars you find, hidden in the most unexpected genres, the taste for realism; it will surely happen that at certain periods that taste will find no genre through which it can flow, but then that deficiency will involve cases of suppletorism or phenomena of cultural pathology that will be homage rendered to the secret permanence of a function of realism.

The first approach therefore takes as reference point a given segment; the second takes as reference point an element that is thought to be found through several segments; both are of equal worth, and the choice between them is only a question of opportunity. A period that has made the "regressive" approach too familiar will be followed by one for which the "recurrent" approach will have more savor. Behind both approaches is the same inescapable aporia; according to the teaching of Plato, one can have no knowledge of becoming as pure becoming, one cannot think becoming except with reference points taken from being. Whence the misfortunes of the historian: knowledge of history is knowledge of the concrete, which is becoming and interaction, but it needs concepts; now being and identity exist only through abstraction.

Let us consider, for example, the history of madness through the ages.[13] Ethnographers began by noticing that from one people to another, the psychic states considered madness—or, rather, the way of treating them—varied; the same psychosis, according to nation, was madness, village idiocy, or sacred delirium. They also discovered that there was interaction, and that the way of treating madness modified its frequency and the symptoms; also, they finally recognized that "the" madness in question scarcely existed, and that it was by convention that a continuity of identity was established between its historical forms. Beyond these forms there is no psychosis "in the wild state," and for a reason; nothing exists in the wild state except abstractions, nothing exists identically and in isolation. But the fact that the kernel of psychosis does not exist in an identical way does not mean that it does not exist; there is no avoiding the question of the objectivity of psychoses. The case of insanity, far from being a privileged one, is the daily bread of the historian; all historical beings—psychoses, classes, nations, religions, men, and animals—change in a changing world. Each being can cause the others to change, and reciprocally, for the concrete is becoming and interaction. Which raises the problem of the concept, revived by the Greeks.

No religion's resembling another, to pronounce the word "religion," is enough to risk conjuring up deceptive associations of ideas. A habit dear to the historians of antiquity shows how conscious they were of this danger: that of using only contemporary terms. They would not say that Lucretius hated religion and that Cicero loved liberty and liberality, but that the former hated *religio* and the latter loved *libertas* and *liberalitas*. It is not that the content of these Latin concepts is directly more explicit than that of their modern equivalents, for to the Romans, sublunary concepts were no less sublunary than they are to us; it is, rather, that the historian relies on the associations of ideas, guaranteed by the period, that the Latin words will evoke among Latinist colleagues and that will prevent him from falling into anachronisms, without having to make these concepts explicit.

The concept is a stumbling block for historical knowledge, because that knowledge is descriptive; history has no need of explanatory principles, but of words to say how things were. Things change faster than words; the historian is perpetually in the position of designers of historical monuments, who must constantly jump from one style to another, forget all they learned at the Beaux-Arts Academy, and make an Egyptian pencil sketch while in front of a Theban bas-relief, a Mayan sketch when standing before a Palenque stela. The true solution would be a complete historization of all concepts and of all categories, which requires the historian to verify the least noun he writes, to be conscious of all the categories he uses without thinking about them. A vast program. One understands how a history book must be looked at: it is to be seen as a battleground between an ever-changing truth and concepts that are always anachronistic. Concepts and categories have to be constantly remodeled, without having any predetermined form, have to be modeled on the reality of their object in each civilization.

Success in this respect is more or less complete; every history book mingles historized concepts with an anachronistic residue arising from unconscious, eternal prejudices. Benedetto Croce has excellently translated this characteristic impression of the mixed and the impure:[14]

History books too often present a curious mixture of true narrative and of concepts that are neither thought through nor firmly sustained; authentic historic local color is mixed with anachronistic notions and conventional categories. On the other hand, when concepts and categories succeed in being adequate for the facts to be interpreted, that purity makes history a work of art, it has reached that almost Taoist point of perfection, as Chuang-tze said, when one can "conquer all things without wounding any."

Appendix

The Ideal Type

The reader might rightly be surprised that we have hardly mentioned the name of an illustrious theory, that of Max Weber's ideal type; we had no need to speak of it, because the ideal type belongs to a problematical position quite different from the one we have taken. It is situated at a much more advanced stage of the synthesis than the one we shall study as "placing in series"; and even, truth to tell, in order to discuss and judge its validity, we would have to begin by clarifying the rich, confused whole that, since Dilthey, has been called hermeneutics and that seems to us the counterpart of historism at the level of criticism. The ideal type is in fact an instrument for interpretation, for hermeneutics, in a problematical position in which history is conceived as the knowledge of individuality.

Today the expression "ideal type" is often (not always) taken in a rather banal sense; it is applied to every historical description in which the event is simplified and seen from a certain angle—which is the case with the least page of history, for one cannot go into every detail, and things are seen in a certain succession. But this meaning is not Weber's; to him the ideal type was not the result of the historian's work, but only an analytical instrument that should not go leave his study and whose use is exclusively heuristic. The definitive account is not an ideal type; it goes beyond it. The ideal type itself is truly ideal, it is a too-perfect event that would go to the end of its logic, or one of its logics, which allows the historian to penetrate more deeply into the logic of a concrete event, to make explicit the non-eventworthy, at the risk of measuring afterward the gap between the ideal and the real.

Weber's texts are very clear: the ideal type (the sect, the city, the liberal economy, the craftsmen) is a "limit concept," a "utopia" that "is nowhere realized," but "serves to measure how much reality approaches or moves away from the ideal picture." Its only value is "heuristic," and it is not the goal of historiography: "it is taken into account solely as a way of knowing" and "the ideal type and history are not to be confused." However, without it, historical knowledge "would remain sunk in the sphere of what is but vaguely felt." The ideal type is not an average, far from it; it reveals the features and is the opposite of the generic. It is very possible to work out the ideal type of an individual.[15]

For a European today, this theory is difficult to understand—not that Weber is not clear, but it is not easy to see the use of all that; one cannot see the psychological truth or the methodological necessity of this way of proceeding. One is tempted to conclude either that Weber unintentionally described his own psychology, his personal habits as a researcher, or that his theory must have had, in the Germany of 1900, harmonics that we no longer discern. The second supposition is the right one. As J. Molino pointed out to me, a whole sector of German thought, from Schleiermacher to Dilthey, Meinecke, and Leo Spitzer, has been unceasingly confronted with the enigma of individuality—"I have already sent you a sentence from which I deduce everything: *individuum est ineffabile*," wrote Goethe to Lavater.[16]

Dilthey was primarily a biographer of genius, the author of the intellectual biographies of Schleiermacher and of the youthful Hegel; the reading of the *Monde de l'esprit*, which is at times a bit baffling when undertaken without knowing this background, becomes exciting when one knows that the example to which Dilthey makes constant reference in his thinking is the understanding of an individual work.[17] The opposition he established between explanation and comprehension, which was almost fatal to the human sciences, is to him a biographer's idea. Now, to the biographer, and very often to the philologist, the "classifications" that are the true basis for the slightest understanding—that *rosa* means "rose" and that Homer writes in verse—most frequently remain implicit, for they pass for primary intuitions; what is seen as a problem is the work in its originality.

The problem of the ideal type is that of understanding individualities taken as totalities and not reduced to classifications that subtend their comprehension. Now the development of an individuality (let us say, of a plot, whether the city, or the liberal economy, or the education of Goethe) is never seen through to the end, and is thwarted by material difficulties or by accidents; as the *Urworte* of Goethe says, it is the play of the "demon" in each one and of his *tyché*. So let us imagine an individuality that carried its logic through to its limit and whose growth was not restrained or halted by any "rub" or by any accident; that individuality would be an ideal type. At the heart of Weber's theory is the idea of the complete development of the individual: "The ideal type is an attempt to comprehend the historical individualities in genetic concepts."[18] For "when it is proposed to give a genetic definition of the content of a concept, there is no other form but that of the ideal type." The fundamental idea of the ideal type method is, therefore, that the perfect individual alone allows the understanding of the imperfect individual.

Chapter VIII

Causality and "Retrodiction"

History is not a science, and its way of explaining is to "make clear," to tell how things happened, which does not result in something substantially different from our usual daily newspaper, every morning or every evening—that is, synthesis (the remainder is the role of criticism, of erudition). If that is so, how is it that historical synthesis is difficult, that it is done progressively and controversially, that historians do not agree on the reasons for the fall of the Roman Empire or on the causes of the American Civil War? There are two reasons for this difficulty. One, which we have just seen, is that it is difficult to surround the diversity of the concrete with concepts. The other, which we are now about to see, is that the historian has direct access to only a tiny proportion of the concrete, the one given him by the documents at his disposal; for all the rest, he has to fill in the gaps. This filling-in is consciously done for a very small part, the part dealing with theories and hypotheses; for a vastly larger part it is done unconsciously because it goes without saying (which does not mean that it is certain). It is the same in daily life; if I read, unmistakably, in a document that the king drinks, or if I see a friend in the act of drinking, it still remains for me to conclude that they are drinking because they are thirsty, in which I can be mistaken.

Historical synthesis is nothing but this operation of filling in; we shall call it "retrodiction," borrowing the word from the theory of incomplete knowledge that is the theory of probabilities. There is a prediction when we consider an event to come: how many chances do I have or did I have of four aces in poker? The problems of retrodiction, on the other hand, are problems of the probability of causes—or, to put it better, the probability of hypotheses: an event having already occurred, how can it be properly explained? Does the king drink because he is thirsty or because etiquette demands that he drink? Historical problems, when they are not problems of criticism, are problems of "retrodiction";[1] that is why the word "explanation" is very popular with historians. To explain is, for them, to find the right explanation, to fill a gap, to discover a break in relations between the Arab East and the West that explains the subsequent economic decline. So all "retrodiction" calls into play a causal explanation (thirst makes the king drink) and perhaps (at least, so it is said) even a true law (whoever is thirsty will drink, if he can). To study the historical synthesis, or "retrodiction," is to study the part played in history by induction and in what "historical causality" consists; in other words, since History has no existence, causality in our daily life, sublunary causality.

Causality or "Retrodiction"

Let us begin with a very simple historical proposition: "Louis XIV became unpopular because the taxes were too heavy." We need to know that, in the practice of the historian's profession, a phrase of this kind may have been written with two very different meanings. (It is curious that, unless we are mistaken, this has never been said. Could it have been forgotten that history is knowledge through documents, and therefore incomplete knowledge?) Historians constantly move from one of those meanings to the other without warning and even without realizing it, and the reconstitution of the past is woven precisely by these comings and goings. Written in its first meaning, the sentence means that the historian knows, from documents, that the taxes were indeed the cause of the king's unpopularity; he has, so to speak, heard it with his own ears. In the second meaning the historian knows only that the taxes were heavy and that, in other respects, the king had become unpopular at the end of his reign; therefore he supposes or believes it is evident that the most obvious explanation for this unpopularity is the weight of the taxes. In the first case he relates a plot to us that he has read in documents: the tax system made the king unpopular; in the second he makes a "retrodiction," working back from the unpopularity to a presumed cause, to an explanatory hypothesis.

Sublunary Causality

To know for a fact that the taxation system made the king unpopular means, for example, going through manuscript memoirs from the time of

Louis XIV in which village priests noted that the poor groaned because of the tax, and secretly cursed the king. The causal process is then immediately understood; if it were not so, the deciphering of the world could not have been begun. It is enough for a child to open Thucydides to understand, as soon as he is old enough to attach some meaning to the words, "war," "city," or "political man"; that child will not spontaneously have the idea that every city prefers to command than to be enslaved— he will learn it from Thucydides. If we thus understand the reason for effects, it is not at all because we carry the equivalent of them in ourselves. We have hardly more love for taxes than had the subjects of Louis XIV, but even if we adored him, it would not prevent us from understanding their reasons for hating him; after all, we understand the love that a wealthy Athenian had for those glorious and crushing taxes that weighed down the rich under the name of liturgies and that the wealthy paid out of pride and patriotism.

To have noted once that the system of taxation made a king unpopular is to expect the process to be repeated: by nature the causal relation goes beyond the individual case, is something other than a fortuitous coincidence, implies some regularity in things.[2] But that does not at all mean that it becomes constant; indeed, that is why we never know what tomorrow will bring. Causality is necessary and irregular; futures are contingent, the tax system may make a government unpopular, but it also may not have that effect. If the effect is produced, nothing will appear more natural to us than this causal relationship, but we shall not be unduly surprised if we find that it does not occur. First of all, we know that there may be exceptions—for example, if a patriotic impulse motivates taxpayers faced with an invasion of their national territory. When we say that taxes made Louis XIV unpopular, we implicitly take into account the situation as a whole in the period (foreign war, defeats, the peasant mentality . . .); we feel that that situation is a special one and that its lessons could not be transferred to another without risk of error.

But does that mean that we are always in a position to be precise about the cases to which the lessons could be transferred or, on the other hand, exactly what particular circumstances mean that they could not be? Not at all; we know very well that, whatever effort we make, we can never specify with certainty what definite circumstances would make the lessons valid or invalid. We are not unaware that, if we tried to do so, we would soon be reduced to invoking, for example, the mystery of the French national temperament—that is, to admitting our inability to prophesy the future and to explain the past. So we always keep a margin of haziness and also of uncertainty: causality is always accompanied by mental reservation; scholastic philosophy was well aware of this, teaching that, in the sublunary world, the laws of physics work only approximately, for the diversity of "matter" prevents them from functioning formally.

It Is Irregular

These truths are not, as we shall see, without interest in discussions on historical causality; every historian can repeat the declaration, which at first sight is contradictory, made by Tacitus in his *Histories:* "I shall cause the reader to learn not only what has happened, which is usually fortuitous, but also the causes of what has happened." Thus, it is all a question of degree: events are more or less disconcerting or foreseeable, causality functions more or less regularly according to the case. So we picture the future with unequal chances of getting it right. Experience has taught us this inequality: we are sure that a thing will fall to the ground (experience taught us that when we were about five months old), unless it is a bird or a red balloon. If we go out into the street too lightly clad, we will catch cold, but that eventuality is less infallible; if we really do catch a cold, we will be sure of the cause, but if we go out without a coat, we are less sure of the consequences. If the government increases or freezes salaries, people will probably be displeased, but the displeasure will go more or less far: a riot is a risk, and only a risk. There is equally some constancy in our actions without which we could do nothing; when we hang up the phone to give orders to the cook, the bailiff, or the executioner, we anticipate the effect of it; there are, however, telephone breakdowns and breakdowns in obedience. This part of approximate constancy means that part of the course of history is reduced to the application of recipes over which the historian passes in silence, since the event is the difference.

Events compose a plot in which everything is explicable but unequally probable. The cause of the riot is the heaviness of the taxes, but it was not sure that things would come to rioting; events have causes, but causes do not always have consequences—in short, the chances of different events happening are unequal. We can even refine this and distinguish risk, uncertainty, and the unknown. There is risk when it is possible to calculate, at least roughly, the number of chances of different eventualities: thus it is when we cross a glacier where a layer of snow hides the crevasses and when we know that the network of crevasses is fairly close together here. There is uncertainty when we cannot state the relative probabilities of different eventualities: thus it is when we do not know if the snowy surface we are crossing is a treacherous glacier or harmless névé. There is the unknown when we do not even know what the eventualities are and what kind of accident may very well occur: thus it is when one sets foot for the first time on an unknown planet. It is a fact that *homo historicus* generally prefers a big risk to a slight uncertainty (he is rather a "stick in the mud") and that he abhors the unknown.

It Is Confused

If every causal relationship is thus more or less constant, if we advance it only with a mental reservation, it is because we have only a global and confused perception of it. Causality is too muddled to be reasoned out by the example of two billiard balls that collide so very simply.[3] We believe in the causal relationship when we see them collide, because the logic of this process is almost as evident as when we see one idea driving away another; on the other hand, we do not take the day to be the cause of the night, although the latter follows it with the utmost regularity. If, in an unknown machine, I see a lever moving down and hear music, I do not infer that the lever causes it, but that the movement of the lever and the music are two successive effects of the same hidden mechanism. But does it often occur to one to speak of a cause? Do I speak of it with regard to an electric switch or the working of a noria? When I turn on the electricity, I am conscious that a global process is produced, and I express no opinion on its breakdown into effects and causes. Everything happens as if the causal relationship were only the global conclusion of a large number of little arguments, as elusive as the "little perceptions" of Leibnitz. If a youngster throws a brick at my window and breaks the pane, I shall very well understand the cause of the effects; I shall even be able to say, if my language is lofty, that the brick is the cause of the broken pane; it would, however, be excessive for me to draw from it a law that says bricks break windowpanes.[4] If I did so, I would only have shown that a sentence can always be put in the plural. Everyday causality is made up of singular causal relationships behind which one sees some generality, but only vaguely. Of course, the fact that projectiles can break windowpanes is not innate knowledge; a newborn child has to learn that glass is fragile. As for myself, I have already seen stones, bullets, and bolts break windowpanes, but no bricks; however, I do not doubt the result, just as I know, on the other hand, that a cork pellet would break nothing. Through some obscure reasoning, I take into account the weight of the object, its volume, its elasticity, and the thickness of the glass, but not its color.

However, I am unable to say exactly what weight, what elasticity will bring about the breaking of the window; in addition, I do not know if there are other conditions unknown to me. It is because it is a conclusion, and a vague conclusion, that causality is always accompanied by uncertainty about its constancy, by mental reservation, and because we are only more or less sure of its effects. For if every effect has its cause, every cause will not always produce its effect; so the Scholastics found it convenient to study in causality not the doubtful possibility of predicting an effect from the cause but, rather, the need to work back from the effect to a cause and to ask themselves "whence came the change," *unde motus primo*.

There is a second reason for the mental reservation with which we surround the prediction: what is called the cause is always just one of the causes that can be separated out of the process; the number of all such causes is indefinite, and their separation has value only in the ordering of discourse. How can we separate the causes and conditions in "James could not take the train because it was packed"? It would be lining up the thousand and one possible ways of relating this little incident. The cause of the broken windowpane may be the brick, the youngster who threw it, the thinness of the glass, or the sorry times in which we are living. How can we enumerate all the conditions necessary for a brick to break a windowpane? Louis XIV became unpopular because of fiscal matters, but, when the nation's territory is invaded, the peasants are more patriotic, or if he had been taller and his figure more majestic, perhaps he would not have become unpopular. So let us beware of stating that all kings become unpopular just because Louis XIV was.

"Retrodiction"

The historian cannot foresee with certainty if a king will become unpopular because of his tax policy; on the other hand, if he has heard with his own ears that one king became unpopular for that reason, there is not a greater case for quibbling about it and alleging that "facts do not exist" (at most he can refine the analysis of the souls of the taxpayers, as we shall see in the next chapter). However, since our knowledge of the past is incomplete, the historian often faces a very different problem: he notes that a king was unpopular, but no document tells him why; he therefore has to move back by "retrodiction" from the effect to its hypothetical cause. If he decides that cause must be taxation, he will write the phrase "Louis XIV bcame unpopular because of taxation" with the second meaning we have seen. The uncertainty is then this: we are assured of the effect, but have we worked back to the right explanation? Is the cause taxation, the defeats of the king, or some third thing of which we have not thought? The statistics of the Masses that the faithful had said for the health of the king show clearly the disaffection felt at the end of the reign; in addition, we know that the taxes had increased, and we bear in mind that people do not like taxes.

People—that is, the eternal man, or ourselves and our prejudices; it would be better if there were a contemporary psychology. Now we know that in the seventeenth century many riots were caused by the new taxes, changes in the value of money, and the high price of grain; this knowledge is not inborn in us, nor do we any longer have the opportunity, in the twentieth century, to see many riots of that kind: there are other reasons for strikes. But we have read the history of the Fronde; the connection between taxes and riots in that is at once visible to us, and the global knowledge of the causal connection has remained with us. So taxation is a likely cause of discontent, but wouldn't others be equally so? What was the strength of patriotism in the peasant soul? Didn't defeats contribute just as much as taxation to the unpopularity of the king? We need a good knowledge of the mentality of the period to work backward, certainly; we shall perhaps ask ourselves if other cases of discontent have other causes than taxation. More probably we shall not reason by so caricatural an induction, but we shall ask ourselves if, according to what is known of the climate of thought at that period, there was a public opinion, if the people considered foreign wars as anything other than a glorious, private affair conducted by the king and specialists, and one that did not concern his subjects, except when they had to suffer for it materially.

One thus reaches more or less likely conclusions: "The causes of this riot, which are not clear, were probably the taxation, as always at that time, in such circumstances." This implies "if things happened according to a regular pattern." "Retrodiction" is in that way related to reasoning by analogy or to that form of prophecy—reasonable, because conditional—that is called a prediction. An example of reasoning by analogy is the following: "Historians constantly use generalizations; if the fact is not obvious that Richard had the little princes killed in the Tower of London, historians will ask, no doubt unconsciously rather than consciously, if it was the custom of monarchs at that time to liquidate their possible rivals for the crown; their conclusion will be influenced very justly by that generalization."[5] The danger in that reasoning is obviously that Richard was personally more cruel than the custom of his day sanctioned. An example of a historic prediction is the following: Let us ask ourselves what would have happened if Spartacus had beaten the Roman legions and had become master of southern Italy. The end of slavery? A slight increase in the rise of production relations?

A parallel suggests a better reply that all we know of the climate of the period seems to confirm; since we learned that a generation before Spartacus, at the time of the great revolt of the slaves in Sicily, those who revolted had established a capital and a king,[6] we can believe that if Spartacus had won, he would have founded one more Hellenistic kingdom in Italy, in which, surely, there would have been slavery, as there was everywhere at that time.[7] For lack of this parallel, another parallel, a less good one, would be the Mamelukes of Egypt. What is valuable in the Sicilian parallel is that one does not see what particular reasons could have driven the slaves in Sicily to found a kingdom, reasons that would have been lacking in the case of Spartacus. The choice of the monarchical regime could not at that period have been thought unusual; the monarchy was the normal constitution of every state that was not a city. On the other hand, the same charismatic and millenarian aura would have surrounded Spartacus and the king of those who revolted in Sicily: this millennarism of the "primitives of revolt" is well known.

Foundation of "Retrodiction"

Thus one ends up with a certain idea of the compossibilities of a given period, with a knowledge of what one can or cannot expect from the people of that period; that is what is called having a historical sense, understanding the soul of antiquity, feeling the climate of a time. All these inferences are most usually unconscious or at least tacit, thanks to the serious attitude and conventions of the genre. Only the epigraphists are lucid enough to speak of "classifying." Indeed, the reasoning that "retrodiction" most closely resembles is classification; when an epigraphist, a philologist, or an iconographist wants to know what the word *rosa* means or what, on that bas-relief, a Roman lying on a bed is doing, he collects all the other occurrences of the word *rosa* and of recumbent Romans, and from the series so constituted he draws the conclusion that *rosa* means a rose and that the Roman is sleeping or eating.[8] The foundation for this conclusion is that it would be surprising for a word not always to have roughly the same meaning and for the Romans not to eat and sleep as the custom of their time demanded.

The foundation of "retrodiction" can thus be seen; it is not the supposed constancy with which effect follows cause, nor is it the foundation of induction, the regularity of natural phenomena. Rather, it is something very empirical; there are customs, conventions, types in history. Here is a recumbent Roman; why did he recline? If men behaved capriciously and were only caprices, the number of possible answers would be indefinite and it would be impossible to "retrodict" the right one. But men have manners and more or less conform to them; in that way the number of possible causes to which one can trace backward is limited. Things might not be so, men might ignore every custom and live only by strokes of genius and strokes of madness, history might be made only of hapax legomena. Then "retrodiction" would become impossible, but the regularity of laws would exist no less and the epistemological edifice would not thereby be modified by one iota.

Fortunately, the human species, or at least each epoch, repeats itself a little, and the knowledge of those repetitions allows "retrodiction." The words of the linguistic code are always used in the same sense; customs make people eat standing up, sitting, or lying down, but not as they wish. The framework of any society is limited, and a manufacturing civilization can with difficulty be chivalrous at the same time, for there is no time for everything and no mind for everything. The species has its instincts—for example, it allows of civil violence, in the manner of rats if not in that of wolves. Those are the constants on which one can count. Other sectors, on the other hand, are known to lend themselves much less easily to classification. With the historian it is as with the detective:[9] when the policeman has before him "an average man" consistent with the model, he knows what he can expect; on the other hand, he can never know what "intellectuals" are capable of inventing. Error, eccentricity, bohemia, genius, and madness are sectors where "retrodiction" is risky. A poor-quality sculpture can be classified, a masterpiece much less so; poetic texts can be reconstituted with less certainty than administrative formularies. War is a truth throughout the known history of humankind, but commercial imperialism is a very narrowly dated phenomenon and it is better not to "retrodict" it for the Peloponnesian War.[10]

The main thing is always to distinguish if one is in a sector where repetition holds or if one cannot count on it. Moreover, there are eccentric or inventive periods in which the divergences are much greater than in others. Practically, the historian constantly oscillates between two extremes: inventing false rules ("a fact of this kind is inconceivable at the period and does not really appear before the eighteenth century") or letting everything go, saying to himself that everything is possible at every period and that custom is not the tyrant it is said to be. One of the tasks of the future historical critic will be to work out a casuistic of "retrodiction."

"Retrodiction" Is "Synthesis"

It is not the first time that we state it, and it will not be the last: the root of the problems of historical knowledge is at the level of documents, criticism, and erudition. The philosophizing tradition in matters of historical epistemology aims too high; it wonders if the historian explains by causes or by laws, but it overlooks "retrodiction," it speaks of historical induction and is ignorant of classification. But the history of a given period is reconstituted by classifications, by comings and goings between the documents and "retrodiction," and the historical "facts" that are apparently the most consistent are in reality conclusions that take in a considerable amount of "retrodiction." When a historian says that taxation made Louis XIV unpopular, relying on the manuscript of a village priest, he uses "retrodiction" by admitting that this evidence was equally valid for the neighboring villages, which supposes a vast inquiry if this induction were properly based and if the sample could be taken as representative. The first "retrodiction" was, in truth, to take three centuries backward a manuscript that exists very materially in 1969, in virtue of the visual and tactile feeling of the historian.[11] This huge proportion of "retrodiction," of interpretation, means that, in certain areas, one can expect any surprise; two centuries ago it was finally admitted that Romulus was legendary and, since 1945, Japanese historians have been able to write that the origins of their reigning dynasty are mythical. There are, indeed, an enormous number of gaps in the historical fabric, because there are a great many between that very special kind of events called documents and because history is knowledge acquired through traces.

We have seen earlier in this book that in no case can a document, even a life of Robinson Crusoe by Robinson Crusoe, coincide completely with an event. So the course of events cannot be recomposed like a mosaic; however numerous they are, documents are necessarily indirect and incomplete, they have to be projected onto the chosen plan and then connected. This situation, though it is particularly perceptible in ancient history, is not peculiar to it; more contemporary history is made of an equally great proportion of "retrodiction," the difference being that this "retrodiction" is here practically certain. But, in short, even if the documents are newspapers or archives, they have to be connected, and we must not attach to an article in *Humanité* the same importance as an editorial in the *Journal des débats,* according to what else one knows of these papers. A tract of 1936 and a few press clippings preserve for us the memory of a strike in a certain suburban factory; since no historical period does everything at the same time, since "sit-down strikes," "wildcat strikes," and "vandalizing strikes" do not happen at the same time, that strike of 1936 will obviously be looked on as being like the other strikes in the same year in the entire context of the Popular Front—or, rather, in the context of all the documents that tell us about those strikes.

On the contrary, in ancient history the apparently most formal document (or the one that seems so because we do not think enough about the proportion of "retrodictions") remains ambiguous for lack of a context. Here is a letter of Pliny the Younger, isolated like a meteorite, that tells us formally that at the beginning of the second century, somewhere in Asia Minor, Christians were very numerous. For lack of a context, we shall not even be able to decide (supposing we think of asking ourselves) if that letter proves that only three generations after the death of Christ, Christianity, at least in highly cultured regions, had almost completed the conquest of souls, or if we should only think that the attention of Pliny and the Roman authorities had just been drawn by an episode of momentary interest: a sudden blaze of conversions in Asia, comparable with an Anglo-Saxon revival or like those epidemics of mass conversions, short-lived ones, that the first missionaries were disappointed to see in Japan, and that the slightest action by the authorities was enough to suppress (however, after the ebbing of the tide there remained on the shore a thin fringe of souls won). Regular rising of the religious tide, or ebb and flow? If we limit ourselves to the Roman documents, "retrodiction" on this point is impossible.

By degrees, documents with fewer gaps allow us to imagine the context of a period (one "gets to know one's period"), and this imagining allows us to rectify the interpretation of other documents that have more gaps. There is here no "vicious circle of historical synthesis," any more than there is a "hermeneutic circle" in the interpreting of literary texts. It is said that there is a circle, that the interpretation of a textual context depends on the details, and that the details assume the meaning one gives to the context.[12] In reality there is no circle at all, since the details on which the provisional interpretation of the context is based are different from the new detail to be interpreted; the interpretation thus progresses as a millipede does. If it were not so, no text would have been deciphered up to now, save by mystic intuition.

Just as there is no "historical circle," so there is no flight into infinity of "retrodictions"; the inferences stumble against the data of the documents. But, if the inferences do not go on to infinity, they at least go very far: to the point of weaving in the head of each historian a little philosophy of personal history, professional experience, in virtue of which he ascribes a particular weight to economic causes or to religious necessity, thinks or does not think of a particular "retrodictive" hypothesis. It is that experience (in the meaning with which we speak of the experience of a clinician or of a confessor) that is taken to be the famous "method" of history.

"Method" Is Experience

For, just as the slightest fact implies a host of "retrodictions," so it implies "retrodictions" of a more general significance that compose a conception of history and of man. The professional experience acquired by studying the events to which it is indissolubly bound is what Thucydides called the ktèma es aei, the ever-valid lessons of history.

Historians thus ultimately make, for their period or for the historical era, a wisdom, and acquire what Maritain[13] calls "a sane philosophy of man, a just appreciation of the various activities of the human being and of their relative importance." Are revolutionary pressures infrequent phenomena supposing a very special social and ideological preparation, or do they happen like car accidents, without the historian having to trouble himself with complicated explanations? Is the discontent born of privations and of social inequality a principal factor in evolution, or does it actually play a secondary role? Is intense faith reserved to a religious elite, or can it be a mass event? What is the famous "simple faith" like? Has a Christianity as Bernanos imagined it ever existed? (Le Bras very much doubts it.) Is the collective passion of the Romans for spectacles and of South Americans for soccer only an appearance hiding political throbbing, or is it humanly plausible that it suffices as what it is? It is not always possible to get the answer to these questions from the documents "of one's period"; on the contrary, those documents will assume the meaning that each one's reply to these questions will give him and the reply will be drawn from other periods, if the historian is a cultured man, or from his prejudices—that is, from the spectacle of contemporary history.

Thus, historical experience is composed of all that a historian can learn in his life, his reading and those with whom he associates. So it is not astonishing that there are no two historians or two clinicians with the same experience, and that endless quarrels are not rare at the sick man's bedside. This is not to forget the naive who think they are working wonders by using techniques in tandem, labeled sociology, religious phenomenology, and so on, as if the sciences in question were deduced from heaven, as if they were not inductive, as if they were not history under a scarcely more general aspect, as if they were not, in a word, the experiences of others that the historian will certainly use for his own profit if he knows how not to let himself be put off by falsely strange labels. That is why the naive who do not forbid themselves access to that experience, under the pretext that sociology is not history, are in fact the really clever ones, and those who make fun of them are only half clever. Historical experience is the familiar knowledge of all the generalities and regularities of history, in whatever wrapping it is fashionable to present them.

The Two Limits of Historical Objectivity

If history is that mixture of data and experience, if it is documentary knowledge, with gaps and "retrodiction," if it is reconstructed by the same fluctuation of inferences as those by which a child gradually constructs its vision of the world, then we can see the limit of historical objectivity; it corresponds to the gaps in documentation and to the variety of experiences.

Documentation

Such are the only limits. One can, indeed, admit right away that history is subjective, as Marrou says, because History does not exist and everything is matter for plots; one can also admit right away the limits of historical objectivity of which Aron speaks, in the sense that these plots are sublunary; that they have a truth, but not a scientific one; and that a page of history will always be more like a page of narration than a page of physics. It must not be concluded that the skepticism of a discerning old-fashioned scholar is fitting or, in the latest fashion, that facts do not exist and that they depend on a correct opinion about the meaning of history. We can only conclude that history is not objective in the same way as science, that its objectivity is of the same order as that of the world that we see.

As F. Chatelet very rightly says:

If we consider the work of present-day historians—and not only the reflections on the history those historians write—we see that the polemics about the impossibility of a historical truth, the conjectural character of history, the irreducible coefficient of subjectivity, have little meaning today. If several presentations of events are possible, it remains true that each of them sheds new light on those events.

We shall not count, among the limits of objectivity, what comes from the division of men's minds into sects: a Marxist will find that economic causes are most important, and others will speak of a search for power or of a circulation of elites. Unlike quarrels between chemists or physicists, that division into sects is of extradisciplinary origin, and reeks of boredom. Nor shall we count the unfinished state of history, which is that of all non-immediate knowledge; nor the fact that analysis can be extended more

(Togliatti) or less (Khrushchev) far into the non-eventworthy, which only proves that there are good historians and others who are less good, and also the fact that historical experience increases.

All that being admitted, it is difficult to see what would prevent people from agreeing on the Seleucid imperialism or on the events of May 1968, apart from lack of documents; historical practice, by its very existence, contradicts the contention that there would be other limits to objectivity, and discussions between historians have never yet ended with the discovery of unsurpassable aporias. Only confused concepts are discovered, problematics less simple than foreseen and questions that had not been thought of; history is not unknowable, but it is extremely complicated, calling for a considerably more subtle experience than that which we can at present acquire. That being said, even the distinction between superficial causes and profound ones is not a question of personal taste or point of view. Certainly, two history papers on the same period are ordinarily quite different; but those differences come from the lighting, from an editorial insistence on a particular aspect of the facts, or from a different choice of what is left unsaid. The same differences would be found between two mathematics papers, or else is really a question of divergences; but then a discussion may very objectively be initiated, and is effectively initiated, that never leads to aporias but only to quarrels.

The Diversity of Experiences

The second limit to objectivity—it is less a definitive limit than an effect of braking, of delaying—is the variety of personal experiences, which are difficult to transmit. Two historians of religion will not agree on "Roman funerary symbolism," because one has experience with ancient inscriptions, with Breton pilgrimages, and Neapolitan devotion, and because he has read Le Bras; the other has developed a religious philosophy based on ancient texts, from his own faith and from St. Teresa. The rule of the game is that you never seek to make explicit the content of the experiences that are the foundation of "retrodiction"; all they can do is to accuse each other of lacking religious sensitivity, which means nothing but is not easy to forgive. When a historian, in order to ground his interpretation, appeals to the lessons of the present or some other period of history, he is accustomed to doing so to illustrate his thought, rather than as a proof; no doubt modesty makes him guess that to a logician, historical induction would appear terribly imperfect, and history a poor analogical discipline.

So we are left free to believe that history is written with one's personality—that is, to say, with confused knowledge. Certainly that experience is transmissible and cumulative, because it is above all acquired from books, but it is not a method (each gets the experience that he can and that he desires), first of all because its existence is not officially recognized and its acquisition is not organized; then, because, if it is transmissible, it cannot be formulated: it is acquired through knowledge of concrete historical situations, from which each one is left to draw the lesson in his own way. The *Ktèma es aei* of the Peloponnesian War is implicit in the account of that war; it is not a penny catechism with plates. Historical experience is acquired by working; it is not the fruit of study, but of an apprenticeship. History has no method, since it cannot formulate its experience in definitions, laws, and rules. The discussion of different personal experiences is thus always indirect; with time the apprenticeships communicate with each other and agreement is finally reached, in the way that an opinion is asserted, but not in the way a rule is given.

Causes or Laws, Art or Science

History is an art, which supposes the apprenticeship of an experience. What is deceptive on this point, what makes us hope constantly that it can one day be brought to a really scientific stage, is that it is full of general ideas and approximate regularities, like daily life: when I say that taxes caused Louis XIV to be hated, I admit by that that it would not be surprising to find the same thing happening to another king for the same reason. We thus approach what is at present the great problem of historical epistemology in the Anglo-Saxon countries: does the historian explain by means of causes or by means of laws? Is it possible to say that taxation caused Louis XIV to be hated, without appealing to a covering law that gives a basis for this singular causality and affirms that every too-heavy tax makes the government levying it unpopular? That would be a problematic whose interest is apparently limited but which in reality contains the question of the scientific or sublunary character of history, and even the question of the nature of scientific knowledge; all the rest of the present chapter will be devoted to it.

Everyone knows that there is general science and that history is full of generalities, but are they "good" generalities? Let us explain first of all the theory of covering laws, for there is more than one thing to remember from its analysis of the historical explanation. We only deny that, despite some appearances, the said explanation has the least relationship with explanation as practiced in science; for, like every reader of G. Granger,[14] we no longer swear except by the opposition between "actual experience" (we have called it the sublunary) and "the formal," the formalizable character of all science worthy of the name. Has the truth of the wisdom of nations, "every too-heavy tax makes the government hated, except when it doesn't," any relationship at all with the formula of Newton? And, if not, why?

The Explanation According to Logical Empiricism

This theory of covering laws in history is due to logical empiricism.[15] This school is convinced of the unity of reason. According to its analysis of explanation in science, every explanation amounts to subsuming events under laws. More precisely, suppose there is an event to be explained: what will explain it is made up of antecedent data or conditions, which are events situated in determined times and places (they are, for example, the initial conditions or the conditions at the limits of physicists); on the other hand there are scientific laws. Every explanation of an event (the diffusion of heat along this iron rod, the more than proportional decline in the price of wheat this year) thus contains at least one law (for wheat it is King's law).

Certainly impeccable analysis; let us apply it to history. Take the conflict of the papacy and of the Empire.[16] Unwilling to undertake a regression to infinity along the chain of events, the historian begins by granting himself data from which to begin: in the eleventh century there exists a papacy and an imperial power, which have a particular character. Each action made from then on by either of the actors in the historical drama will be explained by a law: every power, even if spiritual, wants to be total, every institution tends to get set in its ways. However, it must not be believed that if each separate episode is explained by one or several laws and by the preceding period, all the episodes flow from each other, so that the whole chain will be foreseeable. It is not like that because the system is not isolated: there constantly come onto the stage new data (the king of France and his jurists, the temperament of Emperor Henry IV, the rise of national monarchies) that modify the original data. It follows that if each link is explicable, the concatenation is not, for the explanation of each new datum would take us too far into the study of the chains from which it comes.

Let us congratulate ourselves on having compared history to a dramatic plot: logical empiricism demands it. The data are like characters in the drama; there are also motives that make those characters move—these are eternal laws. New actors often appear in the course of the action, whose arrival, easily explainable in itself, nonetheless surprises the spectators who do not see what is happening offstage; their arrival appreciably modifies the course of the plot, which can be explained scene by scene but is not foreseeable from beginning to end, so much so that its denouement is both unexpected and natural, because each episode could be explained by the eternal laws of the human heart. So we see why history does not repeat itself, why the future is not foreseeable; it is not, as one might suppose, because a law like "all power wants to be total" is perhaps not one of the most absolute and scientific. No: it is only because the system, not being isolated, is not entirely explicable from the initial data. That is a kind of indetermination that the most fiercely scientific mind will not be loath to admit.

Criticism of Logical Empiricism

But, by exposing this scheme, what do we think we have done? Spun a metaphor? Let us come to an understanding:[17] it is not that we have the least nostalgia for the contrast advanced by Dilthey between the natural sciences that "explain" and the human sciences that would only make us "understand," which is one of the most memorable blind alleys in the history of sciences. Whether it concerns falling bodies or human action, the scientific explanation is the same, it is deductive and nomological; we deny only that history is a science. The frontier passes between the nomological explanation of the sciences, be they natural or human, and the everyday and historical explanation, which is causal and too confused to be generalizable in laws.

In truth, the difficulty is to know exactly what logical empiricism means by those "laws" the historian would use. Are they scientific laws, in the meaning everyone attributes to that expression: the laws of physics or of economics? Or are they also truisms in the plural, like "every too-heavy tax . . ."? It is to be noted that, according to the authors and the passages, there is some irresolution on this point. In principle it concerns only scientific laws; but, if the schema of logical empiricism were applicable only to the pages of history that invoke one of those laws, that would really amount to very little. So one is resigned little by little to giving the name "laws" to the truths of the wisdom of nations; so frank is the conviction that history is a serious discipline, which has its methods and its synthesis and all the same provides something other than explanations such as would be found everywhere. When one has thus had to call truisms "laws," one finds comfort in hope: it is a question of a mere "explanatory sketch,"[18] incomplete, implicit, or temporary, in which truisms will gradually be replaced by laws of better quality as science progresses. In short, either one claims that history explains by means of true laws, or one baptizes truisms as laws, or it is hoped that those truisms are sketches of future laws; that makes three errors.[19]

The theory of historical explanation, according to logical empiricism, is less false than uninstructive. There is certainly a resemblance between the causal explanation in history and the nomological explanation of sciences; in both cases recourse is had to data (taxes, Louis XIV) and to a relation that is general (law) or at least generalizable barring exceptions (cause). It is through that resemblance that the historian can utilize causes and laws side by side: the fall in the market price of wheat is explained by King's law and by the eating habits of the French people. The difference is that if a causal relationship is repeatable, one can never formally assert when and under what conditions it will be repeated; causality is confused and gobal, history knows only singular cases of causality that cannot be set up as rules: the "lessons" of history are always accompanied by mental reservations. That is indeed why historical experience cannot be formulated, why the *ktèma es aei* cannot be isolated from the singular case in which it has been verified.

Let us take one of those singular cases; let us undertake, flying in the face of all common sense, to generalize its lesson into a law; let us be resigned in advance to baptizing as "law" the truism obtained. And we still have to obtain one, and it is not so simple, for the causal relationship is global. But we have no criterion at all for analyzing it, so the number of possible decompositions will be indefinite. Let us consider the sanctioned example: "Louis XIV became unpopular because of taxation." That seems simple: the cause is the tax system, the consequence is unpopularity; as for the law, the reader surely knows it by heart. But would there not be two distinct effects and two different causes: the taxes caused discontent, and that discontent became the cause of the unpopularity? A more subtle analysis will yield a supplementary covering law stating that all discontent is carried back to the cause of the fact producing that discontent (if my memory does not deceive me, that law can be read in Spinoza). Then shall we have two laws for one unpopularity? We shall have many more, if we scrutinize "too-heavy taxes" and "king," and if we do not realize in time that our supposed analysis is really a description of what happened.

Moreover, whatever formulation we give it, our law will be false; in the case of patriotic enthusiasm or for every more or less inexplicable reason, it will not work. Scheffler has said:[20] "Let us multiply the conditions and stipulations, and the law will be exact in the end." Let it be tried. To begin with, the case of patriotic enthusiasm will be excepted, the shades of meaning will be multiplied; when the text of the law is several pages long, a chapter of the history of the reign of Louis XIV will have been reconstituted, and it will present the amusing feature of being written in the present and in the plural. Having thus reconstituted the individuality of the event, we shall still have to find its law.

History Is Not a Sketch of Science

Such is the difference between the concrete and irregular causality of the sublunary world and the abstract and formal laws of science. However detailed we suppose it to be, a law can never foresee everything; we call the unforeseeable, which we had not foreseen, a surprise, an accident, an unthinkable fluke, or a last-minute maneuver. It stands to reason that a sociologist cannot hope to foretell the results of an election with greater certainty than that of a physicist foretelling the results of the most ordinary experiments with the pendulum. The physicist is not at all certain of those results; he knows that the experiment with the pendulum can go wrong, the wire of the pendulum can break. Certainly the law of the pendulum will remain nonetheless true; but that airy consolation cannot content our sociologist, who hoped to predict a sublunary event, the real result of the elections, which is unwarranted.

Scientific laws do not prophesy that Apollo XI will come down on the Sea of Tranquillity (it is, however, what a historian wishes to know); they foretell that it will come down there, because of Newtonian mechanics, unless there is a breakdown or an accident.[21] They lay down their conditions and predict only under those conditions, "all things being equal," according to the formula dear to economists. They determine the fall of bodies, but in a vacuum; the mechanical systems, but without friction; market equilibrium, but in perfect competition. It is by separating themselves from concrete situations that they can function as formally as a mathematical formula; their generality is the consequence of that withdrawal, and does not come from putting a singular case in the plural.

Those truths are certainly not a revelation, but they prevent us from following Stegmüller, who, in a book of which it is a pleasure to declare the importance, the clarity, and the moderation, maintains that the difference between the historical explanation and the scientific explanation is only a nuance. The dislike of historians for admitting that they explain by laws would come either from the fact that they employ them without realizing it, or that they limit themselves to "explanatory sketches" in which laws and data are formulated vaguely and very incompletely. For this incompleteness, Stegmüller goes on, there is more than one reason: the laws may be contained implicitly in the explanation, as when the actions of a historical personage are explained by his character or his motives; at other times generalizations are considered to be self-evident, especially when they are drawn from everyday psychology; it happens, too, that the historian considers that his role is not to excavate the technical or scientific aspects of a detail in history. But above all, it is very often impossible, in the present state of science, to formulate laws with precision: "One has only the approximate representation of an underlying regularity or else the law cannot be formulated, because of its complexity."[22]

We totally agree with this description of the historical explanation, except that we do not quite see what is gained by calling it a "sketch" of scientific explanation; in that case, all that men have always thought is a sketch of science. Between the historical explanation and the scientific explanation there is not a nuance but an abyss, because a leap is needed to pass from one to the other, because science demands a conversion, and because a scientific law is not drawn from an everyday maxim.

The Supposed Laws of History

The supposed laws of history, or of sociology, not being abstract, do not have the smudgeless sharpness of a physics formula; therefore they do not function very well. They have no existence in themselves, but only by implicit reference to the concrete context; each time we express one, we are ready to add: "I was speaking in general terms, but I obviously leave room for exceptions and also for the unexpected." It is with them as with the sublunary concepts "revolution" and "middle class"; they are laden with all the concreteness from which they have been drawn, and have not broken the bridges with it. Concepts and historicosociological "laws" have no meaning and no interest save for the surreptitious exchanges that they continue to make with the concrete that they govern;[23] it is precisely by these exchanges that one recognizes that a science is not yet a science.

When I speak of work in statics, I can and must forget what "work" means in everyday usage; the work of physicists, which bears this name only because it had to be given one, is nothing other than the product of a force times the projection of the displacement on the direction of the force; like all scientific objects it is its definition. Science has as its object its own abstractions; to discover a scientific law is to discover, beyond the visible, an abstraction that functions. On the contrary, the "work" of what is experienced cannot be defined; it is only the name given to a concrete thing of which one can at most evoke the confused richness with a virtuoso stroke of the phenomenological pen. It will be defined only to evoke for the reader the memory of that concrete thing, which remains the only authentic text. The *ktèma es aei* thus cannot be formulated independently from an eventworthy context. Let us suppose that the *ktèma* teaches us laws about the revolution, the middle class, or the nobility; the concepts in question having no defined sense and receiving one only from the facts to which they are applied, the *ktèma* would not even be comprehensible without a context.

If we want to know through what space a body falling into a vacuum will pass, we mechanically apply the appropriate formula without wondering what motivations may, in accordance with all we know of apples, move a falling apple through space at a speed proportionate to the square of the time. If we need, on the other hand, to know what lower-middle-class people threatened by big capital will do, we shall not have recourse to the corresponding law, even a materialist one—or, rather, it will be advanced only as a credo or a memory jogger. Rather, we shall repeat to ourselves the reasons that urge the lower middle classes to try, in such a case, to find help in an alliance with the proletariat; we shall expound them according to what we know of those lower middle classes; we shall comment upon what motivates them; and we shall reserve the case in which, because they are too individualistic or blind to their interest, or heaven knows what else, they would not do what was expected of them.

History Is Description

The historical explanation is not nomologic, it is causal; as causal, it contains something general. What is not a chance coincidence has a tendency to reproduce itself; but one cannot state exactly either what will reproduce itself or under what conditions. Compared with the explanation that is characteristic of the sciences, physical or human, history appears like mere description[24] of what has happened; it explains how things happened, it helps us to understand that. It relates how an apple fell from the tree: that apple was ripe, or the wind rose and a gust shook the apple tree; but it is science that reveals why the apple fell. One could try in vain to give a very detailed account of the fall of an apple but never discover the attraction, which is a hidden law that had to be discovered; at most one would reach the truism that unsupported objects fall.

History describes what is true, what is concrete, experienced, sublunary; science discovers what is hidden, abstract, and capable of being formalized. Scientific objects are foreign to our world, they are not the fall of bodies, the rainbow, or the lodestone, which were only the point of departure of the investigation; rather, they are formal abstractions, attraction, quanta, or the magnetic field.

To bring experienced causality and scientific causality to the same logic is to affirm too poor a truth; it is to fail to recognize the abyss that separates the *doxa* from the *epistémé*. Certainly all logic is deductive, and it must be admitted that an assertion relating to Louis XIV logically implies a major premise: "Every tax makes for unpopularity"; psychologically that major premise is foreign to the mind of the spectator of history, but it is not fitting to confuse logic and the psychology of knowledge. And it no more is right to confuse logic and the philosophy of knowledge, although the sacrifice of that philosophy to logic or to psychology is one of the constant features of empiricism.

Logical empiricism has the handicap of all empiricism: it fails to recognize the abyss between the *doxa* and the *epistémé,* between the "experienced" historical fact (the fall of that apple or of Napoleon) and the abstract scientific fact (attractions).[25] So now we are in a position to show that the historical explanation is not a scientific "explanatory sketch" that is still imperfect, and to say why history will never become a science: it is chained to the causal explanation from which it sets out. Even if the human sciences discovered numberless laws tomorrow, history would not be overthrown, but would remain what it is.

Science As Interference

Yet, it will be said, does not history already invoke scientific laws and truths? When we say that a people armed with iron conquered a people armed with bronze, are we not referring to a metallurgical knowledge that can give an exact account of the superiority of arms of iron? Can we not invoke meteorological science to explain the disaster of the Armada?[26] Since the facts to which scientific laws apply exist in experience—indeed, in what other sphere could they exist?—who prevents those laws from being invoked when they are related? So, as science gradually progresses, it will be enough to complete or to correct the explanatory sketches of historians. Unfortunately, that hope misses the main point. History does indeed invoke laws, but it does not do so automatically, just because those laws have been discovered: it invokes them only *where those laws play the part of causes* and are put into the sublunary plot. When Pyrrhus is killed by a tile that an old woman flings at his head, kinetic energy will not be invoked to explain the reason for the effects. On the other hand, the historian will very rightly say, "A macroeconomic law known today explains the economic failure of the Popular Front, yet it remained an enigma to contemporaries who could not avoid it."[27]

History has recourse to laws only when the latter complete the ranks of causes, become causes. Causality is not an imperfect legality, but an autonomous and complete system; it is our life. The world we see is experience, but in it we use scientific knowledge in the form of technical recipes; the historian's use of laws to explain that which is experienced is of the same order. In both cases the historian or the technician starts from the sublunary to reach sublunary effects by utilizing scientific knowledge. Like our life, history, starting from the earth, returns to earth.

If the law does not play the role of a cause, if it only explains an effect already understood, it is a worthless gloss for which history has no use: "Napoleon was ambitious; ambition is explained, as we know, by the presence of one link too many in the deoxyribonucleic acid" would be only a gloss, just as kinetic energy would be in the case of Pyrrhus: the scientific explanation of ambition is knowledge from heaven, and in this matter is of only fairly Platonic interest. On the other hand, "the Corsican customs concerning swaddling and weaning made the future Napoleon the ambitious man we know" would be a historically pertinent explanation; a sublunary fact—too early weaning—by a circuit that anthropological science was to discover one day, ends in a no less sublunary effect—the ambition of the Ogre of Corsica—and, so to speak, falls on our head. To have recourse to the graceful language of atomic ballistics, history, like technics, acknowledges ground-to-ground trajectories (the ambition of Napoleon explains his policies) and ground-air-ground ones (weaning is the scientific explanation of that ambition), but not the air-ground trajectory (Pyrrhus has a fractured head? That is kinetic energy).

I have just seen a documentary film on the Popular Front; I have here the *Histoire économique de la France entre les deux guerres* by A. Sauvy and the *Theory of Political Coalitions* by W. H. Riker.[28] I undertake to relate the successes and failures of the Front; in 1936 an electoral coalition is formed and triumphs: its economic policy will be a failure. The causes of that coalition are clear: they include the fascist thrust to the right and deflation. To add to that twenty pages of the mathematics of the interplay of coalition, which would explain why people who form a coalition do what they do, would be to gloss what is clear; the theory of Riker is thus useless for history—or at least for the plot I have separated out of it. On the other hand, how is the economic failure to be explained? I do not see its causes: Sauvy says that they are to be sought in a macroeconomic law that was unknown in 1936; through that law a sublunary event (the 40-hour week) ends in a no less sublunary effect.

But let us suppose that I have chosen as a plot not the Popular Front, but a subject from comparative history: "coalitions through the centuries"; I shall see if the coalitions correspond with the optimum calculated by the theory of games, and Riker's book will be historically pertinent. Kinetic energy is pertinent to the explanation of an enormous historical event, the acquisition of the most ancient of techniques: that of projectiles, known to the *Sinanthropus,* even to higher apes. The choice of plot decides supremely what will or will not be causally relevant; science can make all the progress it wants, but history clings to its fundamental option, according to which the cause exists only through the plot. For such is the real meaning of the notion of causality. Let us suppose that we have to state the cause of a car accident. A car has skidded after braking on a wet, cambered road: to the police, the cause is excessive speed or worn tires; to the Department of Bridges and Highways, the high camber; to the head of a driving school, the law, not understood by learners, which requires that the distance for braking increases more than proportionately with the speed; for the family, it is fate, which willed it should rain that day or that this road existed for the driver to come and be killed there.

History Will Never Be Scientific

But, it will be said, isn't the truth quite simply that all causes are true, that the right explanation is the one that takes account of them all? Not exactly, and that is the sophism of empiricism: to think that the concrete can be reconstituted by adding scientific abstractions. The number of causes that can be separated is infinite, for the simple reasons that sublunary causal comprehension, otherwise called history, is a description, and that the number of possible descriptions of the same event is indefinite. In a given plot the cause will be the *absence* of the warning "Slippery road" at that spot; in another, the fact that touring cars have no parachute brake. One of two things can happen: when we want a complete causal explanation, we speak either of sublunary causes (there was no warning and the driver was going too fast) or of laws (kinetic energy, the coefficient of the grip of the tires). In the first hypothesis the complete explanation is a myth comparable to that of the geometrical figure of an event integrating all the plots. In the second the complete explanation is an ideal, a regulating idea linked to that of universal determinism;

it cannot be put into practice and, if it could, then the explanation would soon cease to be manageable. (For example, we cannot even calculate the movements of the car's suspension on a cambered road; we can indeed write down double and triple integrals, but at the cost of such simplifications—the suspension will be supposed to have no springs and the wheels to be completely flat—that the theory will be worthless.)

If a complete determination of experience were possible, then it would be impossible and dull to write history. Impossible, because the number and the complexity of the explanations would make them no longer manageable. Dull, because the mysterious economic law governing thought demands that an event for which one has the law now be only an anecdote for us: physics is a body of laws, it is not a collection of exercises and problems. A scientific history would produce the ridiculous effect caused by a certain problem in physics that generations of students have known as "the problem of the muddy cyclist": calculate on what part of the back of a cyclist a bit of mud flung up by a wheel falls (the void, uniform speed, and a perfectly flat road are taken for granted). Or else that dullness would not be: as experience would continue, despite all explanations, to keep its consistency in our eyes, we would go on writing history as before. What erects a barrier between history and science is not attachment to individuality or relationship with values, or the fact that John Lackland will not come that way again: it is the fact that the *doxa,* what is experienced, and the sublunary are one thing; that science is another; and that history is on the side of the *doxa.*

So there are two extreme solutions, in the presence of an event: either to explain it as a concrete fact, to make it "understood," or to explain only certain selected aspects of it, but to explain them scientifically—in short, to explain a great deal, but badly, or to explain a few things, but to explain them well. Both cannot be done at the same time, for science gives an account of only a minute part of the concrete. It starts from laws it has discovered, and of the concrete it knows only the aspects that correspond with those laws: physics resolves problems of physics. History, on the other hand, starts from the plot it has separated, and its task is to make that plot fully understood instead of cutting a made-to-measure problem out of it. The scientist will calculate the effects of coalition on a nonnull sum; regarding the Popular Front, the historian will tell of its formation and will have recourse to theorems only in the very limited number of cases where it would be necessary for a more complete understanding.

The Only Place for Science: The Unintentional Effects

But, finally, what prevents these two extreme solutions from being combined? From our keeping up with the progress of science and gradually replacing comprehensive explanations by scientific explanations, as logical empiricism wants us to? Nothing prevents it, except that the mixture thus obtained would be incoherent, that it would be repugnant to a kind of intellectual need for orderliness, for which it is not enough that propositions be true; let us think again of those relating to the skull of Pyrrhus and to kinetic energy, and we will be satisfied on that point. It is not enough for a truth to have been discovered; it has still to enter into the sublunary system of history without deforming it. We here perceive an artistic level that underlies every intellectual activity: everything happens as if the exercise of thought arose not only from the ideal of truth but also from an ideal of good management that demands that the solutions adopted should be coherent, stable, economical. It is probably at this management level of intellectual activity that there is a relationship, for example, with the idea, as undefinable as indeclinable, of the "beauty" of a language or of a philosophy or of mathematics. Among the inexhaustible interplay of mathematical structures, the infinite number of the systems of compossibles, certain structures are more interesting, instructive, fruitful than others—it is hard to know what adjective to use—fruitfulness and beauty seeming here to be joined by mysterious bonds.[29] It is also this art of intellectual management that forbids mixing history and science, except in the cases where science is called upon by history's own system.

But which are these cases? On what criterion is orderliness in history based? On the criterion of our intentions. One of the most striking features of social life is that nothing ever happens as foreseen, that there is always a great or small interval between our intentions and events—expressed otherwise, that our intentions are not coupled directly with events. The nurse who bound the swaddling clothes of the Bonaparte baby too tightly *did not know* that she was preparing the disasters of 1813, and Blum *did not know* that he was making economic recovery impossible. This interval between the intention and the effect is the place that we reserve for science, when we are writing history and when we are making it. To throw this rough draft into the waste basket, or near it, it is enough for me to will it; to launch a rocket to the moon, the intention is not enough: we appeal to science; to explain the incomprehensible failure of Blum, we appeal to economics.

Like contemplation, science applies itself to giving us explanations of everything, even if we have no use for its explanations; but, in our action, as well as in the knowledge of our action, which is history, we appeal to science only when intentions no longer suffice.[30] Does that mean that history has deliberately decided to see man with human eyes, to take his goals as an irreducible reality, to be a mere re-cognition of what he has experienced? Not at all: let us not take for a goal in itself what is only a measure of administrative prudence; let us not attribute to an existential attitude an option that raises an ideal of intellectual beauty. There is, on the one hand, the sublunary point of view, which, as we see it, is essentially articulated in relation to our intentions; on the other hand, there is the point of view of the *epistémé*, which those intentions do not escape. What must we choose?

The exercise of reason obeys two criteria: truth and the art of management. It is clear that if we had the means of knowing the whole truth about ourselves and of seeing the hidden springs of our intentions, we would not conceal this sight and charitably fling Noah's mantle over it; if we wanted to, we couldn't: from the moment an *epistémé* of history is possible, the historical *doxa* will no longer be anything but an anecdote and an error to us. So when we have a fully equipped human science at our disposal, history will only have to move as quickly as possible from the *doxa* where it lodges at present. But when shall we have that science? So long as a critical threshold is not reached (and it never will be) where that which is experienced can be broadly and conveniently exchanged for the formal, where the explanations of science will be sufficiently complete while remaining sufficiently manageable (which is contradictory), sound management will forbid history to move house, for that would end in chaos.

History is not a science because it is on the side of the *doxa*, and it will remain on that side through a kind of law of coherence. Physical and human sciences can make all possible progress: history will not thereby be modified in its basis; indeed, it will not use the discoveries of the sciences except in a very precise case: *when those discoveries permit us to explain an interval between the intentions of the agents and the results.*

Appendix

The Everyday and the Arranging in Series

"Arranging in series" (the method that consists in gathering, in order to interpret a fact, the greatest possible number of occurrences of that fact: gathering up all the uses of a given word in the extant texts, or all the examples of a custom) is dear to historians and to philologists for many reasons (even when they practice it unknowingly—indeed, like more than one "literary man," without wanting to know it). But among these reasons there is one of such considerable importance, in giving its everyday appearance to that which is experienced and to historiography its seal of authenticity, that we must dwell on it. That reason is that according to whether the occurrences collected are more or less in number, we conclude from them that, for the period being studied, the fact, the custom, the word whose occurrences have been collected, determined or did not determine the *norm* of the period.

Now, in the view people have of their own period, that idea of the norm is of great importance: it gives to their surrounding world its air of familiarity, of everydayness; and that consciousness of everydayness comes to them from the same method of arranging in series that their future historian will use in writing their history. Induction has taught them to make a distinction, in what surrounds them, between the banal phenomena and the peculiarities that stand out clearly. So great is the importance of that impression of everydayness that it is hardly an exaggeration to say that historiography can be summed up in its re-creation of the everyday banality of the past. Let us even go so far as to claim that having a feeling for banality certainly distinguishes a good historian from a less good one.

In our perception of the natural world and of our own society, all determinations "refer to a *normality of experience* that can vary from one universe to the other. In the tropics 'cold' weather means something different than it does in the temperate zone; a 'fast' vehicle, at the time of the stagecoach, something different than in a century of racing cars."[31] We see men and things belonging to our civilization as arranged in types; whence the impression of familiarity they give us. By contrast, an unexpected object will cut across that typology, "where it does not enter a series." Antepredicamental induction has indeed allowed us to constitute a multitude of social, professional, regional types, thanks to which a glance is enough to classify a newcomer. Henceforth, every object will no longer be only what it is; if it does not enter a series, it will further take on a characteristic sense of abnormality.

Thus, to understand the past will suppose that the historian reconstructs in his mind the normality of the period and that he can make it evident to the reader. An event is what it is only in relation to the norms of the period; at every strange fact he reads in history the reader wonders: "Was it as strange to them as to us?" A good historian, by a word or a turn of phrase, will be able to tell him. Even in contemporary history, it is often necessary to re-create normality: recently a historian wrote that in 1970, to make students understand what was shocking about the Ems dispatch, the professor had to put it in a series in the diplomatic style of the day with its immeasurable courtesy. It is here that the truth of the frequently misunderstood affirmation, according to which a period has to be judged by its values, must be sought.

And now let us draw attention to a procedure frequently serving to rouse in the reader that impression of the normality of a period whose meaning might be exaggerated. Let us suppose that I write the following propositions: "Astrology, among cultured Romans, occupied almost exactly the same place that psychoanalysis held with us in the days of surrealism"; "the ancients were very keen on circus spectacles, just as we are on cars." Do I thereby claim that circus and cars satisfy the same anthropological "need"? Or that, following the example of ethnographers, we have to invent a historical category called *focalization*,[32] which will serve as a storeroom for all the phenomena of collective passion whose only common feature is that they astonish societies that do not share that passion? Not at all; I merely mean, by comparing astrology or the circus with contemporary things (which perhaps bear a very vague resemblance to those phenomena) to rouse in the reader the impression that the circus and astrology were felt by the Romans to be as *normal* as what we feel in a passion for cars or psychoanalysis. The reader does not have to exclaim, "How can one be a Roman?"; he does not have to lose his way among turgid speculations on the mass media and antique "modernity."[33] He must feel that, seen from the inside, "to be a Roman" is only very banal.

There are history books that excel in re-creating this everydayness—that is, in making things live; Marc Bloch excelled at it. Others, whom one may like less, present us with a past that is, on the contrary, stranger, sometimes more marvelous, at other times more suspect: anyone who has read anything by Nilsson or A. D. Nock, or by Cumont, will take the hint. If normality is ignored, if the feeling of everydayness is misunderstood or even systematically avoided, that produces the world of Salammbo; that also gives the mixing of the marvelous and of the gibberish of more than one description in ethnography, evoking for us a world of primitives as "barbarous" as the Carthaginians in Flaubert and as improbable as the dreams of Madame Bovary, in which happiness, Naples, and moonlight assumed the density of metal.

Now that does not trouble the reader, for the reader of history knows that history is banal like our everyday life. He knows a priori that, if a god undertook to transport him into another historical period, it would be impossible for him to foresee how he would be occupied in that period: a potlatch, or a battle of flowers, or a crusade, or management. On the other hand, he is sure that he would everywhere find the same everyday style, the same grayness, the same kind of distance in relation to himself and the world that would resound in his soul with an ever future hollowness. The same battle of flowers or the same crusade that seemed surprising to him a minute earlier, when the god had settled him in his new body, seems to him absolutely normal, once he is settled in. From this comes the half-illusion that man has a privileged understanding of man; that, if we explain nature, we "understand" man, we can put ourselves in his place. What is true in this idea is that we know, vaguely or expressly, that the sense of normality plays the same role in the vision of our fellow men as in ours; what, on the other hand, no introspection and no understanding will reveal to us is what that normality is for a given period.

Chapter IX

Consciousness Not the Root of Action

In the study of causality that we have just seen, we made no distinction between material causality (one idea drives out another) and human causality (Napoleon made war because he was ambitious, or to satisfy his ambition); for if we consider only the effects, it is scarcely useful to make this distinction. Man is as consistent as the forces of nature and, inversely, the forces of nature are as irregular and capricious as he is: there are souls of bronze, there are also men and women whose caprices are like those of the waves. As Hume put it:

If we consider how exactly physical and moral phenomena are interlocked to form but a single chain of reasons, we shall have no scruples in admitting that they are alike in nature and that they derive from the same principles; a prisoner being led to the scaffold foresees his death as a consequence as certainly of the firmness of his jailers as of the hardness of the axe.

But there is a huge difference between the axe and the jailers; we pay no attention to the axe, except perhaps in our childhood, whereas we know that men have intentions, aims, values, deliberations, goals, or anyhow else we care to name it. The result is that, in the experience of the historian, human acts occupy a separate place and pose a great number of delicate problems; it is one of the areas where, at present, we feel most keenly that our experience is still too confused and crude—which is tantamount to saying it is now becoming refined and more precise. These problems are numerous: sociology of knowledge, ideology, and infrastructures; value judgments in history; rational and irrational modes of behavior; mentalities and structures—in a word, all the problems of the relations between historical consciousness and action, which, in our present preoccupations, have as big a place as the problem of the relations between soul and body in classical philosophy.

This chapter is much less a sketch of a few aspects of this problematic that it would take volumes merely to set forth; we have sought to suggest but two things: that for a dualist vision (infrastructure and superstructure, mentality and reality) there should be substituted the differential description of particular situations in which the relations between thought and action change from case to case; in short, a casuistic should be elaborated—one hopes a subtle one, for problems that are no less so. Then, that the task of a historian is less to demystify ideologies, to reveal that they hide something else or to say what they hide, than to prepare an original chapter of historical criticism, which, considering the ideologies, mentalities, and any other expressions as outlines, would say precisely what order of facts it is allowable or not allowable to reconstitute from outlines of this kind; a slogan or a proverb is not treated in the same way as a theoretical study or an intonation that betrays the speaker.[1]

Understanding Others

Since we know that an axe has no intentions, but that a man has, and since we are men ourselves, must we not conclude first that our knowledge of man and his works does not follow the same paths as our knowledge of nature, and that reason is not one of those paths? "We explain things, but we understand men," said Dilthey: to him that understanding was an intuition sui generis. It is the point that we must examine first.

Besides the attraction of anthropocentrism, Dilthey's theory of comprehension owes its success to the contradictory character of our experience of man; the latter constantly surprises us, but at the same time he seems to us quite natural. When we try to understand bizarre behavior or an exotic custom, there comes a moment when we declare: "Now I have understood, I need seek no further"; everything appears to happen as if we had in our mind a certain innate conception of man and we cannot rest until we have discovered it in human behavior. We do not perceive that our attitude is the same toward things (when the first moment of astonishment is over, we resign ourselves to admitting everything that happens); that the impression that we have understood, that we have got it right, is an illusion that has also played its part in the discussions on the epistemology of mathematics.[2] We take the resistance of historical or mathematical language to be a resistance of the real, and we take for an intuition the satisfaction of at last having exactly formulated the phrase that encompasses the idea we have of things. Finally, we do not think that, although we flatter ourselves that we understand man, we understand him only after the event, as we do with nature, and that all our supposed intuition does not allow us to foresee, or to "retrodict," or to decree that a given custom (or a given marvel of nature) is or is not impossible. We willingly forget that, as Malraux frankly states, to know men is to be not surprised by them after the event. Forgetting all that, we flatter ourselves that we understand others by a direct method that could not be applied to nature: we can put ourselves in the place of our fellows, get into their skin, "relive" their past. That opinion irritates some as much as it seems obvious to others—that is, it mingles several different ideas that we must try to separate.

First, historians are constantly in the presence of mentalities different from our own, and they are well aware that introspection is not the right method of writing history; our innate understanding of others (a baby from birth knows what a smile means, and answers it with a smile) encounters its limits so quickly that one of the first tasks of iconography is to decipher the meaning of the gestures and of the expression of emotions in a given civilization. The impression of *post eventum* evidence given us by human conduct is undeniable, but that given to us by natural phenomena is the same; if we are told that a proud man overcompensates for his timidity, that a timid man reacts against his proud impulses, or that it is no use preaching to a hungry man, we understand that very well—and we equally understand that two billiard balls knocking against each do what they are doing.[3]

Psychological understanding admits no guessing and no criticism; it is the disguise of an invocation of common sense or of the eternal man, who, for more than a century of history and ethnography, has known nothing but contradictions. The effort to "get into the skin of another" may have heuristic value; it allows us to find ideas or, more frequently, phrases to translate ideas in a "living way"—that is, to transform an exotic sentiment into one that is more familiar. However, it is not a criterion, a means of verification;[4] it is not true that, in the human domain, truth must be *index sui et falsi*. Dilthey's method of understanding is only the mask of popular psychology or of our prejudices; daily life shows quite well how much blunderers undertaking to explain their neighbor's character end up by betraying their own through attributing to their victims their own motivations and, above all, the phantasms of their fears.

It must be admitted that the simplest historical explanation (the king made war for love of glory) is only, for most of us, a hollow phrase that we know only because we have read it in books; we are rarely prepared to experience in ourselves or to ascertain *de visu* the reality of that royal taste and to decide if it is real or only a phrase of conventional psychology. We shall believe its reality when we have read the documents from the reign of Louis XIV in which it sounds sincere, or when we have established that there is no other possible explanation for certain wars. In ourselves, all that we find to shed light on the debate are beginnings of vanity and of ambition, from which we would have to be a Shakespeare to infer sentiments that would prove the royal condition; we can use them to give life to a popular book, but not to settle a point of history. Mimesis is too facile, and we put ourselves into the skin of any role, if it has previously been traced out for us; that is why historians of religion do not succeed in deciding if what is said of the ancient belief in the divinity of the emperor is humanly plausible; they are reduced to accusing each other, in private, of lacking religious sensitivity or a sense of reality. Very fortunately, there is no need to bear in oneself the soul of another person in order to understand it, and St. Teresa makes the mystical experience admirably understood by those who have never had ecstasies (and their name is legion). The idea that man understands man means only that we are ready to believe anything of him, as of nature; if we learn something fresh, we make a note of it. And "so the spiritual marriage of the Seventh House exists, as we are told in the *Castle of the Soul*; we will remember it in case of need, in the course of our work." Comprehension is a retrospective illusion.

Second, what of "to relive" another, to relive the past? It is but a phrase (writing a book of Roman history, I would very much have liked, even for a moment, to replace within me the ideas and preoccupations of a teacher of Latin with those of a Roman freedman, but I did not know how to go about it)—or, rather, it is an illusory and deceptive experience. Can one relive the sentiments of a Carthaginian who sacrifices his first-born son to the gods? That sacrifice is explained by the examples that our Carthaginian saw around him and by a general piety that was intense enough not to recoil at those atrocities; the Carthaginians were as conditioned by their surroundings to sacrifice their first-born as we are to drop atomic bombs on people.

If, in order to understand the Carthaginian, we consider what motives might incite us, living in our civilization, to behave like him, we shall suppose intense feelings where, for the Carthaginian, there was merely conformity; it is one of the most frequent illusions of a certain manner of writing the history of religions, the illusion by which one does not recognize that all conduct stands out from a background of the normality, of the everydayness of its period. We cannot relive the state of mind of the Carthaginian because only the smallest part of consciousness is active and because, in short, there is almost nothing to relive. If we could enter into his thought, we would find there only an intense and monotonous feeling of sacred horror, a colorless terror and a taste of nausea, indistinctly accompanied by the mechanical feeling that is in the background of almost all our actions: "it is done" or "what alternative is there?"

We Know That Men Have Goals

Third, the knowledge of others is mediate; we infer it from the behavior and expressions of our neighbors, taking into account the experience we have of ourselves and of the society in which we live. But that is not the whole truth; it must be added that to man, man is not an object like others. Men, like animals of the same species, recognize each other as fellows; each knows that his neighbor is, within himself, a being like him. And, in particular, he knows that his neighbor has, as he has, intentions, goals; so he can act as if the behavior of the other were his own. As Marrou says, man is at home in all that is human; he knows a priori that behavior in the past has the same horizon as his own, even if he does not know exactly what a given mode of behavior meant: at least he knows in advance that that behavior had a meaning. So our tendency is to anthropomorphize nature and not to do the opposite. It is this comprehension that Marc Bloch set as an ideal for historical science in a page that makes historians tremble for their safety as a phrase of St. Paul made Luther tremble:

Behind the perceptible features of the landscape, the tools or the machines, behind the writings that seem the most frozen and the institutions that seem the most completely detached from those who established them, it is men that the historian wants to comprehend. Whoever does not succeed in that will never be but an unskilled laborer of scholarship. The good historian himself is like the ogre of the legend: where he smells human flesh, he knows that there is his quarry.[5]

Comprehension is not an instrument of discovery, a tripod of the fortune teller (that tripod is the arranging in series), nor is it a criterion of the true and the false, but it allows the goals and the "deliberations" of men to be reconstituted. A page from Taine, who has been so slandered, almost expresses it:

The first operation in history consists in putting oneself in the place of the men whom one wishes to judge, to enter into their instincts and into their habits, to espouse their feelings, to rethink their thoughts, to reproduce within oneself their inner state, to imagine minutely and in one's own body their milieu, to follow in imagination. . . .

We are tempted to interrupt the quotation, for a scientist interpretation will now take the place of deliberations and aims:

[to follow in imagination] the circumstances and impressions that, in conjunction with their innate character, determined their action and guided their lives.

Such a work,

putting one into the viewpoint of the men whose history one is relating, allows one the better to understand them and, since it is composed of analyses, it is, like every scientific operation, capable of verification and perfection.

. . . But We Do Not Know Which Goals

But even if we know a priori that men have goals, we cannot guess which ones. When we know their goals, we can put ourselves in their places, understand what they wanted to do; taking into account what they, at that moment, could guess of the future (they could still hope that Grouchy would arrive in time), we can reconstitute their "deliberations." Supposing, however, that their maxims were rational or at least that we know the way in which they were irrational. On the other hand, if we do not know their goals, introspection will never give them to us or will give us false ones; proof *a contrario*: no goal of a man can surprise us. If I note that when Napoleon joins battle, he tries to win it, nothing seems more understandable; but I am told of a strange civilization (an imaginary one, needless to say, but hardly stranger than many an exotic civilization or than our own) in which, when a general meets the enemy, custom demands that he make every effort to lose the battle. Disconcerted for a moment, I shall quickly find an explanatory hypothesis ("that must be explained a bit like potlatch; in any case, there is surely some humanly comprehensible explanation"). Instead of applying to that civilization the law "Every military leader prefers to win the battle," I shall apply another, more general one: "Every leader and even every man does what the custom of his group prescribes for him to do, however surprising it may appear." One thing leads to another, and our understanding of the man can be summed up in this proposition: "Man is what he is, we must resign ourselves to that, which is to understand him." Such is the secret of history, of sociology, of ethnography, and of other non-deductive sciences.

Thus, the only virtue of the method of understanding is to show us the bias according to which all conduct will appear explicable and banal to us; but it does not allow us to say, of several more or less banal explanations, which is the right one.[6] Indeed, if we cease to give the word "understand" the value of a technical term given to it by Dilthey, and if we come back to its meaning in daily life, we note that to understand is either to explain an action starting from what we know of other people's values ("Durand grew angry at the sight of that presumptuousness; I understand him because I have the same ideas as he has on presumption" or "I don't have the ideas I know him to have on that") or else to understand is *to get information* on other people's goals, perhaps by "retrodiction" and reconstruction. I see Polynesians throwing tin plates into the lagoon of the atoll, and I wonder at it. I am told "It is a competition in prestige, in destruction of wealth; for them that prestige counts for much." Henceforth I know their goals, I understand their mentality.

Value Judgments in History . . .

Thus, the great problem is to learn what were the goals of people, their values, in order to decipher or to "retrodict" their conduct. That means that we shall not escape the problem of value judgments in history. A problem we put now in an epistemological form (Does historiography constitutively include value judgments? Is it possible to write history without judging?), now in a deontological form (Has the historian the right to judge his heroes? Must he remain impassive as Flaubert did?). In this second form the problem very quickly breaks down into moralizing considerations: the historian must become the advocate of the past in order to understand it; must write *laudes Romae* if he is a historian of Rome, must sympathize; or, it will be asked if he has the right to be a party man, "not to attach the same price to what is born and to what is dying," as they like (or used to like) to say in the Party, and to center his plot on the proletariat rather than on the Third Estate, alleging that this centering is more "scientific" than any other. To restrict ourselves to the first formulation of the problem, which is purely epistemological, I believe I discern four aspects of the question, the fourth of which is a very delicate one that will occupy us to the end of this chapter.

First, "the historian has not to judge." Certainly, by definition, history consists in saying what happened and not in judging if what happened is good or bad. "The Athenians did this and the Peloponnesians did that": to add that they acted badly would add nothing and would fall outside the subject. The thing is so evident that, if we come across, in a history book, a development of praise or blame, our eyes jump over it—or, rather, it is so anodyne that at other times it would be artificial to avoid those developments and not to say that the Aztecs or the Nazis were cruel; in short, all that is only a question of style. So, writing military history, for example, if we study the maneuvers of a general and find that he makes blunder after blunder, we will be able either to speak of him with a chilling objectivity or to pronounce the word "blunder" more charitably.[7]

Since history is concerned with what has been, and not with what should have been, it remains quite indifferent to the terrible and eternal problem of value judgments—that is, to the old question of knowing if virtue is knowledge and if there can be a science of goals: can we demonstrate a goal without relying on a further goal? Does not every goal, in the last resort, rest on pure will that is not bound to be coherent with itself or to will its own survival? (It is not because ultimate goals are goals, values, that we can no more discuss them than we can tastes or colors: it is because they are ultimate;[8] we want them or we don't, and that is all.) Indifferent to this problem, history is also indifferent to the more delicate problem of the "judicial" use of the same value judgments.

For it is not sufficient for an act to be bad in itself for its author consequently to be reputed as bad. Was Saint Louis really as holy as he is said to have been? It will not be enough, to decide that, to demonstrate that the Inquisition was bad (or to want it to be bad without demonstrating it). Nor will it be enough to establish that, de facto, Louis IX was the author of the Inquisition: it will be further necessary to appreciate in what measure Louis IX can be held responsible for his acts, and nothing is more delicate to appreciate than a degree of responsibility. Is the fact that the majority of the king's contemporaries, and in particular his teachers, approved of the burning of heretics an extenuating circumstance, and in what proportion? And if the whole period had approved of it, what would remain, in the end, of the king's responsibility? The question is not easy, nor is it a vain one; it is that of our historicity and of our finiteness. However, it does not interest the historian, who will be content to provide the facts for the tribunal (the moral education of Saint Louis, the moral ideas of his time) without judging the degree of culpability of the king or the good or bad character of the Inquisition.

. . . Are Value Judgments in Indirect Speech

Second, "The historian cannot pass value judgments." Certainly, you might as well aspire to write a novel in which values played no part in the actions of the characters; but those values are not those of the historian or of the novelist: they are those of their heroes. The problem of value judgments in history is not at all that of factual judgments versus value judgments: it is that of value judgments in direct speech.

Let us come back to our clumsy general. The only question for the historian is knowing if what he considers blunders were such to the general's contemporaries: were those maneuvers absurd, according to the criteria of the general staffs of the time or, on the contrary, were they in no way out of step in relation to strategic science of the time? According to our answer, our reconstitution of the deliberations and goals will change entirely: Pompey cannot be reproached for not having read Clausewitz. Assuredly Pompey could have had a stroke of genius, gone beyond the level of his century and had a presentiment of Clausewitz: there is a truth in strategy, as in physics, in economics, and perhaps elsewhere too. Thus the historian will judge with truth that that general did not stand out from the mediocrity of his century, but this true judgment is not a historical proposition; it will not intervene in the reconstitution of the deliberations, and will remain Platonic. So the historian will limit himself to noting that people of the period judged in a particular manner; he may add that we judge otherwise.

The important thing is not to mix the two points of view, as is done when it is affirmed that men of other times have to be "judged" according to the values of their times, which is contradictory; we can only judge on the basis of our own values (but that is not the function of the historian) or report how people of the time judged or would have judged on the basis of their own values.

Third, things are not so simple. Our general deliberated on the basis of strategic principles that his period held to be good, as we have just said; it is nonetheless true that those principles, which were bad, were objectively the cause of his rout. The fact of that rout cannot be explained without giving what is, or appears to be, a value judgment that is, rather, the appreciation of a difference; in order to understand the rout, we must know, the historian will say, that the strategy of that time was not ours. To say that Pompey won at Pharsalus because his strategy was what it was is to enunciate a simple fact, like saying that he was conquered because he had no aviation. Thus the historian gives three kinds of apparent value judgments: he relates the values of the time, he explains behavior according to those values, he adds that those values are different from ours. But he never adds that those values were bad and that we have rightly renounced them.

To state the values of the past is to make a history of values. To explain a rout or the atrocity of sacrificing a child out of ignorance of the true strategic or moral principles is also a factual judgment; it is as if to say that navigation before the fourteenth century is explained by ignorance of the compass—which only means that it is explained by the particular nature of celestial navigation. To register a difference between some values and ours is not to judge them. It is quite true that certain activities—such as ethics, art, and law—have meaning only in relation to norms, and that that is a constant fact; at all times men have distinguished between an act of juridical value and an act of violence, for example. The historian, however, is content to report their normative judgments as facts, without claiming to confirm or to set them aside.

This distinction between value judgments properly so called and value judgments related seems to us very important for our problem. In his fine book *Natural Rights and History,* Leo Strauss forcefully recalls that the existence of a philosophy of law would become absurd if it did not imply a reference to an ideal of truth, beyond all the historic states of law. The antihistoricism of this author recalls that of Husserl in *The Origin of*

Geometry or in *Philosophy as a Rigorous Science;* the activity of the geometer would become absurd if there were not a *geometria perennis* beyond psychologism and sociologism. How can we not believe it? Yet it must be added that the attitude of the historian remains different from that of the philosopher or the geometer. The historian, says Strauss, can only formulate value judgments, otherwise he could not even write history; let us say, rather, that he reports value judgments, without judging those judgments. The presence of a norm of truth in certain activities suffices to justify the philosopher who appeals to that presence and seeks to find what that truth is; for the historian the de facto presence of transcendentals in the hearts of men is only the statement of a fact. Transcendentals give to philosophy or geometry—or to history, which has its ideal of truth—a special appearance of which the historian must take account in order to understand what those who cultivate these disciplines meant to do, when he undertakes to write the history of them.

So we can firmly maintain Weber's principle: the historian never utters value judgments in his own name. Wanting to make Weber contradict himself, Strauss writes something like this:

Weber was indignant with the Philistines who saw no difference between Gretchen and a woman of easy virtue, those who remain insensitive to the nobleness of heart in the former and which is lacking in the latter; so he was pronouncing value judgments, in spite of all he might say.

I protest: there he was making a factual judgment; the value judgment would be to decide if free love is good or bad. The factual difference between Faust's lover and a woman of easy virtue is manifest in all the nuances of her conduct; those nuances may become as subtle as you wish and escape the Philistines (on the other hand, we remember that Swann, without seeing her, touched in passing on the idea that Odette was a tart rather than a fast woman), but they must be discernible, so that they can be verified, under pain of not existing. In that case the value judgment itself would no longer have a fact on which to be based.

Fourth, are we at the end of our difficulties? Can the historian always dispense with judging value judgments? Then he would be reduced, says Leo Strauss, to

bowing without murmuring to the official interpretations of the people he is studying. It would be forbidden for him to speak of morality, religion, art, civilization when he was interpreting the thought of peoples or of tribes to whom those notions are unknown. Similarly, he would officially have to accept as morality, art, religion, knowledge, or state everything that claims to be such. With that limitation, we risk being victims of all kinds of imposture on the part of the men we are studying. Before a given phenomenon, the sociologist cannot be content with the interpretation current in the group in which it takes place. The sociologist cannot be forcibly urged to endorse legal fictions that the group in question has never had the courage to consider as mere fictions; on the contrary he will have to distinguish between the group's idea of its governing authority and the real character of the authority in question.[9]

The extent of the problem raised by these few lines can be seen. They seem to us to be of two kinds:[10] first of all, alongside history properly so called, there exists an axiological history, in which we begin by deciding what things really deserve the name of morality or art or knowledge, before writing the history of those things; the other kind of problem has already been touched on when we saw that we cannot take interested parties at their word when it comes to the interpretation they give of their own society, that the history of a civilization cannot be written through that of its values, that the values are some events among others and not the mental doublet of the body social. We can repeat of the body social and of the historical conscience what Descartes said about the individual conscience: in order to know people's real opinion, you have to pay more attention to the way they act than to what they say, because they do not know their real opinion—the action of thought by which one believes a thing is different from that by which one knows that one believes it. In a word, the historical conscience is not at the root of the action, and it is not always a trail that allows the certain reconstitution of historical behavior; the following pages will call to mind some aspects of this problem of historical criticism and of casuistry.

To a Dualism: Ideology-reality . . .

Let us begin with an anecdote. In the last war, in an occupied country, the rumor spread among the people that one of the armored divisions of the occupying power had been wiped out by an Allied bombardment, and the news roused a wave of joy and hope; but it was false news, and the propaganda of the occupying power had no difficulty in proving it. The people, however, were in no way discouraged, and their feelings of resistance against the occupying power were not weakened. The destruction of the armored division was to them not a reason to hope, but a symbol of hope, and if that symbol proved unusable, they would find another; enemy propaganda (probably directed by a herd-mentality psychologist) merely bore the cost of its posters. That interverted logic of the reasoning of passion seems to confirm Pareto's sociology: the reasoning of people is most frequently the vulgar rationalization of their underlying passions, and those underlying "residues" are readily disguised under their own contraries, provided that they last. That is true, but it is only right to add that they are not underlying, that they are visible and belong to experience like the rest; it will be admitted that, among the occupied people, when one man passed the good news to another, his voice, his attitude, and his eagerness betrayed more passion than if he had passed on a piece of bad news or if he had announced the discovery of a new planet; it would suffice for an observer to have some shrewdness to guess that that was logic pertaining to the passions and what would happen if the story was contradicted.

The Marxist criticism of ideologies[11] is the inflation of practical truths that have always been enshrined in proverbs and that demand little understanding; we readily believe what conforms with our interests and prejudices, we find the grapes too green if they elude our grasp, we confuse the defense of our interests and that of our values, and so on. We will willingly admit that if a liqueur and spirits merchant explains that the harmfulness of alcohol is a legend perfidiously spread by the government, his affirmation disguises a corporate interest; we merely claim that he is not a wizard for seeing that, and it does not deserve to be made into a philosophy of history or even into a sociology of knowledge. And that kind of disguise is not peculiar to politico-social ideas, for why should the sphere of class interests have the inexplicable privilege of falsifying our thought more than every other sphere?

The wisdom of the nations has always known that those lies are everywhere, as much among drunkards, who are interested in alcohol in order to drink it, as among capitalists, who are interested in alcohol in order to sell it. The idea of ideological cover is nothing other than the old theory of sophisms of justification found in Book VII of the *Nicomachean Ethics*: the drunkard who wants to drink holds it as a rule that it is healthy to take refreshment, and this major premise of the syllogism, rightly universal, is its ideological cover; similarly the bourgeois defends his income in the name of universalist principles and invokes Man in his major premise. Marx has rendered historians the immense service of spreading to political ideas the criticism of sophisms of justification, which Aristotle illustrated with examples borrowed in preference from personal ethics; in so doing he has incited historians to sharpen their critical sense, to arm themselves against suspicion of the words of their heroes, to enrich their experience of confessors of the past—in short, to substitute the infinite diversity of practical experience for the sectarian dualism of the theory of ideological covers.

. . . Is Substituted for a Concrete Plurality

From then on, all questions become concrete, and are only a matter of subtlety; the field is open for the La Rochefoucaulds of historical knowledge. Were the Crusades a crusade or disguised imperialism? A crusader goes on a crusade because he is a ruined minor noble, because he is temperamentally adventurous, or because he has felt the enthusiasm of faith or the wind of adventure: these two human types are found in all corps of volunteers. A preacher preaches the crusade as an epic of God. All that is gained more easily in everyday life than in concepts; if the crusader were questioned and replied that he went for the glory of God, he would be sincere, because he felt the need to escape from a hopeless situation. Had it not been for the crisis in ground rent, the preacher would have been less successful; but, were it not for the sacred character of the crusade, only a handful of lost children would have set off. When he goes off, the crusader feels he wants to go and fight; he knows that the crusade is an epic of God because he has been told so, and he expresses what he feels through what he knows—as everyone does.

There is no universal instrument for explaining what would be the theory of superstructures; the affirmation of an essential illusion of ideologies will never dispense us from explaining in what concrete ways, different in every case, nationalism or an economic interest could end up in religion. There could not be any mental alchemy about it; there are only particular explanations, which can be entirely expressed in terms of everyday psychology. Did two peoples really fight to find out if communion should be taken under both species? Contemporaries didn't believe it, when they were sincere; Bacon said very happily that "purely speculative heresies" (which he contrasted with politico-social movements with a religious component, like that of Thomas Münzer) involved unrest only when they became the pretext for political antagonisms.[12]

Only theologians, concerned for the interests of theology, and polemicists and partisans, caring more to put the ideological adversary at a loss than to describe the truth of things, seem to reduce the war to a war of religion. As for the combatants themselves, it was useless for them, in order to fight, to admit the real reasons they had for so doing; it was enough that they had them. Yet, since the rule of the game is not to fight without a flag, they left it to their theologians to provide, as a flag, the one of their reasons that divided them least, or else the one that their pious century was ready to recognize as having the dignity of a flag. It thus happens that a group of "ringleaders" gives the signal for war to a crowd that had its own reasons for fighting and that it preserves the eponym of war: our tendency to judge everything according to the official titles makes us explain the reasons of the majority who are fighting according to those of the minority that voice them. We shall then be caught up in a false dilemma: to affirm that men cannot fight for common theological pretexts, or to affirm that a war of religion is necessarily fought for a religious reason.

A thousand other special cases are conceivable. We note or we think we note[13] that in the United States the antislavery campaign that preceded the Civil War coincided with an economic decline of slavery: a mysterious link between economy and thought? petit-bourgeois idealism that was objectively in the service of the North's capitalism? the law of History that would have it that "humanity only sets itself the problems it can resolve" and that "Minerva's owl wakens only at night"? If the facts were true, they would at most prove that in order to attack an institution that still has all its strength, you would have to be a Utopian, even more than a mere idealist, and that Utopians are even scarcer than idealists and succeed even less in getting themselves talked about. Yet it is undeniable that a group defending its most material interests fairly often uses the most idealist rhetoric; is idealism then a lie and a weapon? But, to begin with, exalted justifications are not the most general case; bad temper, arrogance, and defiance are at least as frequent. Then, that idealism deceives no one and convinces only those who are already convinced; it is not a mystification but conduct called forth by the occasion—it plays the part of "threatening information" meant to let the enemy and possible allies know that one is ready to have recourse to escalation to defend a cause one decrees to be holy. Need we add that people are giving up and are near defeat when they cease to affirm the holiness of their cause? It is, rather, the opposite: they cease to brandish that holiness when they no longer feel able to defend it; the idealistic style then becomes inopportune and the hour of the armistice is close.

Consciousness Is Not the Key of Action

It is only too true that all we say of ourselves betrays, in both meanings of the verb, our praxis; we live without knowing how to formulate the logic of our acts, our action knows of it longer than we do, and the praxeology is implicit in the agent as the rules of grammar are in the reader. Thus, one cannot decently expect the average crusader, Donatist, or bourgeois to be able to express, about the crusade, the schism, or capitalism, a truth that the historian would have great difficulty in formulating. The interval between thought and action is a universal experience; if there were a lie, it would be everywhere: in the artist who professes an aesthetic not exactly that of the *Critique of Judgment,* in the researcher who has no methodology in his method. That is why those concerned— artists, researchers, or the lower middle class—protest when the formulation they give of their reasons is blamed: they who "understand each other" know quite well that they are not lying even when they do not succeed in explaining exactly the unbreakable kernel of darkness that their action is to themselves.

Man's action goes considerably beyond his consciousness of it; most of what he does has no counterpart in thought or in affectivity. Otherwise, enormous "instituted" wholes such as religion or cultural life would be reduced to having as their only authentic counterpart separate moments of emotion in the most delicate part of the soul of a small elite. Generally speaking, man has a nature and is not entirely explained by his history. His species and his works are always and everywhere almost the same—or, more exactly, the gamut of his activities and attitudes is less extensive than we might have expected a priori, and his difficulty in getting out of it is much greater; he is not a being by chance. But we do not see in consciousness a sufficient reason for that limitation, which consciousness accepts, serves, or rationalizes more often than it takes a decision knowingly. We do not know what instinctual programs, what praxeological calculations govern most of our conduct without our knowledge. Everywhere we see men living in groups, tribes, cities, or nations, without these categories answering sociological conditions fixed once for all (natural frontiers, linguistic community, economic solidarity); each of those groupings seems to be an original coalition reaction before a "matrix of stakes" whose content changes from case to case and in which the stakes seem to be of nonabsolute importance, but relative to each other. Everything happens as if the omnipresence of political life was explained by one of those instinctual "programs" we know today in animal ethology, which, instead of being simple reactions to a determined sitmulus, spontaneously look for something to which to give the value of a stimulus. So how can we explain the slowness of history, the stability of nations and of classes, and all that Trotsky called the deep conservatism of the masses, which is, taking all in all, the most striking character of history?

So the greatest part of our conduct is directed by nuances that are the unofficial part of reality: we say we had an instinct, mistrust, repugnance that we cannot explain, or that we liked the look of a particular individual. These nuances often make enormous the interval separating the official title of a political or religious movement from the atmosphere reigning there; that atmosphere is being experienced by the participants without being conceived of, is not observed by the sociologists, whose concerns are more highly scientific and leave practically no written traces. One hour's conversation with a Donatist risen from the ranks would be much more useful than to read the Optat of Milev and the theologians of the sect if anyone wanted to determine the proportions of religion, nationalism, and social revolt in the Donatist sect—but on condition that he took account of the intonations and of the choice of words as well as of the content of the discourses. It would be even better to see some of the practitioners at work; when people are massacred because of religious fanaticism, it is not quite the same as when they are massacred because of social hatred.

If we hardly know how to conceptualize those nuances, our conduct knows very well how to react to them. Whatever we say, a follower of Thomas Münzer or a student at Nanterre does not look like a hearer of Luther or a young metalworker; the time is no longer delayed when the theologians write their *Letter to the German Nobility* and when the trade union councils break with student groups. Not without giving a thousand theological or Leninist explanations for the break. Are they mere pretexts, vulgar rationalizations, ideological cover-ups? No. First, the inability to formulate the real reasons save by authorized symbols; then, a tradition demands that political polemics should always assume a folkloric, stereotyped form as strangely ritual as the simulated battles among animals, as domestic scenes or quarrels between neighbours in southern Italy.[14] It is no doubt a show of strength in which stylistic violence makes the muscles ripple under the superficial reasons; and, at the same time, a desire to stick to an agreed scenario, out of diplomatic prudence and to avoid worse.

But, since there remain chiefly texts of the conflicts of the past, it is to be feared that the greatest part of world history is no longer more to us than a skeleton whose flesh is lost forever. Those taking part are the first to forget the noncomforming truth of what they have done and to see what has been through the rhetoric of what is supposed to have been; J. Norton Cru's book has shown this with the memories of witnesses to the First World War.[15] In historical crises those taking part, if they have time and inclination to observe themselves, feel outrun by what they see and by what they see themselves doing. If they are not deceived by the official explanations given to them or those they give to themselves, all that is left to them, once the event is over, is the astonishment at being so upset over it; more often, they believe all that they say and that their theologians proclaim. That version, friend of memory, becomes the historical truth of tomorrow.[16]

Critique of the Idea of Mentality

Faced with the diversity of this clinical experiment, which often seems a challenge to the sanctuary of consciousness, embarrassed and uneasy: how can we restore to man his inner light and his self-determination? By setting up a dualism: to everything that men do there would correspond thoughts they have in mind; a regiment that fights well does so because it is patriotic at heart. To everything a society does there correspond values: this last word owes the richness of its harmonies to the confusion on which it plays. By "value" we mean both a materialized abstraction (the patriotism of troops) and the values that are taught by positive ethics; to explain a civilization by its values is simultaneously to materialize an abstraction, to identify that fiction with positive values, and finally to apply, in totalitarian fashion, the whole to that civilization: one such society will be bourgeois; another, aristocratic.

We are in the presence of a conventional psychology, frequently denounced, that consists of materializing psychic identities. Must we recall once more that in our heads there is nothing, and that mentality is only another name for conduct? We do not have in our mind the considerations that motivate our actions, and if we nevertheless try to express them, it is only after a fashion; far from having the privilege of knowing better than others what we think, we become our own historians for ourselves, with all the risks that involves. Why did the soldiers at Verdun hold on? Was it patriotism? Fear of court-martial? Solidarity with their comrades? If the right way to find out were to question the survivors, we ought to be able to say if it is moral sense, lack of the courage to murder, or fear of the police that prevents us from murdering our neighbor whose television disturbs us.

The patriotism of the armies of 1916 is certainly a reality, and it is what explains why the French front held out. It can easily be seen when the comparison is made with the troops of 1940, whose morale was ruined and the leaders were unaware of it. However, that patriotism was not present in the minds of the participants in the form of values that they could translate into words (when they do try to translate them, as Apollinaire does, it does not ring true—not because it was insincere, but because it is a psychologist's myth). In the heads of the soldiers at Verdun we would find only the anguish of the coming attack and the idea that the relief party with the canteens would not come that night either. You don't say to yourself "I am going to fight out of patriotism" in the same way you say to yourself "I am going to wind the alarm clock in order to get up early tomorrow."

As for the Nietzschean word for values, it is convenient that it has no well-defined meaning. No society is everything at the same time; each sticks to its table of values, certainly, but where can we find that table? What, for example, can the received idea mean, supported as it is by explicit texts, that ancient societies attached no value to work and held it to be despicable? Our societies, on the contrary, think they hold it to be honorable. But how was that ancient scorn of work translated? Ancient societies were not an Eden, they were hives almost as hard working as ours; "not to work" meant above all "to organize, to direct the work of others." The masses worked with their hands, as we do, and the upper class directed public affairs and, owning the means of production, the work of the masses. The disdain for work was reduced to the fact that there was no hesitation to say "work is despicable," whereas we say modestly that all work is honorable in order to react against our first impulse, which is to think that it is not all equally so. The ancient scorn for work is an interesting theme for the historian of proverbs and of social modesty, but it is not a key opening the reality of the ancient organization of work to us.[17] To describe a society, starting with its values, is too frequently to expose oneself to describing, as exotic and strange, features found everywhere and in our own society, but that are not valued there or are differently valued. In ancient society, as in ours, directing the work of others was esteemed more than working with one's hands; as in ours, studying a science to fill one's leisure time was more exalted than studying it to earn a living.[18]

Values are as much as a conventional psychology as a conventional sociology. The ethics professed by a society do not provide the motives and the grounds for all its actions; they are a localized sector, having relationships with the rest that vary from one society to the other. There are ethics that go no further than school desks or the electoral arena, others that want to make a society different from what it is, others that sanctify what it is, others that console it for not being what it used to be, others that are like those in *Madame Bovary*, as is the case with many aristocratic ethics. For example, in Russia in the last century, the legendary "mad prodigality" of the Russian nobles was perhaps an element of the nobles' conception of a decent life-style, "but those who led it were very few. Through social mimesis the idea of it had spread among the nobility, but most of its members had to be content with only imitating this way of thinking, without sharing the way of life. On the other hand, in the remote corners of the provinces they were free to dream, in private or in public, of the prestigious life-style of a few members of their class, for the greater glory of all who belonged to it."[19] Other ethics are not like those in *Madame Bovary*, but falsely terrorist—for example, Puritanism: "The tendency of Puritans to authoritarianism in sexual matters is explained by the necessity they faced to confine themselves to verbal threats and to persuasion: they lacked the sanctions at the disposal of a Catholic clergy."[20]

As can be seen, our representation of ethical sociology is in process of being made considerably more flexible, just as Greek sculpture, about 470, moved rapidly from stiffness to suppleness in the rendering of anatomy; when a book like Jaeger's *Paideia* speaks monolithically of "the" aristocratic ethics that are the key to "the" preclassical Greece, it henceforth has the effect of a masterpiece whose stiffness is a little archaic.

Casuistry: Four Examples

The realism of history requires the acquisition of that flexibility to face one of the most delicate problems of historical criticism: in what cases can one trust the expression that a society gives of itself? In what other cases is the transparency of the historical consciousness specious? This difficulty has been the stumbling block of the present generation of historians: Marxists coming to grips with the nonautonomous autonomy of superstructures, the School of Archivists with its keen sense of the mentalities of other days, religious phenomenology coming to grips with expressions of a ritual or a symbolical type. Given the empirical diversity of things human, historical criticism in this domain takes the form of a casuistry that is a matter of understanding rather than of theory. We are going to analyze four examples of this case of historical consciousness: rites, which are like a thought that no one thinks; a structure with strong affectivity, that of groups submissive to the authority of the ancients, in which there intervene rationalizations and a "secondary" anxiety that is a consequence while it seems to be the first cause; the very important social type that conventionally we shall call "institution," in which necessity becomes a virtue and in which the relationships of society and of the soul are reversed; and routine, whose apparent absurdity conceals a hidden rationalism.

Rites

Almost everywhere in space and time, village lads or those of the tribe ritually tease the newly married men or demand ritual presents from the groom; almost everywhere in space and time they bury with the dead an entire set of furniture and personal possessions they valued—jewels, weapons, pipes, concubines—and food on the grave: this was done in the time of Homer, in Rome in the most enlightened centuries, and it is done at the present time in the devoutly Catholic Calabria.[21] The *meaning* of these rites is clear: *all happens as if* they thought the dead person continued to live in the tomb, all happens as if the village lads considered the newly married man to be taking a possible wife from them, and wanted vengeance or a ransom. But who really *thinks* that? Not those concerned; it is surely pleasant to tease someone or to receive a ransom, and, if the rite did not exist, the village lads would be quite capable of inventing it if they were numerous enough—besides, they had to invent it the first time. But they no longer exactly invent it; they play it like a rite hallowed by usage, and if the teasing were not hallowed by tradition, they might not be bold enough or inventive enough to improvise it. And if they were asked why they inflict this teasing, they would answer, "Because it is the custom, because it is done."[22]

The meaning of the rite is just present enough to their minds to give their reply a touch of self-justification and to make them feel pleasure when they eagerly bow to the tradition of teasing. But their dominant thought is still piously to respect the custom, a respect that in itself gives a specific satisfaction, the ritualism being an anthropological dimension. You see what the error would be if the rite were taken—a thought that no one thinks—for a thought experienced. It is the error committed by religious phenomenology, whose language cries "false" at the very moment it is literally telling the truth; it is the error committed by anyone who, having brought out the meaning of a rite, takes that meaning for a belief explaining the rite:[23] food was brought to the dead because it was believed they were alive underground. Surely the meaning of the rite remains more or less legible to those taking part in it (just as it is legible to the historian), but those taking part live it out as a rite, as a form of behavior sui generis; if teasing of grooms were not ritual, those being teased would revolt. Since that meaning is not being experienced in the same way as ordinary behavior, it can very well happen that a rite contradicts the religions or the ideas professed by those taking part.

In order to escape (quite uselessly) from this apparent contradiction, the history of religions has created the theory of a degradation of rites; skeptical Rome or mystical Rome of the second century and Calabria today obviously do not believe that the dead remain alive in the tomb—Homer did not believe it.[24] Why, then, bury the dead with their household goods? How can we explain that belief without believers? All we can do is to suppose that before the period of our sources, in the archaic religion, they really believed it and that since then that article of faith has constantly been degraded, the rite alone remaining as a survival—a difference of category that is almost mythically transported at the beginning of time. Rites are born as rites, as can be attested by all those who suffered, in the rue d'Ulm or in the barracks, the teasing reserved for "new boys." It is not at all certain that the most primitive of primitive men ever actually believed that the dead ate and lived underground;

when we think about it, it is even unlikely. But he could not resign himself to the thought that they were dead for good, for he also knew that offerings honor and symbolize, and that rites solemnize; as for those rites, he expressed and rationalized them as he could—for example, by saying that the dead were hungry. We see that primitive men were the first inventors of the history of religions.

The Authority of the Elders

Truth to tell, there are no primitives and no archaism; no human happening has a sure date, and all can be called into existence at any period. Let us consider the old political system, the authority of the elders; as we know, the organization of certain societies (the Australian tribes are the classic example) or of certain institutions is founded on the distinction of classes by age, authority being reserved to the elders, as well as on certain privileges (and even, among the Australians, the possession of women). Is this an archaic phenomenon, evidence of a period in the evolution of humanity? That is to take societies for organisms that have their age, whereas they are continued creations in which everything is contemporary. Let us imagine some organization in which the hierarchical criteria are lacking or are insufficient or equivocal, and in which the members are, consequently, more or less left to their individuality. That situation will no doubt raise the need for a more rigorous hierarchy, if the functioning of the institution requires it; if it did not require it, the crumbling into individualities creates the possibility for certain members to form a coalition among themselves and to establish a hierarchy to their own advantage.

In both cases what criterion will serve the coalition as a flag and the hierarchy as a foundation? To put it another way, it is not said a priori that several possible criteria will assume a value *relative* to each other and the best (the most general and least equivocal) will win. It can happen that that criterion is age, as it is in the barracks: the hierarchy of officers is a sufficiently perfected system that no complementary hierarchy is called for; on the other hand, in the inorganic crowd of privates, the "old hands" close ranks before "recruits." Similarly, in a society with an incomplete hierarchy, age will triumph where the hierarchy leaves room for ambiguity—for example in equality of rank; a rule is, in fact, needed, provided it is very clear.

We must beware of all psychologism; it is not a psychosis of old men, *laudatores temporis acti* or uneasy at the rise of the young, that imposes this criterion of age and this authority of the elders. On the contrary, it is the establishment of that criterion, which reasons of organization have caused to be set up, that engenders the psychosis of fear. The criterion of seniority is not archaic: it is imposed because it is relatively the best and there is a reason for it, and it continues as long as that reason remains. As Lévi-Strauss says,[25] the institution creates anxiety and not the opposite; without an institution the psychic tension between age groups does not exist, or is at hardly more than an anecdotal level: cuffs, grumbling, or proverbs. However, it increases when the distinction between age groups serves as a theme for making a hierarchy, because every hierarchy feels threatened. Here we see how much consciousness deforms reality: the consequence is taken for the cause; the anxiety caused by the hierarchy becomes a psychosis of age; finally, when the elders undertake to justify the institution, they will do it by invoking the natural authority of "the elders," a common rationalization in which the true function of the criterion of age is misunderstood.

Since everything is continued creation, we will also prove that a revolt of the young against the system will take place only if the seniority no longer fulfills its function (which is to establish an order, whichever one it may be, provided there is one) or if it has no further function to fulfill— as happens, for example, when white men set up new authorities in the village; it is a dramatic moment, for, the authority of the elders being henceforth but a survival threatening to fall to pieces, the psychosis of age is thereby further augmented. Suffice it to note that in this domain there is no absolute date of institutions, nor is there any longer historical *inertia;* the criteria persist as long as their relative value allows them to persist, and they reappear when that relative value reappears.

Routine

So does there exist, somewhere in society, inertia, habit, customs that endure because they are there? And can that question be formulated with any precision? Can we think that mentalities are like a habit?[26] These are questions to which it is now impossible to give a serious answer, even for a sociologist; one can at most have inclinations, be for tradition or for progress. Yet, however he votes, the historian owes it to himself to apply his principle: to put off the explanation as long as possible, to penetrate the non-eventworthy beyond the latest liberty and the last risk that his predecessors had reached.

Let us, for example, consider routine—is it only a routine? Here are two little facts that allow us to doubt this. In an article published in 1941, Marc Bloch (who, from Paris to Clermont-Ferrand and Lyons, had already chosen the road that was to lead him to torture and to execution) wrote:

> If peasant routine undeniably exists, there is nothing absolute about it; in a great number of cases, we see that new techniques have been adopted, quite easily, by peasant societies, while, in other circumstances, those same societies, on the contrary, have refused other changes that, at first sight, would not seem to have been less capable of winning them over.

We note, on the one hand, that rye, unknown to the Romans, has been planted throughout our countryside since the High Middle Ages; on the other hand, the peasants of the eighteenth century refused the suppression of fallow land—and thus the whole agricultural revolution. The reason for this difference is simple: "To substitute rye for wheat and barley was not to touch the social system in any way"; on the other hand,

> the agricultural revolution of the eighteenth century threatened to ruin the whole social system in which peasant life was embedded. The small farmer was not responsive to the idea of increasing the productive forces of the nation. He was but moderately so to the nearer prospect of increasing his own production or, at least, the part of that production which was to be sold; in the market he felt something mysterious and a little dangerous. His chief preoccupation was, rather, to keep his traditional standard of living nearly intact. Almost everywhere, he considered his fate to be bound up with the maintenance of the old collective servitude; now those customs supposed fallow land.[27]

Another example is taken from industry. It has been found[28] that resistance to change among factory workers, when the management changes the methods of working, is a group behavior; the output of a new worker decreases to be in line with that of other members of the group and not to exceed the more implicitly fixed by the group itself and tacitly imposed on all its members. Indeed, a worker whose output is too high risks becoming a pretext for management to raise the standards for all; the problem of the group is to slow the rhythm so as to produce just the quantity below which they would all risk being paid less as a group. This is an economic problem that is very complex, by reason of the large number of variables to be taken into account, but that the workers in a workshop intuitively succeed in resolving by slowing production in the afternoon if they see that they have done too much work in the morning, and vice versa; this routine is very rational in the means it uses and in its aims.

Every routine has its own logic whose rule is obviously better when expressed and is sufficient to explain why everything lasts in this world. To reduce the risks or the uncertainty, *homo historicus* never proceeds from a tabula rasa (that is done, and with great difficulty, only in scientific research); he is content to choose a solution satisfying certain minimal conditions,[29] and that solution appears to him as written into the nature of things:

Perhaps something better could be found, but, things being what they are, the merit of this solution is that it exists and is acceptable: let us henceforth keep to it; beyond it would lie adventure.

That is why history is not utopia.[30] Action hardly ever presents itself as a fixed goal for attainment of which adequate means would be sought but, rather, as a traditional recipe, to be applied as it is if it is to succeed—or, if need be, to adapt prudently. The data of the slightest problem are so complex that it is impossible to rebuild anew each time—better still, if the recipe did not exist, one would not even think of desiring the goal, or else it would be permanently the system of the flash of genius and of the burst of passion. So if political gatherings, even when they are made up of the elite, do in general take such mediocre decisions as Le Bon would have it—and worthy, according to him, of a lowly populace—that does not at all prove that there was a "crowd psychology" with a specific nature, but only that the kinds of problems that people gather together to solve admit of more mediocre solutions than problems settled in the solitude of a study.

Since a routine, and no doubt all behavior, refers back to hidden reasons rather than to habit, one must resist the temptation to bring back several modes of behavior to some general *habitus* that was like a nature and gave rise to a sort of historic characterology: the noble, the bourgeois according to Sombart. That unity of character does not exist; the antithesis of the noble mentality and the rational, profit mentality is conventional psychology. Because the aristocratic mentality is accustomed to being generous in a certain domain, it does not follow that it cannot prove greedy in another. There are great lords who are always very polite, except where money is involved, and financial sharks who in town are patrons of the arts. Our values are contradictory from one domain to the other because they are the "major premise" that the inverted logic of justifications derives from our conduct, but these different modes of conduct are imposed on us by instincts, traditions, interests, praxeologies that have no reason to form a coherent system. So we can proclaim both that Apollo prophesies and that his prophet is sold to the Persians, or desire "Paradise, but as late as possible." A Hindu moneylender may still have a rather "primitive" mind—he does not know how to do double-entry bookkeeping—and he has perhaps a "qualitative, irrational and traditional conception of time" (at least if the ideas on religion or philosophy that he professes are extended to his real life; apart from that he is like the rest of us, in practice having to wait "for the sugar to melt"—but that vision of temporality certainly does not prevent him from claiming, at the agreed time, the payment of interest with or without the qualitative conception of time[31]).

The "Institution"

We are taking the word "institution" here in the meaning sociologists give it. It does not designate something that is established by formal texts; on the contrary, constituted bodies are only one special case. By "institution" we shall mean everything about which one speaks of a collective ideal, esprit de corps, group tradition, all that presents that mixture of personal ambition and collective censure that makes the group realize more disinterested goals (for better or for worse) than those that would have been pursued by its members individually. Thus governments, armies, the clergy, universities, medical bodies, art or science schools, concentration camps, avant-garde literature, sects of all kinds, and climbers roped together function. Institutions serve aims and are animated by values. Let us not conclude that those values found the institution, for it is rather the reverse: the institution is a trap such that the man caught in it has no other way out than his professional consciousness. In that sense Maurras was not wrong to say that institutions cause the best in us to be prolonged, and Talcott Parsons also has expressed that thought in writing;[32] they also prolong the worst.

That structure of institutions is so important—history owes its monumental aspect to it—that we must dwell upon it. Let us take up again the example of Hellenistic and Roman public benefaction, of which we have already spoken. It all began in the cities, about the time of Alexander the Great, because rich notables were by temperament generous and patriotic, and had reinvented the old aristocratic ideal of excellence and of rivalry. In the Greek cities they devoted their time or their money to the town, offered it buildings, put their influence at its service; in Rome they gave the common people spectacles and feasts, as is right for patriarchal chiefs. This created a tradition (I mean acquired rights and duties of state); following this, a permanent rivalry in ostentatious gifts was established among the notables, while the people began to demand those presents as a due and to claim them from all rich men, even from those not particularly given to munificence; to refuse was difficult in the limited communities that the ancient cities were, in which rich and poor were in daily contact and a noisy demonstration was always possible. The desire for social peace, in those city-states where there were no police, finally made the class of notables impose public benefaction on each of its members as a duty of his rank; the latter did not fail to interiorize that duty, for roles determine not only people's public behavior but also their inner attitudes, since it is not comfortable to live in a state of discord—all sociologists will tell you so.

An individual quality, munificence, thus became a sort of public institution; people acted as benefactors who otherwise would never have done so. The climate of the city was changed by that, and the regime became a moderated aristocracy, condescending in Greece and paternalistic in Rome; the desire for social peace that had made them raise munificence to a duty and even an ideal thus takes on, in retrospect, a Machiavellian aspect. Bread and the circus served to depoliticize the people or, more exactly, to anesthetize them in a sordid materialism; in fact, far from thinking out such a clever plan, the notables had only followed the line of least resistance. The ancient city subsisted on that basis for half a millennium; the notables who governed the town kept the machine moving by dipping into their own purses. That does not mean they all did so willingly. It is not always pleasant to do one's duty but, even if one escapes, one is conditioned to escape with a bad conscience. It is thus that we recognize an institution.

An institution is a situation in which people, starting from motives that are not necessarily idealist—to make a career, not to be at variance with their milieu, not to live in a state of discord—are led to fulfill ideal aims as scrupulously as if they were interested in those aims out of personal taste; so we see that the values at the beginning and the end of the institution are not those that make it last. Whence perpetual tension between the disinterestedness supposed by the goals of the institution and the natural selfishness of its members. Among the public benefactors, some raise the cost of generosity because of noblesse oblige; others try to get out of it and flee to the countryside, not without a bad conscience; others act with the moral health of ambitious men; others escape discord and become an example to all by playing the part of conscientious men who do nothing more than the others, but do so out of pure respect, through a sort of professional morality of benefactors. The origin of that discord is the dialectic of the "all" and of the "each," so frequent in history; if it were in the interest of all the leading citizens that the institution of public benefaction should function well and content the common people, it was also in the interest of each of them not to sacrifice himself to the ideal. They escaped this discord by secreting a class morality, an ideal of public benefaction to escape the dilemma that theoreticians of games of strategy have made famous as the dilemma of the two prisoners:[33] each is interested in the other's doing his duty, but consents to do his only if he is sure that the others will really do his.

From this it will be concluded that psychological explanations are simultaneously true and false. The ideological motives are the true ones when there is an institution: each period makes and praises what conditions and impassions it; one is beneficent out of beneficence, crusades for the crusade, is charitable out of charity. But it is seen, too, that it would be vain to proceed to a public opinion poll and to ask people if they want to be beneficent, and why; the motives are a rationalization of the institution (bread and the circus buy social peace) or a reaction of adaption to it (how much finer, although more difficult, to do one's duty of munificence than to get out of it). Beneficence creates the benefactor, and not the opposite. The key to this evolution is so powerful a human reaction that it is like a calculation of the instinct of preservation: to make a virtue of necessity; to change one's maxims, rather than one's fortune; to assume the attitudes of one's role. Thus, as generations gradually succeed each other, it is easier for them to take up again models that have proved themselves than to reinvent the world.

One more word, of which the reader will see the opportuneness in chapter XII. The analysis of institutions you have just read will no doubt look to you a bit like sociology; indeed, its point of departure is an innocent imitation of Talcott Parsons. The reader may have noted that we, however, have done no more than a historian's work: to explain dated facts through understanding them. Once the historical elements and the incomprehensible plot are eliminated, what remains as a more general and strictly sociological residue? A concept—let us say, rather, a conventional and pseudo-scientific term—that of institution, and a strong maxim worthy of the French moralists: man makes a virtue of necessity, which general sociology expresses in a more scholarly way, saying that statutes and roles are generally interiorized into attitudes. We shall remember that when we study the relationships between history and sociology.

A New Knowledge of Man

We could pursue that casuistry indefinitely; it would suffice to draw on the historiography and sociology of today to multiply the examples: that which testifies to a transformation—or, rather, an enrichment of our experience of man; and that which also suggests the idea of a new dimension of historical criticism.

The age of Paretian or Marxist criticism of ideologies is past; for the dualism of matter and mind, of passions and pretexts, are substituted many particular cases demanding concrete analysis and some experience of collective psychology. That familiarity with collective psychology is one of the acquisitions of present-day culture; it is the discovery of a new domain for man's knowledge. The fruits of that discovery will not be found codified in textbooks, for a "literary" or everyday psychology is in question, not knowledge that can be reduced to formulas; but the proofs of this new familiarity will be found even in newspapers. It is an enrichment following another transformation, that of individual psychology, with Rousseau, Dostoyevski, and Freud; the sense of the dialectics of the ego with itself in humiliation and offense is indeed another characteristic of contemporary culture, as are the struggle of consciences, the paradoxes of compensation and of forward flight. In comparison with this new experience of the individual and collective soul, the old psychology of human contradictions—that of Seneca and of the Christian moralists—as well as the old wisdom of nations about the psychology of peoples, henceforth appear poor and inflexible. There are thus inequalities of rhythm in the acquisition of an experience of man, breaks in the slope.

That ought to entail an increase in historical criticism. Being knowledge obtained through documents, history is what is made of it by the different *types* of traces we have left of the past; but it seems that half of the task of criticism has scarcely been seen. It is one thing to wonder if documents are authentic, sincere, and suitably restored; it is another, in which much remains to be done, to wonder what kind of truth one has a right to draw from a particular type of trace. It would appear that a good number of historical errors come from the overinterpretation of the documents as a result of having asked them questions they ought not to have answered. One cannot conclude a value from a word, an institution from a value, a belief from a rite, a fact from a slogan, a mode of conduct from a proverb, personal faith from a theology, conformity from a faith, the psychology of a people from a linguistic idiom. Perhaps it is even historical criticism of this kind that general sociology, which is the "sick man" of sociology today, would find its true vocation; it would then be reconverted into historical criticism, as we have just seen, and into the historical topic, as we shall see in the next section.

The Main Difficulty of History

It remains that the relationships of consciousness and action present the greatest difficulty in historical synthesis, because they are its most important part; history is centered on our goals, which are obscure to us. In this domain nothing can be systematized: neither reductionism (the religious is not political, or the reverse) nor the clearness of the goals (there are wars of religion that are also political and politicians who are mystics) nor dualism of ideological pretexts and true motives. Practically, we always come back to hesitating between a rationalizing interpretation (routine is a hidden reason) and an instinctive interpretation (the logic of "institutions" finally rests on a survival reflex: making a virtue of necessity; routine is a mere habit); but, most often, both interpretations remain possible at the pleasure of the historian and the facts do not allow the question to be settled. Following is a very simple example, which we borrow from a famous polemic in which the documents are both superabundant and insufficient: the origins of the American Civil War.

None of the causes of that war is really sufficient to explain why the conflict broke out between the North and the South; the opposition of economic interests between Northern capitalism and the planters of the South seems contrived, the quarrel over slavery was too idealist to have political weight, the customs traiffs were a pretext or a detail rather than a casus belli, the contrast in life-styles was not a reason for cutting each other's throats. Let us try a rationalizing interpretation of that war, and let us first state that our mistake was to seek antecedent causes. We will then, very plausibly, suppose that the conflict broke out, not following a particular event, but because the South wondered if it were not going to lose all control of the federal government's policy and if it were not condemned by that, within a more or less short time, to submitting to the Yankee omnipotence; thus the war would be a conflict of authority, preventive in character. Let us further suppose that in that conflict the South was not seeking authority for itself (a society is not a governing class), but wanted to preserve access to the controls of command, so as to ensure its future security; let us finally suppose that the South did not feel that security threatened by some definite risk (ruinous customs tariffs, for example) but by the uncertainty of the future, by the feeling that, the life-styles of the North and South being too different, something could always "happen to it" because of the Northerners and that it had to guard itself "in any case."

None of these hypotheses is unlikely, but how can they be verified? What is to be sought in the documents? It may very well happen that no Southern politician or journalist had developed these themes in writing or orally; what, indeed, is the good of developing them? Why convince those who are convinced? It may well be that none of those who were convinced of the need to fight had expressly those reasons in mind and said to himself, "Here we are, handed over to the North, bound hand and foot"; the threat for the future, the feeling of uncertainty, must not have been translated into an awareness, but into a strong affectivity. When the question of the colonization of the West made patent the future conflict of authority, tension suddenly rose, passions were enflamed. Why? People did not know themselves, any more than a wild beast, driven into a corner of its cage, "knows" why, instinctively, he is afraid and becomes bad-tempered, even if the tamer is not threatening him for the moment.

Thus, we can indifferently ascribe to the Southerners one of these types of motivation: either an irrational, instinctive motive (fear of a foreign master, or hatred of too different a life-style, or a fanatical attachment to an acquired situation) or a perfectly rational reflex, instinctive, seeking security in uncertainty. This ambiguity is found everywhere in history; the routine is perhaps as rational as we have said, but perhaps it is also a mere habit. Fidelity to institutions is a wise calculation or an animal attachment to the alma mater that feeds the man. No fact ever allows a choice between these two types of interpretation, for they are indeed interpretations; our goals are never immediately known, but have to be inferred. Our consciousness is not the faithful witness of our goals; as for our conduct, it expresses them only in a confused way, and does not give their precise formula. The aims are neither conscious nor observable in the pure state.

But, to see the difficulty in its true dimension, it is coextensive with universal history. Everywhere, and particularly everywhere that blood has flowed, we see crusaders, Huguenots, Bohemians, people of La Vendée, or Algerians roused by passions that are as intense as they are obscure and transitory: what, exactly, did they want? We must see at what level the difficulty is; there is still nothing more to be done than to set back to back those who reduce the religious struggles to class struggles and those who claim that they were purely religious. If we approach the problem without prejudice and if we are attentive to the nuances that reveal behavior, we will succeed in disentangling what there was of greed, of politics, and of piety in the Crusades or the wars of religion.

But then the real difficulties will begin: how can we formulate exactly the disentangled aims, and why those aims? With what did the Algerians reproach the French rule? Was it for being foreign? Was it the ethnic difference? Economic domination? With what did the Vendéens reproach the Republic? That it was the Republic and not the king? The very issue of events will not reveal the aims, which will be translated only through compromises, institutions, and failures. Historical passions therefore never appear "in the wild state," to use Foucault's expression; they are always in period costume: the zeal for the crusade, anticolonialism. And one cannot say why, in the sense that they cannot be referred to an anthropological structure, cannot find in them a certain number of permanent goals of man, under pain of returning to the wisdom of nations: the appetite for gain, the sense of propriety, the love of country. Thus, universal history is presented as the recital of a succession of dated caprices ("the nineteenth century and nationalist movements"), the real meaning of which we do not know and that we can describe only by their effects, once we have stated their conventional name.

It is thus because no passion of historical importance is deliberate; to know if the occupying power or the boss is hateful is not the stake of academic debates, and we do not have to admit to ourselves our reasons for hating them: it is enough to have those reasons. So the order of action is not reducible to that of knowledge in the sense that historical consciousness is a deliberation on the means and not information on goals. Our declared ideas and official values are but justifications, rationalizations, consolations—or, better, they are attempts at elucidation: when individuals or societies undertake to elucidate their own reasons for acting, they are at the same point as the historians who undertake it. It is not the intellect that decides the desire, says *De anima;* on the contrary, it has the desire as a principle and deliberates only on the means. Besides, in studying, as we are going to do now, the progress to which historical knowledge is susceptible, we shall be led to make a revealing remark: the human sciences (I mean those that really merit the name of sciences) are sciences relative to the means of action, are praxeologies. They are sciences (or arts) of the organization of means, and they are at least as normative as descriptive; on the other hand, they teach us nothing about human goals.

Part Three

The Progress of History

Chapter X

Lengthening the Questionnaire

The first duty of the historian is to establish the truth, and the second is to make the plot understood; history has a critique but has no method, for there is no method to understand. Each man can therefore improvise himself as a historian—or, rather, he could do so if, for lack of method, history does not suppose one is cultured. That historical culture (it might as well be called sociological or ethnographical) has not ceased to develop, and has become considerable in the last century or two; our knowledge of the *homo historicus* is richer than that of Thucydides or of Voltaire. But it is a culture, not learning; it consists in preparing a topic, in being able to ask oneself more and more questions, but not in knowing how to answer them. As Croce writes, the formation of historical thought consists in this: the understanding of history has become enriched from the time of the Greeks to our own; it is not that we know the principles or the goals of human events; but we have acquired from those events a much richer casuistic.[1] Such is the only progress to which historiography is susceptible.

Progressive Conceptualization

It is difficult to imagine that a contemporary of St. Thomas or of Nicholas de Cusa could have written *Feudal Society* or *The Economic History of the Medieval West:* not only had the example not yet been given of studying economic facts and social relations in the framework of the historical genre but the categories and concepts necessary for doing so were lacking; no one had yet sufficiently considered the facts to see those concepts becoming clear before his eyes. The observation of what has been experienced is indeed a slow and cumulative progress, like the progress in self-knowledge that the private diary allows or like the progressive discovery of a landscape in the course of attentive observation. When Eginhard reread the biographies of the Roman emperors by Suetonius before writing the life of Charlemagne, his protector, he above all saw resemblances between the great emperor and the Roman Caesars, rather than the enormous differences that we see; does that mean that his vision was archetypal, that his conception of history was that events are the repetition of exemplary types? Is it not, rather, that it was archetypal because his vision of the past was poor? You need a great deal of wit, said La Rochefoucauld, to see how original people are. The apperception of the individual, the enrichment of vision, is conditioned by knowing how to ask more questions about an event than the man in the street does; an art critic sees in a picture many more things than does a mere tourist, and the same richness of vision is that of Burckhardt contemplating the Italian Renaissance.

Eginhard surely was not unaware that Charlemagne was different from Augustus and that no one event is the same as another, but he did not take note of those differences or had no words for those nuances; he did not conceive them. The forming of new concepts is the operation through which the enrichment of the vision is produced; in the society of his time Thucydides or St. Thomas could not have known how to see all that we have learned to seek in it: social classes, ways of life, mentalities, economic attitudes, rationalism, paternalism, conspicuous consumption, the link between wealth and prestige and power, conflicts, social mobility, capitalists, landowners, the strategy of the group, social climbing by "short-circuit," nobility in town and country, liquid wealth, unemployed funds, the seeking of security, bourgeois dynasties. They lived these aspects of reality in the manner of the peasant who hardly gives a thought to the shape of his plow, his millstone, and his land, which make three subjects for study and comparison for a geographer. Thus we gradually take an increasingly detailed view of the world of men, and a moment comes when we are astonished that our predecessors did not "realize" what they had, as we do, before them.[2]

History begins with the naive vision of things, that of the man in the street, of the editors of the Book of Kings or of the *Great Chronicles of France*. Little by little, through a movement like the no less slow and irregular one of science and of the *philosophia perennis,* the conceptualization of experience goes on. This movement is less distinguishable than that of science or of philosophy; it is not translated by theorems, theses, or formulable theories that can be contradicted and discussed—to see it, we must compare a page of Weber or of Pirenne with a page of a chronicler of the year 1000. This progress, as little discursive as an apprenticeship, is nonetheless the reason for the existence of the historico-philological disciplines and the justification of their autonomy; it is part of the discovery of how complicated the world is. We would speak of the ever-increasing consciousness that humanity acquires of itself if there were no question, on a smaller scale, of the ever more precise knowledge that historians and their readers get of history.

This progress is the only one about which we are justified in speaking of Greek naiveté or the childhood of the world; in science and in philosophy adulthood is not merited by the extent of the corpus of acquired knowledge, but by the act of foundation. It is not the same with the discovery of the complexity of the world: the Greeks are children endowed with genius but lacking in experience; on the other hand, they had found Euclid's *Elements.* Did not Michelet recognize the modern historian as the instrument of his superiority, "the modern personality so powerful and so much richer"? No modern could be more profound than Thucydides in the area of Greek history, for what has been experienced has no depth, but Thucydides would have learned something from what Burckhardt and Nilsson have written on his own civilization and his own religion; if he had undertaken to speak of them, his phrases would have been much poorer than ours.

So a history of historiography that wanted to get to the heart of the subject would be less concerned with the facile study of the ideas of each historian and more with an inventory of his palette; it is not enough to say that the narration of a given historian is thin or that another shows hardly any interest in the social aspects of his period. The honors list might then have some confusion; old Abbot Fleury, with his *Customs of the Jews and of the Early Christians* would then appear at least as rich as Voltaire, and we would be astonished at the richness of Marc Bloch and at the poverty of Michelet. It would very often happen that that history of history does not unfold among historians, but among novelists, travelers, or sociologists.

The Unequal Difficulty of Apperception

The reason for this age-old education of the vision is a particularity that has supremely modeled the appearance of the historical genre: the different kinds of events are unequally easy to perceive, and in history it is easier to see battles and treaties—events, in the ordinary sense of the word—than mentalities and economic cycles; the ideal of a "non-event-worthy history," of a "pioneering history" is destined to give historians a taste for the difficult and a sense of effort. In politics we easily distinguish wars, revolutions, and ministerial changes; in religion, theologies, gods, councils, and conflicts between Church and state; in economics, economic institutions and proverbs on agriculture that lacks manpower. Society is the juridical statute, everyday life, or fashionable life; literature is a gallery of great writers; the history of science is that of scientific discoveries. That enumeration, which would cause a representative of the School of Archives to faint with horror, is the spontaneous vision of history. The progress of history has been in tearing oneself away from it, and outstanding books were those that conceptualized new categories, from the history of the soil to that of mentalities. It is henceforth possible to judge a textbook of the history of civilization by merely consulting the table of contents: it shows the author's concepts.

The unequal difficulty of perceiving events lies, if I count rightly, in at least seven reasons. First, the event is difference; but history is written from sources whose editors find their own society so natural that they do not divide it into themes. Second, "values" are not found in what people say but in what they do, and the official headings are often deceptive; mentalities are not mental. Third, concepts are a perpetual source of misinterpretations because they vulgarize and they cannot go without caution from one period to another. Fourth, the historian has a tendency to stop the clarification of the causes at the first freedom, the first material cause, and the first chance that come along. Fifth, the real offers a certain resistance to innovation; whether it be a political enterprise or the composition of a poem, a work is done more quickly if it follows in the old ruts of a tradition that seems so natural that it is not conscious. Sixth, the historical explanation is a regression to infinity; when we reach tradition, routine, inertia, it is difficult to say whether it is a reality or an appearance the truth of which is more deeply hidden in the shadow of the non-eventworthy. Finally, historical facts are often social, collective, statistical; demography, economics, customs. They are to be seen only at the foot of a column of figures; otherwise they are not seen or the strangest errors are made about them.

The unusual nature of this list can be seen, a list each one can complete as he likes. This mixing would be enough to warn us that the unequal difficulty in seeing events is a peculiarity of knowing and not of being; there is no substratum of history demanding excavations for it to be discovered. Let us say more precisely that our little list is like the wrong side of the weave of a study on historical criticism, which we think would be the real subject of a study on historical knowledge (the rest, which is treated in this book, is only the tip of the iceberg). At least our list has some heuristic use. History needs heuristics because it is unaware of its ignorance; a historian must begin by learning to see what he is in front of him, in the documents. Historical ignorance does not proclaim itself, and the naive vision of what constitutes an event seems to itself to be as full and entire as the most detailed vision. In fact, where it does not discern the originality of things, historical thought puts anachronistic banality, the eternal man. If in Rabelais we read jokes about monks and, judging his century by ours, we suppose, with Abel Lefranc and Michelet, that Rabelais was a freethinker, it takes Gilson to teach us that

the rule about what was then authorized or excessive as far as jokes were concerned, even religious ones, escapes us and that rule can no longer be determined by the impressions that a professor seeks to prove in the year of grace 1924 when he reads the text of Rabelais.[3]

History has the property of bewildering us, constantly confronting us with strange things that our most natural reaction is not to see; far from finding out that we have not the right key, we do not even see that there is a lock to open.[4] Let me cite a personal example. I have always felt a certain distaste for getting to know those who live on the same floor as my apartment; I salute them with a distant nod of the head when we meet in the elevator, and I never converse with them. I have had to declare, in a tone that was, to my slight surprise, rather satisfied, that I did not even know their names; I have lived in four apartments in five years, and it has always been thus. I have an excellent colleague, an epigraphist like me, whose company I would gladly enjoy more than I do, if we did not live only one floor apart.

My *gnothi seauton* on all that would have remained there if I had not recently read, in a sociological work, that one of the signs that allows us most conveniently to distinguish the middle classes from the lower classes is that among the lower classes, people know each other and neighbors help each other, whereas the middle classes refuse to let purely spatial considerations decide the people with whom they are friendly. Hardly had I read that than I firmly proposed to throw light on it by the electoral notices of Pompeii, where plebeians recommend the candidacy of some notable in these terms: "nominate So-and-So an edile, his neighbours desire it"; for, true of our century, the affirmation of the sociologists is not true of other periods. Pompeii was less like a town of today than a medieval city, with its street communities, or like the suburb of St. Germain in other days, where the duke of Guermantes had good neighborly relations with Jupien the waistcoat maker.

The Historical Topic

The age-old enrichment of historical thought comes from a struggle against our natural tendency to vulgarize the past. It is translated by an increase in the number of concepts at the disposal of the historian and, consequently, by a lengthening of the list of questions he will be able to ask his documents. One can imagine that ideal questionnaire by the example of the lists of "commonplaces" or *topoi* and of "probabilities" made by ancient rhetoric for the use of orators (be it said without the slightest irony: rhetoric was a great thing, and its praxeological significance is surely considerable). Thanks to those lists the orator knew, in a given case, what aspects of the question he had to "think of thinking"; those lists did not solve difficulties: they enumerated all the conceivable difficulties that had to be thought of.

Today sociologists sometimes work out topics of this kind under the name "checklists";[5] another beautiful list of places is the *Manuel d'ethnographie* of Marcel Mauss, which teaches beginners going out to do fieldwork what they have to look at. A historian finds the equivalent of it in the reading of his classics—especially when those classics do not bear on "his period," for, because of the differences in documentation, the topics of different civilizations complete each other; the longer his list of places, the more chances he has of finding among them the right key (or, rather, to notice that there is a lock). As Marrou says, "the more intelligent, cultured, rich in experience, open to all the values of man the historian is, the more capable he will become of finding things in the past, the more his knowledge will be open to richness and truth."[6] Have we not seen before that the work of historical synthesis consisted in performing a "retrodiction," and that this was done by means of a list of possible hypotheses from which he can draw the most probable?

The Topic of Preindustrial Societies

The historical *topoi* are not only useful for synthesis; at the level of criticism, they allow the avoidance of what is most deceptive in the incomplete state of all documentation: the variable place of all gaps. Such a trait, which is common to several civilizations, is directly attested in only one of them and, if one kept to the documents proper to that civilization, one would never think of it for a "retrodiction." Let us suppose that the historian is studying a civilization prior to the industrial era: he will have a topic that will make him know that a priori he will have to ask himself about the absence or the presence of particular circumstances, some of which we shall enumerate. It often happens that the demographic state of those societies—infant mortality, the life span, and the presence of endemic illnesses—is something that we cannot imagine. The products of artisans are relatively so costly that they would be classed today as semiluxury goods (clothing, furniture, and household utensils figure in the inventories of estates, and the garment of the poor person was a secondhand garment, just as today the car of the lower-class person is a secondhand car.[7] Daily "bread" is not a metonym. The job one chooses is normally that of one's father.

The prospect of progress is so absent that these societies consider that the world is adult, completed, and that they are facing the old age of the world. The central government, even if authoritarian, is powerless; away from the capital, its decisions are rapidly bogged down in the passive resistance of the populations (the *Theodosian Codex* is less the work of weak emperors who launch vain edicts than of ideological emperors who proclaim ideals in a kind of mandate). Marginal productivity matters less than average productivity.[8] Religious, cultural, and scientific life is often organized in sects, faithful to an orthodoxy *in verba magistri* (as it was in China and in Greek philosophy). A high proportion of resources comes from agriculture, and the center of power is usually among those who own land. Economic life is less a matter of rationalism than of authority, the landed proprietor appearing above all as a chief who keeps his men at work. The fact of being excluded from public life or of living on the fringes of society singularly favors immersion in economic life (immigrants, heretics, crossbreeds, Jews, Greek and Roman freedmen).

On the other hand, other *topoi* are less frequent than one might think. You cannot prejudge, for example, the size of population (near crowds of people one finds Roman Italy, with about seven million people); you can no longer prejudge the existence and importance of towns nor the intensity of interregional trade (very high in modern China and no doubt in the Roman Empire).[9] The standard of living may also be high (perhaps that of Roman Africa and Asia was near that of our eighteenth century), even in the absence of institutions one would believe to be necessary for an advanced economy, such as paper money or at least bills of exchange. Nor can it be excluded that the population is very largely literate (Japan before Meiji). Those societies are not inevitably immobile, and social mobility may have unexpected importance and assume disconcerting forms: it may pass through slavery (Rome, the Turkish Empire); fatalism and the *laudatio temporis acti* can join forces with each individual's conviction that he can improve his condition thanks to his spirit of enterprise. The "stable poverty" of those societies makes no one ashamed of his place in it, but does not mean that each does not seek to rise. Political life there can be as agitated as in more prosperous societies, but the conflicts are not always struggles between economically different classes; they are more often rivalries for authority between similar groups (two armies, two aristocratic clans, two provinces). There the agitation assumes unexpected forms, obscure styles and false oracles replacing tracts and slogans; it often happens that those who are convinced or mere adventurers rouse the masses by passing themselves off as an emperor or the son of an emperor believed to be dead. It is the type of the "false Demetrius" that we find in Rome with the false Nero, in Russia, and in China. They deserve a study in comparative history.[10]

Non-eventworthy History

The elaboration of topics of this kind is not a common school exercise: the *topoi* are not to be picked up but to be picked out, which supposes analytical, reflective work; they are the result of a non-eventworthy history. Normally, the salient features of a period, those that stare you in the face, those that are important enough to merit being registered as *topoi,* for whatever heuristic purpose it may serve, are what one perceives least. From this difficulty in seeing what is the most important there results one major consequence: most history books are like a low-water mark of events below which they do not even think of pursuing the explanation, and leave it submerged in the non-eventworthy. The existence of this low-water level characterizes what our School of Archives satirically calls treaties-and-battles history or the "eventworthy history"—a history that is more a chronicle than an analysis of the structures. The present evolution of historical studies in all Western countries is an attempt to move from this history of events to a "structural" history.

That evolution may be schematized thus: a history of events will ask the question "Who were the favorites of Louis XIII?"; a structural history will first think of wondering "What was a favorite? How can this political type of monarchies of the Ancien Régime be analyzed, and why did there exist anything like favorites?" It will begin by making a "sociology" of the favorite; it will establish as a principle that nothing is self-evident, for nothing is eternal, and consequently it will strive to extricate what is presupposed from all it writes. Before writing the word "favorite" in order to tell who were the favorites of Louis XIII and that the only favorite Louis XIV admitted to was Marshal de Villeroi, it will realize that it is employing a concept it has not analyzed, though there is surely much to say about it.

For history the role of favorite is not the explanation of the story of Villeroi but, on the contrary, the fact to be explained. The condition of being king—through collusion between the sovereign and a private individual, between the necessities of government and personal feelings, through the monarch's interiorization of his public role, through the conflicts that every organization produces in the soul of each of its members, through the production of the individuality of the monarch on the stage of the court—would engender in kings a very special psychology that it is not easy to "bring back to life"; did the king make a courtier his favorite because he was infatuated with him? Or did the needs of government oblige him to take a man he could trust ("favorites are the best remedy against the ambitions of great lords," writes Bacon)? Would those needs suggest to him, then, to have feelings of affection, so as to justify the public role of an individual who had no public qualification for it?

What reasons make historiography, if it follows its own inclination, normally stop at the low-water mark of "battles and treaties" or "names of the favorites of Louis XIII"? The vision that contemporaries had of the history they were living. A vision transmitted to the historians by the interpretations of sources; history of events is political actuality gone cold. In the seventeenth century, preachers and moralists spoke a great deal about favorites, their eccentricities, their catastrophes, but did not describe the system, for everyone was steeped in it. The memorialists of each period picked out the names of the successive favorites—Concini, Luynes, Villeroi—and the historians continued the practice. On the other hand, since the distribution of landed property or demographic movements had never been part of political actuality, it took historians time to think of looking into it.

You only have to see how we ourselves write contemporary history. There is a book, called *Democracy and Totalitarianism,* that describes the political regimes of industrial societies in the twentieth century; but its author is a sociologist, and it is said that his book is a study in sociology. So what will remain for historians of the twentieth century to do? To pronounce the words "industrial democracy" and "pluralist democracy," which it would be difficult not to use, though one must refrain from saying what things may be considered evident to us. On the other hand, they will relate the accidents that happen to those substances: the fall of a minister here, the overthrow of the central committee over there.

The history of events thus gives itself kinds of essences—the conflict between the Roman emperors and the Senate,[11] the political instability in the third century, the monarchy of the Ancien Régime—and keeps a chronicle of their incarnations. It will relate, consulate after consulate, the suicides and condemnation of senators without giving any clear idea of the reasons and rules of this strange conflict within the ruling class; it will establish a strict chronology of the military and senatorial coups d'état in the third century but without analyzing that instability as that of the Republican regime in France or certain South American regimes are analyzed. It will repeat what Eusebius said about the history of the Church, but will not put the great question: when a population of perhaps 100 million inhabitants is converted en masse to a new religion, what were the reasons? It is a sociological problem of conversion, on which missionaries since the sixteenth century must have formed certain ideas; thus, one could conceive that a historian begins by making a topic of mass conversion (or a sociology or a comparative history, if you prefer), since starting from there he tries, imaginatively, a "retrodiction" of the ancient history of Christianity.

Struggle Against the Optics of Sources

We see what confers their unity on different aspects of the history of non-events: a struggle against the optics imposed by the sources. The School of Archives has produced studies of quantitative history (economic and demographic) on the one hand, and studies of the history of mentalities, values, and historical sociology, on the other. What relationship can there be, at first sight, between such heterogeneous works? Between the curve of the evolution of prices in Lower Provence in the fifteenth century and the perception of temporality at the same time? Where is the unity of the school in question? Let us not seek it in the structure of the development of history (that structure does not exist), in the fact that the school has undertaken to explore the long-term temporal rhythms: to distinguish different temporalities in history is only a metaphor. The unity of these different researches comes from the configuration of the documentation; the curve of prices and the perception of time for people in the fifteenth century have in common that people of the fifteenth century were not aware of either, and that historians who were content to see the fifteenth century through the eyes of those people could no longer be more aware than they were. We state it again: the real problems of historical epistemology are problems of criticism and the center of all reflection on historical knowledge ought to be this: "historical knowledge is what the sources make of it." It too often happens that we attribute to the very existence of events a peculiarity (for example, the distinction between several temporalities) that quite frankly belongs to knowledge, as the sources make it.

When history has broken away from the optics of sources, when the anxiety to make clear everything it speaks of ("So what was a favorite?") has become a reflex for it, history textbooks will be very different from what they are today. They will describe at length the "structures" of a particular monarchy of the Ancien Régime, will say what a favorite was, why and how war was waged; and they will pass very rapidly over the wars of Louis XIV and the fall of the favorites of the young Louis XIII. For, if history is a struggle for truth, it is also a struggle against our tendency to consider that all goes without saying. The site of that struggle is the topic, the lists of places grow richer and more perfect with generations of historians, and that is why one cannot improvise oneself as a historian any more than one can improvise oneself as an orator. You have to know what questions to ask yourself, know too which questions are out of date; political, social or religious history is not written with the respectable, realist, or advanced opinions one has on these things as a private person. There are obsolete ideas to be cast aside, like the psychology of peoples and the invocation of the national genius; there are above all a lot of ideas to acquire, for writing the history of an ancient civilization is not done with the help of humanist culture alone.

If history has no method (and that is why one can improvise oneself as a historian), it has a topic (and that is why it is better not to improvise oneself as a historian). The danger of history is that it looks easy, and is not. No one thinks of improvising himself as a physicist because everyone knows that for that you need training in mathematics; though less spectacular, the historian's need of historical experience is no less great. But, in case of deficiency there, the consequences are more artful: they will not happen according to the law of all or nothing; the history book will have blemishes (unconsciously anachronistic concepts, nodes of abstractions not turned into coin, residues of events not analyzed) and, above all, things missing: it will sin less by what it affirms than by what it has not thought to ask itself. For the difficulty of historiography is less to find answers than to find questions. The physicist is like Oedipus: it is the Sphinx who questions, he has to give the right reply; the historian is like Percivale: the Grail is there in front of him, but will not be his unless he thinks of asking the question.

History as a Recension of Reality

For a historian to be able to answer his question, documents have to exist, but that condition is not enough: one can relate at great length July 14, June 20, and August 10 without a click being produced and without telling oneself that it is not self-evident that the Revolution should take the form of "days," that there must be reasons for it. If the reader is tempted to think, on the strength of that trivial example, that it is a vain editorial work to make the topic advance, we will remind him that Herodotus and Thucydides had all the necessary facts to lay the foundations of social or religious history (including the heuristic comparison with barbarian peoples) and that they did not do so. Did they lack the "intellectual tools"? But we shall say nothing else.

The effort of conceptualization has as its ideal the discursive provision, to the uninitiated reader, of all the data that will allow him to reconstitute the event in its entirety, including its "tonality," its "atmosphere." For initially, a thing produced in a civilization foreign to us has two parts for us; one is expressly read in the documents and textbooks, the other is an aura that the specialist absorbs from contact with the documents, but that he cannot translate into words (so one says that the documents are inexhaustible). The familiarity he has with that aura no less distinguishes the specialist from the uninitiated and allows him to signal the anachronism, the misunderstanding of the spirit of the time, when the uninitiated ventures to reconstruct an event from what has been spelled out for him in textbooks, and recomposes it wrongly because he has not found the essential piece of the puzzle.

The connection between the two principles of historical knowledge that we brought out in chapter IV will be understood: that historical knowledge is worthwhile in itself and that all is worthy of history. Unlike practical interest, which is limited to its particular aims, the characteristic of purely theoretical interest is to realize itself in the sense of a knowledge of the totality of being. It is a general law of thought: the movement of the history of the non-event is also found in geography. The latter has not ceased to attach interest to an ever greater number of categories of features of the countryside: the interval that separates the poverty of a chronicler of the year 1000 and the richness of a present-day historian equally separates the Roman geographer from a present-day geographer. The Ionians designated by the name *historia* the historico-geographical inquiry that is interested in making a census of the world; that census calls for an intellectual effort, for the practical orientation of consciousness makes the conceptualization of reality initially very limited.

An effort that is translated into a discursive result has a cumulative effect and relaunches research; to have separated the notion of attitude toward profit is to have forged an idea of universal use that, born in connection with Western capitalism at the end of the Middle Ages, will at once be put to the test for every other period. By its gratuitousness, its difficulty, the universal character of its topic, and its cumulative acquisitions, history is a half-science, a rational activity, and its real interest lies there. As has been excellently said, the effort to reconstitute the past "has as its aim, not the picturesque, but rationality,"[12] and that rationality "is the basis of the interest one brings to history; real, ordered, readable, the past becomes interesting."[13] That rationalization is translated by a conceptualization of the experienced world, by a prolongation of the topic.

Progress of Historical Knowledge

The enrichment of the lists of places is the only progress that historical knowledge can make; history will never be able to give more lessons than it does now, but it may still multiply the questions even further. It is definitively narrative, reduced to recounting what Alcibiades did and what happened to him. Far from opening on a science or on a typology, it constantly confirms that man is variable matter about which no fixed judgment can be made; it knows no better than on the first day how the economic and the social are joined, and it is still more incapable than in Montesquieu's day of affirming that, given event A, event B will be given too. And so, to characterize the value of a historian, the wealth of his ideas and his perception of nuances count much more than his conception of history; the historian will profess or will not profess the intervention of Providence in history, the guile of reason, history as theophany, etiology, or hermeneutics: it does not matter. A Jewish or a Christian Thucydides would have been able to cap an admirable account with an inoffensive theology without understanding that the plot has been changed by it; conversely, it happens that the historical interest of most philosophies of history is very limited.[14]

It is with the royal road of the historical narrative as with the truth of tragedies: the former can hardly change; essentially, an event will not be related according to another method by a modern than by Herodotus or Froissart—or, more exactly, the only difference that the centuries will have made among those authors is less to be sought in what they say than in what they think or do not think of saying. It is enough to compare the history of King David in the Book of Samuel and in Renan. The biblical account and the one we read in the *Histoire du people d'Israël* are very dissimilar, but we soon see that the most conspicuous difference does not lie in the content, and interests the historian less than the philologist; it relates to the art of narration, to the conception of the account, to the choice of style, to the richness of the vocabulary—in a word, it is due to the evolution of forms, to those reasons of fashion that are so imperious that the most palpable symbol of the passage of time is an old-fashioned garment, and the length of a Greek or Louis XIV type of text that could have been written in the twentieth century is rarely more than a few lines, even if the content is in no way out of date.

Let us leave aside the differences, basically harmless, that are so obvious (they condition literary and intellectual life, in which the garb of modernity is so important), and that philology or the history of art is still far from being entirely able to conceptualize. Let us also leave aside the philosophies of history proper to Samuel and Renan, the acceptance or the rejection of the marvelous and the theological explanation of history; let us also leave the "meaning" that can be given to the history of David, which can be oriented toward Jewish nationalism, toward the Resurrection, and so on. What remains? The essential.

For, in the end, the differences of content are of two kinds: the historical vision is more or less thoroughly investigated, certain things obvious to the Jewish historian are no longer so for a modern historian. The old historian is not very rich in ideas, and when David abandons Hebron and chooses Jebus, the future Jerusalem, as his capital, he has no thought of seeing in that choice all that Renan sees in it:

It is not easy to say what determined David to leave Hebron, which had such ancient and obvious rights, for a poky little place like Jebus. It is probable that he found Hebron too exclusively Jewish. It was not a question of shocking the susceptibility of various tribes, especially that of Benjamin. A new town was needed that had no past.

Then, the event being difference and the light born of comparison, the Jewish historian will not be aware of details that, on the other hand, strike a stranger; he will not write, like Renan:

Certainly a great capital would have been awkward on the site of Jebus, but very large towns were not to the taste and the way of thinking of those peoples. What they wanted was citadels whose defense would be easy.

The old historian obviously could not have at his disposal the topic of capitals. When it is said that Renan, through the biblical account, has rediscovered the true character of David, it is thus not meant that the methods of synthesis have made progress and that our ways of explaining kings and peoples have become scientific, but that Renan could make clearer what was too much taken for granted about the Israelites, on the one hand, and that he could ask questions of which the less political mind of the old historian had not thought, on the other hand. I leave aside, as not germane to the subject of the present book, the obviously greater difference, which is criticism (in its first form and always exemplary of biblical criticism). Setting aside the criticism, the philosophical or theological ideas of hardly any importance from the professional point of view, philological and ideological fashions, and remaining on the plane of historical synthesis, the chasm between Samuel and Renan is the one that would separate the accounts of the same event, by a native and a traveler, on the one hand, and on the other, the man in the street and a political journalist: the chasm is in the number of ideas.

There is no progress in historical synthesis; one understands more or fewer things, but one always sets out to understand them in the same way. A mere description without method, history cannot have those mutations that are the dialectic of the physical and human sciences; thus it cannot be announced that, in the latest news, history has become this or that, that it has discovered temporalities in depth or that it has recognized that breaks are more important than continuities, as one would announce that physics has become quantic or that economics is turning to macroeconomics. The only possible progress of history is the widening of its vision. Its perception of the originality of events has become more refined, and this kind of progress in delicacy is not resounding; outside this increase of a treasury of experience, all the rest is avatars of the conventions of the genre, the day's fashions, or heuristic opportunity. History does not progress, but widens, which means that it does not lose backward the terrain that it conquers forward. So it would be snobbish to take into account only the pioneering zones of historiography; Newtonian physics or Marxist economics is outdated, but the way Thucydides or Godefroy had of writing history is still our contemporary; history is fundamentally erudition, and the names of Martin Nilsson and Louis Robert have exactly as much significance as those of Weber and of the School of Archives to characterize the history of the twentieth century.

How History Is a Work of Art

Can it be that historical synthesis is no more than positivism? It is indeed so, and the most famous books contain no more. It is easily forgotten what an extremely small place general ideas occupy in history books; to what are they reduced in *La société féodale*? To the idea that ground was the only source of wealth and to a few pages that illustrate more than analyze the need of every man to find a protector and the weakness of the central power. In any case there was undoubtedly nothing more to be said. The beauty of *La société féodale* comes from what it reveals: a society with its human types, its habits, and its constraints, in its most irreducible and most everyday originality at the same time; the naturalness of this picture, obscured by no abstraction (few books are less abstract), is what deludes us: as Bloch makes everything understandable, it seems to us that he explains more powerfully than the others. This naturalness is also that of Syme's *Révolution romaine* or of the Hellenistic-Roman civilization shown by Louis Robert, in whom the contemporaries of Cicero, Augustus, or Hadrian are seen with as much realism as a traveler sees a neighboring people that he has come to know well; the characters are in vain in period costumes, their clothes are not more crumpled and dirtied by everyday life. The past then becomes neither more nor less mysterious than the moment we are living.

The interest of a history book is not in the theories, the ideas, and the conceptions of history, packed up to be handed to philosophers; it is, rather, in what makes the literary value of that book. For history is an art, like engraving or photography. To affirm that it is not science, but that it is an art (a minor art), is not to sacrifice to an annoying commonplace or to clear the ground: it would be, if it were affirmed that history, whatever one does, will be a work of art in spite of efforts it makes to be objective, the art being an ornament or incompressible margin. The truth is a little different: history is a work of art *by* its efforts toward objectivity in the same way that an excellent drawing by one who draws historical buildings, who shows the document and does not make it banal, is a work of art to some degree and supposes some talent on the part of its author. History is not one of those arts of knowledge in which, to quote Gilson, it is enough to have understood the method to be able to apply it; it is an art of production in which it is not enough to know the methods: talent is also needed.

History is a work of art because, while being objective, it has no method and is not scientific. Similarly, if one tries to specify where the value of a history book lies, one will find oneself using words that would be applied to a work of art. Since history does not exist, there are only "histories of . . ." and histories of which the eventlike atom is the plot. The value of a history book will depend first of all on the cutting out of that plot, the unity of action it requires, the boldness with which this unity has been extricated from more traditional cutouts—in short, on its originality. Since history is not a scientific explanation, but understanding of the concrete, and since the concrete is one and without depth, a comprehensible plot will be a coherent plot, without the solution of continuity or the deus ex machina.

Since the concrete is a development and concepts are always too fixed, the notions and categories of the historian must try to equalize the development by their flexibility. Since development is always original, you will have to be rich in ideas in order to perceive all its originality and know how to multiply the questions. Since the field of the eventworthy is surrounded by a zone of shadow of which we cannot yet conceive, much subtlety will be needed to explain this non-eventworthy area and to see what is taken for granted. Finally, history, like the theater and the novel, shows men in action and requires some psychological sense to make them alive; for mysterious reasons there is a connection between the knowledge of the human heart and literary beauty. Originality, cohesion, flexibility, richness, subtlety, and psychology are the qualities necessary to say with objectivity "what really happened," to use Ranke's words.

Starting from this, one can amuse oneself by designating the worst history book known—I propose Spengler—and the best—*La société féodale*, for example. The work of Bloch does not mark a final point in knowledge, or progress in the method, for that progress no more exists than does that point. Its merit is in the qualities enumerated above—that is, in its Attic qualities, which a reader seeking in history something other than it can give, would pass by without even seeing them and which, while conferring its objectivity and its naturalness on the work and by being a quality of the historian, are fully revealed only in a literary analysis.

Something Forgotten: Erudition

But the image of historiography as we have so far presented it would suffer from a lack of proportion if we did not add a few words on another orientation of historical knowledge that is very different from narrative history and in which the most irreducible quality of history appears in the pure state; it is about commentary on texts and documents—in a word, about erudition. In erudition, history is reduced to criticism; the effort of conceptualization and the synthesis by "retrodiction" appear only indirectly or implicitly, and the work of the scholar seems to be limited to putting the documents in a state to let the reader see all that they contain and that the reader will be able to see in them. The scholar does not tell stories or comment on the past, he shows it; in fact, he chooses and organizes it, and his work has the false impersonality of a documentary photomontage. Erudition is a variety of historiography to which we give too little thought; two centuries of historicist speculation have excessively associated "history" with "science" or "philosophy," whereas the natural place of history, the documentary knowledge of the concrete, is situated at the opposite pole, that of erudition. To this it must be added that the reading of a work of erudition demands, if not more effort, at least a less conventionally literary effort than the reading of narrative history; moreover, that convention is subject to change, if we are to judge by the current success of collections of documentary history.

A document has a double nature. On the one hand, it belongs by its form to a series: a legal document, to the series of legal documents; a building, to that of buildings; a proverb, to that of proverbs; on the other hand, like every event, it is at the crossroads of an indefinite number of events and is capable of answering an indefinite number of questions. Erudition is concerned only with the first aspect: it establishes the meaning of a document in its series according to the rest of the series; it leaves to the user the task of asking all the questions he wants. Its task consists in showing him only what questions he must *not* ask; one does not question a false act like an authentic one, nor a proverb like a truth established after inquiry; thus erudition is content to adjust the optics of the documents. After that, each person can look in the document and there perceive the past with all the richness of vision of which he is personally capable.

It is the same with axiological history, in which erudition has as its equivalent annotated editions of literary texts, a royal genre particularly cultivated in England, where they really know what poetry is; an annotated edition of *Les fleurs du mal* or of *Seuls demeurent* would be content to explain what the poet meant and has said; it would leave the reader the triple task of enjoying in the text all the beauty he is capable of feeling in it, that of eventually forming sentences to describe that beauty, and that of revealing to anyone interested that it is an insipid university idea to think that poetry can be explained. In short, what bases erudition on reason is that neither history nor poetry takes account of immediate intuition but is perceived through documents or texts that have density and the handling of which is, besides, a source of pleasure or of interest; it may even be considered that it is the taste for handling this dense matter that is the surest sign of an authentic sense of what history or poetry really is.

It can be understood that in those conditions, erudition grows old much less quickly than narrative history or literary criticism; let us say that it grows old naturally, because of the increase in the corpus of documents and not because of changes of fashion or of the raising of young questions. In classical philology, for example, the only works that survive for more than a century or two are exclusively commentaries: those of the scholars of the seventeenth century on the Latin poets, of Godefray on the *Codex Theodosius,* without mentioning those on Aristotle by Alexander of Aphrodisias and by the Scholastics. For a text or a document, posterity can have a thousand ideas for questions that we do not have (the non-eventworthy is only those future ideas), but erudition will not suffer by this lengthening of the questionnaire, for its task is limited to making known, starting no one knows where. For, however advanced an area of knowledge may be, one can always see where one begins not to see, stop at the edge of the unknown, and, without the power to say what future questions are hidden behind the belief in Jupiter, at least not write that Jupiter exists. In fact, the most surprising feature of Thucydides' account is that one thing is missing: the gods of the time.

Beside erudition and commentary, narrative history and the historical synthesis often seem dull. Here are the thousand pages of the *Codex Theodosius*, which are the principal remaining source for the history of the Byzantine Empire; the meaning is difficult, for we do not see to what circumstances all these laws refer and we get lost in the circumlocutions of the chancery rhetoric. The commentary of Godefray is content to smooth away those two difficulties and to explain the texts by texts; immediately the curtain opens on the final drama of antiquity. Is there further need to paraphrase this scene, to relate what everyone can see? Certainly we do not conceive all we see on the stage, but the important thing is to see, and if anyone came to reveal to us that what we see the emperor or the consul doing is called charisma or conspicuous consumption, the comment might seem to us a trifle idle. It may happen that someday the historical genre will die, that narrative history goes out of fashion or that at the booksellers' it falls down to the anecdotal shelf, where the natural history of old has fallen, with bestiaries and lapidaries.

Let us suppose, indeed, that the human sciences develop like the physical sciences have done in the last three centuries. They could not replace history, for an explanation cannot catch up with an account (as we shall see in the next chapter); but they might take all the taste out of history. Let us suppose again that historiography, succeeding in separating itself from the spatiotemporal peculiarity, evolves toward a "general history" that was, to our narrative history, what general geography is in relation to regional geography (as will be seen in the succeeding chapter): in either case there would nonetheless remain an incompressible margin of old-fashioned historiography, for it would indeed be necessary to continue discovering, establishing, and adjusting the knowledge of facts for the use of speculative minds that would question them; that is, the historical genre would then be reduced to its essential and indestructible kernel, erudition.

One dreams then of a metahistory in which the account would be replaced by an assembling of documents chosen with as much flair as Shakespeare had for putting the right words in the mouths of the heroes of his historical plays. If the enterprise could be pushed to its limit, history would be a reconstitution and would cease to be discursive. Which really shows its essence: it relates events, it is a useless repetition of them; it does not reveal things *about* those events. It repeats what took place, in which it is the opposite of science, which reveals what is hidden behind what takes place. History says what is true, and science tells what is hidden.

History Like the Art of Design

What is the ideal of history, then? Is it the conceptualization of what has been experienced? Is it erudition, the interpretation of documents? Is the ideal a *Commentary on the Codex Theodosius* or *La société féodale*? Is the great century of history the Romantic nineteenth century or the erudite eighteenth century? It is more a question of the evolution of taste than a basic problem: whatever the historiographical ideal chosen by a century, it remains true that erudition is the irrecusable kernel of history because it suffices to preserve the memory of the past and to be the archivist of mankind. But it remains nonetheless true that that kernel is not the same thing as the conceptualization and that the latter is not a vain task or a by-product of a really scientific history.

It matters little to know if history as a great genre, narration, is destined to last or if it will only have characterized a moment of the mind, like the epic; very great literary or artistic genres have had only a moment of life, but they are not null and void for all that. If narrative history were destined to fall one day into disuse, it would leave as great a memory as that great artistic moment, the Florentine ideal of "design" in sculpture and in painting; the "design," that perception of the visible world through a very much elaborated experience of the eye in which perspective and anatomy held the place of a topic. The Florentines appreciated anatomy for the simple reason that it was knowledge, that it demanded an apprenticeship, that in that way it was raised above ordinary perception; and they called it a science.[15] The eye of the enlightened amateur "knows" rather than sees; the apprenticeship of a visual questionnaire develops the perception of the human body, thematizes an implicit knowledge, and transforms it into experience. One can even imagine that that apprenticeship has its moment of intoxication when it is taken as a goal in itself: "perspectives" of Piero della Francesca, "anatomical models" of Pollaiuolo.

General sociology represents that moment fairly well; from Simmel to Halbwachs and up to our time, many a page of sociology recalls those studio exercises (with greater hardness in the lines and a firmer drawing in Simmel, more *morbidezza* in Halbwachs). Our reader has seen above an "institutional" anatomical model painted according to a rough sketch by Parsons of which several studio copies are known. One can also imagine an academic degeneration in which anatomy, reduced to a set of rules, would no longer be presented to apprentices at work, in the studio, but would be studied in the academy: from Gurvitch to Parsons in their less good moments, there is no lack of examples.

Like the art of design, history is descriptive knowledge: the reader of a history book feels, when he sees the springs of human affairs working, a pleasure of the same order as a Florentine amateur observing the form and the play of each muscle, of each tendon. Such is the interest of history; it is not of the theoretical or humanist order, nor related to values, nor to the singular existence. The heartfelt cry of the historian, like that of a designer or of a naturalist, would be "It is interesting because it is complicated," because it is not reduced to that form of economy of thought that is deductive science.[16] Vico cursed those Frenchmen who, with their clear, distinct ideas, claimed to make useless the heaviness of libraries.

Chapter XI

The Sublunary and the Human Sciences

But why would it not be possible to raise history to the height of a science, since the facts that make up history and our life are subject to the jurisdiction of science and its laws? Because there are laws *in* history (a body falling in the account of a historian obviously conforms to Galileo's law) but not laws *of* history; the course of the Fourth Crusade is not determined by a law. No more than the history of what happens in my office: the light of the sun becomes more and more slanting, the heat given off by the radiator tends to be stabilized in such a way that the sum of partial derivatives of the second order equals zero, and the filament of the lamp becomes incandescent; that already makes a great number of physical and astronomical laws, which are, however, far too few to recompose this simple event: a winter evening is falling, I have put on the central heating and lit my desk lamp.

Laws and historical events do not coincide; the cutting out of things according to experience is not the same as the cutting out of abstract objects in science. The result is that even if science were completed, it would not be easy to handle, and in a practical way history could not be recomposed with it. The result is also that if science were completed, its objects would not be ours, and we would continue to consult experience, to write history as we do now. And that is the case not by a certain taste for human warmth; we have seen that history is not attached to peculiarities and to values, that it strives to understand, and that it disdains the anecdote. Experience would be no more than an anecdote to it, if it were convertible into science; but it is not practically so, it preserves its density.

In that, the situation of history is not peculiar to it; science does not explain nature much more than it explains history. It does not give an account of a car accident or of a rainstorm in Antibes, one Sunday in February, any more than of the Fourth Crusade, and the resistance that "matter," in the Scholastic sense of the word, offers to its laws is equal to that of human liberty. Science, physical or human, explains *certain* aspects, ready-made for its laws, which it abstracts from natural events or from historical ones; a naturalist would be no more justified than a historian in complaining of it. The original cuttings out of science and of experience are so different that the joining is badly made. The limits of our faculty of knowing are so narrow, the conditions of its exercise are so constraining, that the two cut out are mutually exclusive. You cannot have science of the sublunary save by renouncing the sublunary, by losing the rainbow for the quanta and the poetry of Baudelaire for a theory of poetic language like a hierarchy of constraints with the optimum of convexity; the two cut out will meet only in the infinity of time, when chemistry will replace the cook to predict the taste of a dish. For history to be able to be raised to the level of a science, it would be necessary for science to be the same thing as experience, more scientific and in some way modernized, not to be a break with the immediate and to suffice to scratch an experience a little to find the underlying law. So we are going to show in what way history is not a science; but, since a science of man does exist, we shall also see what relationships history can have with it. To do that, we must first make up our minds on the present state of human sciences.

Scientific Facts and Experienced Facts

If the scientific cutout and the sublunary one do not coincide, it is because science does not consist in describing what is, but in discovering the hidden springs that unlike sublunary objects, function very rigorously; beyond the experience, it seeks the formal. It does not stylize our world, but constructs models of it, gives the formula of it—that of carbon dioxide or that of marginal utility—and it takes as objects the very models whose construction it describes.[1] It is a rigorous discourse that the facts formally obey within the limits of their abstraction. Science also coincides particularly well with the real in the case of the celestial bodies, planets or comets, so much so that this privileged case runs the risk of making us forget that a scientific theory most often remains theoretical, that it explains the real more than it permits handling it, and that technique largely surpasses science, which in turn surpasses it no less greatly in other ways. The opposition between the sublunary and the formal, between the description and the formalization, nonetheless remains the criterion of an authentic science. It is not a research program; discovery cannot be programmed, but it permits knowing from what direction one may hope to hear the intellect whisper and in what direction are the deadlocks, particularly of the avant-garde.[2]

The facts that obey a model will never be the same as those that interest the historian, and that is the difficulty of the question. History, the one that is written and at first that which is lived, is made by nations, crusades, social classes, by Islam and the Mediterranean: all notions of experience that suffice to act and to suffer, but are not ideas of reason. The latter, on the contrary, which a science of man can arrange in rigorous models, are heterogeneous to that experience: strategy of minimax, risk and uncertainty, competitive balance, the optimum of Pareto, the transitivity of choices. For if the world as we see it had the rigor of equations, that vision would be science itself; and, since men will never cease to see the world with the eyes they have, the historicophilological disciplines, which deliberately limit themselves to what has been experienced, will always preserve their justification.

In this respect nothing distinguishes the historicophilological disciplines and the sciences of nature; there cannot be more physics on the plane of perceptible experience than human science on the plane of historical experience. To doubt it, we would have to take literally the empiricist idea of experimental science. If the physical sciences are ready-made in the bottom of test tubes and under microscopes, how is it impossible to disengage a science from historical experience? So it is necessary that human experience should be, in its essence, refractory to all science; let us add as a reminder the belief that only the quantitative are mathematicizable. But we know that experimentation is not the whole of science, that science is the risky interpretation of experiments that are always ambiguous and too rich in details, that it is a theory. And so the impossibility of a scientific history does not depend on the existence of *homo historicus,* but only on the restricting conditions of knowing; if physics wanted to be the mere stylization of the palpable totality, as in the time when it speculated on heat, drought, and fire, all that is said of history's lack of objectivity might be repeated of physical things. Ontological pessimism thus comes back to a gnoseological pessimism.

Because the history of historians cannot be a science, it does not follow that a science of historical experience is impossible;[3] but we see the price of it—what we are accustomed to considering as an event would burst into myriad different abstractions. So the idea of scientifically explaining the revolution of 1917 or the work of Balzac appears as unscientific and as preposterous as the idea of scientifically explaining the department of Loir-et-Cher; it is not because the human facts would be totalities (physical facts also are among them in that case),[4] but because science knows only its own facts.

The Present Position of the Human Sciences

The sublunary and the scientific, the experienced and the formal, are in conflict only in knowing. The contrast Aristotle perceived between the two regions of being—that which is above the circle of the moon and that which is below it—was transported into knowing when modern science was born and Galileo showed that the sublunary had its hidden laws, whereas the moon and the sun were bodies like the Earth and had their "material" imperfections, spots, and mountains. From this it first results that a science of man is possible and that the objections raised to it ("man is unforeseeable spontaneity") sometimes are still the same as those that were made to Galileo when he was told that nature was the Great Mother, the inexhaustible force of spontaneous creation that cannot be reduced to figures. Another result is that a science of man really deserves its name of science only when it is not a paraphrase of the qualities of experience, when it gives itself its own abstractions in a rigorous enough way to be expressed in a well-made language, algebra. Finally, the sublunary continues to subsist as a second mode of knowledge, that of the historicophilological disciplines; it is the essence of science not to be the immediate, and the essence of those sciences to describe the immediate. Between experience and the formal, there is nothing; human sciences not yet formalized are rhetoric, a topic extracted from the description of what has been experienced. When sociology is, wisely, not the history of contemporary civilization; when it wants to be general and to theorize on roles, attitudes, social control, *Gemeinschaft* or *Gesellschaft*; when it measures indices of liberalism, of social cohesion, or of cultural integration, it is like ancient physics, which conceptualized heat and humidity and wanted to make a chemistry with earth and fire.

So we must give up making a science of history, hold a good part of today's human sciences to be unscientific; affirm the possibility of a science of man based on the few pages of that future science that have been written to this day, and maintain that historical scholarship will always retain its legitimacy, for experience and the formal are two coextensive domains (and not two juxtaposed domains of being, that of nature and that of man); science is not the whole of knowledge. Those four ukases arise from a certain sectarianism—or, rather, they are a bet, for we have embarked and cannot not bet—everything is better than the policy of the ostrich or the zeal, on principle, for all novelties.

The present position of the human sciences is that of physics at the beginning of the modern age. Three centuries ago those who thought that the real was mathematicizable could not yet produce, as their justification, more than two or three theorems that seemed very poor beside the rich production of those who interpreted or paraphrased at sight the unintelligible scribble of nature. Galileo won over fewer minds than Paracelsus and, for most of their contemporaries, science was called Paracelsus.

We have to resign ourselves to the unattractive idea that, in an infant science, the law of all or nothing is at work; enormous walls of scientific production that appear in their time to be science itself, may be nothing but ruins. We well know that in a few decades our books of human sciences will appear as strange as the theory of lightning in Lucretius. Let us even say that if today we want to rediscover the freshness and the emotions of ancient physics, to understand the genius it took to distinguish between movement and change, speed and acceleration, heat, light, and temperature, to think out inertia, it is enough to do the following little exercise: try to draw something out of the familiar notions of social class, of depoliticization, or of role (supposing they are less verbal than those of natural place or of perfection of circular movement). He who is surprised that Lucretius so clumsily handled the idea of an equilibrium of natural elements has only to try to do better with the idea of social equilibrium.[5]

Thus one may conclude either that man will always be man and that he will never be reduced to an algebra, or that man has only been a moment in Western thought and that he will be effaced from human brains, and the human sciences with him; these two versions, the classic and the Nietzschean, of the same idea will certainty fascinate the young and the less young. But what is the good of making men unhappy for nothing? The epoch that has seen the establishment of the theory of the minimax, the theorem of Arrow, and generative grammar can legitimately conceive the same hopes as the generation that preceded Newton. Let us run through books on decision theory, relations in organizations, group dynamics, operational research, the welfare economy, the theory of voting. We shall have the feeling that something is being born that brings up the old problems of conscience, of liberty, of the individual, and of the social (but that meets the problem of "rational" conduct); that all the data are present, and more; that the mathematical instrument is ground; and all that is lacking is the flair which let Newton recognize the three or four "interesting" variables.

We can express this in another way, saying that those books are at the same stage of evolution as Adam Smith was: they are a mixture of descriptions, of theoretical sketches, of commonplaces that have come there to die, of developments in common sense, of idle abstractions, and of practical recipes in which all the work of systemization remains to be done, but has become henceforth doable. We have linguistics, of which this is hardly the place to speak; we have economics, a completely constituted human science; psychic science, which has nothing to do with matter (in the Marxist sense of the word this time)—which hardly resembles Marxism, economic history, or the economics page of *Le monde*; it concerns not tons of coal or of corn but the origin of value and the working up of the aims we have chosen in a world where wealth is scarce—and deductive science, in which mathematics is a symbolical language more than the expression of the quantitative. It is the most proper science to make the historian understand in what way history is not a science and to make the ideas on this point get right in his head, that the contrasts should be thrown into relief, that one should begin to see more clearly, that the word "science" may take on a precise sense, and that the affirmation that history is not a science may cease to look like a blasphemy.

We are, therefore, happier than Galileo's contemporaries, who only knew, in the strong sense of the word "know," two or three things about the physical world, the law of falling bodies, or the principle of Archimedes; they could, however, suffice to reveal to them what style they must henceforth expect to find in a real science and that they could cease to torment themselves about problems that until then had obsessed their conception of the world—for example, that of the relations between the macrocosm and the human microcosm.

Possibility of a Science of Man

The objections to a science of man (human facts are not things, science is only an abstraction) might be made about physical science; nothing would be easier than to criticize Galileo unmercifully, as we shall see. The law of Galileo says that the space through which a falling body passes, either vertically or in a parabola, is proportional to the square of the duration of the fall: $e = \frac{1}{2} gt^2$, where the quadratic expression t^2 symbolizes the fact that the space gone through grows bigger and bigger. It is a theory that has the double fault of being unverifiable and of mistaking the originality of natural facts: it does not correspond to experimentation or to an experience. Let us pass over the too famous experiment of the Tower of Pisa; we know that Galileo did not do it (the seventeenth century is full of experiments that were only made in thought, and the experiments of Pascal on the vacuum are among those) or that he did it badly; the results of it are out-and-out false. As for the experiment of the inclined plane, he had recourse to it because he could not make a vacuum in an enclosure; but what right did he have to conclude from a rolling ball to a falling ball?

And why neglect this and retain that, hold that the resistance of the air is negligible and that the acceleration is essential? And supposing that the right key was to be sought in the common-sense idea that a ball falls quickly or slowly depending on whether it is made of lead or of feathers? Aristotle neglected the quantitative aspect of the phenomenon, and he cannot be blamed for it, because Galileo neglects the nature of the falling body. In fact, is his law so quantitative? It cannot be verified for lack of a chronometer (Galileo only had a clepsydra), for lack of an enclosure, and for lack of having determined the value of g. It is as vague as it is abitrary (the formula $e = \frac{1}{2} gt^2$ is true of the pressing of the accelerator by a car driver, as well as of a falling body). But it contradicts our experience. What is there in common between the vertical fall of a leaden ball, the gliding flight of a leaf, and the parabolic trajectory of a javelin flung intentionally, except the word "fall"? Galileo was the victim of a semantic trap.

If there is any evidence, it is the difference between free movements (fire rises, the stone falls) and limited movements (the fire that is blown downward, the stone thrown toward the sky); these latter movements always recover their natural direction, for physical facts are not things. Let us go further, coming back to things themselves. It will be for us a memory that no fall resembles another, that it is not a matter of falls but of concrete objects, that the almost abstract perfection of the fall of a lead ball is a limit rather than a type, that it is too rational a fiction, like *homo oeconomicus*. In fact no one can calculate or foresee a fall; it can only be described ideographically, by writing the history of it. Physics is not a matter of reason but of understanding, of prudence; no one can say exactly how long the fall of a leaf will last, but one can say that certain things are impossible and others not—a leaf cannot remain indefinitely in the air, and a horse cannot be born of a ewe. Nature has no scientific laws, for she is as variable as man; but she has her *foedera*, her constitutional limits, like history (for example, we know that revolutionary eschatology is an impossibility, that it is contrary to the *foedera historiae*, and that anything at all cannot happen; but as for saying what precisely will happen. . . . At most one can think that a particular event "favors" the coming of such another one). Nature or history thus has its limits, but within those limits, determination is impossible.[6]

Our reader understands that these objections to Galileo would have been perfectly reasonable and that Galileo's law was not evidence; it could very well have revealed itself to be false. But he also understands that certain objections must no longer be renewed today in regard to the human sciences. More than one writer has insisted on the irreducible character of human facts that are total, free, and comprehensible, and the knowledge one has of them would be an integral part. Who doubts it? But is that the question? We do not want to relate history; rather, we seek a science of man, but the evolution of the sciences shows sufficiently that the objections of principle made to them in their time in the name of the true nature of things and in the name of the exigency that an object should be approached in conformity with its essence, were the symptom of a still archaic methodology. The eternal error is to believe that science is the double of experience and owes it to itself to give it back to us in an improved version. This error weighed on the beginnings of physics as on those of the human sciences; what does the specific nature of the facts *in* the human sciences matter, since those facts are not those *of* the sciences of man, which, like every science, know only the facts that they give themselves? They cannot prejudge the nature of the facts they will be brought to give themselves.

A choice of variables is shocking to common sense, which will conclude from that that science wants to destroy man, which evidently is enough to alarm us. An economic study will not take into account the ideology of agents, a study of *Les fleurs du mal* will ignore the poetry and the soul of the poet; for that matter, that study did not propose to make us understand Baudelaire, but to discover a formulation of poetic language in terms of programmation under constraints: science seeks objects; it does not explain existing objects. Its only rule is to succeed;[7] sometimes a truism provides the right key, at other times the things that are apparently most simple remain resistant to any formalization (mathematicians have not yet succeeded in formulating an algebra of nodes, whereas for two centuries they have known how to reduce the caprices of the wave to equations). The sign of success is that the formalization adopted gives rise to deductions that work with reality and teach us something new.

In hydrodynamics we start from a few very simple ideas: in a trickle of water the liquid is incompressible, no vacuum forms in it either and, if in thought one cuts out a volume in the current, as much water enters that volume as goes out of it. Starting from these truisms, one writes equations with partial derivatives; those equations can give rise to interesting deductions, they allow it to be foreseen if the water will flow out regularly or not. With man it is not different from the wave. There begins to exist, thanks to a few mathematicians, a formal sociology in which one is tempted to invest as much hope as in economics; when one of those mathematicians, H. Simon, constructs the model of the functioning of a group of administrators and of its level of activity,[8] the variables and the axioms he chooses are of the simplest: the level of activity of the group members, their mutual sympathy, their relations with the outside. It is not by these banalities that the value of the model has to be judged, but by the fact that the formalization leads to deductions that would be inaccessible to verbal reasoning: the possible points of equilibrium for the activity of the group, for the harmony that reigns within it, for its equilibrium with the milieu, and whether those equilibriums are stable.

Before these examples, the historian feels himself in the presence of a kind of mind that is very different from his own; it is no longer a question of critical sense or of comprehension, but of a theorist's flair that is applied indifferently to human conduct and to natural phenomena, and that makes him scent, behind a sometimes trivial paradox, some hidden spring. For example, one can establish retrospectively that the marginalist microeconomics should have been discovered by a curious mind that might have investigated the following paradox: How is it that a famished man does not pay more for the first sandwich he devours, and for which he would have given a fortune, than for the fourth, which satisfies his appetite?

A formalization is not judged by its point of departure, but by its nature and its results. It does not consist in writing concepts in symbolical language—otherwise said, in abbreviations—but in doing operations on those symbols. It must then produce verifiable results, "testable propositions" as the Americans say; otherwise it would be enough to found a formalized erotology that a lover made the following declaration to his loved one: "All charm emanating from you is the integral of my desires and the constancy of my passion is measured by the absolute value of the second derivative."

The flair of the theoretician is, therefore, to guess what aspects of the real are susceptible of being translated into the rigorous and fruitful language of mathematical deductions, what conceptual key will release something that may be minute, that may be very abstract but is nonetheless real, and whose existence had never been suspected. Let us do a little praxeology-fiction. There will have to exist one day a mathematical theory of the state or of public order, as there has existed one of general economic equilibrium since Walras. In the time of the Physiocrats, the mystery of the economy still to be born might be enunciated thus: how is it that the seven hundred thousand inhabitants of Paris each morning find food and have their needs satisfied thanks to the activity of millions of producers and middlemen who act freely and have no understanding with each other and obey no coordinated plan? The key to the mystery was to be found in the equilibrium between supply and demand, in the fiction of an economic life conceived as a vast market translated by a system of equations. The political thinkers, from La Boétie to B. de Jouvenel, have not ceased to be astonished by the miraculous obedience of human groups to ideal rules or to the orders of a handful among them:

Such subordination is enough to strike with astonishment men capable of reflection; it is a singular action, an almost mysterious idea, the obedience of a very large number to a very small number.[9]

To reduce this mystery to science will not consist in using the psychology of authority and of the feelings of dependence in describing the sociological or historical variants of power, with its ideal types, in making a covaried analysis of it; scientific breakthrough will perhaps play, rather, on one unexpected point that gives a grip to formalization—for example, on this paradox: "If the policeman who is on traffic duty wanted to be just, he would interrogate both parties, letting pass the doctor and the midwife; in fact it would be the height of disorder and all would be discontent. And, too, the policeman does not worry about knowing who is in a hurry and why; he simply cuts the flood; he is giving heed to an order as such."[10] Let us dream for a moment about a political mathematics in which the fiction of the crossroads would play the same role of scientific object as that of the market in Walbrassian economics,[11] but let us awaken to remember two things: first, that we must begin by translating that fiction into an algebra, which ought not to be impossible in our epoch, where the queues have just been mathematicized; second, that that algebra ought to allow of verifiable and instructive deductions—that is everything.

The Human Sciences Are Praxeologies

As can be seen, human sciences are really sciences, for they are deductive, and they are really human, for they take man as a whole—body, soul, and freedom; they are theories of all that action is, praxeologies. Economic laws do not concern representation any more than matter; they are neither psychological nor nonpsychological, they are economic. The domain proper to economics begins when we pass from technical productivity to value productivity, and economics is properly a theory of value; it would apply just as well to university diplomas, however dematerialized these may be. The law of diminishing returns has only the appearance of physical law, for it supposes a technological choice and a valorization. The law of decreasing utility is not a psychological law, either;[12] as Schumpeter says, the theory of marginal value is more a logic than a psychology of value.[13] Let us say that value is psychic, if not psychological, in order to indicate that it all the same is more like a representation than like a pebble,[14] for economics is a science of action; value, on the other hand, is an abstraction, a scientific object that is not confused either with prices or with a psychological fact like the desire we have for a thing.

Let us consider the theory of the interest on capital according to Boehm-Bawerk. The fact that the exchange of present goods against future goods is made with the rebate of an interest that is not an objective necessity, an institution, or a psychological move signifies that the logic of the action imposes that rebate. The "requisite" of it is that a less subjective value is attached to future goods; that it is less, means that one thinks of it as such. Finally, let us consider the famous paradox of the water and the diamond: the useless diamond is worth a great deal, while water, which is indispensable, costs nothing; its exchange value is nil, while its use value is considerable. If one accepted, in economics, the making of a distinction between the representation and the functioning, then the inequality of value between the water and the diamond attributable, at first sight, to the representation, should have been driven back to outer darkness—which did not prevent the neoclassicists, a century ago, from discovering the reason for it. Similarly, even yesterday, market strategy, assuredly explicable by the way individuals or groups imagine their partners in the exchange, ought to have been rejected, too, for the too human sciences; now the mathematics of games is interested in theorizing it.[15]

Economics owes its exemplary value to the fact that it goes beyond the dualism of representation and objective conditions; the cleavage it sets up is that which all science sets up—it passes between what it theorizes and what it leaves by abstraction outside the theory and which may be psychological (thus a panic on the Stock Exchange and, more generally, all we call economic psychology) or may not be (thus economic institutions). Psychology and institutions are indeed a requisite, but they are not the requisite for functioning. On the contrary, theory never functions so well as when they are not there; they are the requisite for an insertion of theory into the concrete. Similarly, Newtonian mechanics has as a requisite the existence of a moon, of a sun, and of planets: similarly again, if you want the Kantian categorical imperative to act on reality and the pure respect of "you must" makes you deliver a deposit entrusted to you, it takes a psychological requisite (love of virtue or fear of the police) and an institutional requisite (the existence of the thing called deposit).

Like every theory, the economic theory is theoretical. So it is quite useless to condemn once again the fiction of a *homo oeconomicus* moved by his egotistical instincts alone.[16] The fiction, in this matter, is not that of selfishness, but of rationality. Let us put ourselves into the neoclassical perspective, rather out of date today but preserving its value as an example. Economic analysis does not study what men do to attain, more or less efficaciously, their economic goals, but what they would do if they were *homines oeconomici* more rational than they generally are, independent of the aims they have chosen and of the psychological motives that made them choose them; for an apostle, if he is an organized man, a penny is a penny, as it is for a loan shark. Economics retraces the logic and the limit of action; as in the case of Kantian morality (in which a moral action, insofar as it proceeds from an inclination of the agent, "has no real moral value, however much it conforms to duty, however praiseworthy it may be"), one may think that "no action up to today" has been accomplished by pure economic rationality, any more than the pure bodies of chemistry exist in nature. But that does not prevent Kantian morality, economics, and chemistry from accounting for a considerable part of the concrete and from isolating clearly the part that escapes them; to the "you must" of economic rationality, if man replies "And if I don't?" economics can answer, "The event will avenge me."

The theory is thus an instrument of analysis and intervention; whether man is rational or not, it explains what will come of it, and why. For example, it demonstrates that the theory of interest on capital remains true in a Communist system, where the economic institutions of capital and loan do not exist; since 1889, Boehm-Bawerk has very clearly demonstrated it.[17] For to choose rationally between two plans whose dates of payment are more or less distant, the planner will be obliged to create on paper, under what word is not important, an index that will be equivalent to the rate of interest, so as to calculate the comparative costs of the tying up of public credit. The Soviet economists, for whom this problem is the principal anxiety at the moment, have recognized that if the theory has clean hands, it nonetheless has hands.

The misunderstanding of *homo oeconomicus* is repeated about each praxeology. It is not quite true that the *Critique of Practical Reason* reveals a moral doctrine of pure respect that would be opposed to the ancient eudaemonism or to an ethics of values. Rather, it gives, in Kant's words, a "formulation" of morality; it analyzes the logic of the ethical act independently of the mentality of the agent, of his philosophical or religious rationalizations, of his motives, and of all that would be read in a sociology of the ethical life.[18] Kant does not teach what the moral agents must do, and he does not go in for a paraenesis; instead, he states the significance of what they effectively do. If those concerned judge otherwise, it is because they cannot disengage the formula of what they do. So one cannot object to Kant that observation does not confirm that man acts out of pure respect, or interpret Kantism as a sublimation of the Protestant or petit-bourgeois mind. One might as well believe that the *Critique of Judgment* advocates formalism in art; it is content to bring out the formula of aesthetic judgment as such, and all sociology of art that dissolved the aesthetic praxeology into sociology would empty itself, the activity it claims to describe having no more meaning.

The neoclassic economists are not the ideologists of liberal bourgeoisie[19] any more than Clausewitz is a doctrinaire of war to the death: all he does is to formulate the abstract in "absolute violence" of "clashes"[20] of "real war," the logic and the limit of all armed conflict. Each domain of action has its hidden logic, which guides the agents independently of the consciousness they have of it, motives that are their own or rationalizations that their society gives of it; mentalities and structures are not the ultima ratio, and sociology is not the tribunal of the world. The different doctrines of political authority and of Weberian sociology of power, with its three ideal types, merely turn around the irreducible fact of political authority, whether it be traditional, constitutional, or charismatic. To study human action only sociologically is to resign oneself to understanding nothing about it. The two *Critiques*, or Clausewitz, or economic theory, or the still-confused whole designated by the name of operational research is the remains of a future science; thus is gradually built, beyond psychology and sociology, in a still unnamed no-man's-land, a science of action that is at present the clearest hope of the human sciences.[21]

Why History Aspires to Science

But is it a hope for the historian? What can he expect of the human sciences? He would like to expect a lot of them, for he lives in the uneasiness given him by the lack of a theory, and at present we see the despairing attempts to escape from that uneasiness multiplying in the windows of bookshops; that is called the "mode" of human sciences. The slightest line of an account (the oppressed rose, the oppressed resigned themselves to their lot) calls for a double justification. So it is that human nature includes the thing termed "oppression" that will involve or not involve a rising (and there is necessarily a "why" to this difference); one cannot be indefinitely content to state that, according to Weber, oppression "favors" revolt. From Thucydides, who had experienced the attraction of Ionian physics and medicine, to Marc Bloch, who begins by prowling in Durkheim's direction, the theoretical uneasiness, though constantly repressed, remains nonetheless visible. "John Lackland has passed that way" is a historical proposition if ever there was one; that he won't go that way again is understood, but how can we not ask why he passed that way? From the psychoanalysis of John Lackland to the sociology of pilgrimages, without forgetting the commercial routes and the phenomenology of temporality in the English nobility, we will try everything to answer that "why."

We shall thus end up by knowing, about the journey of John Lackland, exactly as much as we know about the journey of one of our neighbors or about a journey we have taken ourselves; it takes no more to live, so it needs no more to write history. The historian will end by finding amply sufficient the simple fact that John passed that way and, first of all, by establishing it, but it will not be without repressing the regret not to have done better. Yet he resigns himself to it because he has soon established it, for so long as he relates his history in all simplicity and does not require from his pen more than a novelist would ask—that it explain—all is well; all goes badly, on the other hand, as soon as he tries to do more, to recapture the principles of his explanations, to generalize, to examine deeply—all eludes his grasp, all becomes verbal or false. The regret, however, remains with him, for the need for determination is as imperious as the reason. Therefore he will remain ready to believe in all hope: structuralism, functionalism, Marxism, psychoanalysis, sociology, phenomenology.

The Confusion of Essences

There is more: the contemplation of a historic landscape is like that of a terrestrial landscape; not only are the forms of relief like the statement of a problem, but they further seem to suggest solutions or indicate where a future science lies. For, after all, apples might not fall to the ground,[22] and men might not obey some of the solutions. Authority, religion, economics, art have a hidden logic, are so many regional essences.[23] Their relief is not the result of chance; their slopes are not oriented haphazardly; there is some rugged exigency in them. The most astonishing characteristic of this scenery is its hugeness; everything in it turns to the institution, to differentiation, or to diffusion, everything in it develops and grows complicated: empires, religions, systems of relationships, economics, or intellectual adventures. History has a curious tendency to raise giant structures, to make human works almost as complicated as those of nature.

The result is that, even if one writes from beginning to end the history of a human work, one has not yet the feeling of having really explained it: the historian spends his time turning round essences that have their secret praxeology, without ever knowing the last word of what he is speaking about. He has to admit, on the one hand, that there is not much in common between an ancient "state" and the modern state; that when he speaks of the Greek religion and of the Christian religion, he is misusing a homonym. But, on the other hand, he does not cease to feel that there is an essence of public authority or of religion behind their historical variations; no one knows what those essences are, yet to want to write history while pretending to be ignorant of what is known immediately by any traveler who, disembarking on an unknown island, recognizes that the mysterious gestures made by the natives are a religious ceremony, is to reduce history to chaos. So, from Plato to Husserl, history, like all experience, has not ceased to pose the problem of the essence; our vision of experience is a vision of essences that, although confused, alone give a meaning to the scene.

In brief, we never, in histoy, succeed (and what historian has not known the exasperation of what powerlessness?) in finding what Wittgenstein calls the hard of the soft, to seize which is the condition and the beginning of all science; everywhere, on the contrary, experience is at hand. Doubly so. First, causality is not constant (a cause does not always produce its effect; moreover, as will be seen in the next chapter, they are not always the same causes—for example, economic causes, which are the most efficacious). Second, we do not succeed in passing from the quality to the essence. We can recognize that a certain conduct may be termed religious, but we cannot say what religion is; this inability is translated in particular by the existence of confused frontier zones—for example, between the religious and the political, where one is reduced to platitudes ("Marxism is a millenarist religion") that one cannot resign oneself to formulate, but that one also cannot ignore, for they contain, somewhere, a bit of truth. However, that bit slips through the fingers in quarrels about words, as soon as one tries to determine it. This jumble, these contradictions, this confusion induce us to state, beyond experience, the order of the formal, of the scientific; for science is born of contradiction and of the confusion of phenomena, much more than it is inferred from their resemblances. Thus there is repeated unceasingly the old conflict between Aristotelian experience and Platonic formalism; all science is more or less Platonic.

The historian keeps to experience, so he has constantly to resist the temptation to settle its confusions, at least expense, by going in for reductionism. Yet it would be simple to explain everything by bringing everything back to something else, the wars of religion will come back to political passions. Those passions will not be related to a sickness of the body social, as such, which the individual feels within himself and which, through anguish or shame, prevent him from sleeping even if he does not suffer from them in his private life; they will be reduced to the sphere of his personal interest, and that interest itself will be of the economic order. That is a materialist reductionism, but there are others that will be idealist and that are worth nothing more. Thus politics will be reduced to religion; instead of considering that the Roman emperor or the king of France was surrounded by a charismatic aura (the cult of the imperial, the annointing and coronation, the curing of sorofula) because he was the sovereign, because the love of the people for the sovereign is a feeling expressed in all times, and because all authority appears more than human, it will be thought that the monarchic cult was the "basis" of royal power. Similarly, economics will be reduced to psychology: if primitive peoples exchange goods, it will be in virtue of a psychology of the countergift and of a seeking for prestige. Everything will be brought back to something more banal than itself. If emperors were accustomed to leave behind monuments of their reign—triumphal arches or Trajan's column—it will not be out of a desire to leave a trace of their reign in the open and to proclaim their glory, even if no one listens; it will be for "imperial propaganda."

We may consider that, today, the personal education of a historian, the acquisition of that clinical experience of which we were speaking before, is largely spent in getting rid of those reductions that are in the air and in rediscovering the originality of different essences. To reach a contradictory and deceptive conclusion: each essence is explained only by itself—religion by the religious sentiment, and monuments by the desire to leave monuments. The human soul is formless; it does not have a hierarchical structure that would allow the bringing back of these diverse sentiments to one more profound sentiment, class interest, or innermost religion. And yet, although one sees no foundation for them, those sentiments persist no less fiercely; they coexist, independent, arbitrary, and irreducible as old nations. The surprising contrast between their absence of principles and their tenacity can be explained only by some hidden reason and reference to a future science.

It Has Little to Expect from Science

But what will be the effect of that future science on the historian's profession? It will be weak, because, as we are not unaware, there are no laws *of* history. The result is that the historian will have "to know everything," like the ideal orator or like the detective and the criminal, but will be able to be content, like them, to know as amateurs. The detective and the criminal must have information on everything, for they cannot foresee to what lengths the execution or the reconstitution of a criminal plot may take them. But if that plot can work up scientific knowledge, at least there is no science of the plot itself, whose unfolding has no laws. How far away it already seems, the epoch, only half a century old, when Simiand advised that in history one should seek generalities and regularities, in order to draw from them an inductive science of wars and revolutions; when it was hoped to succeed one day in explaining the growth and evolution of a given society.

Not only is no event enfiladed by a law, but even laws that interfere with the course of an event will never explain more than a small part of it. Parsons spoke truly, more than he perhaps thought, when he wrote[24] that history is "an empirical, synthetic science which needs to mobilize all the theoretical knowledge necessary to explain the historical processes." To put it more precisely, "the knowledge that is necessary"—laws in detail—in the measure that they complete the understanding of the plot and are inserted in sublunary causality. Spinoza's dream of a complete determination of history is only a dream; science will never be able to explain the novel of humanity, taking it in whole chapters or only in paragraphs. All it can do is to explain a few isolated words of it, always the same ones, that you come across on many a page of text, and its explanations are sometimes instructive for the understanding, sometimes only idle commentaries.

The reason for this separation between history and science is that history has as a principle that all that has been, is worthy of it; it has not the right to choose, to limit itself to what is susceptible of scientific explanation. The result is that in comparison with history, science is very poor, and repeats itself terribly. Whatever economy or whatever society you describe, the general theory of the state as a crossroads and of the economy as the market equilibrium will be true; for the equations of Walras to become an event, the Earth would have to become an Eden in which goods would no longer be scarce, or a demi-Eden where they would all be substitutable for each other. What would be the use of a future mathematics of political authority to a historian of the Roman Empire? Not to explain that the emperor was obeyed for exactly the same reasons that every government is obeyed. That theory would, rather, do him a negative service; it would help him not to give way to reductionism and to false theories, not to speak too much of charisma. It would, in short, render him the services of a culture. Let us conclude, with L. von Mises, that "when history brings into play certain scientific knowledge, the historian has only to acquire an average degree of knowledge (a moderate degree of knowledge) of the science in question, a degree that will not exceed what is normally possessed by every cultured person."[25]

So much the more because science may be so abstract that one has no real idea of what to do with it. The theory of games of strategy is presently as magnificent as it is useless, like the calculation of probabilities in Pascal's time; and the whole problem is to succeed in applying it to something. You have only to see the precautions of writers who are tempted to use it, their way of touching it gingerly.[26] It is so easy, indeed, to get burned by it. Here is the famous "dilemma of the two prisoners": two suspects know that if they both keep quiet, they will get off with a light punishment, but that if one of them confesses, he will be released, whereas his comrade will receive a severe sentence because he was not the first to confess.[27] There is enough there to excite anyone who has the slightest sociological imagination. That is, therefore, why social life is sustained by a dialectal of "all" and "each";[28] all want the government to work, but no one wants to pay taxes if he is not sure that the others will pay too. That is why authority, order, is needed; that is the explanation of the solidarity, of the prudence of *homo historicus*; that is the definitive refutation of anarchism; and that is why revolutions do not happen. Better still, from that insoluble dilemma will be deduced the necessity for a formal rule: "do what you have to do, come what may," and you will have created the Kantian ethic. It is too beautiful, there is too much of it, it is nothing more than an allegory; the slightest monographic study in which the dilemma would have testable effects would suit us much better. Alas! Man is so wavering and diverse a being that the human sciences cannot be other than very abstract, for they have to go very far before finding an invariant.

Example: Economic Theory and History

The human sciences will explain little history and will remain too abstract for the historian, which is confirmed by the example of one of those sciences that already exists, economic theory. We know it poses a dilemma. Either it is deductive, and can then rightly boast of remaining "eternally" true, beyond the diversity of institutions, in which case its practical or historical applications are very poor, or else it has applications, more or less laborious and approximate, but at the price of dated institutional content, which makes it unusable for the historian, who can no longer transpose it into "his period" without anachronisms. Neoclassic economics embodies the first horn of the dilemma fairly well, and macroeconomics since Keynes is nearer the second; the essential concern is to make the right distinction, and it is to that that we shall apply ourselves.

It is common knowledge that many economic historians do not know much economic theory and that they are none the worse for it. Economic history is much more interested in describing the economic facts than in explaining them; it reconstitutes curves of prices and of wages, calculates the distribution of real estate, describes economic institutions, commercial or fiscal policies, and economic psychology; it retraces the economic geography of the past. When it speculates on monetary problems (as Charles Wilson does in masterly fashion), it is much more like a know-how of technicians than a knowledge of theoreticians; a pure economist would see in that know-how only "materials" for a quantitative theory of money.

To speak the language of logical empiricism, the mass of institutional and historical "data" is very much larger, in economic history, than that of "laws." Theory can hardly serve to reconstitute facts; it comments upon rather than explains them. We are not, all the same, going to talk again of the prestige of von Thünen each time it is a question of the distance separating two economic metropolises.[29] On the other hand, theory will have a very important negative role: it will prevent us from falling into the preconceptions of common sense. Was it not born, after all, of a reaction against preconceptions about money and customs protectionism? Today it can teach a historian of Rome that the too famous affirmation of Pliny, "the latifundia have ruined Italy,"[30] has exactly no value for economic history (except for that of popular ideas on economic ethics); that we must weigh our words before saying that Roman Italy was ruined by the competition of the rest of the Empire; that the problem of inflation is not simple; and that it is not absurd to think that the counterfeit money of the third century could have favored the poor.[31]

In short, theory plays the part of a culture, teaching that "things are always more complicated than that." But as for saying what they are. . . .[32] Let us not be the dupes of the successes of the macroeconomics of our present-day governments; know-how is not knowledge. Because a finance minister knows recipes for a healthy currency, it does not follow that the quantitative theory of money is achieved. But then the historian will not be able to transpose into the past the lessons of present economic practice, because you do not knowingly transpose what you can deduce; if you do not know why a recipe succeeds, how do you know if the conditions of its success were realized in the past? The historian who took literally, in Keynes, the words "law relative to the propensity to consume" (according to which consumption increased less quickly than income) would be preparing disappointments for himself, for the supposed "law" is only an empirical finding that has been contradicted by the facts of our own age.

If one transposes only what can be deduced, the quantity of economic science that historians can use with certainty is reduced like the ass's skin (see Balzac, *La peau de chagrin*); this considerable impoverishment is the ransom of the anachronisms we are avoiding. As we see it, neoclassic economics constitutes the culture most appropriate to the needs of a historian,[33] if only because the neoclassicists had an acute methodological awareness and strongly maintained the distinction between pure theory and the institutional and empirical data, between "what belongs to the nature of the economic system in the sense that that flows necessarily from the action of economic factors left to themselves" and what, while being of an economic order (an institution or panic on the Stock Exchange) is "foreign to the sphere of pure economics."[34] This distinction is all the more necessary because economic theory, even if it is pure, nonetheless has as its starting point contemporary economic life (and, more narrowly still, the national economy, the "wealth of nations").

It is thus that, reduced to its pure part, neoclassic economics cannot teach the historian anything on two points that particularly interest him: consumption and the social distribution of wealth. Or, rather, it leaves him all the work, for, as he sees it, these questions are exclusively psychological or institutional—that is, empirical, descriptive, historical. It may be the consumption of goods, the use that a society makes of its wealth: dams, superhighways, wars, temples, or potlatches. Economics cannot teach us anything about which of these uses a society elects or about the motives that make it elect that use; all that an economist can do is ask people to what use they mean to put their wealth. The scale of their preferences and the income of each one being known, he will then draw curves of indifference and will suppose that the consumer intends to get the maximum out of his means. He will indicate to the consumer the optimal combination that his income permits: so much butter and so many guns, according to what is known about the taste, keener or less keen, of the consumer for one or the other of those products. So, under the name of theory of consumer behavior one must not confuse what is really theoretical and what is only the psychosocial description. The true economic analyst cannot go further than the transitivity of choices,[35] the indifference curves, and the effect of substitutions;[36] to explain the choices themselves is not his business, for economics does not study the economic aims, but the consequences of those aims in a world where goods are scarce and imperfectly substitutable for each other.

Some of the studies on the consumption function is no more economics than a study of the technological data of the productions function would be; those studies, in truth, are sociological, and a historian cannot expect much of them, for he will no doubt prefer to make the sociology he needs. A sociologist of economics tells him that certain consumers buy an expensive product because it is expensive, so as to prove to all that they are rich enough to do so, and that this conduct is called conspicuous consumption.[37] But to the historian that is not enough; conspicuous consumption can assume very different forms, and he will want to know who consumes conspicuously, why, and whom to bluff. Another economist reveals to him that a class or a nation feels frustrated at the sight of a class or a nation richer than itself, that its propensity to consume increases in consequence, and that that reaction is called demonstration effect. This baptism is too much, if it only gives a name to the most banal of reactions; it is not enough, if one wants to understand this reaction (to see it at work in a historical context): the lower middle class aping the upper class or unrest in the Third World in opposition to American civilization. The sociological economist being content to put names on truisms, all the work remaining to be done is for the historian.

Another Example: The Distribution of Wealth

The case of the distribution of wealth is different from that of consumption; it is concerned with a problem within the sphere of pure economics and of its deductions. It does not claim to give an account of the effective historic distribution of wealth among the members of a society; it wants to deduce an abstract model that the historian or the sociologist will always be able to confront with reality. It is the difference between the concrete object and the object of knowledge. Unfortunately, nothing is more easily obliterated than the consciousness of that difference; then you come to be astonished that a theory is theoretical. Certainly, to Schumpeter, it is immediately evidence that the theory can only deduce the theoretical distribution;[38] on the other hand, to other writers it will be a statement or even a shocking discovery. Clearly, we are here in the presence of two different or unequally lucid conceptions of the nature of economics.

In distribution, as in everything else, pure economics is not the description of what is happening, but the deduction of what would be happening if the economic mechanisms were left to themselves and were isolated from the rest (a hypothesis that, in the case of liberal capitalism, is a little less far from reality than in other economic systems); it is for the historian to measure the distance between that fiction and reality and, if that distance is too great, to say how the logic of economic action has avenged itself for the disdain it has suffered. That seems clear; unfortunately, a permanent risk of confusion exists between the point of view of the theoretician and that of the historian. Since the macroeconomics revolution, and since state intervention in the economy has become more and more important, there has developed a sort of neofiscalism that has transformed the economists into counselors of the government or into constructors of models of growth; now, when he speaks of distribution, the economist, according to whether he is a fiscalist or a theoretician, does not use this same word about the same thing. The theoretician considers only the economic agents, their incomes, their salaries, their quasi incomes, and their eventual profits; the fiscalist starts with reality, the table of the national income of his country, the basic document for all economic policy. Thus he will be brought to consider the salaries of civil servants and the wages of domestic servants, which figure in his table but which the theoretician ignored (except when he undertook to reduce them to theory).[39]

The difference between the theoretical distribution and the historical distribution is so great that the theory of distribution hardly forms a chapter of its own; the "salaries" and the "incomes," rather than the true salaries and incomes, are sorts of indexes that measure the marginal productivity of work and of the soil, and the distribution is only an appendix to the chapter on production. At this degree of generality one can no longer distinguish slavery from wage earning. It is admitted that, theoretically, the salary of the worker is equal to the marginal productivity of his work;[40] but this wage earner is scarcely only a reasonable being who possesses just the minimum of individuality necessary to facilitate the study. In reality his salary is surely very different from that productivity, which is difficult to measure precisely, and it is fixed by the employers, the trade unions, and the governments. But the "true" salary remains the theoretical one, in the sense that it will take its revenge if one moves too far from it.

What, then, will happen in a slave state where the worker receives no wages? It will be considered that his salary is pocketed by the slave's owner, provided he feeds the slave;[41] this is a means of calculating the income of the owner, of seeing if slavery is profitable. Or, rather, it would be such a means, if the calculation was possible in practical terms. But the slave regime itself escapes theory—or, rather, the theory is imposed on it as a datum given—so distribution calls not for a scientific explanation, but for a sociohistorical description of which the *Répartition du revenu national* of Marchal and Lecaillon[42] remains the classic example for the contemporary world. Such is the cleavage between the experienced and the formal, between the sublunary and the scientific, between the *doxa* and the *epistémé*.

Historical Truth and Scientific Truth

History can be transformed by the human sciences in a measure comparable with that by which our lives can be transformed by technology; we have electricity and atomic energy, but our plots remain composed of causes, ends, and chances. No manner of writing history can be revolutionary, any more than life can cease to be daily. Linguistics is of no use for understanding texts better, any more than the theory of light is of use in educating the eye about colors; philology is therefore not an application of linguistics, which, like all theory, has no end other than itself. Semiotics perhaps will teach us tomorrow what the beautiful is, which will satisfy our curiosity but will not change our way of perceiving beauty. Like philology or geography, history is a "science for us," which knows true science only in the measure that it intervenes in experience. It experiences no aesthetic or anthropocentric complaisance in holding to this point of view; if, practically, it could exchange the *doxa* for the *epistémé*, it would not hesitate to do so.

Unfortunately, it is characteristic of our faculty of knowing that the two planes of knowledge do not succeed in meeting, in spite of a few interventions of detail. Being is at the same time complicated and rigorous; one can either undertake to describe that complication, without ever finishing it, or seek a beginning of rigorous knowledge, without ever recognizing the complexity. He who clings to the plan of experience will never escape; he who constructs a formal object sets out for another world where he will discover something new, rather than finding there the key of the visible.

We have no complete knowledge of everything; the event with which we are most personally involved is still known to us only by traces. We can resign ourselves to having no complete knowledge. We sometimes succeed in reproducing limited models of the real; scientific knowledge, which is everywhere possible, even about man, dispenses us from that of the concrete, which is never complete. It remains true that things do not invest themselves fully in us, that they figure there only partly or obliquely; our mind reaches strict or ample knowledge of the real, but it never contemplates the original text of it.[43]

History is a palace whose full extent we do not discover (we do not know how much of the non-event remains to be historicized) and of which we do not see all the suites at once; thus we are never bored in that palace where we are imprisoned. An absolute mind would be bored there, one that knew the geometric form of it and had nothing more to discover or describe there. This palace is a true labyrinth to us, for science gives us well-constructed formulas that will allow us to find the exits, but will not give us the plan of the premises. The idea that science is perpetually unfinished must be taken with its full force; this does not mean only that we are sure of nothing, that the totality of our knowledge is not safe from error, but that there is no totality—science adds discovery to discovery, and never draws a line below the addition. Scientific affirmations are limited to themselves, and suppose nothing of what they do not say. Let us consider Newtonian gravity, which seemed to suppose the unthinkable idea of action at a distance. Certain contemporaries had concluded from that that Newton was mistaken, for gravitation seemed to suppose another mystery, the force of attraction. Voltaire concluded from this that such must be the essence of things, and that the Creator had given this force to matter.[44]

That view was accepted until the day Einstein discovered that it is more general to say that, in physical space, the shortest way between two points is a curve and that attraction is just that. Let us not conclude that space is truly curved, for physics will not leave it at that; one day relativity must come out of the magnificent isolation that at present is its own. Similarly, when Walras and Jevons discovered the law of marginal utility, people did not fail to give a realistic version of it, invoking the decrease of our needs, the law of Weber and Fechner. Nor were objections lacking; certain needs, they remarked, grow with satisfaction instead of decreasing. Some concluded that marginalism was useless or false; others, more wisely, called attention to the fact that the important thing was the verifiable deductions that could be drawn from this. Now the mathematics of games perhaps permits the deduction to rise higher and to be interpreted otherwise.

A result of this is that historical truth is very different from scientific truth; both are provisional, but not in the same way. If science, it will be said, is perpetually unfinished, is it not the same with history? Are not historical truths that pass as established susceptible to being upset by new discoveries? Physicists or historians, we are never sure of anything. That is true, but one feels at the same time that these arguments miss an essential difference. Science is unfinished because it never puts a total, and history is unfinished because its totals are subject to revision if an error or an omission is found. The case of the physicist is a little like that of an ingenious savage[45] who, by dint of fiddling with the controls of a car, may have discovered that by turning on the ignition and pressing the starter, he can start the engine, which remains invisible to him under the tightly closed hood. Beginning with his "model" of starting, he will not fail to make hypotheses about what that engine can be, but he will never see the engine with his own eyes. It may even happen that he has elucidated the working of all the knobs and that he has nothing more to discover on the dashboard; but he will never be able to know if his science of the engine is complete, and it would be vain for him to wonder, for it is vain to question ourselves on what escapes our grasp.

To affirm that space is curved is not really to affirm that it is curved; on the contrary, to affirm that Socrates and Jesus existed and are not myths, is really to say that they existed. The affirmation is to be taken literally, and there is nothing more to know; it may one day show itself to be false. Every historical process can always be revised, but it cannot be deepened; the verdict will be translated by a yes or a no. An epistemologist would say that an empirical fact is a fact; on the other hand, a scientific theory is not positively true—it is, at most, not invalidated. A Christian would say that there may be a conflict between history and Revelation, but not between science and faith.

Chapter XII

History, Sociology, and Complete History

B ut have we not aimed too high? Does not history resemble geology rather than physics? The formalized sciences are not all science, and it cannot be claimed that there is nothing between the *mathemata* and history-philology; there are sciences that, without being hypothetico-deductive, are nonetheless scientific, in that they explain the concrete, starting from an order of concrete facts that was hidden and that they have discovered: geology explains the present relief by structure and erosion, biology explains the mechanisms of heredity by the chromosomes, pathology explains infectious illnesses by microbes. The question of the possibility of a scientific history or of a scientific sociology would become this: does there exist an order of facts that, at least broadly, *controls* other facts? Can history become a geology of human evolution?

As we shall see, to find such an order of facts is an old dream that has been sought successively in climates, in political regimes (*politeiai*), in laws, customs, economics; Marxism remains the best known among these attempts to constitute a geology. If we succeeded in constituting it, history and sociology would become sciences, they would allow intervention or at least foresight; they would, respectively, resemble the history of the Earth and general geology, the history of the solar system and astrophysics, the phonetics of a given language and phonology. They would cease to be descriptions and would become explanations, history being the application of the theories of sociology. We know that, unfortunately, that dream is only a dream. There is no order of facts, always the same, that would constantly control the other facts; history and sociology are condemned to remain comprehensive descriptions. Or, rather, history alone really exists; sociology is only the vain work of codifying the *ktéma es aei,* the professional experience that knows only concrete cases and does not permit those constant principles that alone would make it a science.

How does it happen, then, that sociology exists and that its utility is superior to that of a phraseology for the use of historians? From the fact that history does not do all that it ought to do, and leaves it to sociology to do, at the risk of going beyond the goal. Limited by the perspective of events from day to day, contemporary history abandons to sociology the non-eventworthy description of contemporary civilization. Limited by the old tradition of narrative and national history, the history of the past is too exclusively bound to the account followed by a spatiotemporal continuum ("France in the seventeenth century"); it rarely dares to repudiate the unities of time and place and also to be comparative history, or what is called that ("the city through the ages"). Now one can see that, if history decides to be "complete," to become completely what it is, it makes sociology useless.

Certainly, it would hardly matter if a part of the legitimate domain of history were put under the name of sociology; the interest of it would be all but corporative. The misfortune is that this error of attribution entails consequences: history does not do enough of it (the unities of time and place limit its vision, even within the domain of which its ownership has always been recognized) and sociology does too much. For lack of having recognized that it is history without the name, it believes itself obliged to do science; the same can be said of ethnology. Sociology is a pseudoscience, born of the academic conventions that limit the freedom of history, and its criticism is not even always an epistemological task: it is a task for the history of genres and conventions. Between a history that was at last complete and a formal science of man (which at the moment looks like a praxeology), there is no room for any science. To become a complete history is the true vocation of history, which has before it an inexhaustible future, since to describe the concrete is an infinite task.

Conditions for a Scientific History

"Scientific history" may designate two very different enterprises: to explain events scientifically, by the different laws to which each of them is subject, or to explain history as a whole, to discover its key, to find the driving force that makes it advance as a whole. We have just seen that the first enterprise is impossible; the explanation would be extremely incomplete or would not be manageable. The second enterprise is notably that of the Marxists. Is it possible to explain a piece of history as a whole, or, if you prefer it, to find behind each event, whether it be the 1914 War, the Russian Revolution, or cubist painting, one identical order of causes: the capitalist relationships of production? Instead of circumstantial explanations in which the nature of causes would not be the same from case to case, can one not discover a certain category of facts, always the same, which, at least roughly, would explain the other facts of history? It will thus be considered that history functions according to a categorical structure, is articulated as economics, social relationships, law, ideology, and so on; thus, the eighteenth century wondered which of the two categories, laws and customs, explained the other.

In geology, when you want to explain the relief of a region, you do not study the singular adventure of each pebble—this one has been loosened by frost and that one by a sheep grazing there—you are satisfied with studying the structure and the type of erosion, because it happens that a study of them suffices to account for the essential: the climate, the flora, and human activity have much more limited effects or else rarely have far-reaching effects. Similarly, in history you will consider that a category of causes, economics, has much more powerful effects than the others, which assuredly may react on it, the volume of those reactions remaining limited, however. And, in the same way that a geologist has a presentiment of the nature of the subsoil, when he sees what vegetation covers the ground or that the habitat is grouped round the few water holes, the geologist of history, seeing the strange flowers called *Don Quixote* or Balzac, would have a presentiment of the infrastructures on which they grow.

That Marxism was only a hypothesis, but a reasonable one; all came back to a question of fact: does a certain category of causes constantly have more powerful effects than the others? In geology the answer is yes, as we have just seen; in medicine it would be no: when you seek the explanation of a noninfectious illness, you are referred from anatomy to physiology, from physiology to histology, and from histology to biochemistry, without any of these instances being more decisive than the others.[1] If there were to exist, in history, one decisive instance, it would be reasonable to think that it was economics, for beyond the confusion of great events and of great events and great men, it is clear that the greatest part of human life is spent in working in order to live.

It remains to be determined if economic activity, which is so important in relation to other activities, goes as far as controlling them—that is, explaining them. But what does "explaining" mean? There is no explanation unless there is constancy. You can explain when you can say roughly what causes regularly produce a given effect, or else when you can say roughly what effect will be regularly produced by given causes; all hangs on this "roughly": the margin of approximation must not go beyond a certain level.[2] The laws of physics are such that, if I put a saucepan of water on to boil, I can regulate only the quantity of water and of heat and obtain precisely the desired effect. And, if I am an artillery man, the most precise leveling will not prevent my shells from scattering, but only within the well-known limits of the calculation of probabilities; so I shall end by scoring a bull's-eye.

Why It Is Impossible

If it happened that the economic relationships of production were, at least in the main, a cause on which you could count or if they produced, at least in the main, effects that came up to our expectations, Marxism would be right and history would be a science. It would be necessary, for example, for the Revolution to be assured, sooner or later, while the causes leading up to it (attitude of the proletariat, national peculiarities, general line of the Party) would vary only within reasonable limits; it would surely be necessary that a precise infrastructure (capitalism) was answered by diverse infrastructures (realist novel or escapist novel) but not miscellaneous ones (not the epic). But we know that it is not like that, that Marxism has never foreseen or explained anything, and we shall not linger on it. But it must be seen exactly what its failure means for the epistemology of history; that failure does not at all mean, for example, that poetry cannot be explained by economics, but only that it is not so *constantly* and that in literary history, as everywhere in history, there are only circumstantial explanations. That poetry has its own value and life is too evident, but by what right can we prophesy that it will never happen that a poem is principally explained by economics? That poetry never eats of that bread? It would be an edifying style, or a metaphysical prejudice that would contradict the principle of interaction.

Culture, like all history, is made of particular events, and you cannot prejudge the explanatory structure that each requires. That is why you cannot make a theory of culture or of history, nor can you set up as a category what common sense—or, rather, modern languages—calls "culture." It is even a characteristic feature of social life, and a source of endless discussions, that this semifluid state where nothing is constantly true, where nothing is decisive, where everything depends on everything else, as so many proverbs express it: "Money does not make happiness but contributes to it"; "the subject of a novel is neither good nor bad in itself"; "the superstructure reacts on the infrastructure." This reduces politics, even if assured of its goals, to a matter of visible government, and history to not being a science; a historian knows from experience that if he tries to generalize an explanatory diagram to make a theory of it, the diagram yields under his hand. In short, the historical explanation does not follow roads laid out once for all; history has no anatomy. We cannot find in it "the hard of the soft."

It is not possible to classify causes in a hierarchy of importance, even roughly, and to consider that economics has, all the same, more powerful effects than have the vaguer rumblings of the history of ideas; the relative importance of the categories of causes varies from one event to another. We have seen a national humiliation bring back to an unsurpassed stage of barbarianism the people who for a century and a half had been the Athens of Europe, and a lower middle-class man fallen into a bohemian existence unloose a world war with two aims: to annihilate the Jews, which is a form of the history of ideas, and to conquer for his people lands to cultivate to the east.[3] The latter is an aspiration of agrarian societies of the past and of the old "hunger for land," which one is astonished to find in an industrial and Keynesian century. The absence of a constant hierarchy of causes is well shown when we try to intervene in the course of events: too low a level of working-class education, and the five-year plans and the superiority of socialism are reduced to nothing. The most different causes take the leadership, turn and turn about, with the result that history has no sense nor cycles, that it is an open system; that is a point on which our cybernetic age begins to be able to say precise things.[4]

Another result of this is that there cannot be a science of history, for it is not enough that there should be determinism for a science to be possible; a science is feasible only in the sectors where universal determinism (which it is everywhere impossible to follow in its inexhaustible detail) is presented with more global, comprehensive effects and can then be deciphered and handled by an abridged method that applies to macroscopic effects: that of models and that of predominant effects. If determinism is not found to allow those effects in the sector under consideration, then deciphering is impossible and the corresponding science is not feasible.

Let us imagine a kaleidoscope; nothing more is determined than the variety of figures that the little bits of colored paper form. One can recount the history of the succession of those figures, but could one have a science of them? Yes, but under one or the other of these conditions: the kaleidoscope would have to be constructed in so specific a way that one could find, behind the variety of figures, certain recurrent structures whose return could be calculated; or that there is, as happens with loaded dice, a particular gesture of the hand that always produces a certain figure. If these conditions are not fulfilled, one can only tell the story. One can, it is true, give oneself the task of constructing a topic for those figures, to enumerte the colors of the bits of paper and the general types of configurations they form; in short, one will be able to make a general sociology of them. A vain enough task, since those colors and those configurations exist only in words, and are cut out as "subjectively" as the constellations that tradition cuts out on the vault of heaven.

History not having more of an anatomy and of predominating causes than it has laws that would be proper to it, we must give up the idea of Comte that it is for the moment at a prescientific stage and is waiting to be raised to the rank of a science, that science being sociology. Under that name Comte obviously did not mean the formal science of certain sectors of human activity, to which there is a tendency at present to give the name of praxeology. His sociology was a science of history "as a whole," a science *of* history; it was to establish the laws of history, like the "law of the three estates," which is the description of the movement of history taken as a whole. But that science of history has revealed itself to be impossible (not for metaphysical reasons—human freedom—but for factual reasons of "cybernetic" order). What is done today under the name of sociology is not a science; it is sometimes a description, a history without the name, at other times a topic of history or a phraseology (it is general sociology). Faced with this confusion, is it indicated that historians and sociologists should be invited to an everyday more necessary interdisciplinary collaboration? That historians or economists should be invited to use the results of present-day sociology (for one does wonder what those results are)? The clarification seems more urgent than the collaboration, and history, in this matter, needs to be clarified no less than does sociology.

Sociology Has No Object

All science has an object; what is the object of sociology? It appears that it has none. We know how Durkheim puts the problem in the *Rules of Sociological Method*:[5] for a sociology to be possible, there must be social types, social species. If, on the other hand, "the nominalism of historians," which holds those types to be cutouts ad libitum of the real, were true, then "social reality could be the object of only a vague, abstract philosophy, or of purely descriptive monographs," works of historians and travelers. This view can equally be expressed thus: for a sociology to be possible, the present must not be only what the past has made of it; it cannot be, no matter what, at the will of antecedents, but it must always have its own structure. It must resemble an organism rather than a kaleidoscope. For that, a certain order of dominant facts must give it a form. Marx attributed that preponderance to the forces of production; Durkheim attributes it to what he calls the "social milieu," provided with properties that he metaphorically calls "volume" and "concentration." At every moment this milieu exerts a "kind of preponderance" over the other concomitant facts; thanks to it, the social body is not the mere result of its past, but has a definite anatomy, "just as the whole of the anatomical elements constitutes the internal milieu of organisms." This milieu explains events: "The primary origin of every social process, of whatever importance, must be sought in the constitution of the social milieu."

If that preponderance of a certain order of facts did not exist, then sociology would find it "impossible to establish any relationship of causality"; better still, it would have nothing more to say: all would be history. But that is not so; on the contrary, at whatever moment of history you make a cross section of a society, you will find in it social types and a global structure, which are not reducible to antecedents. Those are the proper objects of sociological science. Let us even say that those two objects only make one, for "if there are social species, it is because collective life depends above all on concomitant conditions that present a certain diversity"; there are, in fact, different forms of organization, which sociology must describe. A particular social milieu, which confers a particular anatomy on a society, also causes it to have a particular type of organ; all is not found with everything. Sociology is a sort of biology of societies; let us also represent it as a *Spirit of Laws* in which the preponderant factors would be the volume and concentration of the milieu.

Three-quarters of a century have passed since those beautifully lucid pages were written. If it is true that since that time sociology has discovered no social type, no preponderant order of facts, if we have to go as far as a mathematical praxeology to discover invariables, then we must conclude that the "nominalism of historians" was true and that sociology has no object. Since it exists, however, or at least sociologists exist, it is because the latter do under that name something other than sociology. It is not possible to explain a society or a portion of history as an organism; there exists only a dust of events—the coalition of 1936, the recession of 1937, the fall of a tile—each of which requires its special explanation. French society in 1936 has only nominal reality; there is no science that can explain the articulation of its components, there is no science that gives a total explanation of the numberless physicochemical facts of every kind that occur at every moment within a perimeter arbitrarily carved out on the terrestrial surface. We have seen above that the words "scientific knowledge of history" could be taken in two different senses: explanation of history as a whole or explanation of each event in its category. So either a society is explicable as a whole, which supposes that an order of preponderant facts confers on it a form—then sociology is possible and history is no more than an applied sociology (the unfolding of the life of a society will be comprehensible, in essentials, starting from the knowledge of its organism)—or else the different events form a whole only in words—then sociology has no justification, for there is nothing for it between the nominalism of history and the scientific explanation of events by means of the different laws to which each event belongs.

The dilemma of sociology, which is that of nominalism, was stated in a book by Hans Freyer, which bears the significant title "Sociology as Realism."[6] Either the sociological types, the archaic "community," clan, or *gens* and modern "society," are only points of view concerning the real, neither more nor less legitimate than numberless other possible points of view—in that case sociology is reduced to an accumulation of empirical data (let us say, historical)—or else those types really exist, and in that case one must discover them in history. Sociology is a biography of humanity; it shows how men have passed from the clan community to the ordered society or to social classes. That is not to say that at a given time, in a single group, community and society could not exist simultaneously—but then their coexistence was not that of two partial points of view in the mind of the sociologist; it was that of two incompatible forms of organization, which resulted in social antagonism. Thus, to believe Freyer, is the crisis of the contemporary world to be explained. We then wonder in what way the sociology of Freyer merits the name of sociology: under that name he has in reality written a history of social organization over two or three millennia.

But sociology persists in being something other than history. The result of that ambition is that sociology has nothing more to say, and so it speaks emptily or it speaks of something else. In short, the books published as sociology can be arranged under three headings: a political philosophy that does not admit to it, a history of contemporary civilizations, and a seductive literary genre, of which the *Cadres sociaux de la mémoire* of Halbwachs is perhaps the masterpiece and which has unconsciously been the successor of the moralists and the tract writers of the sixteenth–eighteenth centuries; general sociology comes almost entirely under the third heading. For the first heading sociology allows the exposition, as being science itself, of liberal or conservative opinions on politics, education, or the role of the mob in revolutions; it is in that case a political philosophy. On the other hand, and this is the second heading, if a sociologist makes the statistical study of the student population of Nanterre and draws from it an explanation of the university revolt of May 1968, he is doing contemporary history, and future historians will have to take his work into account and study his interpretation; and so we humbly ask pardon of that sociologist for the evil we seem to speak of sociology, and beg him to consider that we are disputing the flag and not the goods.

There remains general sociology. Just as part of the present philosophical production succeeds edifying literature and collections of sermons that represented, in the sixteenth–eighteenth centuries, a considerable part of publishing (about half of the books published at certain periods), so general sociology carries on the art of the moralist. It tells how society is made up, the sorts of groups, the attitudes of men, their rites, their tendencies, just as the maxims and treatises on man or the mind described the variety of conduct, of societies, and of the prejudices of man. General sociology paints the eternal society as the moralists painted the eternal man; it is a "literary" sociology, in the sense that we speak of the "literary" psychology of the moralists and novelists. It can, like the latter, produce masterpieces; after all, the *Homme de cour* of Balthasar Gracian is a sociology (written, like Machiavelli, in normative language). However, the greatest part of this literature of tract writers is not destined to survive, and even less to initiate a cumulative process; it can save itself only by its artistic or philosophical qualities. In fact, moralists or general sociology, it is always a question of descriptions of the known. But the law of economy of thought refuses to store in its treasury a description, however truthful it may be, if that description is only one possible among an infinity of others that are also true, and if each man bears within him the means of making one for himself, if need be; it keeps in its treasury only the "matters of memory," history and philology, and scientific discoveries.

General sociology can be nothing but a "literary" sociology, a description, a phraseology. None of these descriptions can be truer than the others, or more scientific. Description, not explanation; let us very didactically recapitulate the three degrees of knowledge. The formula of Newton explains the laws of Kepler, which explain the movements of the planets; microbe pathology explains rabies; the weight of taxes explains the unpopularity of Louis XIV. In the first two cases we have scientific explanations and, in the third, a description and understanding. The first two demanded discoveries, and the third is a child of memory. The first two permit deductions or predictions and interventions, the third is a matter of prudence (it is not political except in understanding). To the first category there correspond very abstract concepts, "work" or "attraction"; to the second, scientific concepts issuing from a purification of concepts of common sense (the "coast" of geologists is much more precise than that which everyday language designates "coast," and conventionally it would be opposed to *cuesta*). To the third explanation there correspond sublunary concepts. This third explanation is history. As for sociology, which is neither the first nor the second, it can be only history or a paraphrase of history. Now historical descriptions are made of words, of concepts, of universals. One can always extract one of those series of universals to make of it a general sociology; one can always undertake to employ only those universals, which will open the way for a deductive sociology. Which, though deductive, will be no more a science than Spinoza's *Ethics,* or than law or theology. The result is always the same: general sociology is a phraseology and the possible sociologies are indefinite in number, as the result has proved.

Sociology Is Only a Description

Sociology, writes Parsons, is a group of descriptive categories, "a carefully elaborated system of concepts applicable in a coherent manner to all parts and all aspects of a concrete system."[7] It is too little or too much ambition. If only all social life must be described, any of the existing languages will do, because each of those languages permits one to say everything; if a language whose coherence is never baffled by the contradiction of phenomena is needed, that language will be the object of a complete general sociology—it will not be, as Parsons believes, the preliminary to that great work. Then, too, the "system carefully elaborated" by Parsons is worth neither more nor less than another; one will only wonder if it is more convenient, if not truer, as one wonders about Esperanto. Certainly it is fine to describe society, as Parsons does, by putting everywhere the five words structure, function, control, role, and rule. That does not prevent the language of L. von Wiese, though older by a good third of a century, from being no less good, using everywhere wishes, attitudes, and situations.

Is it now a question of describing human groups? No one will deny, as Tönnies would have it, that human relations oscillate between two ideal types, that of community or *Gemeinschaft* and that of society or *Gesellschaft.* The first is founded on the impulse of sentiments (*Wesenwille*), and the second on a rational will (*Kürwille*); but Parsons is not wrong to consider that the same relations oscillate between abstract and universalist rules and personal and total bonds. The first description means that the family bond is not the one that links the shareholders of an industrial company, and the second means that the bond linking a Roman client to his patron is not that of a civil servant in relation to his government. Sociology has the merit of all language: not only does it permit all things to be said, but it allows them to be seen better, allows us to become aware of implicit aspects. That is why general sociologies have a tendency to multiply: every professor tends to attach special importance to the aspects of things that he has had the greatest difficulty in conceptualizing.

Sociological theory being but a description, it was foreseeable that the sociological explanation should culminate in what has dominated the intellectual scene for some fifteen years: functionalism.[8] Does the latter not consist in explaining things by what they are? If, then, electoral corruption can be described as ending at least in a happy result, that of protecting marginal individuals, one will conclude that the function of corruption (latest function, different from its conscious function) is that of protection. Since a social fact has as a function what it is, and since a social fact is a group fact, it can be said that all facts have, finally, a great function, that of integrating the individual into the group, which is true of national holidays and of anarchical revolts that seal the sacred union against them and are an outlet necessary to equilibrium. It will be the same with cufflinks; Kluckhorn wondered, in fact, what was the function of those links, and he found it: they fulfill the function "of preserving customs and of keeping up a tradition."

In general, in fact, we have a feeling of security if we have "the impression of following orthodox and socially acknowledged customs"[9]— an impeccable explanation, in terms of the criterion of verification of functions, according to Parsons. In order to test a functional explanation, one must ask oneself "what, for the system, would be the differential consequences of two or several mutually exclusive results of a dynamic process, if those consequences are expressed in terms of maintaining stability, of producing change, of integrating or breaking up the system."[10] Which means, clearly, that functionalism consists of calling functions the effects of every social fact on society; since bread and the circus integrate the common people into the social body, their function is to integrate them. Parsons seems to want us to consider society as Kant considered nature: as a work of art executed according to goals; he does not add, like Kant, that that finalism will never teach us anything about nature or society.

Uneasiness of Sociology

And so it is a secret from no one that sociology lives today in uneasiness and that the *melior et major pars* of sociologists no longer takes seriously anything but "empirical work"—that is, the history of contemporary society. For what are we to think of the other sociology, which is not a history without the name? What are we to think of a discipline that on the one hand is studied by distinguished minds, that fills thousands of pages, that gives rise to serious discussions, and that, on the other hand, is a false genre of which it can be prophesied that its products are still-born, like those of 1800 psychology? In fact, nothing more like something of Gurvitch or of Parsons than the *Traité des facultés de l'âme* of Laromiguière, of which the reader will be convinced if he will read the relevant note.[11] He will find there the content and spirit of those volumes of sociology whose pages one forces oneself to turn, struggling against the boredom of the always-known, of that mixture of truisms, of approximations, of logomachy and not-even-false that one peruses because one may fish up at long intervals an instructive little fact, an ingenious idea, or a happy expression; these volumes that, in most cases, are collections of truisms (read Linton's *L'homme*) and that, in the best cases, would have the interest of all historical or ethnographical description if, unfortunately for us, the author had not believed he had to be more than a historian, if he had not insisted on showing himself to be a sociologist, on putting his interest not in what he relates, but in the words he uses to relate it, which leads him to delineate in a flabby style, to swamp and banalize the contours for the pleasure of replacing everywhere the same concepts.

Sociology, I mean general sociology, does not exist. There exists a physics, an economics (and only one), but there does not exist *one* sociology; every person makes his own, just as each literary critic makes himself a phraseology to his taste. Sociology is a would-be science, but one of which the first line has not yet been written and whose scientific balance sheet is exactly nil; it has revealed nothing that was not already known: no anatomy of society, no causal relation that common sense did not know. On the other hand, the contribution of sociology to historical experience, to the lengthening of the questionnaire, is considerable, and it would be even more so if shrewdness was the best-distributed thing in the world and if scientific preoccupations did not sometimes stifle it; all the interest of sociology is in that shrewdness. The basic theory of personality in Kardiner is as vague as it is wordy; the relations he wants to establish between "primary institutions" and that personality are sometimes evident, sometimes arbitrary or even naive, but his description of the native soul in the Marquesas Islands is a fine exotic page of contemporary history. The result is that, in a book of sociology, the developments that professionals would criticize as literary or journalistic are the best in the work and the qualified professional developments are the dead part; the shrewd are not unaware of it and, when they write on the solitary crowd or the sociology of photography, they maintain a wise balance between what is pleasing to the two categories of readers.

Sociology Is a False Continuity

In short, sociology is only a word, a homonym, under which heterogeneous activities are placed: phraseology and topic of history, political philosophy of the poor, history of the contemporary world. Thus, it provides a fine example of what we have called false continuities; to write the history of sociology from Comte and Durkheim to Weber, Parsons, and Lazarsfeld would not be to write the history of a discipline, but that of a word. From each of these writers to the other there is no continuity of basis, object, purpose, and method. Sociology is not a unified discipline that has evolved; its continuity exists only through its name, which establishes a purely verbal link between intellectual activities that have a single common point in having established themselves on the fringe of traditional disciplines. There was a void between those disciplines (history was incomplete history); there was also the temptation to do some "scientific" political philosophy and the temptation to found a science of history. In that vague ground between the old disciplines there have camped successively, on different sites, heteroclite enterprises that, owing to their fringe position, have received the same name of sociology.

The question, then, is not to know, for example, what the sociologist Durkheim has in common with the sociologist Weber, for they have nothing in common, but why the latter took the name of sociologist (it was because his conception of history was narrowly limited by his theory of related values). At the beginning sociology was, according to Durkheim, a very lucid enterprise that had its conditions of possibility very precisely defined. Those conditions have little by little revealed themselves to be impossible to use, but the name of sociology remained and has passed to other, often less lucid, enterprises. Was there not a field of social facts to study? Every activity relating to this field and that did not admit to being history or philosophy was baptized "sociology." It might be a question of legitimate activities that filled the gaps of a historiography that was too eventworthy or that introduced new methods in contemporary history (questionnaire, opinion poll); it might have been a question, too, of less legitimate temptations. The evolution of sociology being that of the uses of its name, there is an abyss between the evolution of a true science, geometry or economics, which constantly changes "dialectically" while remaining faithful to its foundation, and the evolution of a vague place like sociology, which is dependent on semantics. Sociology belongs to the history of contemporary culture, but not to the history of the sciences.

All can be said in a word: sociology has never discovered anything; it has revealed nothing that could not be found in a description. It is not one of those sciences that were born or, rather, have truly been founded as the result of a discovery; it is still saying to itself: "Here are social facts, let us study them," and not "Let us proceed along the way of discoveries." Social facts theoretically give rise to a science, like chemical or economic facts; but it is not enough, in order to have that science, to see what those facts resemble and to relate them scrupulously—that way, one will simply have done natural history or history. A human science that discovers nothing is not a science; it is either history or philosophy (for example, political philosophy), whether it accepts that or not.

Since there is no discovery to put to the account of sociology, one understands that there remains nothing of three-quarters of a century of sociology, except ways of speaking; the more the reader would be tempted to reproach us for summarily condemning, and as a whole, an immense intellectual activity that was extremely varied in terms of authors and national schools, the more he must remember that that variety has a common characteristic, that of having left nothing in the hollow of our hand. What remains of German sociology, from Tönnies to Nazism, save for a few convenient expressions (*zweckrational* or "charismatic") that all the same cannot pass for a theory of action or of authority, and a few philosophemes, like the opposition of the ethics of intention and those of responsibility? One sign does not deceive: to study sociology is not to study a body of doctrine, as one studies chemistry or economics; it is to study the successive doctrines of sociology, the *placita* of present and past sociologists. For there are reigning doctrines, national schools, styles of a period, great theories fallen into disuse, others that are sociology itself so long as the "big boss" who is its author controls access to sociological careers—but there is no cumulative process of knowledge.

Sociology Is History or Rhetoric

We must finish by resolving to draw the lesson: sociology has failed to do more than what history did or ought to have done. History is also the more interesting because it is less sociological and more historical, because it is limited to the relation of events. Let us take a classic chapter of the most widespread doctrine today, the theory of the social role, renewed from the Stoics. If we look round us, we see that our fellowmen, whether they are bakers, voters, or subway riders, are limited in their freedom of action by their fellows (that is their status), and generally act in conformity with what is expected of them (that is their attitude); if they took it into their heads to act otherwise, their deviations would be repressed (that is control). This rigorous vocabulary (a necessary condition for the progress of all science) allows the discovery, for example, that a professor of Latin will have the ambition of a professor of Latin rather than that of a worker in lead or zinc or of a polo player; for the level of the tasks a person assigns to himself depends on the idea he has of himself. This idea is generally inspired by the status of that person.[12]

Even more instructive conclusions are possible. There is an important study on the effects of change in roles on the attitudes of role occupants.[13] We will see how history, topic, and phraseology are mingled in it. The writer begins by recalling that, according to Newcomb, Parsons, and other theoreticians, the interior attitude of a person is influenced by his role; is it not said "You wouldn't recognize him since he became senior clerk?" All the same, the common observation is not a scientific demonstration; certainly, we have already beginnings of proof: "S. A. Stouffer, for example, has discovered that career officers are more in favor of the Army than draftees."[14] But the relationship of cause and effect still remains to be explained. The writer, starting from the very democratic principle that what people freely say of themselves must be taken as true, distributed a questionnaire to 2,354 workers in a plant and discovered that 62.4 percent of the foremen and the trade union leaders had opposite attitudes toward the management of the plant: the foremen were for; the trade unionists, rather against. It remains to explain this, and the writer thinks of two factors: "One of those factors is bound up with the influence of the reference groups: a change of role implies a change of reference group, which leads to a change of behavior; the other factor is based on the postulate that it is necessary to have attitudes, inside one, in agreement with one's external behavior."

Neither of these two explanations will be a revelation for our reader, who knows why the taxes made Louis XIV unpopular and who is not unaware that an infinity of other explanations of the same kind would be possible; he knows equally well that the majority of people play their role sincerely, for he has been able to verify that the larger part of humanity does not live in a state of schizophrenia or pouting or withdrawal from the world. Finally, what does this statistical study produce? First of all, a contribution to the history of the American workers' movement: around the middle of the twentieth century, two-thirds of the trade union leaders were hostile to management; next, an experiment on factory life, a *ktèma:* so such hostility is thus a thing consistent with human nature, or at least with that nature in the twentieth century, and it can be "retrodicted" elsewhere. As for saying whether the attitudes influence the roles, or conversely, and whether those words have only one meaning, it is not important, although that is the real sociological aspect of that study.

As F. Bourricaud[15] excellently writes, there is a science when one discovers in a process a hypothetico-deductive system that imitates the *rules of the game* (that is what economics does); on the other hand, to seek there general categories that can be applied to every situation is only to seek in what vocabulary one can describe social life, is only to discover everywhere attitudes and roles just as Ionian physicists found water and fire everywhere, it is only to make analogy triumph. From such phraseology nothing can be deduced or predicted; to contribute something, it must be determined hypothetically, receive a content instead of being formally valid—in short, it must have a historical insertion, for this pseudoscience lives on its "surreptitious exchanges" with the concrete, is concrete in the inflated mode. But, as in the concrete, causal explanations are never assured and are always surrounded by mental restrictions, they can never be generalized and cannot be separated from a particular conjuncture.

Sociology is a history without knowing it and, methodologically speaking, is still at a pre-Thucydidean stage. Being history, it cannot go further than the probable, the likely; at most it can say, like Thucydides, that "in the future, events, by virtue of their human character, will present similarities or analogies with events of the past." But those probabilities are only truisms if they are isolated from the historical context where they were effectively true. That is why Thucydides did not speak of laws of history or of the sociology of war; he only spoke of probabilities. To quote J. de Romilly, *The Peloponnesian War* is subtended by a complex and coherent system of suggested probabilities, but not by formulated laws, for that kind of generality does not allow adequate formulation.[16]

Thucydides is thinking unceasingly of laws—we know that the historian thinks unceasingly that he sees laws and regional essences in the scenery of the past—but he never enunciates them. This refusal to formulate them is "a refusal to impoverish" and to become insipid, for "the general lessons drawn from history would be suspect, inexact, partial." There is no general knowledge independent of the account, and there cannot be. Is it not striking that the same Thucydides who sees in the *ktèma* the most precious thing brought by his book, does not tell us what that *ktèma* is, what its analogies are? No doubt, knowing that the *ktèma* was indefinite, he meant to leave to each reader the task of getting it out of the narrative; for that *ktèma* is different each time, it changes as a function of the war with which each reader compares the Peloponnesian war. Thucydides did not want to go beyond the plane of experience of an individual case; although a contemporary of the physicists and of the sophists, he refrained from writing an art of history, a *technè*, a sociology. His book thus poses the key question of historical knowledge: how is it that, while one thinks he perceives lessons of history everywhere, it is yet impossible to enunciate, in black and white, those lessons without falling into falsity or platitudes? We know the answer: historical nominalism, the vague character of sublunary causality, makes it that no order of causes constantly imposes itself as more decisive than the others.

And so many a book of sociology is worth more for the historical data it utilizes than for the ideas it gets out of them. Montesquieu is irreplaceable when he describes the monarchy or the moderate aristocracy or when he does the non-eventworthy history of the estates of the Ancien Régime under the timeless chapter titles; on the other hand, when he tries to explain that history by variables and laws, he interests only the history of ideas. The *Esprit des lois*, in its sociological aspects, is an out-of-date book, but it survives triumphantly as a book of comparative history; it completes the history of the estates of the Ancien Régime, which historians of the eighteenth century wrote too much as eventworthy.

Sociology Results from Too Narrow a Conception of History

The situation has not changed over two centuries. Sociology is born and lives on the incompletenesses of history; when it is not an empty phraseology, it is contemporary history or comparative history without the name, and good sociology, the one that deserves to be read and is read with interest, is one of those histories. It is therefore proper that historians should be conscious that sociology is history that they neglect to write, and whose absence mutilates what they do write, and which sociologists and ethnographers understand that they cannot make more scientific than the historians. We have seen before how eventworthy history of the past is a prisoner of the perspective of documents, registered in their time by the news, the events day by day; taking up that story, contemporary history forms it in the same perspective and leaves to sociology all that is not political chronicling.

Yet it is hard to see why a book titled *Phénomène bureaucratique* would be sociology whereas the phenomenon of public beneficence would be history, why the book *Auxerre en 1950* should be less historical than Auxerre in 1850; what can really distinguish the *Boys in Blue Jeans* from a book on the Hellenistic ephebi, and a study on kinship among the present-day Kariera from a study on Byzantine relationships.[17] We are not, all the same, going to take the distribution of academic chairs in the Sorbonne for a system of the sciences, or to imagine that the diversity of the documents that make known to us the experience (here the Hellenistic inscriptions, there an opinion poll, over there a whole Kariera tribe) would mean that that experience would lend itself more readily here than there to being transformed into science. Certainly, since history is written by means of documents, and one and the same man cannot easily master both Greek epigraphy and the statistical method, the present linking of disciplines, which is mainly based on the differences of the documentation,[18] has every reason for existing; but it is not necessary to take the difference of the documentation for an epistemological difference.

Yet that is what is often done. A sociologist tells himself that, since he bears the name sociologist, he must do better than "accumulate empirical data" (*rein empirische Erhebungen, Materialhuberei*)—let us understand that to behave like a historian, he must rise to a science of society, reach eternal or at least "almost eternal" laws (*fast ewige*), as L. von Wiese has put in. Similarly, if instead of studying the ancient Athenian family as a historian, you study the contemporary Kariera family, and if you bear the name of ethnographer, you will believe you are authorized or invited to philosophize on anthropology; the primitive, as its name suggests, no doubt reveals man more profoundly. If you study the associative phenomenon in the contemporary world, you will feel obliged to draw from it a theory of associativity. The contemporary world is not, like history, an inert museum piece in its showcase; it is the very thing about which you can think. On the contrary, if you study the associative phenomenon in the ancient world, you will believe you are dispensed from reflecting and from asking what the sociologists have said about the associative phenomenon (they have said interesting things, even of capital importance, about it; they have made excellent non-eventworthy history). Such is the weight of the conventions of genre on our minds, of *geprägte Formen;* we have seen gods born of a pun and false sciences born of a traditional division into genres.

The Two Conventions that Mutilate History

History, a few millennia ago, made a bad start. It has never completely freed itself of its social function, that of perpetuating the memory of the life of peoples or of kings. Although, very soon, it became a work of pure curiosity for specificity that Herodotus at once allied with history, contemporary history and non-eventworthy history, it has nonetheless remained under the influence of two kinds of conventions. The first convention had it that there was no history, save of the past, of what is lost if the memory of it is not preserved; the knowledge of the present seemed, on the contrary, to go without saying. The second convention had it that history related the past life of a nation, was centered on the special individuality of the latter, and established itself in a spatiotemporal continuum: Greek history, the history of France, history of the sixteenth century; it was not thought that it was quite as legitimate to carve out historical matter in items: the city through the centuries, millennarism through the ages, peace and war between nations.

The first convention has accustomed us to oppose the present, which would be the thing itself, and the past, which is affected by a historical index that makes it half unreal. This false opposition is at the origin of two pseudosciences, sociology and ethnography, that divide the history of contemporary civilization between them, the former taking those of civilized peoples, the latter those of primitives (Herodotus, more discerning, described conjointly the civilization of the Greeks and that of the barbarians); not being affected by the historical index, these two disciplines evolve freely in an eternal present: to study "roles" in a contemporary society is to study the "roles" themselves. It is obviously not naiveté, but the convention of the genre. Besides, from time to time we see a sociologist dive into the past; he comes back with a book in the preface of which he does not fail to declare that he wanted to show that comparative history could procure new "materials" for sociology. We are, as can be seen, in the Hades of confusion, in one of those situations where things are half thought out, enough for one not to be able to be accused of naiveté, not enough to dare to clarify the arbitrary conventions and the false consequences drawn from them.

If ethnology and sociology are right to ratiocinate on man, why does history not do so? If history is right not to do so, why should sociologists and ethnographers have more right to do so? The existential opposition of the present and the past also models the traditional aspect of geography and economics. Geographers chiefly describe the present state of the earth's surface; as soon as the number of kilometers of railway lines increases in some country, they hasten to update the figure they will teach in their lectures. There *is* a historical geography, but it is a poor relation (a pity, because a "Human Geography of France in 1813" would be as interesting as feasible). As for economics, it is not for nothing that it is called "national economy" by the Germans and "wealth of nations" by Adam Smith; although disengaging eternal laws, it is spontaneously contemporary and national.[19]

The second convention, that of the unities of time and place, binds history to the continuum and makes of it above all the biography of a national individuality. In different degrees the greatest part of history written today is carved out of the history of a nation; that which avoids the convention of the continuum is called comparative history. History is in the situation in which geography would be if the latter limited itself almost exclusively to regional geography and if general geography was held to be a poor relation or else a spearhead technique. It is the same in literary history, where the perspective of national literatures still reigns, so much so that when literary history avoids that tradition, ignores frontiers, and becomes fully itself, it gives the impression of constituting a separate discipline, which we call comparative literature. Yet neither comparative history nor comparative literature is anything but history or literary history in the most ordinary sense of the word; more exactly, they are the complement of traditional histories, which are mutilated. They are not new disciplines that must replace traditional histories; they add to the latter to form at last a complete history, a history that has pulled itself away from the continuum, that gives itself full freedom in the choice of the plot and for which the unities of time and place, the history of a century or of a people, are no longer anything but one possible cutout among others.[20]

We have seen that time is not essential to history, but only specificity; respect of the unities, attachment to spatiotemporal singularity, is the last survival of the origins of history as a conservancy of national or dynastic memories. In the same way that the problem of oppressed minorities is in reality that of oppressing majorities, comparative history (called also general history) and comparative literature are not fringe disciplines; they are, on the contrary, national portions of history that must not be taken as the whole of history. If, since the seventeenth century, geography has become a complete discipline and has admitted the full legitimacy of general geography, it is probably because, unlike history, which is first of all national, geography for obvious reasons is first of all the geography of foreign nations, "a history of travel." The genius of Varenius has done the rest.

The Example of "General" Geography

The geographers have one great principle, from which the historians have the most absolute duty to get inspiration: never to consider a phenomenon without comparing it with related phenomena that are spread over the other points of the globe; if one is studying the Talèfre glacier in the massif of Mont Blanc, one will not fail to compare it with other Alpine glaciers, even all the glaciers of the planet. From comparison, light is born; the "principle of comparative geography" establishes general geography and gives life to the regional.[21] Geographers call "horizontal dimension" and "vertical dimension" these two possible orientations of all description,[22] one of which follows a continuum that is the region, whereas the other proceeds by items: glacier, erosion, or habitat. The epigraphists know those two orientations that they call regional classification or classification by series. This dualism is also that of history versus comparative history, and of literary history versus comparative literature; all these descriptive disciplines have as their object facts succeeding each other in time or space and, if they are considered from an adequate angle, often offer similarities among themselves. Thus one can either describe a portion of space or of time with the facts it contains, or describe a series of facts offering some similitude. Literary facts may be related like a popular history (the novel in France, literature and society in eighteenth-century France, European literature) or by categories: the the first-person novel, literature and society.[23]

It makes no difference which of these two orientations one chooses; one is not more general or sociological than the other. The "field" of historical or geographical facts has no depth, it is quite flat; one can only carve out bits that are more or less big and that are or are not all in one block: "the French novel" or "first-person novels," "the Greek city" (the Greek cities) or "cities throughout history." But practically, whatever orientation is chosen, it implies the knowledge of the other orientation. Anyone who would take it into his head to study the Talèfre glacier without knowing, by observation of other glaciers, what a glacial system is, would not understand anything about his glacier or would perceive only the most anecdotal features of it. He who studied the ancient novel, imagining that comparative literature is a marginal discipline that does not concern him, would only end up sterilizing his study. He who studied the favorites of Louis XIII without studying the "series" of favorites of the Ancien Régime, would misunderstand the system of favorites represented by the favorites of Louis XIII: he will be doing narrowly eventworthy history. In order to understand a single favorite and tell his story, several must be studied; consequently he has to come out of his period, to take no more account of the unities of time and place. Only comparative history allows an escape from the perspective of sources and the making explicit of the non-eventworthy.

The prejudice of the unities of time and place has thus had two troublesome effects: comparative or general history has, until recently, been sacrificed to "continuous" or national history, which has resulted in incomplete history; for lack of comparison, that national history has mutilated itself and has remained a prisoner of too eventworthy a perspective. What is then to be wished? That comparative history should have full freedom of the city? That books entitled *Primitifs de la révolte, Messianismes révolutionnaires du Tiers Monde*,[24] the *Culture of Cities, Political Systems of Empires* should multiply? Certainly, for they are good books. However, it remains possible to do comparative history within the most traditional, most "continuous" history; it suffices not to relate a single fact without having first studied it within its series. To study several revolutionary messianisms comparatively, is only to do the history of each of them in a better way.

So it is to be wished that we shall see a history developing that is the counterpart of general geography and vivifies "continuous" history, as general geography vivifies the regional one and teaches it how to see. The abandoning of the unities gives history freedom to carve out, to invent new items, which is a source of indefinite renewal. Let us even wish that continuous history becomes the least part of history, or that it should no longer be the framework of works of erudition. In fact, if the unities of time and place are abolished, the unity of plot becomes the essential one; but it is rare for traditional carvings-out to provide coherent, interesting plots. Geographers have long since given up carving out regions according to political frontiers; they carve them out as functions of proper geographical criteria. History owes it to itself to imitate them and to take complete freedom of itinerary through the field of events, if it is true that it is a work of art, if it is true that it is interested purely in the specific, if it is finally true that it is purely interested in the specific, if it is true that "facts" exist only through a plot and that the carving out of plots is unrestricted. The first duty of a historian is not to treat his subject, but to invent it. That history in freedom, rid of its conventional limits, is complete history.

Complete History Evacuates Sociology

Complete history makes sociology useless: it does all that the latter does, and does it better. The frontier between the two disciplines has already become elusive; for a good third of a century, historians, under the name of the non-eventworthy (in France) have done what previously would have been called sociology.[25] But they do it in a more interesting manner: the accent is not on concepts, as is done in speech, but on the historical matter, on the things of which they speak; the concepts bear their full weight through deliberate exchanges that they maintain with reality.

If we want to see, on the other hand, where a sociological approach to historical problems leads, we must glance through Eisenstadt's book on the political and administrative systems of the ancient empires.[26] How can we not expect much from this comparative history, where the description of each of those empires must have gained in acuity by resemblance to, or by contrast with, the study of all the others? And how can we not deplore that so much work and penetration ended up in a comparative picture softly drawn, uninstructive, depending narrowly on what is most conventional in this historiography of the eventworthy? What fate willed that the writer, too much a sociologist, be interested above all in separating out a network of universals, instead of freshening up and accentuating the pictures of history? The fault is not the writer's: historians would be mistaken to reproach a sociologist for having tried to cultivate a field that they were wrong to leave fallow.

The Historical Work of Weber

On the whole, to become complete, history ought to free itself of three limitations: the opposition between the contemporary and the historical, the convention of the continuum, the eventworthy perspective; salvation is thus on the side of the "sociology" and the "ethnography" of contemporary societies, of "comparative" history—in short, of the history of the non-eventworthy, with its decomposition of the "temporalities in depth." A history that becomes complete in that way is really sociology. The most exemplary historical work of our century is that of Max Weber, which wipes out the frontiers between traditional history, of which it has the realism; sociology, of which it has the ambitions; and comparative history, of which it has the span. Weber—for whom history was related to values—is not less paradoxically the one who has led the evolution of the genre to its logical end: to a history completely freed from spatio-temporal singularity and, since everything is historical, a history that freely gives itself its objects.

The work of Weber—who, a sociologist "by understanding," does not seek to lay down laws—is truly history. It owes its falsely systematic aspect to the fact that it is a comparative history subtended by a topic; it gathers and classifies particular cases of a single type of event through the centuries. *La cité* is a broad comparative study of the urban habitat through all periods and all civilizations. From the comparison Weber draws no rules; at most he notes that, for understandable reasons (and consequently reasons not separable from a concrete historical situation with which the formal rule maintains surreptitious exchanges), a particular kind of event "favorizes" a particular other one. The oppressed classes naturally have a certain affinity with a particular kind of religious belief, a warrior class has difficulty with a rational religious ethic; it is humanly understandable that it should be so, and no less comprehensible that the rule has exceptions. All is degraded thereby, into *more or less,* as always in history; the general propositions in fact only set forth "objective possibilities which, according to the cases, are more or less typical or more or less close to an adequate causality or to a faintly favorable action."[27]

In short, Weber traces out a network of variants: a charismatic power, he will say, for example, can remain in force and become hereditary or, on the contrary, disappear at the death of the beloved leader; historical accidents will decide it. So it is not astonishing that these *topoi* are the least part of the work; it would give a disproportionate idea of the aspect of the works of Weber if it were not said that they form, on the whole, only a few phrases that appear here and there in the course of long pages of historical description, and that the aim of the work is more in those comprehensive descriptions than in the enunciation of conclusions of that kind. Truth to tell, pronouncements of the same kind are found in historians, if they have a sententious turn, and it is not they who could have made men think that the work of Weber was something other than history without the name. What makes this work not resemble history as it is traditionally conceived comes of three things: the break with the continuum, Weber going to seek his wealth in every flowerbed; the flippant tone of this outsider who ignores all the corporative customs, and the conventional style that serves as a sign of recognition to the specialists of each period; the fact that the comparison brings him to ask questions that those specialists do not always think of asking.

Thus, as L. von Mises writes,[28] the sociology of Weber is, in fact, history under a more general and more summary form. To him, sociology could not be more than a history of that kind, since, in his eyes, human things could not have universal laws and gave rise only to historical propositions, to which he refused the appellation "historical" only because they were comparative and non-eventworthy. To him they were sociology, science, because there could not be any other science of man. We know, in fact, what had been the epistemological position of Weber, the heir of Dilthey and of historicism, in "the quarrel of methods" in which the partisans of economics as pure theory and the partisans of economics as a historical and descriptive discipline confronted each other. Weber, to whom economic theory was not deductive knowledge, but an ideal type of the economics of liberal capitalism, and to whom the human sciences were not on the same plane as natural sciences, could keep the ample manner of writing history that he had for a science of man, and reserve the name of "history" for an eventworthy history. Things have become clearer in the last three-quarters of a century; we are now inclined to see history in *Économie et société* or in *La cité*, and to reserve the name of science for economic theory and, more generally, for mathematical praxeology.

There comes a moment, in the evolution of ideas, when old problems are basically liquidated, even if we go on speaking of them out of habit. We continue to talk of the analysis of the historical object, to conjure up the phantom of a scientist conception of history, to dread the specter of historicist relativism, and even to wonder if history really has a meaning; but visibly conviction is no longer there, either because those ideas are accepted (like the analysis of the historical "fact" and the nonscientific character of history) or because they are outdated or have become a thing of ideological or religious belief. On the other hand, two new problems at a much humbler level have become central: history is what documents make of it, history is what the conventions of the genre make of it, unknown to us.

Notes

Chapter I.   Only a True Account

1. *Traité de l'enchaînement des idées fondamentales dans la nature et dans l'histoire* (repr. Hachette, 1922), p. 204.
2. P. Ricoeur, *Histoire et vérité* (Seuil, 1955), p. 29.
3. H. I. Marrou, "Le métier d'historien," in coll. Encyclopédie de la Pléiade, *l'Histoire et ses méthodes*, p. 1469.
4. "Frontières du récit," in *Figures,* II (Seuil, 1969), p. 30. History admits the ethos and the hypotyposis, but not the pathos.
5. On this theme, rather different from the ancient distinction between nature and convention, *physis* and *thesis*, see Leo Strauss, *Droit natural et histoire*, Fr. trans. (Plon, 1954), pp. 23–49; the theme is also found in Nietzsche (ibid., p. 41).
6. *Souvenirs d'un voyage dans la Tartarie, le Thibet at la Chine* (ed. of Ardenne de Tizac, 1928), IV, p. 27.
7. Dilthey, *Le monde de l'espirit,* trans. Rémy (Aubier, 1947), I, p. 262.
8. This sort of aestheticism of the event is basically the attitude of Rickert, who against physical sciences opposed history as the knowledge of the individual. But he was thinking less of the individual as an event singularized in time than of the individual as a museum piece. According to him, a famous diamond like the Regent would be an object for history, as opposed to a piece of coal, which, if broken up, would not lose an individuality that it does not possess; the same would be true of Goethe, as opposed to the man in the street. What makes these objects into so many personalities is the value they have for us. History is related to values—that is one of the great ideas of German historicism, as we shall see in chapter IV; it is the reply to the central question of historicism: What makes a fact "historic"? Rickert is thus obliged to explain why the historian does not speak only of diamonds and of men of genius: the reason would be that beside "primary" historical objects, like Goethe, there would be indirectly historical objects, such as Goethe's father. In chapter IV we shall see the influence of these ideas on Max Weber. On Rickert, see M. Mandelbaum, *The Problem of Historical Knowledge, an Answer to Relativism* (Harper Torchbooks, 1938; repr. 1967), pp. 119–161; R. Aron, *La philosophie critique de l'histoire, essai sur une théorie allemande de l'histoire* (Vrin, 1938; repr. 1969), pp. 113–157.

9. Husserl, *Recherches logiques,* trans. Élie (P.U.F., 1959), I, p. 260; B. Russell, *The Analysis of Matter* (Allen and Unwin, 1954), p. 177.
10. Let us say that three moments are discernible in historical work: the reading of the documents, the criticism, and the retelling. (1.) I can undertake a work on the history of China without being a Chinese scholar; if the sources are translated, I can read and understand them as well as anyone else, and, by the mere reading of these sources, the "synthesis" of the events will immediately be made in my mind, as when I open my daily newspaper. (2.) But I shall have to learn, from criticism, whether the inscriptions on tortoise shell are authentic, and whether the works grouped under the name of Confucius are really his; I will also have—and that is the delicate part of criticism—to learn to distinguish, in the Chinese texts, the propositions that are to be taken literally from those that are metaphorical, conventional, or the results of illusions that Chinese society had about itself. (3.) Events being always known by partial and indirect *tekmeria,* there will be many gaps that I will fill in the retelling; a particular emperor abdicated in order to retire to a Taoist hermitage on a mountain, but why did he do it? Is this the Chinese way of saying he was shut up in a monastery by some palace official? Or did it really happen that at the end of his life a man of letters, though an emperor, wanted a retreat to prepare his soul for philosophy, as was done in Rome? Alone the retelling, based on a "classification" of similar cases and on the probability of different causes, will allow me to reply. Synthesis in reality consists of filling in gaps in immediate comprehension. As a result the distinction between major history and "auxiliary discipline" is deceptive.
11. On the tripartition of the successors of Aristotle—true, seemingly true, unbelievable—see R. Reitzenstein, *Hellenistische Wundererzählungen,* pp. 90–97; A. Rostagni, "Aristotele e l'aristolelismo nella storia dell'estetica antica," in his *Scritti minori,* I, pp. 205–212; W. Knoll, *Studien zum Verständnis der römischen Literatur,* p. 61. In the article *"Histoire"* in the *Encyclopédie,* Voltaire wrote: "History: it is the recital of facts given as true, unlike the fable, which is the recital of facts given as false."
12. See, for example, G. R. Elton, *The Practice of History,* 2nd ed. (Collins, Sydney University Press, 1969), p. 20.

Chapter II.   History Does Not Exist

1. *La pensée sauvage* (Plon, 1962), pp. 340–348; we quote these pages very freely, without indicating omissions.
2. To illustrate a few confusions, let us quote these lines of A. Toynbee: "I am not convinced that a sort of privilege should be given to political history. I know quite well that that is a widespread prejudice; it is a trait common to Chinese historiography and to Greek historiography. But it is quite inapplicable to the history of India, for example. India has a great history, but it is a history of religion and of art, it is no way a political history" (*L'histoire et ses interprétations, entretiens autour d'Arnold Toynbee* [Mouton, 1961] p. 196). We have countless cheap color prints of Indian temples; how could we judge as being not great a political history that, in India, for lack of documents is almost unknown? And, above all, how could we judge what "great"

may mean? To read Kautilya, that Machiavelli of India, makes us see things differently.

3. The mathematician Mallory, who disappeared while climbing Everest in 1924; it is not known if he had reached the summit.

4. For example, the history of the arts, in the *Natural History* of Pliny the Elder.

5. A. Koyré, *Études d'histoire de la pensée scientifique,* pp. 61, 148, 260 (n. 1), 352ff.; *Études newtoniennes,* p. 29; cf. *Études d'histoire de la pensée philosophique,* p. 307.

6. The French peasant (tr.)

7. See the objections of Max Weber to Eduard Meyer, *Essais sur la théorie de la science,* trans. J. Freund (Plon, 1965), pp. 272 ff.

8. The idea that all the events of the same epoch have the same features and form an expressive whole is widespread; likewise, to us, each district of Paris or all the countryside in Umbria has the same local color. Spengler appealed to a kind of tact (the word is his own), to an intuition that he flattered himself he possessed to an exceptional degree, to perceive the originality and the discontinuity of the seasons of history. About 1950, French phenomenology hoped that, just as the world of perception forms a kind of melodic unity, so we might one day understand the unity of style that, no doubt, suffused all the events of the same period. It is nonetheless curious to see on what basis this illusion rests; it is as naive as that of "Gay Paris" or of the Belle Époque. It comes especially from the rhetorical color, from the phraseology of the sources: the clarity of classical Greece, the ornate simplicity of the Ciceronian era where great lords strolled under porticoes, speaking about the immortality of the soul. Let us take the Byzantine Empire, which we see as laden with jewels, sparkling, baroque, stifling, atrocious, seemingly unlike the Roman Empire. The origin of this physiognomy is solely the Kafka-like rhetoric of the Byzantine Empire common to Ammianus Marcellinus, St. Jerome, the Theodosian Code, and the inscriptions that E. Auerbach has so closely analyzed (*Mimésis,* French trans., pp. 70–77). Besides, when we read the papyruses of the Roman Empire, the rare decrees that are extant, or the *Acts of the Martyrs,* the same impression of dreadful heaviness appears: the cruelty of all the empires in which administration—distant, corrupt, and passing lightly over the peasant masses—makes up for its powerlessness by its cruelty and its majestic posing; it is the same in the Turkish and Chinese empires. Likewise, we would like to know what is real behind the somber aspect of the century of Villon and dances of death, and at what level of reality the admirable study of physiognomy by Huizinga can be placed. That dark color, that obsession with death is attributed to the circumstances of the fifteenth century—to plague, wars, to the Great Schism. So I ask, if things were so simply linked, what physiognomy ought the literature and the painting of the centry of Auschwitz and of Hiroshima to have?

9. The philosophy of history is today a dead genre, or at least a genre that survives only among epigones of a rather popular sort, like those of Spengler. For it was a false genre; unless it is a revealed philosophy, a philosophy of history is a useless repetition of the concrete explanation of facts and will refer one to the mechanisms and laws that explain those facts. Only the two extremes are viable: the providentialism of the *City of God* and historical

epistemology; all the rest is spurious. Let us suppose that we have the right to affirm that the general movement of history is directed toward the kingdom of God (St. Augustine), or that it is formed of seasonal cycles that recur in an eternal return (Spengler), or that it conforms to a "law"—in effect, to an empirical proof—of the three states (A. Comte), or else that, "in considering the movement of liberty, one would discover in it a regular course, a continuous development" that leads humanity to live free under a perfect consitution (Kant). There are two alternatives: Either this movement is merely the outcome of forces that shape history, or else it is caused by a mysterious external force. In the former case the philosophy of history is a useless repetition of historiography—or, rather, it is only a historical statement on a large scale, a fact that needs explanation like every historical fact; in the latter case, either this mysterious force is known through revelation (St. Augustine) and men will try, with varying degrees of success, to rediscover traces of it in the particulars of events unless, more wisely, they give up guessing at the ways of Providence, or else (Spengler) the fact that history goes round in a circle is a curious, unexplained fact that has been discovered by looking at history itself. But then, rather than being frightened, it is fitting to explain this strange discovery, to see what concrete causes make humanity go round in a circle. Perhaps those causes will not be found; then the discovery of Spengler will be a historical problem, an unfinished page of historiography.

Let us return to the philosophies of history that, like Kant, note that on the whole the movement of humanity follows or tends to follow a particular road, and that this orientation is due to concrete causes. Certainly noting this is of only empirical value; it is as if, for partial knowledge of the Earth and the continents, there were suddenly substituted a complete planisphere on which the contour of the continents appeared as a whole. To know the whole form of the continent would not lead us to modify the description we had already given of the part already known; in the same way, to know the future of humanity would in no way lead us to modify our way of writing the history of the past. Nor will that bring us any philosophical revelation. The main lines of the history of humanity have no specially didactic value—if humanity takes more and more the direction of technical progress, that is not necessarily its mission; it may be due to banal phenomena of imitation, of "snowballing," at the risk of a Markov chain or an epidemic process. The knowledge of the future of humanity is of no interest in itself—it would refer back to the study of the mechanisms of historical causality; the philosophy of history would send us back to the methodology of history. For example, Comte's "law" of the three states refers back to the question of knowing why humanity goes through three states. And that is what was done by Kant, whose very lucid philosophy of history is presented as a *choice* and sends us back to a concrete explanation. In effect, he does not hide the fact that the plan of a philosophical history of mankind will not consist in writing the whole of history philosophically, but in writing the part of that history that comes into the perspective selected: that of the progress of freedom. And he takes care to seek the concrete reasons that cause humanity to move toward that goal; it is, for example, that even when there are momentary returns of barbarism, at least a "seed of light" is transmitted to future generations and that man is made in such a way that he is good ground for the growth of those seeds. And that future of humanity, though it is possible and probable, is in no way certain. Kant meant to write his philosophical History to work toward that future, to make its coming more probable.

10. For example, W. Dray, "The Historian's Problem of Selection," in *Logic, Methodology and Philosophy of Science, Proceedings of the 1960 International Congress* (Stanford University Press, 1962), pp. 595–603.

11. K. Popper, *Misère de l'historicisme*, French trans. by Rousseau (Plon, 1956), pp. 148–150.

12. E. Gilson, *Linguistique et philosophie* (Vrin, 1969), p. 87: "The mere name of Aristotle suffices to irritate those who cannot forgive him, having come before them, for seeing and uttering simple, solid, evident truths, almost naively evident, that today one can but rediscover, through inability to go beyond them easily. . . . This simple and direct objectivity allowed Aristotle to say things as he saw them. There has never been an Aristotelian philosophy: The reality to be spoken of served him instead of a system."

13. On the origins of historism—or historicism, if you prefer—from Voltaire and Ferguson to Herder and Goethe, the classic book is that of F. Meinecke, *Die Entstehung des Historismus*, which is *Worke*, III (Oldenbourg, 1965). But the tastes of the Prussian scholar ran rather to individuality and the Goethean sense of the individual than to "totalitarianism," historical or otherwise (see Werke, IV, pp. 100–101, which he had the courage and the nobility to publish in 1939); Meinecke thus represents a particular current of historism, and nationalism occupies a restricted place in his book, which also does not treat Hegel. (In his review of the work, Croce rejected the thesis of Meinecke and put Hegel at the beginning of historism; that review is reproduced in *La Storia come pensiero e come azione*.)

14. On the origins of the historical sense from the eighteenth century on, see H. Butterfield, *Man on His Past, the Study of the History of Historical Scholarship* (Cambridge University Press, 1955; 1969), p. 33; let us add the name of Abbot Fleury, whose work is deserving of study. For a general history of the historical genre, see Fritz Wagner, *Geschichtswissenschaft*, which is Orbis Academicus, I, pt. 1 (Karl Alber, 1951; 1966), which studies historians, from Hecate of Milet to Max Weber, insisting on the importance of German historism. For a picture of the tendencies of present-day historiography and for recent writers, see A. Marwick, *The Nature of History* (Macmillan, 1970).

Chapter III.   **Plots, Not Facts or Geometrical Figures**

1. Cf. J. Vialatoux, quoted by J. Hours, in *Valeur de l'histoire* (P.U.F., 1963), p. 69, comparing the logic of the story with the logic of history.

2. *Scientisme et sciences sociales*, trans. Barre (Plon, 1953), pp. 57–60, 80; cf. K. Popper, *Misère de l'historicisme*, trans. Rousseau (Plon, 1956), pp. 79–80 and n. 1.

3. On the problem of cutting up the earth's surface into geographical regions, see the impressive article by H. Schmitthenner, "Zum Problem der allgemeinen Geographie," *Geographia Helvetica*, 6 (1951), esp. pp. 126 and 129 (reproduced in W. Storkebaum, ed., *Zum Gegenstand und zur Methode der Geographie*, vol. LVIII in the series Wege der Forschung (Wissenschaft-

liche Buchgesellschaft, 1967), pp. 195, 199–200: "The découpages made on the basis of different geographical categories cross each other in the most varied manner"; the idea that there would be natural regions is an illusion of naïve perception, fixed by toponomastics. The conceptual elaboration of the geographer breaks this cutting up in a variety of ways, according to the criterion chosen, and it in no way leads to finding regions that would this time be scientifically based, each one forming an organic whole on which the criteria would be superimposed (by what miracle could they in fact be superimposed?); to want to find the "true" regions is "to want to achieve the squaring of the circle."

The article by Schmitthenner is also an excellent introduction to an epistemology of geography, the interest of which would exactly equal that of an epistemology of history. There is nothing stranger than the following fact: Whereas the parallelism of geography and history is strict, the epistemology of history is looked on as a noble, moving, philosophical subject, the epistemology of geography would assuredly find few readers. Yet the problems of the two disciplines are fundamentally the same (dissolution of the "fact," causality and interaction, liberty, relations of explanation and intervention with the sciences; geology or economics, the practical aspect; politics or the arrangement of the territory, problems of concept, type, and comparative method, the "sublunary" aspect); the unequal popularity of history and geography measures the impact of romanticism on our vision of history; what makes historical epistemology a "noble" subject is the romantic idea that history would be the tribunal of the world (or, if you will, it is because we no longer believe in the theory of climates, in which geography governed human freedom and had the same value as a lesson in relativism that we attribute today to history; ethnography continues that lesson). Decidedly, history must shed its romantic halo.

In fact, the Toynbee of geography has existed. He was the geographer Carl Ritter, whose point of departure was the lesson of Herder (cf. the French geographical school dreaming in the margin of Michelet's *Tableau de la France*) and, according to him, natural regions were realities, individualities created by God, who gave them to man, with the latter's task being to make them habitable in conformity with the destiny the Creator had assigned to them. Ritter, moreover, has left a positive work whose importance and originality are stressed by geographers.

4. H. Bolkestein, *Wohltätigkeit und Armenpflege im vorchristlichen Altertum* (1939).
5. A. Wolfelsperger, *Les biens collectifs* (P.U.F., 1969).
6. A. Toynbee, in *L'histoire et ses interprétations*, p. 132.
7. In the same way, the geographers most conscious of the methodology of their science have recognized the subjective character of the notion of region (which in geography plays a part exactly corresponding to that of the plot in history), and have reacted against the Toynbee of geography, Ritter, who believed in the reality of the regions of the Earth. See, besides Schmitthenner's article, quoted in note 3, the remarks of H. Bobek and H. Carol, published in W. Storkebaum, ed., *Zum Gegenstand und zur Methode der Geographie*, pp. 293, 305, 479. For the division of the spatial continuum, the geographer can choose among numberless points of view, and those regions

have no objective frontiers and existence. If we undertake, like Ritter, to find the "true" division into regions, we fall into the insoluble problem of an aggregation of points of view, and into a metaphysics of organic individuality, or into a physiognomy of the landscape (the idea of a geometrical projection being the edulcoration of those superstitions).

Practically, the aggregation of points of view is done in confusion, either by surreptitiously jumping from one point of view to another in the course of the account, or by cutting out from the continuum for the sake of a point of view arbitrarily or naively chosen (whether inspired by toponomastics or by administrative geography). In geography and in history, the idea of subjectivity—of liberty and equality of points of view—brings a definitive clarification and tolls the knell of historicism. On the other hand, it does not follow (and Marrou protests against this confusion) that what has happened in time is subjective; just as nothing is more objective than the earth's surface, the object of geography. Geography and history are nominalisms: whence the impossibility of a history à la Toynbee and of a geography à la Ritter, for whom regions or civilizations really exist and are not a question of points of view.

8. H. I. Marrou, *De la connaissance historique* (Seuil, 1954), pp. 63 f., 222 f. H.-W Hedinger, *Sujektivität und Geschichtswissenschaft, Grundzüge einer Historik* (Duncker and Humblot, 1970), is not very useful.

Chapter IV.   Pure Curiosity about the Specific

1. Max Weber, *Essais sur la théorie de la science*, trans. J. Freund (Plon, 1965), pp. 152–172, 244–289, 298–302, 448.
2. *Essais*, p. 448.
3. *Essais*, pp. 244–259.
4. *Essais*, pp. 244, 247, 249.
5. We saw in ch. III that every "event" is the crossroads of an inexhaustible number of possible plots; that is why "the documents are inexhaustible," as is rightly repeated.
6. *Essais*, p. 302, cf. pp. 246, 279.
7. H. Kelsen, *Théorie pure du droit*, trans. Eisenmann (Dalloz, 1962), pp. 42, 92, 142.
8. In the same sense, M. Oakeshott, *Rationalism in Politics* (Methuen, 1962; University Paperbacks, 1967), pp. 137–167: "The activity of being an historian"; that activity is "a process of emancipation in relation to the practical attitude to the past which was the first and remained for a long time the only one."
9. However, if singularity—individuation by space, time, and separation of consciousness—has no place in the history the historian writes, it makes all the poetry of the historian's profession. The general public, which loves archaeology, is not mistaken. It is singularity, too, that most often decides the choice of that profession; we know the emotion aroused by an ancient text or object, not because it is beautiful, but because it comes from a period that has disappeared and because its presence among us is as extraordinary as a meteorite (except that objects from the past come from a "gulf" even more "out of range of our soundings" than the sphere of invariables). We also

know the emotion given by historical geography studies, in which the poetry of time is superimposed on that of space; to the strangeness of the existence of a place (for a place has no reason for being there rather than elsewhere) is added the strangeness of the toponymy, in which the arbitrariness of the linguistic sign is in the second degree, which means that little reading is as poetic as that of a geographical map. On that is superimposed the idea that this same spot that is here was formerly something else, though it was at that moment the same place one sees here now; the ramparts of Marseilles attacked by Caesar, the ancient road "along which the dead have passed" and which followed the same course as the road one has now under one's feet, the modern dwelling that stands on the site and carries on the name of an ancient dwelling. The carnal patriotism of many archaeologists (like Camille Jullian) undoubtedly had no other origin. History thus occupies a position between scientific universality and inexpressible singularity; the historian studies the past out of love for a singularity that escapes him because he studies it and that can be the object only of reveries "outside work." It is no less confusing that one has wondered what existential need could explain the interest we have in history and that one has not thought that the simplest answer was that history studies the past, that gulf forbidden to our sounding lines.

10. The distinction between the singular and the specific recovers in part that made by Benedetto Croce between history and the chronicle: *Théorie et histoire de l'historiographie,* trans. Dufour (Droz, 1968), p. 16.

11. *The Parts of Animals* I, 5, 644b.

12. This is the place to pay homage to Annie Kriegel, *Les Communistes français* (Seuil, 1968).

13. Schopenhauer, *Le monde comme volonté et représentation,* III, supp. ch. 30: "Knowledge, though coming from Will, is nonetheless corrupted by that same Will, as the flame is obscured by the material being burned and the smoke that it gives off. And so we can only conceive the purely objective essence of things and the ideas present in them by taking no interest at all to the things themselves, because they then afford no relation with our Will. . . . To understand the idea in the midst of reality, we must in some way rise above its interest, make an abstraction of its will, which needs a particular energy of intelligence. . . ."

14. Inaugural lecture, Collège de France, chair of molecular biology, 1967: "Today we hear on all sides men defending pure research, free of any immediate contingency, but that precisely in the name of praxis, in the name of powers still unknown that it alone can reveal and harness. I accuse scientists of having often, too often, maintained that confusion; of having lied about their true design, invoking power in order, in reality, to feed knowledge, which alone matters to them. The ethics of knowledge is radically different from the religious or utilitarian systems, which see in knowledge not the goal itself, but a means of reaching it. The only goal, the supreme value, the sovereign good in the ethics of knowledge, is not, let us admit it, the happiness of humanity, even less its temporal power or comfort, nor even the Socratic *gnôthi seauton*—that is, objective knowledge itself." Saint Thomas, *Summa contra gentiles,* 3, 25, 2063 (ed. Pera, III, p. 33; cf. 3, 2, 1869 and 1876) in this contrasts knowledge to the game, which is not an end in itself.

That knowledge is an end in itself does not mean that it cannot be used occasionally for other ends, useful or enjoyable, but that in any case the end it is to itself is always present and always sufficient, and also that it is constituted in function of that one end—that is, truth alone. To Thucydides, history, which reveals truths that will always be true, is a definitive acquisition in the order of knowledge and not in the order of action, where a singular situation is to be judged, which renders useless the too general truths of the *ktèma es aei*: J. de Romilly has strongly stressed this important point (misunderstood notably by Jaeger), by contrasting Thucydides-type history with that which claims to give lessons to men of action (Polybus, Machiavelli). Similarly, according to a known saying, Plato wrote the *Republic* to make the cities better and Aristotle, on the other hand, wrote the *Politics* to make a theory better.

15. B. Croce, *Théorie et histoire de l'historiographie*, trans. Dufour (Droz, 1968), p. 206. Similarly, H. Bobek very rightly notes, geography, whatever is frequently said, is not the science of space; it is the science of regions (which are to the geographer what plots are to the historian). The spatial character of the region is understood but is not essential); to know that a given town is north of another is not geography, any more than knowing that Louis XIII preceded Louis XIV. See H. Bobek, "Gedanken über das logische System der Landeskunde," in the collection of W. Storkebaum, *Zum Gegenstand der Geographie*, p. 292. To misuse the unnecessary idea that geography is the knowledge of the spatial character of phenomena would lead to vapidity—for example, finding it enough, for a "geography of law," to say that Anglo-Saxon laws are found in such and such a region, instead of saying *how* that comes about, how that juridical geography is understood. Let us add that just as a historical event is individualized, is made singular by time, and only by that, so a geographical fact (that glacier) is individualized only by its position in space; everything else, all the "individual qualities" or what are supposed to be such, of the glacier have to be explained and are specific. Historical or geographical individuality is a combination of specific qualities that are repeatable separately and in combination; the only thing differentiating two identical combinations would be their localization at different points in space and time.

16. Compare, in the criticism of art, E. Cassirer discussing the ideas of Rickert: "Zur Logik der Kulturwissenschaften," *Acta Universitatis Gotoburgensis*, 48 (1942), pp. 70–72.

Chapter V.   **Intellectual History**

1. The lengthy pages that Heidegger devotes to history, at the end of *Sein und Zeit*, express a conception widely held today: Historical knowledge (*Historie*) is rooted in the historicity of the *Dasein* "in a special and privileged manner" (p. 392); "The selection of what must become a possible object for *Historie* is already present in the choice of the existential facticity of the *Dasein*, from which it rises in the first place and in which alone it can exist." We recognize the central problem of historism (and already, in one sense, of Hegel in the *Lessons*); since not all is worthy of history, what events deserve to be chosen? Heidegger's conception of history takes into account that time

is there; it also takes into account what has been lived (man is Care, and he has fellow men and even a *Volk*), but only partly so (the Heideggerian man, unlike the man of St. Thomas, feels he is mortal; on the other hand, he does not eat, does not procreate, and does not work). Finally, it allows us to understand that history can become a collective myth.

But if the temporality of the *Dasein* and the *Mitsein* were sufficient as a foundation of history, in that case the perception of space as "near Guermantes" and "near Méséglise" would be the foundation of every geographical monograph on the district of Combray. Such telescoping of the essence in the interests of the foundation ends in a conception of history that is not so much false as uninteresting. For example, it will justify any collective stupidity. Let us note one detail for our research: if History has as its root the future of the *Dasein*, can one still write contemporary history? Where can one find a rationality organizing the historiography of the present moment? If my people have not yet decided whether they will annex a particular province, how can the history of that province be written in the sense of the future my people will choose concerning it? So Heidegger begins by "setting aside the question of the possibility of a history in the present, in order to attribute to historiography the task of opening up the past." The idea that there is an essential difference between the history of the past and that of the present has been a source of endless confusion in the methodology of history; it will be seen at the end of this book that it is central to a criticism of sociology.

2. On the huge variations of that fringe, see M. Nilsson, *Opuscula selecta*, II, p. 816. About 1900 the peasants of a Danish village had preserved the exact memory of an episode in the Thirty Years' War relating to their village; they had forgotten the general circumstances of the episode and its date.

3. But the philosopher does think about it: "Foundations and ruins of states, customs of all kinds, in conformity with or contrary to good order, different culinary customs, changes in food and drink, have occurred all over the world; there have been a thousand kinds of climatic changes that have transformed in a thousand ways the original nature of living beings." Plato, *Laws*, 782a.

4. The world is completed. Let us go further—everyone can state that everything is less good today than it was yesterday (the land is exhausted; men are shrinking; there are no more seasons; the level of grades on examinations is continually going down; piety, respect, morality are being lost; workmen of today are no longer those of former days, who so lovingly fashioned the stretcher of a chair. Compare Shakespeare's *As You Like It* II, iii, 57, with that famous page of Péguy, and it must be concluded that the world is not only mature but near its old age and its end. Texts on the exhaustion of the world are numberless and frequently misunderstood. When the Emperor Alexander Severus speaks in a papyrus of the decadence of the Empire in his own reign, that is not a courageous admission or a blunder, both admirable on the lips of a head of state; it is a commonplace, as normal at that time as it is today for a head of state to speak of the peril that the atomic bomb presents for humanity. When the last pagans, in the fifth century, paint Rome as an old woman with a wrinkled face, *vieto vultu,* and say that the Empire is crumbling and is near its end, it is not the spontaneous confession of a social

class condemned by History and feeding on the feeling of its own decline, but a well-worn theme; moreover, if Rome is an old woman, she is a venerable old lady deserving the respect of her sons.

Aubigné was not a decadent skeptic when, speaking of *the tragedies* of the martyrs of his party, he wrote: "An autumn rose is more exquisite than any other, you have gladdened the *autumn of the Church*." The Augustinian idea is known: that humanity is like a man living the sixth of his seven ages (see, for example, M. D. Chenu, *La théologie au douzième siècle* [Vrin, 1957], p. 75; Dante, *Convivio* 2, 14, 13). The chronicle of Otto of Freising has the refrain "we who have been placed at the end of time"; let us not conclude from that that there was anguish in the twelfth century. That thought endured until the nineteenth century, when the idea of progress introduced into the collective consciousness one of the most impressive mutations in the history of ideas; the eighteenth century still considered that the world is close to demographic and economic exhaustion (despite the protests of the Physiocrats, who contrast Columelle with Lucretius). The most surprising text comes from Hume's *Essay on Miracles;* the English philosopher wants to oppose unbelievable facts and strange things that can be believed: "Suppose that all writers of all periods agree in saying that from January 1, 1600, there was complete darkness for a week over the whole earth; it is evident that we philosophers of today, instead of doubting this fact, ought to receive it as certain and seek its causes whence it came—the decline, the corruption, and the dissolution of nature are . . . made probable by so many analogies that any phenomenon seeming to lead to that catastrophe comes within the limits of human witness."

This idea of aging is only a variation of the fundamental idea that the world is completed, mature; it is thus that we relate the history of the human species as that of the passing from monkey to man. The monkey became man as we know him; that is done, the tale is told—we have given an account of the genesis of the human animal. Now that is exactly how Lucretius sees the history of civilization at the end of book V of *De natura rerum*. It has frequently been asked if, in those famous lines that describe the political and technological development of humanity, Lucretius "believed in progress" and also if he approved of material progress or held it to be in vain. We have first to see what was intended in book V. Lucretius is there proposing an experiment in thought: to prove that the theories of Epicurus are enough *to account wholly* for the construction of the world and of civilization; for the world is constructed and completed, the techniques for inventing are invented, and the rest of history could not pose new philosophical problems. This idea of the completion of the world, which from now on can only grow old, is the most widespread and natural of the philosophies of history; by comparison the conceptions studied by L. Löwith (cyclic time or marching forward in a straight line to eschatology) are more intellectual, less natural and widespread.

5. The idea of a historicist mutation and the halo that for a century has surrounded the word "history" arise in part from the custom of connecting with this word different problems that are not all new and in other days were expressed in other terms; since these problems are of no interest to historical methodology, we will be satisfied with enumerating them.

1. To begin with, the various themes of historical relativism: relativity of values or frameworks of thought; therein lies a world of ideas extending from Collingwood or the ideas of Renan on the relativity of the beautiful, to certain tendencies of Nietzsche. Relativism does not consist in establishing the existence of variations in values, but in refusing to put the question of right to this subject. Now, since the historians' only task is to describe those variations and not to judge them, this problem does not interest them; for them the mutation of history has consisted not in admitting that values vary, but in recognizing that all that varies is worthy of history.

2. The problem of responsibility and of action (the sense of history, historical morality versus individual morality, Marxist morality). Today this problem of morality and politics is expressed in historical terms, and it is reexpressed each time it is admitted that since politics is the architectonic science, the problem of individual morality comes back to a perfect *politeia*.

3. The problem of man's essence; you will find many books that, with a title in which the word "history" figures, treat man as a reasonable animal, as a political animal, and as a being existing in time; is man only a part of nature? Is he free, is he the author of his collective destiny?

4. The problem of truth as history in the works of the Italian neo-Hegelians, Croce and Gentile: "Knowledge must give place to knowledge *in fieri*, just as to extrahuman truth, extratemporal truth, there succeeds human, temporal, worldly truth—that is, the truth that is history" (F. Battaglia, *La valeur dans l'histoire*, trans. Roure [Aubier, 1955], p. 121).

5. History (or culture) versus nature—that is, thesis versus physis.

6. The Husserlian problem of a history of science and of the insertion of truth into time ("foundation" of a science, the community of scholars throughout history); far from being absolute minds, we are incapable of anticipating the future development of knowledge, and yet that knowledge will be absolutely true. This problem is posed to us in historical terms; in the thirteenth century it would have been seen, rather, as a "psychological" problem, that of the intellect as agent (the progressive discovery of knowledge, passing from the potentiality to the act, presupposes an intellect totally in act, preceding in actuality and by right the intellect of the knowing subject; this intellect as agent, which has always thought all that it thinks and contains no truth not actualized, which exists in time while "impassively" escaping any historical modification, and which exerts on human intellects effects that are not always the same because of the historical and "material" differences of those intellects—that intellect allows humanity to discover progressively what is true. Better still, it seems that it is one for all men throughout time; around this one reservoir of truths there gathers the community of intelligences. It would be attractive to draw a parallel between the *Krisis* of Husserl and the *Monarchy* of Dante).

7. Hegel's *Lessons on the Philosophy of History*. But this difficult text, around which legends abound (on this I fully believe my old friend Gérard Lebrun, having had the advantage of hearing the remarkable talks given by him on those *Lessons*), shares the fate of the *Philosophy of Nature;* it loses its import and its savor if separated from the system as a whole. Moreover, it is concerned with political philosophy even more than with that of history.

6. Play by Sartre (trans.)

7. Plato, *Hippias Major*, 285e.
8. It happens, too, that patriotism is but a noble pretext; the numerous and huge volumes of the *Monumenta Germaniae historica* appeared under the motto *Sanctus amor patriae dat animum;* in fact, love of country gives the courage to die, but not to compile.
9. Hegel, *Leçons sur la philosophie de l'histoire*, trans. Gibelin (Vrin, 1946), p. 63.
10. Will it be only a citizen who will write history? I doubt it. Where does the citizen, the politically active man, begin? The subjects of absolute monarchies make history of the glory of their king, of the affairs of foreign princes, and are interested in genealogies; people have always had politics as their favorite spectacle (La Bruyère said this in speaking of "newsmongers" before David Riesman attributed the same taste to 'inside-dopesters" of advanced democracies—sociologists, that is your doing). A tribe of "primitives" makes war or parley; are they not politically active? A serf crushed in apolitical passivity will not write history, but is it not because he is also crushed into intellectual passivity? On the other hand, a courtier, a contemporary of that serf and as politically passive as he is, will write the history of the despot or of his court.
11. See the common-sense objections of P. Vidal-Naquet, "Temps des dieux et temps des hommes," *Revue de l'histoire des religions*, CLVII (1960), p. 56.
12. The transposition in terms of consciousness of the cultural activities of the primitives has wrought havoc and will remain as a characteristic style of the ethnology and the history of religions in the first half of this century; forgetting that thought is divided into genres (a tale is not a theologism, a theologism is not implicit faith, a pious hyperbole is not a belief), all thought has been reduced to being a *cosa mentale* of unbreathable density. Thus was born the myth of the primitive mentality or of a Sumerian weltanschauung that seems to be the thought of a termite in its hill, or the myth of mythical thought: sacerdotal cosmogonies proper to some religious professionals, who believe in them in the measure that an idealist philosopher believes in daily life that the exterior world does not exist, individual elucubrations like the all too famous *Dieu d'eau* of Griaule, edifying stories, tales for an evening or for a harvest gathering in which men no more believe than the Greeks believed in their own mythology—all that is taken in bulk and called myth (the antidote is found in B. Malinowski, *Trois essais sur la vie sociale des primitifs* [Payot, 1968], pp. 95 f.). Behind every hyperbole is placed, in the name of religious feeling, the full charge of implicit faith—can you imagine a study of Louis XIV treating the theme of the Sun King with as much seriousness as that of the solar nature of the Roman emperor or that of the divinity of the pharaoh (the antidote is in G. Posener, "De la divinité du pharaon," *Cahiers de le société asiatique*, XV [1960]). Where have I read, or dreamed, of that young ethnographer, the Fabrice del Dongo of ethnography, who was almost taken unaware and had reasons for wondering if he had "really witnessed" a scene from the life of the primitives? He had gone to study a tribe who, it had been explained to him, "believed" that if its priests for one moment ceased playing a certain musical instrument, the cosmos would at once die of lethargy (that music was one of those rites that are said, in the history of religions, to maintain the cosmos in being or to promote the prosperity of the

collectivity, for example). Thus, our ethnographer expected to find, among the musician-priests, people who would withhold the detonator of an atomic bomb; he found ecclesiastics performing a sacred, ordinary task with the bored professional conscience of a good worker. In the *Upanishad* we similarly read that if the morning sacrifice was not offered, the sun would not have the strength to rise; this hyperbole in seminary style is to implicit faith what Déroulède is to patriotism; only a naive person taking everything literally will find in the *Upanishad* the Indian vision of the world and an authentic document on the archaic mentality.

13. See, for example, pp. 80 f. of the very useful vol. XXIV, *Geschichte*, of the *Fischer-Lexicon* (Fischer-Bücherei, 1961).

14. The famines of former days were even more besetting than the economic crises between 1846 and 1929. Economic history was born of erudition and economic theory. In 1753 and 1754, Michaelis and Hamburger studied prices among the Hebrews and the Greeks; for erudition, in the eighteenth century, was more non-eventworthy than "great" history meant for the general public (it is still true of classical epigraphy in the twentieth century). The *Ideen über die Politik, den Verkehr und den Handel der vornehmsten Völker der alten Welt* of A. H. L. Heeren first appeared in 1793. In 1817 the big volume by Boeckh on the political economy of the Athenians definitively founded the genre. The most widely read theoretical models were indubitably those of Adam Smith and J. B. Say.

15. Cf. an interview with Sartre, 17 March 1969: "In the present-day perspective [meaning the history of the present time, in both senses of the term], we cannot force the study of the Crusades, whether from a selective compulsion or a humanist illusion (which, justifiably, conceals the selection) of universal knowledge. But nothing says that, in a truly revolutionary, nonselective society, in which knowledge emerges in practice instead of being monopoly and justification for reaction, all history would be restored—not, as was done in earlier days, in its affable display, but with telescopings, abridgments, obstructions, according to the importance that the society accords to its own past." These views are scarcely Peripatetic.

Chapter VI.   **Understanding the Plot**

1. We can imagine, for example, that if Italy abandoned the market for second-quality pottery to Gaul in the first century of our era, it was not because the Italian economy was crushed by the technical superiority of the provinces or by the cheapness of labor there, but because, in other sectors, Italy had a crushing superiority over the provinces and because, although she could have produced better and cheaper pottery than Gaul, her interest lay relatively in specializing in the sectors where her advantage was great. Let us hasten to add that this is purely hypothetical. I merely want to show that the others are just as much so, and that it is wise not even to begin the study of them. One can only register facts, and even very few of those would stand up to criticism.

2. Aristotle, *De interpretatione*, IX, 18B30; M. Merleau-Ponty, *Sens et non-sens*, p. 160: "True objectivity, then, requires one to examine, in order to give them their rightful role, the subjective components of the event, the

interpretation of it given by the protagonists. . . . We must awaken the past, put it back into the present."

3. R. Aron, *Introduction à la philosophie de l'histoire, essai sur les limites de l'objectivité historique,* p. 183: "That liberty to reconstruct shows itself further in the choice of level. One historian will put himself on the same plane as the actor, another one will neglect microscopical analysis and will follow the combined movements leading to the event under consideration. The problem of the proximate origins of the 1914 War will have less range and interest for a Marxist. The capitalist economy, European politics of the twentieth century, secreted, so to say, a conflict, the incidents of the last days are of little importance."

4. Compare what Trotsky says of Nicholas II in *Histoire de la Révolution russe,* I, at the end of the chapter "The Death Throes of the Monarchy."

5. History is narration; it is not determination nor is it explanation; the opposition of "facts" and "causes" (Taine, Langlois, and Seignobos) is an illusion rising from a misunderstanding of historical nominalism. That history is not determination goes without saying (when one thinks it has been proved that "Napoleon could not" take a certain decision, it would remain true that, during the night before the decision, the emperor might have had a fit of mysticism or one of apoplexy). There is, on the other hand, a widespread idea that a historiographer worthy of the name and truly scientific must pass from "narrative" to "explanatory" history. For example, in Josef Gredt's textbook of Aristotelian-Thomist philosophy, we read that history is not truly a science in the sense that its object is a mass of factual data that it does not deduce, but that it does become scientific in a certain way by connecting those facts with their causes. But how would it not connect them with their causes, since every account immediately has a meaning, since it is impossible to gather a fact without bringing its causal roots with it, and since, conversely, to find a new cause of "a" fact is to disengage, in the form of a consequence, a new aspect of "the" fact in question?

To find economic causes of the French Revolution is to shed light on the economic aspects of that revolution. The illusion comes from believing that the Revolution is "a" fact other than nominally; that it is not *a* fact means it is not a *fact,* since "being and one are convertible"—it is a nominal aggregate. Certainly, when one writes "What are the causes of the Revolution?" and when one is hypnotized by this statement, one has the impression that the fact is there and that it remains to find its causes; thus one imagines that history becomes explanatory and that it is not directly comprehensible. The illusion disappears as soon as the word "Revolution" is replaced by what it covers: an aggregate of little facts. As R. Aron writes (more or less) in his *Dimensions de la conscience historique,* "the" causes taken together do not entail "the" Revolution as their resultant; there are only *detailed* causes that each explain one of the numberless *detailed* facts grouped together under the name "Revolution." Similarly, when Max Weber related puritanism to the beginnings of capitalism, he did not claim to discover the several causes or the one cause of "the" capitalism; he simply brought to light one aspect of capitalism that was misunderstood before his time and whose cause he simultaneously indicated: a religious attitude. This aspect is not a perspective on the geometrical figure that capitalism might be, for that geometrical figure does not exist; the aspect in question is only a new historical fact that will quite naturally integrate with the aggregate we call capitalism. In other words, under the same name of capitalism we shall continue to designate an event that in reality is no longer quite the same, because its composition has been enriched.

We shall see, in chapter X, that the progress of history is not to pass from narration to explanation (every narration is explanatory), but to push narration further into the non-eventworthy.

6. G. Granger, "L'histoire comme analyse des oeuvres et comme analyse des situations," in *Médiations*, I (1961), pp. 127–143, which states: "Every human work is something more than the product of its conditioning, but, on the other hand, that something in no way obliges us to hypostatize the frameworks of consciousness to subordinate to them all apprehension of reality."

7. The classical example is the formal analysis of St. Paul's speech before Areopagus by E. Norden, *Agnostos Theos, Untersuchungen zur Formengeschichte religiöser Rede* (1923; repr. 1956).

8. H. Wölfflin, *Principes fondamentaux de l'histoire de l'art: Le problème de l'évolution du style dans l'art moderne*, Fr. trans. (Plon, 1952), pp. 262 f., 274 f. The work of A. Warburg, with his study of the *Pathosformeln*, gives a fairly similar meaning.

9. J. G. Droysen, *Historik* (1857), ed. Hübner (1937; repr. Munich: Oldenbourg, 1967), p. 180.

10. A. Siegfried, *Tableau politique de la France de l'Ouest sous la Troisième République* (repr. A. Colin, 1964).

11. H. Mendras, *Sociologie de la campagne française* (P.U.F., 1959), p. 33.

12. The method of differences and remainders leads nowhere, because it is impossible to make clear all the causes. Yet few illusions are as tenacious as the idea that wonders are to be expected from this method, and nothing is less rare than desires in this direction; see Morris Ginsberg, *Essays in Sociology and Social Philosophy* (Peregrine Books, 1968), p. 50; L. Lipson, "The Comparative Method in Political Studies," *The Political Quarterly*, XXVIII (1957), p. 375; R. S. Cohen in P. A. Schilpp, ed., *The Philosophy of Rudolf Carnap* (Cambridge, 1963), p. 130.

13. For the police, see Trotsky, *Révolution russe*, I, *Février*, ch. "Les cinq journées," trans. Parijanine (Seuil, 1950), p. 122; for Lenin, ibid., p. 299: "It remains to be asked, and the question is not unimportant: how would the Revolution have developed if Lenin had not been able to reach Russia in April 1917? . . . The role of individuality is here revealed to us in gigantic proportions; we must only understand that role exactly by considering individuality as a link in the historical chain."

14. Polybius, 2, 7; Machiavelli warns against similar imprudence, *Discorsi sopra la prima deca di Tito Livio*, I, 27.

15. Th. Schieder, *Geschichte als Wissenschaft* (Munich: Oldenbourg, 1968), p. 53: "History as the justification of what has been, that is the greatest danger threatening the historian."

16. The census taker clings to Syme's prosopographic method, which puts the role of individuals in the foreground. But prosopography has never been a method; it is a procedure for explaining—how would that procedure have prevented Syme from advancing the great problems of the period, if he had

wanted to do so? And how can one describe individuals and their actions without describing at the same time their social world and its problems?

17. A society is not a pot in which matters of discontent, by dint of boiling, make the lid fly off; it is a pot in which an accidental moving of the lid gives rise to boiling, which makes it shoot off. If the initial accident is not manifested, the discontent remains diffuse, though visible if the spectator is a man of good faith and has no interest in seeing nothing (I have very exact memories of the Muslim unrest in Algeria in August 1953); it is true that the onlooker can predict nothing about the passage from the diffusion to the explosion.

18. On this tripartite division (nature, practical or poietic activity, fortune), traditional among the commentators of Aristotle see, for example, Alexander of Aphrodisias, *De fato ad imperatores*, IV, *Alexandri Scripta minora reliqua*, p. 168, 1–24 Bruns, in *Supplementum Aristotelicum*, II, pt. 2 (repr. 1963); Themistius, *Paraphrasis in Physica*, p. 35, 10 Shenkl, *Commentaria in Aristotelem Graeca*, V, pt. 2, which distinguishes the *physis*, the *tyché*, the *techné*, and the *proairesis*. The tradition of this tripartite division explains the line of Dante, *Inferno*, 32, 76: *Se voler fu o destino a fortuna, non so* (with the assimilation of *destino* with nature, which also comes from Alexander of Aphrodisias). Compare the proverbial division, nature-art-chance, in Plato, *Laws*, 888e, and Aristotle, *Metaphysics*, 1032a10 and 1070a5 (to *techné* will be added *proaieresis* aiming at singular goals); *Protreptics*, B12 Düring; *Nicomachean Ethics*, 1112a30, with the commentary of St. Thomas; *In Ethica*, 466 (p. 131, Spiazzi), which distinguishes *natura* (including the supralunary *necessitas*), *fortuna*, and *quod per hominem fit;* compare *Summa contra gentiles*, 3, 10, 1947b: *naturalis, fortuitus, voluntarius*. In Tacitus we find here and there the tripartite division of common sense: *mores, fortuitum, fatum*. For Humboldt, see Wilhelm von Humboldt, *Werke in fünf Banden* (Cotta, 1960), I, *Betrachtungen über die bewegenden Ursachen in der Weltgeschichte*, p. 578.

19. Since readings are fashionable, I shall risk a Peripatetic reading of Sartre's *Questions de méthode*, at least of chs. 2 ("The Problem of Mediations") and 3 ("The Progressive-Regressive Method"); in ch. 2 we find substance as the only efficient cause (Let us quote: "When we say: there are only men and real relations between men—for Merleau Ponty I add: things, too, and animals—we only mean that the support of collective objects must be sought in the concrete activity of individuals"; "the swift and diagrammatic explanation of war under the Legislature as an operation of the mercantile middle class causes those men whom we know well, Brissot, Guadet, Vergniaud, to disappear, or in the last analysis makes them purely passive instruments of their class"); in ch. 3 we find causality, *proairesis*, deliberation, finality ("We declare the specificity of the human act crossing the social milieu while preserving the determinations and transforming the world on the basis of given conditions. To us, man is characterized above all by his going beyond a situation, by what he succeeds in doing with what has been made of him, even if he never recognizes himself in his objectivation").

20. M. Merleau-Ponty, *Éloge de la philosophie et autres essais* (N.R.F., 1968), p. 116; for the Husserlian "imaginary variation," see R. Toulemont, *L'essence de la société selon Husserl* (P.U.F., 1962), pp. 22, 37, 90, 192, 289.

21. Compare Wölfflin, *Renaissance et baroque*, Fr. trans. (N.R.F., 1968), p. 169:

"The road that leads from the cell of the scholastic philosopher to the studio of the architect is not obvious." Among other reasons for doubting Panofsky's hypothesis is that this historian seems to have given way to a retrospective illusion. To us, the bulk of the *summas* and the method of implacable subdivisions are physiognomical features of scholasticism. But what about in the eyes of people of the thirteenth century? It must not be forgotten that the *summas* were only school textbooks, and that the philosophical works that marked an epoch in the Middle Ages were most often only the size of an ordinary book or of a short treatise, as is true today. When Panofsky compares the articulated multiplication of the cathedrals to that of the *summas*, he is obviously thinking of the *Summa theologica*. But let us, rather, open the *Summa contra gentiles*, which is not a textbook but a pioneering work, one of the five or six greatest philosophical works in the world—and whose authentic title was *Liber de veritate fidei*. Instead of a Gothic forest, we shall find a big book made up of short chapters with a fairly flexible plan and that, by the elegant precision of its style, does not suffer from pedantic insistence about subdivisions; we might call it Cartesian, if it were not much clearer than Descartes. Consequently, Panofsky is like a scholar undertaking, round the year 3000, to make a relationship between the art and the philosophy of our century; having taken as an example a philosophy textbook meant for use in the first years at the university, he would conclude from it that the method of numbering the paragraphs and of typographical stressing were to us basic traits of a philosophical statement, which could easily relate to structuralism in the painting of Mondrian, Vasarely, and the geometrical abstractionists.

22. Compare Canguilhem's criticism of Borkenau, *La connaissance de la vie*, 2nd ed. (Vrin), pp. 108–110: "Descartes consciously rationalized a mechanical technique, much more than he unconsciously translated the practices of a capitalist economy." It must be admitted that few works are as overrated as that of Borkenau (at present being reprinted), unless perhaps the work of Lukacs.

23. Which is more important, laws or mores? The discussion goes back to Plato, *Laws*, 793a–d; compare 783b; see, for example, A. Boeckh, *Économie politique des Athéniens*, trans. of the 1st ed., I (Paris, 1817), p. 3; Hegel speaks of a reciprocity of action (Lefebvre and Gutterman, *Morceaux choisis*, no. 110).

24. *Cours de linguistique générale*, p. 121.

25. *Histoire de l'idée de la nature* (Albin Michel, 1969), p. 31. Let us hasten to add that this is a posthumous work of this well-known historian of modern science.

26. On the illusion of the unity of style, see ch. II, note 7.

27. A. Shalom, *Colingwood philosophe et historien* (P.U.F., 1967), pp. 107, 172, 433.

Chapter VII.   Theories, Types, Concepts

1. O. Hintze, *Staat und Verfassung: Gesammelte Abhandlungun zur allgemeinen Verfassungsgeschichte* (Göttingen, repr. 1962), esp. pp. 110–139: "Typologie der ständischen Verfassung des Abendlandes; also see Th. Schieder,

Staat und Gesellschaft im Wandel unserer Zeit (Munich: Oldenbourg, 1958), p. 172: "Der Typus in der Geschichtswissenschaft"; R. Wittram, *Das Interesse an der Geschichte* (Göttingen, 1968), p. 46: "Vergleich, Analogie, Typus"; B. Zittel, "Der Typus in der Geschichtswissenschaft," in *Studium generale*, V (1952), pp. 378–384; C. G. Hempel, "Typologiste Methoden in den Sozialwissenschaften," in *Theorie und Realität, ausgewählte Aufsätze zur Wissenschaftslehre*, Hans Albert, ed. (Tübingen: Mohr, 1964).

2. See the movement of thought in A. R. Radcliffe-Brown, *Structure et fonction dans la société primitive*, trans. Marin (Éditions de Minuit, 1968), pp. 65–73.

3. On comparative history, which is one of the liveliest and most promising directions of contemporary historiography (less in France, it is true, than in Anglo-Saxon countries), but on which ideas are still not clear, see the bibliography of Th. Schieder, *Geschichte als Wissenschaft* (Munich: Oldenbourg, 1968), pp. 195–219; E. Rothacker, "Die vergleichende Methode in den Geisteswissenschaften," *Zeitschrift für vergleichende Rechstwissenschaft*, LX (1957), pp. 13–33.

4. Compare Marc Bloch, *Mélanges historiques*, I, pp. 16–40: "For a comparative history of European societies," esp. p. 18. One must carefully distinguish between this comparative history of religions in the manner of Frazer, which is comparative in the way that comparative history is (the comparison is used to complete a fact) and the comparative history of religions in the manner of Dumézil, which is comparative in the way that comparative grammar is (the comparison allows the reconstitution of an anterior stage of the religion or the language, which is the origin of the different languages and religions under consideration). In general, on historical reasoning *per analogiam*, see J. G. Droysen, *Historik* Hübner ed., pp. 156–163; Th. Schieder, *Geschichte als Wissenschaft*, pp. 201–204; R. Wittram, *Das Interesse an der Geschichte* (Göttingen: Vandenhoeck und Ruprecht, 1968), pp. 50–54. But the study ought to be taken up again within a theory of "retrodiction" and induction.

5. Compare Barrington Moore, *The Social Origins of Dictatorship and Democracy*, French trans. (Maspéro, 1969), p. 9.

6. On the contrary, when comparative grammar confronts Greek and Sanskrit, it is to find something else in them: Indo-European, which could not be discovered even by the most penetrating mind scrutinizing only one of these two terms. However perspicacious one may be, one will never see Indo-European in Greek alone.

7. On the recent character of the coincidence of fatherland and state, see A. Passerin d'Entrèves, *La notion de l'état*, French trans. (Sirey, 1969), p. 211. The work of Dion is thus divided between Greek nationalist propaganda and propaganda for the Roman emperor. So we shall distinguish the loyalist nationalism of Dion from a different movement, a popular and perhaps a social one (the Cynics criticize wealth under the pretense of ascetic morality), which was that of those popular orators in the public square (the Cynics) who preached revolt against the Empire. At the height of the century of the Anthonys, the Cynic Peregrinos Proteus "tried to persuade the Greeks to take up arms against the Romans" (Lucian, *The Death of Peregrinos*, 19); he set himself on fire before the crowd, like the sages of India. Compare W. Mühlmann, *Messianismes révolutionnaires du Tiers Monde* (Gallimard,

1968), p. 157: "Today, in Islamic countries, the Mahdist millenarism, very common in the lower classes that surround popular preachers, is in contrast to an official and rationalizing doctrine of nationalism, which is a luxury doctrine created by upper classes." To the luxury nationalism of Dion, to the popular or leftist nationalism of the Cynics, let us add a third attitude, the "collaborationism" of another publicist, Aelius Aristides, who thanks Rome for having strengthened her domination by associating the local elites with the power.

8. R. Wittram, *Das Interesse an der Geschichte*, p. 38: "In the word 'nationality' rings all the nineteenth century, the reader hears the cannons of Solferino, the trumpets of Vionville, the voice of Treitschke, he sees uniforms and dress clothes, he thinks of the national struggles in the whole of Europe . . ."; the same author points out that the word one so often reads today "has not the same meaning for the people of that period and for us," is more recent than we might think. Droysen, in the humanist tradition and under the influence of Hegel, still lived in an intellectual universe of fixed concepts.

9. *Treatise of Human Nature* (Everyman's Library), p. 31.

10. P. Laslett, *Un monde que nous avons perdu: Famille, communauté et structure sociale dans l'Angleterre pré-industrielle,* French trans. (Flammarion, 1969), p. 31. See also pp. 26; 27 ("capitalism, one of those numerous imprecise words that make up the vocabulary of historians"); 30 ("it is unfortunate that a preliminary study like ours should be preoccupied with a concept so difficult, so controversial, and so technical as that of social class"); 61 ("associations of ideas").

11. Kant, *Critique de la raison pure,* trans. Tremesaygues and Pacaud (P.U.F., 1967), p. 501.

12. Compare R. Stark and C. Y. Glock, "Dimensions of Religious Commitment," in R. Robertson, ed., *Sociology of Religion, Selected Readings* (Penguin Books, 1969), pp. 253–261.

13. R. Bastide, *Sociologie des maladies mentales* (Flammarion, 1965), pp. 73–81, 152, 221, 248, 261.

14. B. Croce, *L'histoire comme pensée et comme action,* trans. Chaix-Ruy (Droz, 1968), p. 40.

15. M. Weber, *Essais sur la théorie de la science,* trans. J. Freund, pp. 179–210 and 469–471 for all the quotations that follow. On the ideal type see especially R. Aron, *La sociologie allemande contemporaine,* 2nd ed., pp. 103–109.

16. This sentence from Goethe to Lavater is the epigraph of Meincke's *Entstehung des Historismus.*

17. R. Aron, *La philosophie critique de l'histoire, essai sur une théorie allemande de l'histoire* (Vrin, repr. 1969), p. 108: "Biography is considered [by Dilthey] as a historical genre par excellence, because the person is the immediate and supreme value and the periods are given shape only by the geniuses who give a finished form to the scattered riches of a collectivity. Biography is, finally, a period seen through one man."

18. Elsewhere, Weber contrasts genetic concepts and generic concepts, a probable allusion to the "generic history" that Karl Lamprecht wanted to contrast with "individual" history.

Chapter VIII.   Causality and "Retrodiction"

1. We shall refrain from urging the very debatable comparison between historical "retrodiction" and the calculus of probabilities of hypotheses; but see H. Reichenbach, *L'avènement de la philosophie scientifique*, trans. Weill (Flammarion, 1955), p. 200. Let us also note Peirce's study on probabilities and historical criticism, "Logic of history," in *Collected Papers of Charles Sanders Peirce* (Harvard University Press, 1966), vol. VII, pp. 89–164 (it will be noted that Peirce limited himself to the "frequency" conception of the basis of probabilities).

2. W. Stegmüller, *Probleme und Resultate der Wissenschaftstheorie und analytischen Philosophie*, vol. I, *Wissenschaftliche Erklärung und Begründung* (Berlin and Heidelberg: Springer, 1969), p. 440, and, in general, pp. 429 ff. Let us point out that pp. 335–427 of this important work are henceforth the starting point for all thinking on the epistemology of history.

3. Compare A. Michotte, *La perception de la causalité*, 2nd ed. (Louvain: Studia Psychologica, 1954).

4. Compare P. Gardiner, *The Nature of Historical Explanation* (1961; Oxford Paperbacks, 1968), p. 86, and, in general, pp. 80–98; W. Dray, *Laws and Explanation in History* (Oxford: Clarendon Press, 1957 [1966]), chs. 3, 4.

5. E. H. Carr, *What Is History?* (1961; Penguin Books, 1968), p. 63.

6. L. Robert, *Annuaire du Collège de France* (1962), p. 342.

7. Let us hasten to say that the word "slavery" is equivocal; slavery is sometimes an archaic juridical bond applied to the relationship of being in domestic service, sometimes the slavery of the plantation, as in the southern United States before 1865. In antiquity the first form was by far the most widespread; plantation slavery, which concerns only the forces and relationships of production, is an exception peculiar to Italy and Sicily of the low Hellenistic period, just as plantation slavery was an exception in the nineteenth century; the rule in agrarian matters was, in antiquity, as M. Rodinson said, free peasantry or serfdom. Spartacus, after destroying the plantation economy, would obviously have permitted, as did all his period, domestic slavery.

8. For the classification that seems to merit the attention of philosophers and of which there are fine examples in chs. I and VII of Spinoza's *Theologico-Political Treatise*, the simplest thing would be to study the work of a philologist who uses it without naming it, like Eduard Norden, or of a historian who uses and names it, like L. Robert. Here is an example of that very complex inference. The Greek word *oikeios* in the classical language means "peculiar, proper to"; in epitaphs of the Roman period, one very frequently finds the expressions *oikeios adelphos* or *oikeios pater*, which one is at first tempted to translate as "his own brother" or "his own father"; but the work occurs so often that one soon guesses that, with the passage of time and the wear and tear on words, it had become a simple possessive, and one must just translate it "his brother" or "his father." The implicit reasoning has been as follows: the occurrences of *oikeios* have been classified and it has been noted that they were more frequent than the number of times one could reasonably expect to see epitaphs feel the need to stress the "ownness" of this fraternity or paternity. But what does "reasonably" mean? It is an unacknowledged

classification: for *oikeios* to be a simple possessive and no longer to require a nuance of insistence, epitaphs have to be put together in a simple style and not in the Kafkaesque style of the Byzantine Empire, which puts all its weight on the slightest word; to interpret *oikeios* thus supposes that one has judged the style of the whole context—that is, that one has compared it with other styles of the time. Such is the enormous complexity of the mini-reasonings supporting the simplest affirmation.

9. The comparison between historical criticism and the police inquiry is imperative: we find it in H. Reichenbach (cited in note 1) or in Goblot's *Traité de logique*. We shall not here go into the question of knowing the nature of historical inference, which is neither deduction nor induction—see Goblot; also see A. Xénopol, *La théorie de l'histoire* (1908), which is in no way to be disdained, although one more and more rarely finds it quoted—for the nature of this inference, it seems that light is to be sought in Peirce and his description of abduction.

10. See, on this, P. Vidal-Naquet, "Économie et société dans la Grèce ancienne," *Archives européennes de sociologie,* VI (1965), p. 147.

11. We shall not go into the problematics of verification by prediction of past events, and we shall also leave to professional philosophers the problem, as it occurs in history, of protocolary statements; we shall be content to refer to A. C. Danto, *Analytical Philosophy of History* (Cambridge University Press, 1965; paperback, 1968), chs. IV, V.

12. A. Boeckh, *Enzyklopädie und Methodenlehre der philologischen Wissenschaften,* vol. I, *Formale Theorie der philologischen Wissenschaft* (1877; Teubner, 1968), pp. 84 f., in contrast with Dilthey, *Le monde de l'esprit,* trans. Remy (Aubier-Montaigne, 1947), vol. I, p. 331.

13. J. Maritain, *Pour une philosophie de l'histoire,* trans. Journet (Seuil, 1957), p. 21.

14. G. Granger, *Pensée formelle et sciences de l'homme* (Aubier-Montaigne, 1960; 1968); compare "Évènement et structure dans les sciences de l'homme," in *Cahiers de l'Institut de science économique appliquée,* no. LV (May–December, 1957), p. 47. On the theories in physics, on the pseudo theories in sociology, on the human sciences as praxeologies, see A. Rapoport, "Various Meanings of 'Theory,' " in *American Political Science Review,* LII (1958), pp. 972–988.

15. The fundamental work is C. G. Hempel, The Function of General Laws in History" (1942), in H. Feigl and W. Sellars, eds., *Readings in Philosophical Analysis* (New York: Appleton-Century-Crofts, 1949), and in P. Gardiner, ed., *Theories of History* (Glencoe, Ill.: Free Press, 1959); in the same line, I. Scheffler, *Anatomie de la science,* trans. Thuillier (Seuil, 1966), ch. VII; compare K. Popper, *Misère de l'historicisme,* trans. Rousseau (Plon, 1956), p. 142. See the very subtly varied positions in P. Gardiner, *The Nature of Historical Explanation,* and in W. Dray, *Laws and Explanation in History,* already cited, as well as in A. C. Danto, *Analytical Philosophy of History,* ch. X. But the best exposition of Hempel's theory is that of Stegmüller, *Probleme und Resultate der Wissenschaftstheorie,* vol. I, pp. 335–352. Logical empiricism and neopositivism have multiplied the studies on this question, and we certainly do not flatter ourselves that we know them all.

16. Compare Stegmüller, pp. 354–358 and 119; for the deductive-nomological theory of explanation, *ibid.*, pp. 82–90.

17. Stegmüller, pp. 360–375: "The So-called Method of Understanding"; compare R. Boudon, *L'analyse mathématique des faits sociaux* (Plon, 1967), p. 27.

18. On the "sketches of explanation," see Stegmüller, pp. 110, 346.

19. We return to the question as a whole in ch. X, where the discussion can be completely unfolded. The main concern, as we see it, is that what is taken from experience (fire, Islam, the Hundred Years War) has nothing in common with abstract cuttings from the formal (the quanta, the magnetic field, the amount of movement), that there is a chasm between the *doxa* and the *epistémé* and that what is taken from experience does not even allow the application of scientific laws to history, except for details: it is precisely what Stegmüller basically recognizes, when he shows that there are laws *in* history (that is, in daily life: the tile that falls on Pyrrhus' head obviously obeys the law of falling bodies), but not laws *of* history (p. 344); there is no law that would explain the unfolding of the Fourth Crusade. We agree with G. Granger, *Pensée formelle et sciences de l'homme*, pp. 206–212.

20. I. Scheffler, *Anatomie de la science, études philosophiques de l'explication et de la confirmation* (Seuil, 1966), p. 94: "[A defective generalization] can be replaced by some other true generalization, implying supplementary conditions." Let us hasten to add that to an author like Stegmüller this procedure will only result in a pseudo explanation (Stegmüller, p. 102) of the type "Caesar crossed the Rubicon in virtue of a law according to which every individual finding himself exactly living the part and in the circumstances of Caesar would inevitably cross any river exactly like the Rubicon.

21. It is the distinction made by K. Popper between prophecy and prediction: "Prediction and Prophecy in Social Sciences," in *Theories of History*, P. Gardiner, ed., p. 276.

22. Stegmüller, p. 347. How can we help but think of the criticism of Hume, made by Stegmüller himself, p. 443 (compare p. 107): "It is a hopeless undertaking to cling to everyday modes of speech and, without rising above the level of these everyday modes, to want to draw from them more precision than they in fact have." Let us quote also his admissions on p. 349 ("an incomplete 'sketch of explanation' is less often completed than replaced, with the progress of science") and p. 350 ("The replacing of a sketch of explanation by a full explanation almost always remains a Platonic exigency").

23. We borrow the expression and the idea from J. Molino's brilliant critique of R. Barthes, "La méthode critique de Roland Barthes," *Linguistique* (1969), no. 2.

24. On the opposition between "to explain" and "to describe," see Stegmüller, pp. 76–81; compare p. 343.

25. Compare Ernst Cassirer, *The Philosophy of Symbolic Forms*, vol. III, *Phenomenology of Knowledge*, trans. Manheim (Yale University Press Paperback, 1967), p. 434: "The statements of empiricists about science are very far from what science really is; the only point in common with truth is negative in nature: the rejection of a certain metaphysical ideal of knowledge; modern physics, like empiricism, has given up hope of penetrating the se-

crets of nature, if by 'secrets' we mean the ultimate substantial source whence empirical phenomena derive. But, on the other hand, physics draws a much firmer line between perceptible appearances and scientific experience than do the systems of dogmatic empiricism—those of Locke, Hume, Mill, or Mach. If we consider the material, the 'matter of fact' as these systems describe it, we see no methodological difference between the facts of the theoretical sciences and historical facts; that uniformization avoids the real problem of the nature of facts in physics. Physical facts are not on the same footing as those of history."

Similarly, on p. 409, Cassirer shows in its true light the famous "John Lackland will not pass that way again"; it must not be said that a historical fact is *not* repeatable (the fall of Napoleon) and that a physical fact *is* (the fall of *that* apple); these two falls are on a par, both being historical facts. What is repeatable is not the fact (the fall of *one* sovereign, the fall of one apple), but an abstraction based on the fact (the law of the fall of heavy bodies); by abstracting, physics *makes* repeatable the abstraction that it takes henceforth to be fact. "There is nothing like facts in the pure state; on the contrary, what we call a fact must always be oriented in a particular theoretical sense, be seen in relation to a definite system of concepts that implicitly determine it. The theoretical means of determination are not *added* to some raw fact, but constitute it; thus, the facts of physics are directly distinguishable from those of history by their specific intellectual perspective" (p. 409). We shall see that in history, where the system of reference is the plot, the perspective of causality is specific, and that one can reach legality only by a total change of the system.

26. These are the two examples given by Stegmüller, p. 344.
27. For the economic history of the Popular Front, see A. Sauvy, *L'histoire économique de la France entre les deux guerres*, vol. II (Fayard, 1967); this masterly book clarifies the relations that can exist between history and a human science.
28. Yale University Press, 1962 and 1965. In truth, we here speak metaphorically, for Riker's book, whose aim is theoretical, treats only the interplay of coalitions without stakes, and so cannot be used for the Popular Front, since the radical party had divided interests, so that the sum of the stakes was not null. But one knows that games with not-worthless stakes are very difficult from the point of view of an uninitiated like the author of these lines. A different and complementary approach to the problem is found in H. Rosenthal, "Political Coalition: Elements of a Model, and the Study of French Legislative elections," in *Calcul et formalisation dans les sciences de l'homme* (Éditions du C.N.R.S., 1968), p. 270.
29. A. Lichnerowicz, *Logique et connaissance scientifique*, in Coll. Encyclopédie de la Pléiade, p. 480.
30. Compare K. Popper, *Conjectures and Refutations: The Growth of Scientific Knowledge* (Routledge and Kegan Paul, 1969), p. 124.
31. Husserl, *Expérience et jugement, recherches en vue d'une généalogie de la logique*, trans. Souche (P.U.F., 1970), p. 233; compare R. Toulemont, *L'essence de la société selon Husserl* (P.U.F., 1962), pp. 70, 188–192, 239.
32. On focalization, see the excellent work of M. J. Herskovits, *Les bases de l'anthropologie culturelles* (Payot, 1967), ch. XV; R. Linton, *De l'homme,*

trans. Delsaut (Éditions de Minuit, 1968), speaks, rather, of "investments."
33. See the amusing satire on the sociology of modernity by P. Bourdieu and
J. C. Passeron, "Sociologues des mythologies et mythologies des sociologues," *Temps Modernes* (1963), p. 998.

Chapter IX.   Consciousness Not the Root of Action

1. The bibliography of such a subject is indefinite; let us refer to only two general studies that are situated on historical ground: G. Duby, "Histoire des
mentalités," in Encyclopédie de la Pléiade, *L'histoire et ses méthodes* (1961),
pp. 937 f.; and W. Stegmüller, *Probleme und Resultate der Wissenschaftstheorie,* vol. I, *Wissenschaftliche Erklärung und Begründung* (Springer Verlag, 1969), pp. 360–375, 379–427.
2. N. Bourbaki, *Éléments d'histoire des mathématiques* (Paris: Hermann,
1960), p. 30: "Whatever may be the philosophical nuances with which the
conception of mathematical objects is coloured by a particualr mathematician or philosopher, there is at least one point on which they are unanimous:
that those objects are *given* to us and that it is not in our power to attribute
arbitrary properties to them, just as a physicist cannot change a natural phenomenon. In truth, there no doubt enter into these views, on the one hand,
reactions of a psychological order known to every mathematician when he
exhausts himself in vain efforts to find a demonstration that always seems
to escape him; from there to assimilating that resistance to obstacles that
the world of the senses puts in our way, there is but one step."
3. Compare R. Boudon, *L'analyse mathématique des faits sociaux* (Plon, 1967),
p. 27.
4. Stegmüller, p. 368.
5. *Apologie pour l'histoire ou métier d'historien* (A. Colin, 1952), p. 4.
6. Stegmüller, p. 365; Boudon, p. 28.
7. Leo Strauss, *Droit naturel et histoire,* trans. Nathan and Dampierre (Plon,
1954; 1969), ch. 2.
8. The fundamental text is *Nicomachean Ethics,* VII.8.4.1151a10; St. Thomas
summarizes it thus: "In the domain of appetites and operations, the end be-
haves in the same way as the undemonstrable principles in speculative matters" (*Summa contra gentiles,* bk. I, ch. 80; compare 76. It follows that "the
man who errs on principles cannot be brought back to the true by more
certain principles, whereas the man whose error bears on conclusions can be
brought back" (*Summa,* IV, 95; compare 92).
9. Strauss, p. 69. As we have seen, regarding axiological history, the pure historian is content, as Weber says, with seeing in the object the *insertion* of
possible value judgments. He sees, in a given ancient religion, that there is
a difference between the attitude of a believer who tries to gain the goodwill of the gods by rich offerings and that of another believer who offers the
gods his purity of heart. The historian can say, "Another religion—Christianity, for example—would see an abyss between those two attitudes."
(Naturally, he can also note that factual difference in the form of a value
judgment, and write: "In that religion interested in base matters, almost no
difference was made between that impure attitude and that exalted one."
No matter, it is only a question of style: as a historian, we read him to learn

what was the nature of that religion, and not in order to learn how it ought to be judged.)

10. We leave aside for the moment a third problem, relating to the phrase "on peoples," to which the idea of morality or the notion of civilization would be unknown; it is the problem of the false continuities and categories treated in ch. VII; it is also the one of "regional essences" (politics, art), which will be treated in ch. XI.

11. The criticism of ideological pretexts, unduly limited to the collective consciousness (or even to class consciousness, as if the word "class" were other than a vague, equivocal, sublunary notion) must in reality be brought back to two philosophies: the theory of the sophisms of justification (*Nicomachean Ethics*, VII.3.8.1447a17 f.) and the Kantian idea of a horizon of consciousness, of a community of minds. For what need would the drunkard or the bourgeois have to justify himself ideologically and to draw a universal major premise from his conduct, if he did not feel the very idealistic need to convince other reasonable beings? Men need flags; ideological sophism, the inverted logic of passion, is homage rendered by bad faith to the ethical City. In that way one will avoid the supposition that an ideological pretext has a function, that it serves some purpose, like deceiving people (when in reality it first of all answers a need to justify oneself before the ideal tribunal of reasonable people); it can be seen that an ideological pretext ordinarily is useless, because it deceives no one, because it hardly convinces anyone except those already convinced, and because the *homo historicus* does not really give in to the ideological arguments of his opponent when his interests are at stake.

The idea of a defensive function of ideology is a Machiavellian fiction that has led research to a dead end.

12. *Essays*, "On the Vicissitude of Things."

13. It is believed less and less, it seems; in a recent number of the *Annales*, it is said to be thought today that at the time of the American Civil War, slavery had in no way exhausted its economic capacity.

14. For example, in Rome at the end of the Republic, political quarrels took the form of low invective, bearing on the private life and sexual morals (the philippics of Cicero, of Sallust); it was stereotyped conduct rather than a *logos*, and enemies of the day before, after heaping invective on each other, could easily become reconciled as the best of friends; the defamatory accusations, which had deceived no one, were much more easily forgotten than political grievances full of dignity would have been. In India today, we know similar verbal strife between parties, of which F. G. Bailey has given an amusing description in *Stratagems and Spoils, a Social Anthropology of Politics* (Oxford: Blackwell, 1969), p. 88. Among ourselves we cannot for a moment doubt that the type, style, and arguments of our motions and petitions are much more like a convention than like their requirements.

15. J. Norton Cru, *Du témoignage* (Gallimard, 1930). See especially his criticism of the *topos* of the bayonet attack; that *topos* figures in nearly all the witnesses. But if Norton Cru is to be believed, the bayonet attack was never practiced—or, rather, was immediately abandoned; but it had been, before the war, a great symbolical theme of military valor.

16. We are astonished, for example, to see how little, in the memories of resisters

or of militants those conflicts of authority are contemplated that are nonetheless the plague of underground organizations (or of religious sects). The violence of these memories often absorbs more energy than the struggle against class enemies, colonizers, or occupying powers; that forgetfulness, which is sincere, is no doubt explained by an unconscious decency, and above all by the fact that the interested parties, at the very moment they are the victims of this rage, do not understand what is happening to them, for these conflicts arise less from their intentions than from a lack of organization. The memory easily forgets what is does not understand, something to which it cannot assign a recognized status. See, however, J. Humbert Droz (former secretary of the Comintern), *L'oeil de Moscou à Paris* (Julliard, 1964), p. 19, with a division worthy of Thucydides between the observer and the partisan.

17. On the ancient scorn for work, see, above all, the unconventional work of A. Koyré, *Études d'histoire de la pensée philosophique* (A. Colin, 1961), pp. 292, n.2; 296–301.

18. A form of traditional erudition, the study of words and ideas, cannot therefore make known anything but words and notions, or slogans, or rationalizations; it does not explain the conduct or the aims of men. If I study *concordia* or *libertas* in Cicero, I shall know what he said about them, what views he held on the subject, what he wanted men to believe, or even what he believed to be the reality of his conduct; but I shall not learn the true aims of that conduct. When a specialist in modern French studies the vocabulary of the electoral manifestoes under the Third Republic, he knows it by experience; but a specialist in antiquity does not have that experience, and he is impelled by a scholarly tradition to take literally the interpretations that ancient societies give of themselves after a fashion, as we ourselves do.

19. M. Confino, *Domaines et seigneurs en Russie vers la fin du XVIIᵉ siècle, études de structures agraires et de mentalités économiques* (Institut d'études Slaves, 1963), p. 180.

20. P. Laslett, *Le monde que nous avons perdu,* p. 155.

21. Here is a Calabrian lament published by De Martino: "And now I must tell you, you who were the treasure of the women, what I have put you in your coffin: two shirts, one new and the other mended, your towel to wash your face with in the next world, and then I have put in your pipe, for you loved tobacco so much! And now, how can I send you cigars into the next world?" Also see Father Huc, *Voyage en Chine*, Ardenne de Tizac, ed., vol. IV, p. 135.

22. C. Lévi-Strauss: *Le totémisme aujourd'hui* (Gallimard, 1962), p. 102.

23. On the priority of the rite in relation to the myth, E. Cassirer, *The Philosophy of Symbolic Forms*, trans. Manheim, vol. II, *Mythical Thought*, pp. 39, 219.

24. E. Rohde, *Psyché, le culte de l'âme chez les Grecs et leur croyance à l'immortalité*, trans. Payot, p. 15.

25. *Le totémisme aujourd'hui*, pp. 96–103, to be toned down by A. R. Radcliffe-Brown, *Structure et fonction dans la société primitive*, trans. Marin (1969), p. 239.

26. Against the idea of social inertia, see Barrington Moore, *Les origines sociales de la dictature et de la démocratie* (Maspéro, 1960), p. 384, which de-

nounces the vicious circle (the mentality creates the structure that creates the mentality) and the verbal nature of the problem (whence do mentalities come? from heaven?). He directs his criticism against the idea of inertia in Talcott Parsons; literally, the reproach is not well founded: Parsons insists that his theory of inertia is not an empirical generalization, but a theoretic axiom; see *The Social System* (New York: Free Press Paperback, 1968), pp. 204, 251, 481. In fact, things are rather worse—the description of Parsons is so verbal that, more anxious to fix a vocabulary than to describe a process, he only runs into more problems with words: once set down on paper, words are inert, even if the things they designate are not.

27. M. Bloch, *Les caractères originaux de l'histoire rurale française,* vol. II (A. Colin, 1956), p. 21.

28. I recall the facts at second hand, because I have no access to the review *Human Relations,* I (1948), in which they were set out.

29. Compare M. Crozier, in his preface to J. G. March and H. A. Simon, *Les organisations, problèmes psycho-sociologiques* (Dunod, 1964), p. XII; or M. Oakeshott, *Rationalism in Politics* (Methuen, 1967), pp. 95–100. We know that Plato contrasted the innovative *epistémé* and the routine *techné.*

30. Compare, on economic equilibrium, J. Schumpeter, *Theory of Economic Development* (Oxford University Press, 1967), p. 40: "Once the system of values has been established, the economic combinations given once for all are always the point of departure for each new economic cycle and have, as it were, a presumption in their favour. That stability is indispensable for the economic behaviour of individuals; in practice, in the great majority of cases, they cannot do the thinking needed to reelaborate their experience. We verify, in practice, that the quantities and the values of things during the previous cycles determine the quantities and the values for each of the following cycles. But this fact alone would not be enough to explain stability: the main fact is obviously that those rules of conduct have gone through the trial of experience and that individuals think that, in the main, they cannot do better than to conform to them. The empirical mode of action of individuals is, thus, not an accident, but has a rational basis." On the existence of such unconscious calculations leading to rational conduct, see G. Granger, *Pensée formelle et sciences de l'homme,* p. 101 (theory of apprenticeship); Davidson, Suppes, and Siegel, in *Decision Making, Selected Readings,* ed. Edwards and Tversky (Penguin Books, 1967), p. 170; W. Stegmüller, *Probleme und Resultate,* vol. I, p. 421. Present-day human sciences being presented as techniques of efficacious intervention aiming at an optimum, the study of human behavior consists of making allowances for rational modes of behavior that intervene rationally and are a hidden *praxeology* and for "irrational" modes of behavior, in the sense that they do not conform to our present models of intervention, and in that way belong to a descriptive ethology, that is, are an inoffensive residue.

31. Against mentality as a general *habitus,* see the protest of M. Confino, *Domaines et seigneurs en Russie,* p. 257.

32. T. Parsons, *Éléments pour une théorie de l'action,* trans. Bourricaud (Plon, 1955), pp. 193 f.; compare p. 40. On the separation between mentality and structure in institutions, compare A. Gehlen, *Studien zur Anthropologie und Soziologie* (Berlin: Luchterhand, 1963), pp. 196 f.

33. Two suspects know that if they both keep quiet, they will get away with a light sentence, but that if one of them confesses, he will be freed, while his comrade will be given a heavy sentence for not having been the first to confess. Ought he to speak first, or should he trust the other? We return to this in ch. XI, where references will be found.

Chapter X. Lengthening the Questionnaire

1. B. Croce, *Théorie et histoire de l'historiographie*, trans. Dufour (Droz, 1968), p. 53.
2. Astonishingly well rendered by P. Laslett, *Un monde que nous avons perdu*, p. 13.
3. E. Gilson, *Les idées et les lettres* (Vrin, 1955), p. 230.
4. Cf. Droysen, *Historik*, ed. Hübner, pp. 34–35, 85: "The art of heuristics obviously cannot get information that does not exist in the sources, but there is not only information that we see at the first glance and the ability of the researcher will be shown in his art of finding it where others saw nothing and will perceive it only when they are shown what they have in front of them."
5. For example, at the end of the study by J. G. March and H. A. Simon, *Les organisations, problèmes psycho-sociologiques*, trans. Dunod (1964). In the book by Jean Bodin, *La méthode de l'histoire*, trans. Mesnard (Publications of the Faculty of Letters, Algiers, 1941), an old masterpiece still worth close reading, ch. III is entitled "How to Determine Exactly the Commonplaces or Rubrics of History." Droysen's "systematics" is also a list of *topoi*: the races, human goals, the people, the language, the sacred (*Historik*, pp. 194–272). Or else see the list of topics (learnedly called "variables") made by S. N. Eisenstadt at the end of his big volume, *The Political Systems of Empires* (Glencoe, Ill.: Free Press, 1967), pp. 376–383. (This book is a history of comparative administrative history, called "sociological analysis"; it aims at promoting a "historical sociology.") In truth, few ideas are as useful and as neglected as that of the topic, that kind of list destined to facilitate invention; Vico complained that in his time, historians and philosophers of politics neglected the topic to the advantage of criticism alone. For a renewal of the topic in the human disciplines, see W. Hennis, *Politik und praktische Philosophie, eine Studie zur Rekonstruktion der politischen Wissenschaft* (Berlin: Luchterhand, 1963), ch. VI: "Politics and Topic," with the reply of H. Kuhn, "Aristoteles und die Methode der politischen Wissenschaft," *Zeitschrift für Politik*, XII (1965), 109–120 (this discussion is of an exceptional level and interest). There is place for a topic everywhere that things are not organized *more geometrico*. The aim of the topic is to allow invention—that is, to (re)discover all the considerations that are necessary in a particular case; it does not allow the discovery of anything new, but the mobilization of cumulative knowledge, not to neglect the right solution or the right question, to omit nothing. It is a matter of understanding, of prudence. Sociology was born of the idea that there was something to say about social facts and that that something was not to be confused with the history of those facts. Unfortunately, as we shall see, those facts do not lend themselves to classification or to an explanation other than diachronic, historic, and do not give rise to a science: all that can be said of them is of the

topic: sociology is a topic unaware of itself. The sociology of Max Weber is a topic.

6. H. I. Marrou, *De la connaissance historique* (Seuil, 1954), p. 237.

7. Here is a passage from Adam Smith that may interest any archaeologist who finds traces of furniture in a house: "The houses, the furniture, the clothes of the rich, after some time, serve the middle classes or the lower classes; these latter are in a position to buy them when the upper class is tired of using them. If you go into the houses, you will still find there fine furniture, though of antique shape, but very good for use and not made for those who use it" (*Wealth of Nationals*, trans. Garnier-Blanqui, I, p. 435). Smith, in the context, is speaking of mansions that have been divided into apartments and are now lived in by the lower classes.

8. Average productivity is, as we know, the average yield per unit of production, and marginal productivity is the productivity of the last unit of production that it "is still worthwhile to have produced." When technique is deficient and production insufficient to meet elementary needs, the least favored producer is still necessary to the subsistence of the collectivity; it cannot do without him even if his yield is much below the average. Equilibrium is not fixed by the lower limit, and it is the average yield that determines prices and wages. It will happen that a producer who cannot live on his work, but whose work is necessary to the community, may be maintained from other resources. Compare K. Wicksell, *Lectures on Political Economy*, ed. Robbins (Routledge and Kegan Paul, 1967), I, p. 143; N. Georgescu-Roegen, *La science économique, ses problèmes et ses difficultés*, trans. Rostland (Dunod, 1970), pp. 262, 268: J. Ullmo, "Recherches sur l'équilibre économique," *Annales de l'Institut Henri-Poincaré*, VIII, fasc. 1, pp. 6–7, 30–40.

9. Which urged Rostovtsev, very conscious of the high economic level of the Roman Empire, to explain it by an advanced economic system and to transpose to antiquity what is known of the origins of modern capitalism; as could be read in a recent number of the *Revue de philologie*, Rostovtsev imagined the economy of the ancient world on the model of contemporary capitalist economy, "with a few zeros less." But account has to be taken of a detail of history: the plurality of paths. The problem of a "single way" in economics is at rest, in practical terms this time, when we are talking about a people of the Third World developing: does development necessarily move along the single way of industrialization? Georgescu-Roegen doubts it in the pages cited in the preceding note and, for the historian of the Roman world, the interest of those pages is considerable.

10. A study one would imagine somewhat like that of E. Hobsbawm, *Les primitifs de la révolte dans l'Europe moderne*. In Rome a false son of Tiberius is known (Tacitus, *Annals*, II, 39), as is a false Nero who seeks to impose himself on the Parthians under Vespasian. The ease of these attempts is explained by the fact that Italy and practically the whole Empire have no police: it is the army or nothing (Tacitus, *Annals*, IV, 27; Apuleius, *Metam.*, II, 18). We have to imagine the crowds ready to be roused by the strangest rumors (see the astounding anecdote of Dionysius Cassius, LXXIX, 18) and "to burn witches" (Philostrates, *Life of Apollonius*, IV, 10). The first "false Demetriuses," about which one can read the book of P. Merrimée, appear

in the Hellenistic period (Alexander Balas, Andriscos of Aramyttion). In England let us cite Perkin Warbecken (1495).

11. The "conflict of the emperors and the Senate" does not exactly resemble either a conflict of authority (it is not, as might be imagined, the inevitable conflict between two naturally enemy powers, the imperial monarchy and the old Republican aristocracy) or a struggle between political tendencies, or a class struggle with repercussions in the machinery of state, or simply the rivalry of clans to share the benefits of power. It is, rather, a phenomenon of political pathology, a kind of tragic misunderstanding like the "trials" of the 1950s behind the Iron Curtain (but not like the Moscow trials, in which there was a struggle between tendencies). In the latter Stalin had executed not those opposing him, but people he thought were doing so, while they were hardly doing so and did not understand what was happening to them. That misunderstanding supposes that two conditions were fulfilled: that the apparatus of government is such that there are those who, out of interest or mere professional conscience, are disposed to execute the will of the autocrat; and that the autocrat is placed or has placed himself in so uncomfortable a political situation or that he is so obsessed by the memory of former opponents that he is always on the verge of a nervous breakdown, and he sees conspiracies everywhere around him. Thus, if, just once, he loses his head, the infernal machinery is set in motion, and no longer stops. Each emperor in Rome was free to set it or not set it in motion; so in Tacitus and Pliny we sense the fear of an infernal machine, and we foresee an anguished haste to put the reigning emperor on his guard against the fatal error of setting it in motion (they repeat to him that he is a good prince and that those fatal errors belong to a past that is over). Under Hadrian, with the affair of the four consuls at the beginning of his reign, it looked as if everything were to begin again. What made possible that infernal machinery was the fact that the ruling group does not distribute to itself the benefits of power, but receives them from the emperor; and so the members of this group support each other by the threat of reprisals (if A plays a dirty trick on one of my allies, I shall do the same to an ally of A). Thence a clan can push into the service of the emperor by ruining another clan, without fearing reprisals.

12. F. Chatelet, *La naissance de l'histoire, la formation de la pensée historienne en Grèce* (Éditions de Minuit, 1962), p. 14.

13. Eric Weil, quoted by Chatelet, *ibid.*

14. This may be the opportunity to recommend, on the other hand, a forgotten book the knowledge of which I owe to J. Molino: the four remarkable *Mémoires sur la philosophie* (that is, on the method) *de l'histoire* that a follower of Leibniz, Weguelin, published from 1770 to 1775 in the *Nouveaux mémoires de l'Académie royale des sciences et belles-lettres* of Berlin. There will be found, among many other things, a study on historical induction (1775, p. 512) and one on inertia in history (1772, p. 483). Weguelin seems to have been rapidly forgotten; Droysen does not know him.

15. Kenneth Clark, *Le nu*, trans. Laroche (Livre de Poche, 1969), I, p. 298; II, p. 204.

16. Leibniz, *Théodicée*, II, 124: "Virtue is the noblest quality of created things, but it is not the only good quality of creatures; there is an infinity of others

which attract the love of God. From all those loves there results the greatest good possible, and it happens that, if there were only virtue, if there were only reasonable creatures, there would be less good. Midas was less rich when he had only gold. Besides, wisdom must vary. To multiply only the same thing, however noble it may be, would be a superfluity, a sorry thing. To have a thousand well-bound Vergils in one's library, to sing always the operatic tunes of Cadmus and of Hermione, to eat only partridge, to drink only Hungarian wine: would that be called reason? Nature needed animals, plants, inanimate objects; there are, in those creatures without reason, marvels that serve to exercise reason. What would an intelligent creature do if there were no movement, no matter, no sense? What would it think about if there were no nonintelligent things? If it had only distinct thoughts, it would be a god, its wisdom would be limitless."

Leibniz is here remembering the Scholastic readings of his youth; the distinction of beings was a problem for the School men: "the perfection of the universe demands that there be contingent beings; otherwise the universe would not contain all the degrees of beings" (*Summa contra gentiles* I, 85; see especially II, 39–45 or III, 136: "If spiritual substances are superior to corporeal ones, it would nonetheless be an imperfection for the world to include the former").

Chapter XI.   The Sublunary and the Human Sciences

1. See for example, J. Ullmo, *Le pensée scientifique moderne* (Flammarion, 1958), chs. 1, 2; and "Les concepts de la physique," in Encyclopédie de la Pléiade, *Logique et connaissance scientifique*, p. 701.

2. For example, structuralism, on which see G. Granger, "Événement et structure dans les sciences de l'homme," in *Cahiers de l'Institut de science économique appliquée,* no. 55 (May–Dec. 1957); and preface to the 2nd ed. of *Pensée formelle et sciences de l'homme* (1968); R. Boubon, *À quoi sert la notion de structure?* (Gallimard, 1968).

3. G. Barraclough, "Scientific Method and the Work of the Historian," in *Logic, Methodology and Philosophy of Science, Proceedings of the 1960 International Congress* (Stanford University Press, 1962), p. 590: "The choice made by the historian between the ideographic attitude and the nomographic attitude, and in particular his refusal to pass from descriptive narration to theoretical construction, is not imposed on him by the nature of the facts, as Dilthey and others have tried to prove. It is a purely voluntary choice. It is not difficult to show that there is no essential difference, from this point of view, between the facts used by the historian and the facts used by the physicist. The difference is only in the accent an observer puts on individuality."

4. F. von Hayek, *Scientisme et sciences sociales*, p. 78.

5. The idea of social equilibrium, convenient and elusive, like all that arises from the wisdom of nations, from those proverbs in which Aristotle saw the most ancient philosophy, has been the object of at least an attempt at elaboration: E. Dupréel, *Sociologie générale* (P.U.F., 1948), pp. 263–274. The problem is transformed by game theory, in which a very abstract notion of equilibrium may be rethought, starting from the "characteristic function" of the division of winnings.

6. On the Epicurean *foedera naturae,* which are not laws but constitutional limits (a horse cannot be born of a ewe; that said, nature has the right to do all that the *foedera* do not forbid it to do), see P. Boyancé, *Lucrèce et l'épicurisme* (P.U.F., 1963), pp. 87, 233.

7. Whence the humorous statement of N. Chomsky, *Syntactic Structures* (Mouton, 1957), p. 93, trans. by Baudeau, *Structures Syntaxiques* (Seuil, 1969), p. 102: "Great efforts have been made to try to answer the objection "How can you construct a grammar without appealing to sense?" And yet the question is in itself badly put, since the postulate that one evidently can construct a grammar by appealing to sense is not justified by any effective realization. . . . The true question that should have been raised was this: "How can you construct a grammar?"

8. H. A. Simon, German trans., "Eine formale Theorie der Interaktion in sozialen Gruppen," in Renate Mayntz, ed., *Formalisierte Modelle in der Soziologie* (Berlin: Luchterhand, 1967), pp. 55–72; R. Boudon, *Analyse mathématique des faits sociaux* (Plon, 1967), p. 334.

9. Necker, quoted by B. de Jouvenal in *Du pouvoir,* 2nd ed. (1947), p. 31. The stability of the coalitions does not seem explicable in the framework of games with no stakes. W. H. Riker, *The Theory of Political Coalitions,* p. 30.

10. Alain, *Propos,* Jan. 3, 1931 (Pléiade, p. 985).

11. L. Walras, *Eléments,* p. 43 f.

12. J. Schumpeter, *History of Economic Analysis,* p. 27; and *The Theory of Economic Development* (Oxford University Press, 1961), p. 213. On the law of decreasing returns as translating the fact that the factors are not completely interchangeable, see Joan Robinson, *The Economics of Imperfect Competition* (Macmillan Papermacs, 1969), p. 330. As F. Bourricaud says (preface to his translation of Parsons' *Elements for a Sociology of Action,* p. 95), it can be said that economics, as a system of rules that determine the alternative uses of scarce goods, is both subjectivist (since there is a choice) and behaviorist (since there is a "preference revealed" by the behavior of the consumer). Economists pay no heed to it, for they do not claim to make the theory of the totality of a behavior; their theory is abstract—that is, deliberately partial.

13. *History of Economic Analysis,* p. 1058. On the psychic nature of economics, also see L. von Mises, *Epistemological Problems of Economics* (Van Nostrand, 1960), pp. 152–155; F. von Hayek, *Scientisme et sciences sociales,* p. 26.

14. L. Robbins, *Essai sur la nature et la signification de la science économique,* Fr. trans. (Librairie de Médicis, 1947), pp. 87–93.

15. See the accounts, very different from each other, of R. D. Luce and H. Raiffa, in *Games and Decisions* (Wiley, 1957), p. 208; of G. Granger, "Epistémologie économique," in Encyclopédie de la Pléiade, *Logique et connaissance scientifique,* p. 1031; and of W. J. Baumol, *Théorie économique et analyse opérationnelle,* trans. Patrel (Dunod, 1963), p. 380.

16. Examples of attacks against the *homo oeconomicus* are B. Malinowski, *Une théorie scientifique de la culture,* Fr. trans. (Maspéro 1968), p. 43; E. Sapir, *Anthropologie,* Fr. trans. (Éditions de Minuit, 1967), I, p. 113. On the other side, L. Robbins, *Essai sur la nature et la signification de la science économique,* p. 96; and Ph. Wicksteed, *The Common Sense of Political Economy*

(Routledge and Kegan Paul, 1910; repr. 1957), pp. 163, 175. A curious remark made by Wickstead has been, no doubt independently, developed by Riker in *Theory of Political Coalitions*, p. 24: When we manage our own money, we can very well conduct ourselves as bad *homines oeconomici* and waste our money or give it away; but whoever manages the money of others (that of the state or of a ward) is morally obliged to conduct himself as a pitiless *homo oeconomicus;* now, since in modern societies money is most managed by third persons, *homo oeconomicus* tends to become more and more real. On the *vexatissima quaestio* of utility and egoism, we must cite at least chapter 5 of *Fondements de l'analyse économique* of P. A. Samuelson, trans. Gaudot (Gauthier-Villars, 1965); but certainly I do not flatter myself that I understand this book, the mathematical level of which is serious.

In the present situation of the human sciences, the question is not at all that of "matter" and of "perception" and of knowing if the "representations" are or are not a simple requisite of objective processes; one may hold these old questions to be absolutely out of date. The question, as we know, is that of rational and irrational ways of behaving. The human sciences, as they exist today, are, as Granger says, techniques of intervention; they partake simultaneously of the descriptive and the normative—they are praxeologies. Through their hypothesis of rationality, they remain human, have a human significance beyond their apparent meaning. If two tribes of primitives exchange goods in a potlatch, the sociologist will describe the ceremonial and psychological aspects of this exchange, will write paragraphs full of subtlety on the meaning the gift has for those people, whereas the economist will draw out the economic significance of that exchange: to maximize the profit, to earn a "consumer's surplus" by the exchange. Whence the diagnosis of Granger (*Pensée formelle et sciences de l'homme*, p. 66): "The double temptation lying in wait for the human sciences is to limit themselves to events experienced, or else, in an ill-adapted effort to reach the positivity of the natural sciences, to liquidate all meaning in order to reduce the human fact to the model of physical phenomena. The constituent problem of the sciences of man may thence be described as the transmutation of meanings experienced in a universe of objective meanings."

This raises several problems: (1) The human sciences are at present as much normative as descriptive; that is why Eric Weil (*Philosophie politique*, p. 72, n. 1) can desire the formulation of a hypothetico-deductive theory of politics that is comparable with economics and would be a science of intervention. It remains to be seen in what measure man conforms or does not conform to the normative optimum; all normative praxeology must be accompanied by a descriptive ethology comparing the real behavior with the norm. (2) Is not rational behavior the least part of human behavior? In the same way that instinct has its failures, its absurdities, doesn't human behavior have its own? (See Stegmüller, *Probleme und Resultate*, p. 421.) Whence the just objection of F. Bourricaud to the eclecticism that Parsons proves in his "great theory": can one now build a theory of action that holds good for nonrational as well as rational modes of behavior? (3) Is not the fact that the human sciences are at present techniques of intervention and draw out a human significance merely a provisional state in their development?

From Galileo to the end of the eighteenth century, physicists often thought that nature acted in such a way as to follow the simple mathematical paths, to adopt mathematically elegant solutions; but they themselves had begun by discovering the simplest laws. It does not, therefore, seem sure that the notion of significance is essential to the human sciences; but it must at present be the most opportune.

17. E. Von Boehm-Bawerk, *Positive Theorie des Kapitals,* 1889 ed., pp. 390–398; Pareto only repeated the demonstration.
18. H. J. Paton, *Der kategorische Imperativ, eine Untersuchung über Kants Moralphilosophie* (De Gruyter, 1962), pp. 41, 77.
19. Formulated thus, this kind of affirmation obviously is related to the popular diatribe; but it also conceals a serious problem. (Similarly, the popular idea that the human sciences are the instrument of heartless technocrats hides the problem of their nature, which at present is half normative.) The problem in question is none other than the famous *Methodenstreit:* Is economics a historical science, as German historicism thought it was, or a theoretical science? To Max Weber, economics was a mere ideal-type of a historical reality, liberal economics. As a reaction against that historical and institutional tendency of the German school (still a very living tendency), Austrians from Boehm-Bawerk to Schumpeter, von Mises, and von Hayek have stressed the theoretical, "pure," rigorous character of the doctrine and have marked the distinction between the universal laws and the empirical, psychological or institutional data, to the point of denouncing Keynes as an empiricist in disguise. F. A. Hayek, *The Pure Theory of Capital* (Routledge and Kegan Paul, 1941; 1962), represents an "Austrian" attempt to translate Keynes into the language of pure theory.
20. The metaphor of the frictions, found in Clausewitz, *De La guerre,* trans. Naville (Éditions de Minuit, 1955), pp. 109, 671, is found again in Walras, *Éléments d'économie politique pure,* 4th ed. (1900; Dalloz, 1952), p. 45.
21. G. Th. Guilbaud, *Éléments de la théorie mathématique des jeux* (Dunod, 1968), p. 22.
22. The story of Newton's apple is authentic: A. Koyré, *Études newtoniennes* (Gallimard, 1968), p. 48, n. 35.
23. Compare the pluralist materialism of J. Freund, *Essence du politique* (Sirey, 1965). Of course, we do not give the words "regional essence" the very precise meaning they have in Husserl.
24. Parsons, *The Social System,* p. 555.
25. *Epistemological Problems of Economics,* p. 100. Let us stress the great interest of this book for the epistemology of history and of sociology; we deplore not having been able to get *Theory and History,* by the same author (Yale University Press, 1957), which is out of print. The clarity of mind regarding the epistemology of history, shown by the authors whose education is primarily scientific (either physics, like Popper, or economics, like Mises or Hayek), is a lesson to be meditated on.
26. For instance, G. Granger, *Essai d'une philosophie du style* (A. Colin, 1968), p. 210. Another example: in *Théorie économique et analyse opérationnelle,* p. 395, W. J. Baumol declares that the "game of the two prisoners" reveals the fundamental reason for the prolongation of state control in the most

democratic society; on that he refers to his book *Welfare Economics and the Theory of the State* (Longmans, 1952). When we have read the latter book, we note that there is not the slightest reference to the theory of games, but the reader will find many situations described there to which he might be tempted to apply that theory, as the author himself was surely tempted to do when writing his book.

27. R. D. Luce and H. Raiffa, *Games and Decisions,* p. 94; W. J. Baumol, *Théorie économique* . . . , p. 395; W. Edwards, "Behavioral Decision Theory," in W. Edwards and A. Tversky, eds., *Decision Making* (Penguin, 1967), p. 88. The *Times Literary Supplement* has announced the publication of a book by A. Rapoport and A. Chammath, *Prisoner's Dilemma* (Ann Arbor: University of Michigan Press, 1970).

28. Sartre, *Critique de la raison dialectique,* pp. 306–377.

29. Von Thünen's *Der isolierte Staat* appeared in a new edition by the Wissenschaftliche Buchgesellschaft in 1968.

30. Let us merely say, to come back to it in another piece of research: (1) That Pliny had at his disposal no archive document allowing him to affirm such a thing. An affirmation of quantitative, demographic, or economic order demands archives and the work of a statistician. The Roman state had at its disposal no archives of that kind, and statistics did not exist. (2) Even if Pliny had had archives at his disposal and had compiled columns of figures, to draw from them the conclusion that large estates were responsible for the ruin of agriculture in Italy, it would have demanded a technological and economic study inconceivable at that time; even in our day it would be a theme for endless scientific discussions. But economics did not exist any more than statistics in Pliny's time. The value of his phrase for the economic history of Rome is exactly equal to the value for a physicist an affirmation of Lucretius on a point in physics. Here we find again the problem of criticism we mentioned at the end of chapter VIII: on what kind of facts a given type of document gives us information. Pliny's affirmation is not a source for Roman economics, but it is a source for the history of popular ideas in Rome about economics and social ethics. For this affirmation is exactly comparable with a modern slogan like "What is good for General Motors is good for our country" or "Trusts are ruining the French economy" or "The return to the land will be the salvation of the French economy"; at this level the discussion or the simple statement of the question is not even possible.

31. Counterfeit money favored the poor who were in debt; see Marc Bloch, *Esquisse d'une histoire monétaire de l'Europe,* pp. 63–66. Before criticizing the theory of S. Mazzarino in the name of proverbial prejudices about counterfeit money and inflation, F. A. Hayek's *Prices and Production* (Routledge and Kegan Paul, 1935; 1960), should be read; it shows that the influence of an injection of money on prices depends on the point at which that injection is made into the system.

32. No economic theory will allow us to *better* Rostowzew on the Roman economy; but it will no doubt bring people to say *less.*

33. A. Marshall, *Principles of Economics,* 8th ed. (1920; Macmillan Papermacs, 1960); J. Schumpeter, *History of Economic Analysis* (Allen and Unwin, 1954; 1967); and *The Theory of Economic Development,* trans. Opie (Oxford: Galaxy Book, 1967), probably the masterpiece of the master and of the whole

school—there is also a French translation; K. Wicksell, *Lectures on Political Economy,* trans. Classen (Routledge and Kegan Paul, 1934; 1967).

34. Schumpeter, *Economic Development,* p. 218; compare pp. 10, 220–223. The Austrians distinguished the endogenous changes, which are born within a system, and the changes external to the hypotheses posed.

35. A consumer who prefers guns to butter and atomic bombs to guns ought to prefer those bombs to butter, on pain of being incoherent and of making calculations very difficult.

36. On the effect of substitution and of income, see J. R. Hicks, *Valeur et capital,* Fr. trans. (Dunod, 1956), pp. 23 f.

37. Th. Veblen, *The Theory of the Leisure Class, An Economic Study of Institutions* (1899; New York: Modern Library, 1934). But see the ingenious remarks of R. Ruyer, *Cahiers de l'Institut de science économique appliquée,* no. 55 (May–Dec. 1957).

38. *Economic Development,* pp. 145–147, 151. I have not been able to see Schumpeter's study "Das Grundprinzip der Verteilungstheorie," in *Archiv für Sozialwissenschaft und Sozialpolitik,* XLII (1916–1917).

39. J. Ullmo does this in "Recherches sur l'équilibre économique," in *Annales de l'Institut Henri-Poincaré,* VIII, fasc. 1, pp. 49–54; compare Schumpeter, *History,* pp. 939n. and 630n.

40. More precisely, that, economic facts being left to themselves, competition being perfect, and equilibrium being achieved, the rate of salary, through offer and demand for work, is established at the level of marginal utility for the consumer of the part of the product that can be imputed to the marginal worker of each enterprise. Another formulation, much more institutional, is this: this rate is "institutional," fixed by custom or political struggle, and will be written, in the form of an abscissa, as an independent variable, the volume of the employment being one of the dependent variables. The rate of salaries then escapes the mechanism of imputation (for the Austrians the value "again descends" the stages of manufacture, from the finished product to the raw materials; a raw material is not exploited if nothing salable can be gotten from it); on the other hand, the machines, another dependent variable, do not escape the mechanism of imputation.

41. Schumpeter, *Economic Development,* p. 151; on the doubtful profitability of "plantation" slavery, see Marshall, *Principles,* Papermac ed., p. 466.

42. J. Marchal and J. Lecaillon, *La répartition du revenu national,* 3 vols. (Librairie de Médicis, 1958 f.); another, very interesting type of economic-sociological analysis is that of J. Fericelli, *Le revenu des agriculteurs, matériaux pour une théorie de la répartition* (Librairie de Médicis, 1960), pp. 102–122, for instance. German historicism, relayed on this point by logical empiricism, continues its fight against pure theory and prolongs the *Methodenstreit* in a book by Hans Albert: *Marktsoziologie und Entscheidungslogik, ökonomische Probleme in soziologischer Perspektive* (Berlin: Luchterhand, 1967), esp. pp. 429–461.

43. M. Guéroult, opposing Leibniz to Spinoza: *Spinoza,* vol. I, *Dieu* (Aubier-Montaigne, 1969), p. 10.

44. On the contrary, on this point Euler preserved a wise reserve and was content to say: "everything happens as if . . .", he writes in his *Lettres à une princesse d'Allemagne sur divers sujets d'histoire et de philosophie,* II, 68:

"To avoid all confusion that the way of speaking might cause, one ought rather to say that the bodies of the world move in the same manner, as if they really attracted each other."

45. One will recognize here a pastiche of the famous analogy of the watch, tightly shut in the case, in Einstein and Infield, *L'evolution des idées en physique,* trans. Solovine, p. 34.

Chapter XI.   History, Sociology, and Complete History

1. F. Dagognet, *Philosophie biologique* (P.U.F., 1955); compare W. Riese, *La pensée causale en médecine* (P.U.F., 1950).
2. D. Bohm, *Causality and Chance in Modern Physics* (Routledge and Kegan Paul, 1957; 1967).
3. Such were the two principal war aims of Hitler. To avenge Versailles is only a preliminary stage; he had to destroy France and England to have his hands free to the east. See H. R. Trevor-Roper: "Hitlers Kriegsziele," in *Viertel-jahrshefte für Zeitgeschichte* (1960); E. Jäckel, *Hitlers Weltanschauung, Entwurf einer Herrschaft* (Tübingen: Rainer Wanderlich Verlag, 1969).
4. E. Topitsch, "Gesetzbegriff in den Sozialwissenschaften," in R. Klibansky, ed., *Contemporary Philosophy,* vol. II, *Philosophie des sciences* (Florence: La Nuova Italia, 1968), pp. 141–149. On the question of whether it is possible to perceive a general evolution in human history, we will find different views, but equally reasonable, in K. Popper, *Misère de l'historicisme,* sec. XXVII, adding to it the important note supplied by the preface to the French edition, p. x; J. Maritain, *Pour une philosophie de l'histoire,* trans. Journet (Seuil, 1957); N. Georgescu-Roegen, *La science économique, ses problèmes et ses difficultés,* trans. Rostand (Dunod, 1970), p. 84.
5. Durkheim, *Règles de la méthode sociologique,* pp. 76, 111–119. Perhaps that is a reply by Durkheim to a page where Stuart Mill poses, as a condition of a sociological science, the simple existence of determinism, each state of things, at each moment, simply resulting from the previous state. The object of sociology, then, according to Mill, would be to discover uniformities of succession; in that case "the mutual correlation between different elements of each state of society is only a derived law, which results from the laws regulating the succession of the different social states" (*A System of Logic,* bk. VI, ch. 10). It is true that Mill soon adds that, in order to foresee a social evolution, "our task would be greatly facilitated if it were found that one of the elements of social life is preeminent over all the others and that it is the prime agent of social evolution." Then he discovers that that element exists: it is "the state of the speculative faculties of the human mind," for Mill sees, in the progress of technique and knowledge, the axis of universal history, the motive power of history being thus "the advance in knowledge, or in the prevalent beliefs."
6. Hans Freyer, *Soziologie als Wirklichkeitswissenschaft: Logische Grundle-gung des Systems der Soziologie* (1930; Wissenschaft. Buchgesellschaft, 1964). However, Freyer does not put the problem, *expressis verbis,* in terms of nominalism; but it can be transcribed thus.
7. *The Social System* (Free Press Paperbacks, 1968), p. 20.
8. On functionalism, see A. R. Radcliffe-Brown, *Structure et fonction dans la*

société primitive, trans. Marin (Éditions de Minuit, 1968); R. K. Merton, *Éléments de théorie et de méthode sociologiques,* 2nd ed., trans. Mendras (Plan, 1965), pp. 65–139 (compare R. Boudon, *À quoi sert la notion de structure?,* p. 186); the functionalism of Malinowski must be set apart, *Une théorie scientifique de la culture,* French trans. (Maspéro, 1968). One remembers that the *Structures élémentaires de la parenté* are as much functionalist as "structuralist." For the criticism of functionalism, see E. E. Evans-Pritchard, *Anthropologie sociale,* French trans. (Payot, 1969), ch. 3; K. Davis, *Le mythe de l'analyse fonctionnelle,* French trans., in H. Mendras, *Éléments de sociologie, textes* (A. Colin, 1968), pp. 93 f.; G. Carlsson, "Betrachtungen zum Funktionalismus," in *Logik der Sozialwissenschaften, herausgegeben von E. Topitsch,* 6th ed. (Kiepenheuer und Witsch, 1970), pp. 236–261; and especially W. Stegmüller, *Probleme und Resultate . . . ,* vol. I, *Wissenschaftliche Erklärung und Begründung* (1969), pp. 555–585. We take the liberty of referring to our own stance on structuralism and functionalism in *Annales, économies, sociétés, civilisations* (1969), no. 3, pp. 797 f.

9. Quoted by Merton, p. 79.
10. *The Social System,* pp. 21–22.
11. "The system of the faculties of the soul is composed of two systems, the system of the faculties of understanding and the system of the faculties of the will. The first includes three special faculties: attention, comparison, reasoning. The second also comprises three: desire, preference, freedom. As attention is the concentration of the activity of the soul on an object, in order to acquire the idea of it, so desire is the concentration of that same activity on an object in order to acquire the enjoyment of it. Comparison is the bringing together of the two objects; preference is the choice between two objects that have just been compared. Reasoning and freedom do not seem to offer at first the same analogy; however. . . ." Quoted by Taine in his admirable *Philosophes classiques du XIXᵉ siècle en France,* p. 14.
12. Compare J. Stoetzel, *La psychologie sociale* (Flammarion, 1963), p. 182.
13. S. Lieberman, "The Effect of Changes in Roles on the Attitudes of Role Occupants," translated in H. Mendras, *Éléments de sociologie, textes,* p. 377.
14. Let us understand: it is not at all superfluous to establish that professional officers in the American army, about the middle of the twentieth century, were more in favor of the army than were draftees, for it was not certain in advance and it is precisely the kind of thing where social legends abound. What is less convincing is to want to establish by that not a point of history, but a point of doctrine about the correlation of roles and attitudes.
15. In the preface to his translation of the *Éléments pour une théorie de l'action,* pp. 94–104, published in 1955. There is great merit in having seen clearly into these matters as early as that year.
16. J. de Romilly "L'utilité de l'histoire selon Thucydide," in Hardt Foundation, *Entretiens sur l'Antiquité classique,* vol. IV, *Histoire et historiens dans l'Antiquité* (Geneva, 1956), p. 62. In that way Thucydides "avoids crossing two dangerous thresholds": "presenting as necessary the series which he elucidates. An account, even repeated, could not pass from frequency to constancy," since that constancy is "rendered impossible by the freedom of man and by chance surprises"; the second danger is to "present those probabilities as independent, isolated and self-sufficient," whereas, in practice, the

data of the context "complete it, limit it, support it" (J. de Romilly, p. 59). Chapter VIII of this book is a commentary on this Thucydidean practice.

17. M. Crozier, *Le phénomène bureaucratique;* Ch. Bettelheim and S. Frère, *Auxerre en 1950;* N. de Maupeou-Abboud, *Les blousons bleus.* One of these books has been reproached with being not speculative enough, sociological, and content to collect facts, explaining them in too "literary" a way (let that be understood as "historical"). Would not that be rather a compliment?

18. It is inevitable that periodization, in history, should be largely modeled on the nature of the documentation. The break between the Roman Empire and the Byzantine Empire is that between a literary and epigraphic documentation and a documentation made up of patristics and of the *Codex Theodosianus.* The political history of the contemporary period and the social history of the same period (or "sociology") use very different documents and methods. The role unconsciously played by the nature of the documentation in our carving out of the historical field must be considerable, and a history of historiography ought to attach a great deal of importance to it.

19. J. Robinson, *Philosophie économique,* trans. Stora (N.R.F., 1967), p. 199.

20. A retrospective comparison may be drawn from the evolution of philology: a century and a half ago E. Boeckh, in his *Formale Theorie der philologischen Wissenschaft,* undertook to reform philology—that is, to bring philology, as philologists had founded it, to a state of greater coherence by pushing to the end the philologists' own principles: thus, as we know, are sciences reformed. To do that, he had to challenge the then absolute break between the study of antiquity and that of the moderns, and impose the idea, a surprising one at that period, that to comment on Shakespeare or Dante was not different from commenting on Homer or Vergil.

21. A. Bonifacio, in Encyclopédie de la Pléiade, *Histoire des sciences,* p. 1146.

22. On the distinction between "horizontal" and "vertical" orientation, see Schmitthenner and Bobek in W. Storkebaum, *Zum Gegenstand und Methode der Geographie,* pp. 192, 295.

23. To the convention of the continuum, in literary history, a second one is added: the field of literary events is cut out according to the language in which the works are written; the language, and the pride that a nation draws from its national literature, ordinarily break up the literary field into national cells. Comparative literature is the name given to all literary history that frees itself, either from the convention of the continuum (and can then study the items: "the first-person novel," "literature and society through the ages") or from the convention of national literatures; see Cl. Pichois and A. M. Rousseau, *La littérature comparée* (A. Colin, 1967), p. 176. Putting it otherwise, comparative literature is two things: either a "general literature" in the sense of "general geography" (which has nothing general about it: it only cuts out in items instead of cutting out according to the continuum) or a literary history that follows the continuum (as does traditional historiography or regional geography) but does not cut out according to national frontiers: it will study Hellenic-Roman literature, or Greco-Latin literature in the Roman Empire, or European baroque.

24. E. Hobsbawm, *Les primitifs de la révolte;* W. E. Mühlmann, *Messianismes;* L. Mumford, *Culture of Cities;* S. N. Eisenstadt, *Systems of Empires.* Nothing shows better the futility of the distinction between history and ethnog-

raphy than the book of Mühlmann; the French title is rather ethnographical, but the original title, *Chiliasmus und Nativismus*, is more historical. The writer declares, on p. 347, that he wanted to animate the study of historically known revolutionary messianisms, of which the documents of the Middle Ages and of today give us only a faint and distorted idea, by means of what observation allows us to note today among the underdeveloped peoples.

25. One example out of a thousand of these overlappings between history and sociology, and the too-narrow conception that sociologists sometimes have of what history is today: in an interesting and humorous book, *Strategems and Spoils, a Social Anthropology of Politics* (Blackwell, 1969), F. G. Bailey declares this: if we study the fall of Asquith in 1916, when the unionists in his Cabinet went over to the coalition of Lloyd George, we do not have, being an anthropologist, to study the personal history of each one of them, to discover what experiences determined their attitude to authority, to the Welsh, what little quarrels and enmities may have influenced their acts: that is the business of historians. Generalizing sciences, like politics or anthropology (the French say, rather, ethnography), interest themselves for preference in the cultural code according to which these people acted, described, and justified their acts. So we will first seek the reasons invoked in 1916, in the United Kingdom, for such political maneuvers, and then we will seek the kind of grammar that is behind this language. It will become evident that this language was constituted by normative themes. On the contrary, among the Pathans (a Pakistani people whose political way of acting the writer studies in another chapter) they change camp to ensure their safety, for material reasons of the same order as the one that can be invoked to justify the acts of one's private life. In certain Indian villages, on the other hand, the normative themes are different: the winners are those who can show that they acted honorably, in the general interest, and that their adversaries have been selfish or dishonest. The culture of the period of George V, like the Victorian culture, also favored the language of "the general interest." We will raise two objections. First, far from limiting themselves to the anecdote (the personal history of each politician), the historians, in our century, study the political language or grammar of a given period—that is, non-eventworthy history; the philologists have done so since the last century (history of ideas in classical antiquity, history of words). Second, it is hard to see how a relative proposition "in the United Kingdom in 1916" could be qualified as "generalizing"; it can only be a historical proposition.

26. S. N. Eisenstadt, *The Political Systems of Empires* (New York: Free Press, 1963; 1967).

27. A. Aron, *La sociologie allemande contemporaine*, 2nd ed. (P.U.F., 1950), p. 150.

28. We fully share the position of L. von. Mises, *Epistemological Problems of Economics* (Van Nostrand, 1960), p. 105; compare pp. 74, 180 (and, for the word "praxeology," preface, p. viii): "Weber has composed great works that he styled as sociological. We cannot grant them that title. That is in no way an unfavorable judgment; the research that is brought together in *Économie et société* belongs to the elite of German scientific production. It remains that, for the greatest part, they are not what we used to call sociology and what we now prefer to call praxeology. But neither are they history in the usual sense

of the word. History speaks of a city, of the German cities, or of the European cities of the Middle Ages. Before Weber, we had seen nothing like the brilliant chapter of his book that deals purely and simply with the city in general and that is a study of the urban habitat at all periods and among all peoples. Weber could never admit that a science aims at universally valid propositions, so he considered that he had done science: and to underline our distinction, we are going to give another name to what Weber called sociology: the most suitable is no doubt "general aspects of history" or "general history." I have preferred to avoid the deceptive epithet "general," for "general" history or geography is no more general than the history of a period or regional geography. I would prefer to speak of "history by items" or "categorical history."

Index